Praise for

RESTLESS SOULS

"In our perplexing age of religious revivals and conservative politics, this brilliant book lays bare the deep Emersonian roots of quintessential figures and movements of American spiritual seeking—figures like the inimitable Walt Whitman, Felix Adler, Vida Scudder, and Howard Thurman, or movements at Greenacre and Pendle Hill, who combined mystical quests with progressive politics. Schmidt's profound genealogy of our Spiritual Left is a source of hope in our present-day crisis."

— Cornel West, Ph.D., author of *Democracy Matters*

"*Restless Souls* should help correct the misimpression created by the religious right that liberal forms of spiritual experimentation play an inconsequential part in U.S. religious history. On the contrary, as Schmidt argues, their roots are deep, complex, longstanding, and no less central to a proper understanding of what American spirituality has been, is, and should be all about."

— Lawrence Buell, Harvard University, author of *Emerson*

"*Restless Souls* immerses the reader in a history of spiritual seeking. No other book gives us so broad a grasp of this lineage from Emerson to Oprah. Informative and fascinating reading."

— Wade Clark Roof, J. F. Rowny Professor of Religion and Society, University of California, Santa Barbara

"Leigh Schmidt offers an historical tour of American spirituality that is a tour de force—and written in a lovely and lucid style that befits its subjects."

— Ronald C. White Jr., author of *The Eloquent President: A Portrait of Lincoln Through His Words*

"Can you will a book into being? For the longest time now I've wished someone would write the history of America's 'other' spirituality, but Leigh Schmidt's *Restless Souls* is even better than I'd imagined such a book might be. It pleases me in so many ways, not the least being the respect, verging at times on tenderness, with which these quirky, quintessentially American visionaries are portrayed."

— Carol Lee Flinders, author of *Enduring Grace: Living Portraits of Seven Women Mystics*

"Nowadays millions of Americans claim to be 'spiritual, not religious,' and Schmidt's capacious, entertaining history reveals how deeply this sentiment has been plowed into American culture over the last two centuries. *Restless Souls* breaks new ground in detailing how in the United States secularity and religiosity have bolstered rather than battled one another. Must reading for anyone intrigued by the profound cultural accord that underlies our ongoing cultural wars."

—Richard Wightman Fox, author of *Jesus in America*

"In this rich and fascinating study, Leigh Schmidt pioneers in illuminating the spiritual and mystical themes in American religious history and, just as usefully, makes a convincing case for the vital importance of an oft-slighted liberal religious movement."

—William Hutchison, Warren Research Professor of American Religious History, Harvard University, and author of *Religious Pluralism in America*

"The culture of liberal spirituality has long been stigmatized as an oxymoron by the Christian right and a therapeutic capitalist conceit by the academic left. With energy, cogency, and compassion, Leigh Schmidt has restored this almost lost nineteenth-century tradition of the quest for spiritual experience, cosmopolitan religion, and social justice. *Restless Souls* is an urgently needed book for a restless and fragmented time."

—Charles Capper, Professor of History, Boston University, and author of *Margaret Fuller: An American Romantic Life*

"Leigh Schmidt's wonderful new book rescues the Sheilas of the American world and points unmistakably to their seriousness as religious seekers—with a long lineage in liberal Protestantism. Written with wit and verve and a wealth of details, Schmidt's work superbly documents the combinative world of networks and meetings out of which the contemporary spirituality movement emerged."

—Catherine L. Albanese, Professor of Religious Studies, University of California, Santa Barbara

"Liberal religious spirituality gets short shrift from Christian conservatives and secular cultural critics alike, who dismiss it as a fraud and a fad, but Leigh Schmidt provocatively proves it to be a significant American faith tradition—one that over a century and a half has produced deep thinkers and even saints."

—Dean Grodzins, author of *American Heretic: Theodore Parker and Transcendentalism*

RESTLESS SOULS

RESTLESS
SOULS

———— ◆◆◆ ————

THE MAKING OF
AMERICAN SPIRITUALITY

———— ◆◆◆ ————

LEIGH ERIC SCHMIDT

HarperSanFrancisco
A Division of HarperCollins*Publishers*

HarperCollins books may be purchased for educational, business, or sales promotional use. For information please write: Special Markets Department, HarperCollins Publishers, 10 East 53rd Street, New York, NY 10022.

HarperCollins Web site: http://www.harpercollins.com

HarperCollins®, ■®, and HarperSanFrancisco™
are trademarks of HarperCollins Publishers.

FIRST EDITION

Library of Congress Cataloging-in-Publication Data
    Schmidt, Leigh Eric.
        Restless souls : the making of American spirituality / Leigh E. Schmidt.—
    1st ed.
            p.   cm.
        Includes bibliographical references (p.   ) and index.
        ISBN-10 0–06–054566–6
        ISBN-13 978–0–06–054566–6
        1. United States—Religion.   I. Title
    BL2525.S33   2005
    204'.0973—dc22   2005046078

05 06 07 08 09 RRD(H) 10 9 8 7 6 5 4 3 2 1

To

John F. Wilson

Mentor, Colleague, Friend

The stern old faiths have all pulverized. 'Tis a whole population of gentlemen and ladies out in search of religions.

    —Ralph Waldo Emerson, "Worship," 1860

America is an opportunity to make a Religion out of the sacredness of the individual.

    —John Weiss, *American Religion*, 1871

I have worshiped in an Evangelical church when thousands rose to their feet at the motion of one hand. I have worshiped in a Roman Catholic church when the lifting of one finger broke the motionless multitude into twinkling motion, till the magic sign was made, and all was still once more. But I never for an instant have supposed that this concentrated moment of devotion was more holy or more beautiful than when one cry from a minaret hushes a Mohammedan city to prayer, or when, at sunset, the low invocation, "Oh! the gem in the lotus—oh! the gem in the lotus," goes murmuring, like the cooing of many doves, across the vast surface of Thibet.... I do not wish to belong to a religion only, but to the religion; it must not include less than the piety of the world.

    —Thomas Wentworth Higginson,
      "The Sympathy of Religions," 1871

To know the universe itself as a road, as many roads, as roads for traveling souls.

—Walt Whitman, "Song of the Open Road," 1856

The ripeness of Religion is doubtless to be looked for in this field of individuality, and is a result that no organization or church can ever achieve. As history is poorly retained by what the technists call history, and is not given out from their pages, except the learner has in himself the sense of the well-wrapt, never yet written, perhaps impossible to be written, history—so Religion, although casually arrested, and, after a fashion, preserved in the churches and creeds, does not depend at all upon them, but is a part of the identified soul.... I should say, indeed, that only in the perfect uncontamination and solitariness of individuality may the spirituality of religion come forth at all. Only here, and on such terms, the meditation, the devout ecstasy, the soaring flight.

—Walt Whitman, *Democratic Vistas*, 1871

CONTENTS

PREFACE

Typos are among the petty annoyances of teaching and writing, but sometimes they become a source of accidental light. I had a student once who wrote an excellent paper on the Burning Man festival, that flourishing carnival of the arts and neo-pagan spirituality held each September in the Nevada desert, and the essay contained one of those fortuitous slips in its subtitle: "Reviving Community Through Shard Experiences." I knew, of course, that she meant *shared,* but the absent *e* made the phrase more probing and paradoxical. Did this effervescent experiment in New Age festivity generate community or reflect fragmentation? Was it an emblem of spiritual awakening or of cultural incoherence?

The typo effectively crystallized a long-standing tension in American religious life. "I once heard a preacher who sorely tempted me to say, I would go to church no more," Ralph Waldo Emerson had commented in his infamous Harvard Divinity School address in 1838. Was Emerson's growing alienation from the church—he had already resigned from his Boston pastorate in 1832—a sign of welcome freedom, a liberation of the spirit from stunting institutions, authorities, and rites? Or was it an indication of self-reliance gone awry, a spiritual seeking that went everywhere and arrived nowhere? It is that kind of pointed questioning—a doubled perspective at once open yet critical—that I have brought with me to the historical and contemporary ferment surrounding spirituality in American culture.

That is not to say that this history feigns dispassion: would one really want a view from nowhere when it comes to a topic as freighted as "spirituality"? My own Emersonian and Whitmanite colors will become apparent soon enough, and conservative critics no doubt would be quick to paint me with them, should I not own up to those affinities explicitly here. A highly productive alliance among liberals, progressives, and spiritual seekers has long been evident in American culture, and I count myself among those Americans who would like to see such associations remain vital in order to provide an essential counterpoint to all the values talk of the Religious Right. This book probes the ways in which the very development of "spirituality" in American culture was inextricably tied to the rise and flourishing of liberal progressivism and a religious left. Perhaps, indeed, it would be better to call this a Spiritual Left, since the now prevalent notion of being spiritual but not religious is itself primarily a seeker's code for the rejection of the exclusive salvation, moral correctness, and institutional apparatus of conservative Christianity.

I teach in the Department of Religion at Princeton University—an affiliation that carries with it no formal religious ties as well as a stout defense of intellectual independence. That professional identity, though, hardly lifts me above the history that has conjoined spirituality and progressivism in American culture. In crucial ways, academic freedom and the (not so) "new spirituality" are both parts of a liberal inheritance. Often, indeed, the intellectually engaged stance of the American scholar and the spiritually open stance of the Transcendentalist seeker have been the fruit of the same vine. I write, in short, from within an American tradition that has given us Emerson and Whitman—and also William James.

Still, this is primarily a work of cultural history, not public philosophy. Precisely because the inner life is so laden with religious and political conflict—in the twenty-first century as much as in the sixteenth century or the fourth century—it has been crucial for me to speak first and foremost as a historian. In a spirit of free and fair-minded inquiry,

I imagine this book as a guide especially for those who are curious about the origins of the current boom in spirituality and who seek a sympathetic depiction of its many expressions. Perhaps, like the émigré poet and NPR commentator Andrei Codrescu, you fondly recall the friends you have lost to gurus—and would like to place their quests in perspective. Or perhaps you are grateful for the friends you have found in fellow seekers and wonder if there is a shared history that joins your otherwise disconnected journeys. Or perhaps you are already a steady member of a religious community but you nonetheless puzzle, as Emerson did, about the relationship between "the Church" and "the Soul." Whatever the case, this book provides a historical map of the still open roads of American spirituality.

I have been fortunate in the pursuit of this project to have the support of generous institutions and foundations: Princeton University, the Lilly Endowment, the American Council of Learned Societies, and the Center for the Contemplative Mind in Society. Each helped me have the time to research, write, and teach the history of these restless American souls.

Among colleagues, I owe a special debt to Laurie Maffly-Kipp and Mark Valeri, codirectors with me of a multiyear project on the history of American Christian practice and, more importantly, valued friends. My gratitude is extended as well to our coconspirators in that enterprise: Catherine Brekus, Anthea Butler, Heather Curtis, Kathryn Lofton, Michael McNally, Rick Ostrander, Sally Promey, Roberto Lint Sagarena, Tisa Wenger, and David Yoo. Chris Coble was absolutely crucial in helping to bring us together and in keeping us on track. Other scholars and friends provided me with various leads, correctives, and confirmations: Dorothy Bass, Ann Braude, Richard Wightman Fox, David Hackett, David Hall, Charles Hambrick-Stowe, Amy Hollywood, Robert Orsi, Stephen Prothero, Albert Raboteau, Gary Scharnhorst, Ann Taves, Bradford Verter, David

Watt, and Christopher White. Three historians, in particular, offered close readings of the whole manuscript and gave me extensive comments, all for the small recompense of my appreciation: Dean Grodzins, William Hutchison, and Kathryn Lofton. Kathleen Holscher and David Passiak helped me get my research started, and Emily Mace provided vital assistance as it came to a close. Rosanne Adams-Junkins, Jacalyn Blume, Roger Dahl, Sue Hodson, Anne Gordon Perry, Diana Franzusoff Peterson, and Wesley Wilson offered indispensable guidance to archival materials as well as the wisdom bred of long intimacy with such documentary and photographic records. Above all, R. Marie Griffith has been both rigorous critic and indispensable confidante.

At HarperSanFrancisco, Stephen Hanselman and John Loudon were the first to pursue the idea of this project with me. Eric Brandt, soon taking it under his wing, saw the book through to completion as my editor; Kris Ashley also offered critical assistance at each step of the way. I am grateful for the support of all four.

The book is dedicated to John F. Wilson, professor emeritus at Princeton. No doubt it raises his eyebrows to see his good name associated with something as potentially emotive as spirituality. Perhaps it is even a little galling to have a cradle Californian lay so much of this history at the feet of a tradition close to his own heart and mind, religious liberalism, which was nowhere more at home than in his own New England. But John is a master of tact and subtle indirection, so I have no doubt that he will find a delicate way of letting me know where I have erred. As Whitman observed, "The indirect is always as great and real as the direct." Talk about the circuitous: I voice my deep respect and regard for him through the pages of a book.

SPIRITUALITY IN THE MAKING

ONE DAY I WOKE UP and wondered: maybe today I should be a Christian, or would I rather be a Buddhist, or am I just a *Star Trek* freak?" So one woman playfully told a sociologist who studies contemporary American religion. Reports on the mushrooming growth of a culture of spiritual seeking have become a journalistic commonplace. As the *Utne Reader* asked in a cover story in 1998 called "Designer God," "In a mix-and-match world, why not create your own religion?" Eclectic devotions, creedal crossings, consumer sampling, and individualistic expression are widely seen as the religious order of the day. "I cannot describe my spiritual practice as Buddhist,... or as Hindu or Catholic or Sufi, though I feel that in a sense it is all of these," the feminist spiritual writer Carol Lee Flinders concludes of her wayfaring. "I meditate as best I can on Native American prayers and Taoist verses, on passages drawn from the Bible or the Upanishads, on passionate love songs composed for the One Beloved by a Spanish monk or an Indian princess-turned-minstrel." Flinders's spiritual exertions are hardly uncommon these days. The

1

act of journeying across the bounds of traditions, denominations, and institutions has emerged as a familiar, if still creative, course of exploration for many Americans. From Jewish-Buddhist contemplatives to yoga-performing Methodists, more and more seekers have been finding spiritual insight through a medley of practices and pieties.[1]

While sociologists, pollsters, and journalists have provided steady commentary on the blossoming of spiritual seeking in American culture, these observers offer a quite limited historical perspective on how such a religious world took shape in the first place. The majority confine themselves to a watershed view of the 1960s and 1970s, a baby-boomer dividing line between a nation of ensconced churchgoers and a culture of unhinged seekers. How over the longer term did the United States become a land of spiritual questing? How was it that so many Americans became so intensely absorbed in something amorphously called "mysticism" or "spirituality"? *Restless Souls* shifts the prevailing focus away from rambling boomers (let's hope our self-esteem can handle it) and makes the recent spiritual upsurge a matter of cultural and intellectual history. In other words, this is not a story about a rootless generation of seekers, a sardonic tour through the spiritual marts of the New Age, or an arch essay on a bourgeois-bohemian "Soul Rush." All those have been done—and done well. Too well, really, since today's "pastiche spirituality" has come to be seen almost invariably as a marker of a current social trend, a leading indicator of a new religious transformation rather than a historically shaped tradition of its own. The American fascination with mountaintop mysticism and seeker spirituality goes much deeper than any generational fixation allows.[2]

If one temptation is to make newness the basis of any news on spirituality, another is to treat such religious experimentation as timelessly American, part of an intrinsic pioneering spirit that has been mapped onto inner frontiers. It is possible, in other words, to regress too far. Put in historical terms, these contemporary spiritualities of seeking are not predictable from the Protestant-heavy colonial world of British North America or even from the sectarian sauna that became so steamy after the American Revolution. The Protestant right of private judgment, the original prerogative of a believer to interpret Scripture by his or her own lights, was a topsy-turvy notion, but the principle had various stabilizers, not least the primacy of the Christian Bible itself. If that oft-exercised right made for an exegetical madhouse full of contradiction, at least most of the faithful shared the same cell of canonical restraints. (The Bible is for infant baptism; no, it is for believers' baptism only. The Bible supports slavery; no, it vows prophetic justice and equality. The Bible demands that women keep silent in public worship; no, it licenses the prophesying of godly sisters. And so on.) Debates were everywhere, but the authority and sufficiency of biblical revelation were not up for grabs in early American Protestantism. Sure, pilgrims wandered ceaselessly into new interpretations of Christianity—with their Bibles firmly in hand.

Protestants, of course, were not only intense and often eccentric Bible readers, but also practitioners of rigorous self-examination and introspective journaling. Aren't the spiritual pilgrimages of Puritan saints the foundations of American interiority, the ghosts that linger still, across that vast spectrum of evangelical Christianity from the Baptist Jimmy Carter to the Methodist George W. Bush? How can a story about the making of American spirituality pass over (rather than through) the lives of such worthies as Ann Bradstreet, David Brainerd, Jonathan Edwards, Sarah Osborn, Phillis Wheatley, or other exemplars of Puritan and evangelical practices of piety? The spiritual disciplines these early Protestants enshrined—Sabbath observance, private prayer, diary writing, sacramental meditation, communal narration of conversion experiences, Bible reading, and covenant keeping—were vastly influential and remain so within various strands of contemporary Christianity. The point is not to diminish their importance, but to recognize that American "spirituality," as the term is now broadly configured in the culture, was invented through a gradual disentanglement from these model Protestant practices or, at minimum, through a significant redefinition of them. Only through some dissociation from those Protestant habits does the term *spirituality* come to be distinguished from religion; only at a step removed from evangelical Christianity does *spirituality* begin to refer to "direct mystical experience" and "an individual's solitary search" for "the absolute or the divine."[3]

In colonial America, few were seeking "spirituality" per se. Not a term found in Scripture itself, the word showed up in the title of only one American publication before 1800. Even in that case *spirituality* fronted a collection of hymns in which it referred to a quality of corporate worship, not the interior lives of individual pilgrims: namely, James Maxwell's *Hymns and Spiritual Songs … Design'd to Promote the Spirituality of That Part of Christian Worship* (1768). Instead, Puritans and evangelicals emphasized practices of piety; they pursued devout, holy, or godly lives; like the Apostle Paul, they juxtaposed the spiritual with the carnal, but rarely did they label their regimen of sanctification "spirituality." Far from being a keyword in the early Protestant vernacular of personal devotionalism, *spirituality* was usually employed as a theological term in opposition to *materiality*. It pointed, in other words, to the fundamental contrast between the physical and metaphysical worlds, matter and spirit. In allied usages, *spirituality* sometimes referred to a specific attribute of God—alongside omnipotence or patience—or to the immaterial quality of the soul as opposed to the body.

The connotations that *spirituality* carried a century later were largely absent from early American Protestantism. "I should say, indeed," the great American poet Walt Whitman exhorted in *Democratic Vistas* in 1871, "that only in the perfect uncontamination and solitariness of individuality may the spirituality of religion come forth at all." The poet wanted "the subterranean fire" that seemed smothered under the "corpses" of institutions, traditions, and forms. What he wanted, in brief, were "the divine ideas of spirituality," compared to which "all religions," including Christianity, were "but temporary journeys."

Likewise, the Harvard philosopher and poet George Santayana, one of whose earliest pieces was a meditation on Whitman, easily marked out spirituality as the "higher side" of religion in his monumental *Life of Reason: or, The Phases of Human Progress* in 1905: "This aspiring side of religion may be called Spirituality." A model for a life of simplicity, creativity, and equanimity, in Santayana's view, "spirituality likes to say, Behold the lilies of the field!" That poetic prospect, affording such clarity about spirituality's elevation over religion, remained a largely unimagined terrain among Puritans and evangelicals. Here is the bottom line: the American invention of "spirituality" was, in fair measure, a search for a religious world larger than the British Protestant inheritance.[4]

If it is not particularly fruitful to ground the history of American "spirituality" in early American Protestantism, then what about the iconoclastic religion of the American Enlightenment, the intellectual world that produced the religious and political ruminations of Thomas Jefferson, Benjamin Franklin, and James Madison? Certainly, these American founders as well as their British and European colleagues offered crucial formulations of religious privacy and voluntaristic freedom. "My own mind is my own church," the revolutionary pamphleteer Thomas Paine insisted with plenty of bravado, but little overstatement. It would be hard to find a more important taproot of anticreedalism and anticlericalism than the enlightened ideology that these cosmopolitan statesmen both embodied and broadcast. Still, these freethinking leaders were not religious seekers, but natural philosophers. Their sense of religious privacy was a matter of political principle, not devotional solitude; their God was a distant technician, a watchmaker, not an immanent spirit, an intensifier of feeling. As deists, they viewed God as the supreme architect of nature's laws, not an intimate listener to outpoured prayers. Only when Enlightenment freedom, happiness, and autonomy were refracted through a romantic prism did the life of the spirit come to matter experientially to rational souls. Only then did the absence of religious enthusiasm seem a graver peril than its presence. "Nothing great was ever achieved without enthusiasm," Emerson would insist.[5]

But what about the Enlightenment's shadow, the esoteric world of Freemasons and gentlemanly inquirers into the occult, the alchemical underside of both the Renaissance and the Age of Reason? Surely, the secret sources of modern American spirituality are to be uncovered in the mystery-shrouded world of Western esotericism. That kind of claim, in actuality, is often little more than a distraction. It serves two purposes that are particularly at odds with good history: First, it is used to reinforce an orthodox perspective on history that imagines an ageless battle between the truths of Christianity and the false claims of occultists and heretics. New Age spirituality, from this perspective, becomes little more than the latest instance of ancient deviations from orthodoxy, which early modern adepts transmitted through clandestine brotherhoods and which now need to be fought against as they have always been fought against. The second purpose is the inverse of the first: ancient esoteric sources, carefully tended for centuries by secret societies and elite initiates, make contemporary searches seem venerable, even timeless. That certainly appears to be the point for the famed literary critic Harold Bloom when he announces that he is a latter-day Gnostic and that indeed the American religion at its best is a Gnostic gospel of divinized souls, each imbued with a "spark or transcendental self that is free of the fallen or created world." It is a lot less grandiose—and a lot more accurate—to admit more immediate and mundane sources than to mystify origins with tales of ancient magi and esoteric lore. Equating the "new spirituality" with the persistence of occultism or the revival of Gnosticism is all too often either heresy-hunting or mythmaking. Much less often is it light-bearing.[6]

All right, enough negations: what really counts in the invention of modern American spirituality? The history that matters the most, by far, is the rise and flourishing in the nineteenth century of religious liberalism in all its variety and occasional eccentricity. Seeker spirituality—excitedly eclectic, mystically yearning, perennially cosmopolitan—is an artifact of religious liberalism, especially in its more radical stripes. Included in that company of nonconformists were Transcendentalists, romantic Unitarians, Reform Jews, progressive Quakers, devout disciples of Emerson and Whitman, Spiritualists, questing psychologists, New Thought optimists, Vedantists, and Theosophists, among sundry other wayfarers. Many of these newfangled pilgrims traveled several different religious paths in succession; some traversed more than one simultaneously; more than a few expressly saw themselves as the makers, immodestly enough, of the religion of the future, a universalized spirituality. Almost from first to last, they charted a path—at least, so they imagined —away from the old "religions of authority" into the new "religion of the spirit." From the democratic vista of religious liberalism, a much clearer and more precise history of American spirituality comes into view.[7]

Even with that specified point of departure, getting a grip on spirituality is hardly an easy task. John W. Chadwick, a New England minister close in outlook to Emerson, already felt "helpless" in pinning the term down in 1891, sounding a little bit like the desperate judge trying to define pornography: "You call upon me to explain what I mean by 'spirituality.' ...I seem to know spirituality when I meet it in a man or book, but if I should attempt to define it, my definition might be as vague as that 'kind of a sort of something' which the hard-pressed obscurantist offered as his definition of the Trinity." When Chadwick did try to make sense of what "spirituality" had come to signify, he referred back to Transcendentalists like Theodore Parker and Emerson who had led the heady revolt against New England's established religious order in the 1830s and 1840s. It is a strategy pursued in these pages as well, and one can only hope that it is done with less feebleness and greater clarity here than Chadwick mustered in this halting moment of perplexity.[8]

In a recent article called "A Seeker's Guide to Faith," the magazine *Real Simple* provided a helpfully concrete illustration of the historical threads pursued here. The connection came in an interview with

Stephanie Jones, an artist living in Brooklyn, who had grown up attending the African Methodist Episcopal Church. Gradually she has moved away from the intermittently observed Christianity of her youth into an everyday practice of Buddhist chanting, prayer, and meditation. In calling her daughter Emerson in honor of America's paradigmatic nineteenth-century seeker and liberal dissident, Jones witnessed to her own spiritual journey and tugged on the twine that ties twenty-first-century quests to nineteenth-century emancipations. "Emerson was the prophet of spirituality," an admirer wrote already in 1882, a sentiment that Jones has effectively incarnated through her daughter's given name. To paraphrase the Concord sage himself, the here and now is intimately tied to the there and then.[9]

Or take the story of Elizabeth Lesser's search, which she relates at the outset of *The New American Spirituality: A Seeker's Guide* (1999). There she tells of a concerted quest for meaning and community that takes her through a series of religious affiliations in the 1960s and 1970s. Trading off between Thomas Merton's contemplative Catholicism and the meditative practices of a Zen center, Lesser eventually settles upon a westernized version of Sufism after meeting the guru Pir Vilayat Inayat Khan in 1972. It is through this encounter and the ongoing workshops of the Omega Institute in Rhinebeck, New York, that Lesser gradually finds her spiritual longing for "mindfulness," "heartfulness," and "soulfulness" satisfied. Could there be a more paradigmatic tale of a new generation of seekers?

It does not take long, though, to see beneath the surface of the contemporary in Lesser's search for "a new kind of spirituality." Among the devotions she undertook with Pir Vilayat and her fellow travelers were "universal worships," in which "each of the major world religions, and many of the minor ones as well, were honored with scripture and practice. In one Sunday service we might read from the Koran, Hindu and Buddhist texts, Sufi stories, and the Old and New Testaments of the Bible, and then chant mantras, do traditional Jewish dances, and wash each other's feet in the spirit of Jesus washing the feet of his disciples." Those services, however trendy they might sound, were not a recent experiment of the counterculture. Pir Vilayat's father, Hazrat Inayat Khan (1882–1927), who first brought his message from India to the United States in 1910, was actually responsible for introducing the practice. Marrying a near relation of Mary Baker Eddy, the founder of Christian Science, in 1912, Khan quickly attracted his own eclectic circle of American inquirers into Sufi music, dance, and devotion. At the outset of one of his lecture tours in 1925, the *New York Times* offered an account of Khan's "spirituality" in an article entitled "Indian Mystic Offers One Religion for All." "My ancestors were Moslems," Khan explained to the reporter. "I have no religion. All places of worship are one to me. I can enter a Buddhist temple, a mosque, a church or a synagogue in the same spirit. Spirituality is the tuning of the heart."

In his lectures in New York and elsewhere across the country, Hazrat Inayat Khan justified his innovations through an appeal to the increasingly pervasive ideals of religious liberalism: spiritual liberty, mystical experience, meditative interiority, universal brotherhood, and sympathetic appreciation of all religions. Indeed, in the very years surrounding Khan's American sojourns, Martin Kellogg Schermerhorn, an industrious Unitarian minister from Poughkeepsie, was promoting, with the backing of the philanthropist Andrew Carnegie, various collections of hymns, scriptures, and prayers for the celebration of "universal worship" services. For Schermerhorn as much as Khan, modern religious identities would be regrounded only through an undoing of ethnic, racial, and religious tribalism, including Christian and Muslim exclusivism. Hence Schermerhorn busied himself in compiling the liturgical materials for the universal religion as he imagined it would find expression in new "Cosmopolitan Churches" and within the private devotions of eclectics like himself and Khan. Just this quickly, then, Elizabeth Lesser's recent seeking can be resituated in a century-long perspective: not so much a rootless baby-boomer quest, but instead a more deeply grounded and complex exploration of a cosmopolitan spirituality.[10]

Anecdotes aside, the argument offered in these pages about the centrality of religious liberalism may seem at best counterintuitive. At least at an institutional level, conservative Roman Catholics and evangelical Protestants dominate the current scene. The Christian Right and its high-profile allies in Washington grab the headlines and occupy the public square with confidence and flair. At the same time, new immigrants—whether Muslims, Buddhists, Hindus, Sikhs, or Korean Christians—lobby with growing effectiveness for a fuller voice in civic life. The so-called liberal or mainline denominations have over the last half-century fallen on very hard times, suffering an almost staggering erosion in membership and public influence. Meanwhile, beyond the thinned ranks of liberal Protestants, New Agers have been so satirized as quirky crystal gazers, left-over hippies, and self-absorbed spiritual shoppers—David Brooks, a pundit for PBS and the *New York Times,* has called them "vaporheads"—that even neo-pagans and Wiccans feel compelled to disown the New Age epithet.[11] Why would anyone beyond the hallways of Harvard Divinity School or the streets of Santa Monica think that liberalism still explains much of anything about American religion?

Few commentators would dare to wear liberal Protestant blinkers anymore, let alone raise a paean to the foundational importance of America's liberal tradition. In theology, as in politics, liberalism is the hobgoblin of orthodoxies, possessing a fearsomeness for conservatives and traditionalists little removed from John Henry Newman's mid-nineteenth-century conjuration: "The more serious thinkers among us ... regard the spirit of Liberalism as the characteristic of the destined Antichrist." Perhaps given the endless polemics and the very slipperiness of the term, *liberalism* is a label best retired. Perhaps it would be less contentious, if more cumbersome, to refer to this larger religious impulse, under William James's rubric, as "the personal and romantic view of life." Or perhaps it would be better to think of this as the rise of "cosmopolitan," "eclectic," or "ecumenical" perspectives on spirituality. Yet, as a term of considerable resonance in nineteenth- and twentieth-century religious thought, *liberalism* allows an array of movements, within Christianity and beyond it, to be considered under the same umbrella. However difficult, it is still possible to use the *liberal* epithet in contextual, evenhanded ways without necessarily launching another theological or political Last Judgment in which fundamentalist sheep are separated from modernist goats (or vice versa).[12]

Liberalism had intellectual progenitors from Baruch Spinoza and John Locke to Adam Smith and Jeremy Bentham, but, as a distinct religious and political ideology, it was an invention of the nineteenth century, not the seventeenth and eighteenth centuries. A broadly diffused movement, it was always as much a religious vision of emancipated souls as a political theory of individual rights and civil liberties or an economic calculus of the beneficence of free markets. In the United States, liberalism cohered first in the 1820s as a radical form of Protestant Christianity that then over the next few decades readily edged beyond Christianity itself. It was the volatile currency of religious innovators and critics of orthodoxy who, though spanning a wide spectrum of allegiances, remained convinced of their own essential affinities. Individualistic in their understanding of authority, religious liberals were generally contemptuous of creeds and scorned uncritical submission to scriptural texts as ignorance or even idolatry. Moving beyond mere toleration as an ideal, they led the way as eager sympathizers with other faiths. With a grand sense of human freedom and potentiality, they were committed to progress in the domains of spiritual consciousness, social organization, and scientific knowledge. For religious liberals, unlike their secular cousins, a deepened and diversified spirituality was part of modernity's promise. Materialism and scientism might challenge this unfolding religion of the spirit from one side and reactionary pieties and politics from another, but, to its proponents, those perils only made the inward dimensions of liberalism more important. Religious liberalism, with its motley bedfellows of romantics and reformers, led the way in redefining spirituality and setting out its essentials.

Getting a handle on "liberalism," of course, is no easier than pinning down "spirituality." The Harvard-educated metaphysician Horatio Dresser, one of the many architects of the "more spiritual phase" of American progressivism around 1900, dubbed the nineteenth century "the epoch of religious liberalism." He saw it as a momentous movement that affected one denomination after another and that decidedly opened up the spiritual life to Emersonian self-reliance and therapeutic well-being. He quickly added, though: "The history of liberalism is so comprehensive that it is always a question nowadays what we mean when we use the term." Then, as a succinct definition, he offered: "To be liberal is to be of the new age." It was not a bad effort, but the basics of religious liberalism require at least a few more brushstrokes. The rudiments, at least for spiritually inclined progressives like Dresser, included

- individual aspiration after mystical experience or religious feeling;
- the valuing of silence, solitude, and serene meditation;
- the immanence of the transcendent—in each person and in nature;
- the cosmopolitan appreciation of religious variety as well as unity in diversity;
- ethical earnestness in pursuit of justice-producing reforms or "social salvation";
- an emphasis on creative self-expression and adventuresome seeking.

An interlocking group of precepts and practices, these could pass under various names—from the Transcendentalist Newness to the

Universal Religion to the New Spirituality. *Religious liberalism* remains particularly serviceable as shorthand for this conglomeration.[13]

Imbued to varying degrees with these principles, emancipated souls set out less on a pilgrimage toward otherworldly salvation and more on an individualized search to imbue this life with spiritual meaning and depth. Liberal pilgrims still made progress, but they did so not through the perilous landscape of damnation in John Bunyan's seventeenth-century representation of the journey to the Celestial City. Instead, they traversed an increasingly disenchanted and divided terrain that they sought to reanimate and make whole through a universalized religion of the spirit. That new topography had its own hazards, of course—mires of alienation, lost identity, and nihilism—that sometimes made hell seem more real than the spewing of any fire-and-brimstone evangelist. As Whitman observed in *Leaves of Grass,*

> *Down-hearted doubters dull and excluded,*
> *Frivolous, sullen, moping, angry, affected, dishearten'd, atheistical,*
> *I know every one of you, I know the sea of torment, doubt,*
> *despair and unbelief.*

In opening up new roads for traveling souls, religious liberals regularly confronted those psychic risks and sometimes even overcame them.[14]

In a moment of irrational exuberance all his own, Thomas Jefferson once predicted that Unitarianism, as a newly minted denomination of "liberal Christians" in New England, would come to dominate American religious life as a great force of reason. With its emphasis on Jesus as moral exemplar more than divine being, its optimism about human nature, and its refined educative vision, Unitarianism would, Jefferson believed, set the tone for the new republic's unfolding improvement and advancing knowledge, its freedom from superstition and intolerance. "I confidently expect," he wrote from Monticello in 1822, "that the present generation will see Unitarianism become the general religion of the United States."[15] That ascent did not come close to happening and now sounds downright laughable as a prediction (in a nation of about 150 million church members, Unitarian Universalists account for just over 150,000 of them). Looked at another way—say, from the far reaches of Emerson's influence—disaffected Unitarians and their liberal kin did have a sweeping effect on American religious life and the spiritual aspirations of vast numbers of Americans.

The spiritual life, as religious romantics imagined it, was nothing if not personal, and any adequate history of these developments has to emerge out of the inner lives of distinct figures. Many of those who people these pages are familiar (Ralph Waldo Emerson, Walt Whitman, Henry David Thoreau, Margaret Fuller, W. E. B. Du Bois, and William James), others somewhat less so (Thomas Wentworth Higginson, Lydia Maria Child, Felix Adler, Rufus Jones, Ralph Waldo Trine, Swami Vivekananda, Howard Thurman, and Thomas Kelly), and some all but forgotten (William Rounseville Alger, Anagarika Dharmapala, Sarah Farmer, Protap Mozoomdar, and Max Ehrmann). Attributable to this diverse group of thinkers, writers, and organizers were most of the fundamental innovations: the transformation of "mysticism" and "spirituality" from obscurity to prominence, the revamping of the seventeenth-century notion of "seekers," the locating of religion's essence in the solitary individual, as well as the sympathetic capacity to appreciate and appropriate other religious traditions as spiritual resources. The following chapters pursue four generations of liberals who helped create an expansive, unsettled culture of spiritual seeking: the Transcendentalists of the 1830s and 1840s, their radical heirs of the 1850s to 1880s, the realizing agents of liberalism's universal vision between 1890 and 1910, and the seekers who brought to fruition the emergent spirituality after 1910.[16]

Restless Souls opens with a chapter that dives into the heart of the Transcendentalist love of "mysticism." The English term came into being only in the mid-eighteenth century as part of the polemics over the place of ecstatic experience in the Christian life, and its associations were initially more negative than positive. A century later, it was an important and colorful fragment in the spiritual kaleidoscope. The eighteenth-century Swedish visionary Emanuel Swedenborg, whose accounts of his extensive conversations with angels were more popular in death than in life, was one important contributor to this transformation; he reached the height of his American influence in the 1840s and 1850s. Homegrown mystics became increasingly prevalent, and many of them emerged at the intersections of the Transcendental Club and the Harvard Divinity School, a place, as one of its own deans admitted, "made up of mystics, skeptics, and dyspeptics." By the time the pioneering American psychologist William James embraced "mysticism" as a prominent part of his *Varieties of Religious Experience* (1902), he had a sustained lineage upon which to build. James's exploration of mystical consciousness represented a culmination in the ascent of the new mysticism from Emerson forward—a climb that had been swift and momentous in its effects. The United States was a country, a critic sighed in 1906, where "mysticism" and "a craving for spiritual experiences" had "run mad."[17]

One of the most important Transcendentalist innovations, charted in the second chapter, was the remaking of the hermit's solitude into a much more expansive spiritual trope. Before Emerson celebrated lonely strolls through nature in the 1830s and before Thoreau took to the woods at Walden Pond in the 1840s, the hermit had suffered a fall from grace, with Enlightenment philosophers and Protestant critics alike attacking the "monkery" of Catholic anchorites. In the early American republic the hermit, as a social type, also stood as an outcast who sought solitude as a refuge for lonely suffering, and the tales that circulated had a tragic cast of violence, lost love, and ominous mystery. Hermits were no longer enviable or heroic embodiments of religious dedication, austerity, or vision; they more often evoked bemused curiosity than pious awe; and sometimes that curiosity turned into outright contempt, especially when the self-mortifying practices of the ancient desert saints were in view. In the half-century or so after the 1840s, however, solitude reemerged as a defining feature of the spiritual life in American culture, an oasis of redemptive isolation amid the myriad alienations of modernity. It became such an entrenched habit of mind, if not body, that such grand theorists as William James and Alfred North Whitehead made solitary experience the core of religion itself. Aptly enough, James even noted one quirky seeker he had come across in his combing of spiritual narratives for whom the very mention of "the word *hermit* was enough to transport him."[18]

The third chapter explores the growing conviction that all the religions of the world were cut from the same cloth, that at bottom they shared a common spirituality. The Transcendentalists, eclectics to the core, were the first Americans to dabble with Asian religions as a source of personal inspiration and spiritual aspiration. From Emerson, Thoreau, and Whitman on down, they distanced themselves from orthodox Christianity (and unorthodox Christianity for that matter) through appeal to the religions of the East. Thomas Wentworth Higginson, a second-generation Transcendentalist, was especially prominent in crafting an absorbent, inclusive religion out of the various religions of the world. Higginson, a radical abolitionist who led an African-American regiment during the Civil War, made a signal religious contribution through a frequently republished essay called "The Sympathy of Religions." Higginson and his numerous colleagues—among them the fellow radical Lydia Maria Child—happily offered up the gems of sacred wisdom to all liberal souls for their enrichment and through such offerings imagined themselves immersed in nothing less than "the piety of the world." The creation of that cosmopolitan, sympathetic disposition fueled one innovation after another in American spirituality. It was a sine qua non of a seeker culture.

One of the results of the growing American encounter with Asian religions was a heightened emphasis on the practice of meditation and the value of the concentrated mind, and that distinct history is chronicled in the fourth chapter, "Meditation for Americans." The importation of yoga as a serious practice began in the 1890s, and much of its popularity centered on the disciplines of mental focus and composure in a swirling, rushed, anxiety-ridden culture. Significantly, Americans took up yoga in the context of an increasing interest in the implications of positive thinking for health, harmony, and well-being. In 1902 William James surmised that it was not evangelical Protestants but "mind-curers" who were responsible for the growing presence of "methodical meditation" in American religious life.[19] He was right about that: meditation came to more and more Americans not through a retrieval of venerable Christian practices, but through the rise of "New Thought," as the optimistic gospel of mental healing and positive thinking was then dubbed. The burst of interest in meditation involved a peculiarly American conversation among Transcendentalists, liberal Protestants, Reform Jews, Vedantists, Buddhists, and mind-cure metaphysicians. A significant swath of New Thought was simply liberal propositions put into practical dress. Ralph Waldo Trine, one of the most popular American guides to a contemplative mind and a harmonious body, shared much more than his first and middle names with Emerson.

In the fifth chapter the saga of Sarah Farmer and her grand experiment unfolds. Inspired by the World's Parliament of Religions in Chicago in 1893, a much-watched international gathering of religious representatives of different faiths, Farmer set out to create an ongoing center of learning at which leading spiritual teachers from diverse traditions would congregate in pursuit of a global spirituality. To that end, she created a summer community called Greenacre in Eliot, Maine, in 1894, a gathering that would throb from one year to the next with religious variety and innovation. Under pines and in tents, mental healers communed happily with Hindu swamis, Buddhist practitioners, university professors, accomplished artists, and Concord sages. Though a stunning success—the Greenacre gatherings thrived for more than two decades; the World's Parliament lasted all of seventeen days—the community nonetheless fell into division. A fault line cracked open between those who remained loyal to the original design of eclectic seeking and those who came to favor submission to one claimant to universal spirituality. Farmer's pilgrimage into the Bahá'í faith—"the Persian Revelation," as she called it—capped a life of religious inquiry in which elements of everything from Buddhism to Spiritualism commingled. Her new allegiance sorely tested liberal notions of freedom and open-mindedness, even though the movement she embraced echoed the wider values of peace, harmony, and universal brotherhood. The brouhaha at Greenacre raises in sharp relief the still relevant question of whether seekers are to keep on seeking for seeking's sake or to identify an end point to their search. Can a solid religious identity be achieved only through the particularity, integrity, and discipline of one tradition? Was the point of pursuing the spiritual life self-expansion, artistic creativity, and endless curiosity or instead self-surrender, obedience, and resignation to God?

Even as Greenacre's influence declined, other spiritual retreats arose. Among the more important and lasting was Pendle Hill, a community of contemplatives, activists, and seekers led by the Society of Friends (Quakers) and founded in 1930. In the final chapter, an influential group of Quaker intellectuals, all of whom doubled as spiritual guides at Pendle Hill and elsewhere, is explored. Between 1900 and 1940 Rufus Jones, a professor of philosophy at Haverford College, pioneered the liberal transformation of the Society of Friends. He remade them as the archetypal "seekers" in part by resurfacing that category from the seventeenth-century literature of English sectarians and then applying it in a universalized way to the modern religious world. Any number of twentieth-century seekers might suggest the earnestness of these striving souls, but certainly an excellent exemplar is one of Jones's own acolytes, Thomas R. Kelly, who swerved desperately out of academic philosophy into devotional discipline in the late 1930s. He stands in a long line of Quaker-connected spiritual writers in the twentieth century: from Douglas Steere, Howard Thurman, and Elton Trueblood to Richard Foster, Parker Palmer, and Mary Rose O'Reilly. The mysticism of Jones and Kelly as well as the broadly in-

clusive retreat at Pendle Hill made the Society of Friends dispropor-
tionately influential in the shaping of a contemporary American spirituality of seeking. In unpredictable ways, these mystic Quakers even
became entangled with an estimable group of émigré writers in Southern California, including Gerald Heard, Aldous Huxley, and Christopher Isherwood, all of whom were quintessential seekers on the
opposite coast.

The story, of course, continues well beyond Kelly (he died young
in 1941). But the culture of seeking was, by then, in place, and after
Kelly (and this includes the much ballyhooed rupture of the 1960s) it
is historical epilogue. The continuing popularity of Max Ehrmann's
"Desiderata," a prose poem first published in 1927, suggests some of
the echoes still resounding from the seeker culture of the early twentieth
century. Its imperative of being gentle on oneself and finding serenity
amid chaotic social churnings became a widely quoted spiritual motto
on posters and plaques in the 1940s and 1950s; it even climbed the pop
charts in the early 1970s as the title piece of a Grammy-winning album
of Les Crane's; and it continues to circulate now as a "survival guide"
for twenty-first-century life. Widely seen as symptomatic of the therapeutic, privatized, and individualistic bankruptcy of today's seeker
spirituality, Ehrmann's piety proves, on closer inspection, much
harder to caricature. Draining the puddle of syrup and surmounting
the heap of satire that have overwhelmed Ehrmann is more than a
concluding historical exercise. The recovery of his story serves as a
closing parable for a much larger project: namely, the serious reen-
gagement of the interwoven history of liberalism, progressivism, and
spirituality in American culture. Given the ease with which the Religious Right now monopolizes "moral values" as their own distinct
turf, it is all the more important to know the history of the Spiritual
Left in order to reclaim an alternative vista from which to view the
outworking of American democracy.

Throughout the book, the American spirituality crafted by these
seekers is taken with the seriousness of the introspective brooding

and liberating vision that gave it birth. Much of the contemporary commentary on American religion is suffused with the tropes of the marketplace—as if economic models of free competition, entrepreneurial promotion, and consumer demand are the most reliable guides to the spiritual ferment. From this perspective, all this spiritual sampling is but an inner mirroring of the surfeit of choice in America's megamalls. Religious seeking becomes comparable to test-driving various automobiles to see which delivers the most satisfaction on Whitman's open road. This book resists such analogies and analysis not because they are irrelevant, but because they now seem all too obvious. In an age in which conservative pundits caricature liberalism as a shallow ideology of trendy consumerism—"latte liberals" or "Volvo liberals"—it is especially important to probe deeper than brand labels in exploring the cultural import of seeker spirituality.[20]

Already in 1930 Woodbridge Riley complained in *The Meaning of Mysticism* about the "sordid" and "ridiculous" aspects of "commercialized mysticism," which "spends not hours with the mystics, but minutes with the mystics." Notwithstanding the thinness of his own book, he was caustic about how the market trivialized "a genuine search for the interior or hidden life." "Go to any large department store and ask for books on mysticism and they will offer you books bearing such titles as these, 'How to Strengthen Your Will,' ...'Silent Exercises' and the like. By means of such apparatus adults can do their daily dozen in mental gymnastics." In a market society, spiritual practices can be turned into commodities as much as spoons, handguns, or Halloween treats. This book takes for granted that commerce has been a powerful agent in the production and distribution of everything from Bibles to balloons; likewise, inner quests, even for off-the-grid simplicity or spiritual enlightenment, never transcend the market. Indeed, the consumer culture all too clearly feeds those very yearnings in its advertising images of spas, sports-club yoga, and alpine retreats.[21]

How else to understand the "Off-the-Cuff Philosophy" bracelet available from a recent catalog called *Signals: Gifts That Enlighten and*

Entertain? In sterling silver, the bracelet features the engraved words of Ralph Waldo Emerson, "beloved author, minister, activist, poet, philosopher, and lifelong believer in America": "What lies behind us and what lies before us are tiny matters compared to what lies within us." How else to fathom the advertisement for the Chevy Tahoe that promotes it as the perfect vehicle for "self-discovery" with a line from Thoreau's *Walden*? Thoreau's words—"I never found the companion so companionable as solitude"—bless the image of the forest-tucked SUV. The consumer culture encourages spiritual desires, just as it cultivates any number of other desires, and then offers the goods to assuage (temporarily) those cravings and anxieties. But a cynical narrative about commercialization is hardly the primary story of modern interiority. At this point it seems appropriate to give the trope of spiritual shoppers a much-deserved rest. And the same goes for all the smorgasbord, buffet, cafeteria, and deli imagery that one hears in relation to contemporary spirituality—as if religious seekers were little more than spiritual gluttons gobbling up anything and everything that they can heap on their plates.[22]

Even as it offers an inner history of restless souls, this book remains inextricably tied to outer lives. It is a recurring rap on the "new spirituality" as well as on the eccentric individuality of Whitman and friends that they quickly sink into solipsism and become politically and ethically weightless. Narcissism and consumerism are serious issues—in the study of American spirituality as in the study of other aspects of American culture—but they are not uniquely Emersonian, romantic, or liberal problems. Evangelical Protestantism, which has produced more than its share of critics of the "new spirituality," has also given rise to more than its share of Bible-based diets, gospels of wealth, and guides for the maximized erotic pleasures of married heterosexual couples. In other words, a therapeutic culture of self-realization and a consumer culture of self-gratification are at least as much "evangelical" as they are "liberal." Yoga studios and aromatherapy hardly hold a candle to the conglomerate of T-shirt fashions, aerobics videos, and apocalyptic best sellers that makes up the Christian Booksellers Association.

The same liberal spirit that led to a critique of conventional Christianity and organized religion readily energized strenuous activism and self-denying social engagement, including innumerable reform causes from abolition to suffrage, from international relief to workers' rights. Commonly contained within this seeker spirituality was a critical social and political vision; repeatedly, self-reliance and solitary retreat were held in creative and effective tension with a sharply honed social ethics. By the 1920s and 1930s, the joining of "prayers and pickets" was a given of liberal spiritual practice. The religious and political vision of Martin Luther King Jr. in the 1950s and 1960s gained much from that combined inheritance from Thoreau to Mohandas Gandhi. A handful of nineteenth-century religious liberals, after all, had led the way in creating an open spiritual and ethical exchange with like-minded leaders in India and threw their support behind the anticolonial Buddhist revival in Ceylon (Sri Lanka). The ongoing call to "Free Tibet," the fruitful alliance between American religious progressives and the Dalai Lama, has a history behind it that a bumper sticker can hardly compress. Or when Rabbi Michael Lerner speaks now of the possibilities of an "Emancipatory Spirituality," when he sets that vision against the reactionary dimensions of American religion and politics, he is engaging the historical idiom long joining the material work of liberal progressivism to lived spiritual practice.[23]

It does not require a commitment to religious liberalism to recognize its historical importance in giving birth to modern American spirituality. It is quite possible that traditionalists of whatever flavor will read this history as a tale of religious loss and cultural incoherence, a long train of evidence that self-reliance has run roughshod over community in the United States. It is equally possible that those who cherish a newfound spiritual eclecticism will read this history as a tale of far-seeing prophets to be acclaimed for their vision of progress and cosmopolitanism. Poised with the historian's caution between criticism and celebration, *Restless Souls* strives for a fair-minded depiction of the origins and unfolding of the American preoccupation with spirituality. That judiciousness, though, is not to be confused with indifference or neutrality. For those who see themselves as spiritual seekers, religious liberalism presents a self-critical tradition still very much worth contemplating and engaging. For those who are settled, yet desirous of something more from their religious homes, it invites curiosity, exploration, and inquiry. For those who continue to see it as a dangerous license, it offers, as ever, a challenge and a dare.

CHAPTER ONE

MYSTIC CLUB

A ONE-TIME SPY FOR THE DANISH military, Carl H. A. Bjerregaard (1845–1922) hastily left Denmark in 1873, a twenty-eight-year-old lieutenant absent without leave, and headed for New York. In the United States Bjerregaard started a new life, first as a factory worker in New Jersey, and then through employment at the Astor Library (soon to form the core of the New York Public Library). In Denmark he had briefly helped curate a natural history museum, so his joining the library staff in 1879 to classify books and recatalog them was not wholly out of character. Soon his military service faded into the past; he spent the rest of his career with the New York Public, eventually heading up the main reading room. That was only his day job, though. In his spare time, with all the library's resources at his fingertips, Bjerregaard fashioned himself into a philosopher, artist, and mystic.

By the 1890s, he was lecturing widely on mysticism, nature worship, and kindred topics. "I address you as Pilgrims of the Infinite," Bjerregaard told an audience in Chicago in 1896, "for you are pilgrims; I can see that on your faces. You are not pilgrims either *from* or *to* the Infinite, but you are *of* the Infinite. *From* and *to* indicate space and time relations, but in the Infinite we recognize neither time nor space; there is no to-day and to-morrow; no here and no there. Eternity is no farther off from the Mystic, than the moment in which he speaks. You are Pilgrims OF the Infinite." Bjerregaard's summons to explore the "Mystic Life" was heady stuff. It was, among other things, an affirmation of the supreme freedom of spiritual aspirants to seek the truth for themselves and within themselves. The call seemed to resound everywhere: Bible passages, Taoist sayings, pine trees and cones, Jewish Kabbalah, Zoroastrian fire imagery, yoga, Sufi poetry, American Transcendentalism, and the Christian mythology of the Holy Grail.[1]

Bjerregaard's spirituality, like the faith of Ralph Waldo Emerson (1803–1882), was especially in synchrony with the American lecture

Sarah Farmer's Greenacre community in Maine, with its tent village surrounding a large inn on the shore of the Piscataqua River, provided the setting for C. H. A. Bjerregaard's lectures on mysticism and spirituality in the 1890s. (Eliot Bahá'í Archives, Eliot, Maine.)

circuit. Bjerregaard's favorite place to speak was Greenacre, the summer community that the visionary Sarah Farmer (1847–1916) founded in Eliot, Maine, in 1894. He saw Farmer's experiment as a realization of his ideas about a universal mysticism and was lavish in his praise of its design. When he gave personal examples of his own exalted experiences, they almost always circled back to Greenacre, whether to a sunrise worship service led by the Zoroastrian Jehanghier Cola or to barefoot walks on the dew-drenched grass. "Greenacre is a revelation," Bjerregaard remarked. "When you rise from the cool waves of the Piscataqua [River], you rise out of the quiet place of your own soul." As a lecturer, Bjerregaard believed in presentations that were personal and experiential; like Emerson, he did not want to offer secondhand news or disinterested scholarship. Make lecturers, he said, "give their own experiences and not something they have read in books and only poorly digested…. In soul life no abstract teachings are worth much."[2]

His time at Greenacre in the 1890s provided him with that firsthand material. Of one glistening experience there in 1896, Bjerregaard was especially jubilant:

> The first evening I spent at Greenacre, I watched the sunset from "Sunrise Camp," and it happened to me as it did to Wm. Blake, I did not see with my eyes, but through my eyes came to my soul the essence of that Golden Ball, and I heard it as "Glory to God on High" — "Peace on Earth" — "Good-will among Men." It was July 5th, 1896, never to be forgotten. It was a gorgeous sunset. All the heavens and the earth were still; the fleeting colors of roseate hues and ashen gray played in incalculable series of mutations. Behind the passing scenes, the glorious orb, incomparable emblem of Being, sank majestically down behind the distant White Hills, and before the scenes, as if in midair, I felt the Becoming. My reason could not arrest the movement, my understanding could not declare what it perceived. The glorious tints, the melting into one another, the lack

of fixedness or duration, the deep, yet eloquent and sonorous silence spoke from Heaven and whispered Eternal Harmony.

His lone epiphanies at sunset converged with the corporate prayers of the gathered seekers as they all softly chanted together a newly minted mantra, "the now famous Greenacre Uplift": "Omnipresence manifest Thyself in me." There on the banks of the Piscataqua River in a tent village, surrounded by fellow Pilgrims of the Infinite, Bjerregaard found his spiritual element.[3]

Mysticism mattered in the 1890s, as Bjerregaard's eager audiences in Chicago and at Greenacre made plain. Across a wide swath of religious liberalism, mystical experience had become a hallmark of religion at its most awesome, profound, and desirable. The new universal mysticism (to which Bjerregaard gave representative expression) served, in turn, as the foundation upon which the contemporary love of spirituality would be constructed. "The mother sea and fountain head of all religions," the psychologist William James (1842–1910) wrote in a letter in June 1901, "lies in the mystical experiences of the individual, taking the word mystical in a very wide sense." Understanding how mysticism took on such a wide significance over the course of the nineteenth century is an important step in fathoming how spirituality became such an expansive part of America's religious vernacular in the twentieth century. As Bjerregaard concluded in another series of lectures on mysticism in 1896, "A study of the mystics will prove a key by which you can open the doors that lead to Universal Consciousness and Cosmic Emotion, to everything of the New Spirituality, revealed in our day." Bjerregaard's very nomenclature makes plain that the "new spirituality," talked up so much as a recent development, is more venerable than novel. He himself stood right in the middle of this transformation, a bridge figure who joined nineteenth-century "mysticism" to twentieth-century "spirituality."[4]

As a matter of course, Bjerregaard saw the mysticism he was preaching as timelessly true. By the 1890s, it had become common intellectual fare to imagine the mystical writers as part of an everlasting coterie, essentially unaffected by "clime or creed." Their writings sparkled with eternal verities and ineffable insights into the Absolute; ageless classics, they had "neither birthday nor native land." "Mysticism has no genealogy," Robert Alfred Vaughan (1823–1857) commented in his influential *Hours with the Mystics* in 1856. "It is no tradition conveyed ... down the course of generations as a ready-made commodity. It is a state of thinking and feeling, to which minds of a certain temperament are liable at any time or place, in occident and orient, whether Romanist or Protestant, Jew, Turk, or Infidel."[5]

Such claims only got bolder with time. "A history of Mysticism is an impossibility," one writer remarked in 1918 with startling assurance. "It has no history." Mysticism as monotony—it was so universally the same that it was almost boring: "When you see [mysticism] here or there, early or late, you feel perfectly at home with it. You say, 'Here is the same old thing.' It suffers a little, perhaps, from sameness." It would come closer to the truth simply to stand such antihistorical suppositions on their head. The kind of timeless mysticism that Bjerregaard was trumpeting, one could say with a playful contrariness, actually had a very precise American birthday. In May 1896, when Bjerregaard published his first series of lectures on the subject, mysticism would have celebrated its fifty-eighth birthday, its nativity seven years (almost to the day) before Bjerregaard's own birth.[6]

So, when and where was "mysticism" born in the United States? On May 20, 1838, in Medford, Massachusetts, in the old parsonage of Caleb Stetson (1793–1870), a seasoned pastor of high ambitions and modest achievements. On that day the Transcendental Club, a symposium of liberal Christian ministers and New England intellectuals in its third year of existence, met specifically to take up, in Ralph Waldo Emerson's phrase, "the question of Mysticism." In addition to Emerson, on hand for this late-into-the-night discussion were such illuminati in the making as Theodore Parker (1810–1860), Jones Very (1813–1880), and George Ripley (1802–1880). Within months of the

Amos Bronson Alcott, an enthusiastic member of the Transcendental Club, went on to found his own Mystic Club as a successor. (Concord Free Public Library.)

gathering, Very, as poet and oracle, would take off on his own distinct mystical flight, roaming from Cambridge to Concord, offering to baptize people with the Holy Ghost and with fire, much to the dismay of his friends and colleagues. Three years later Ripley would leave his pastorate over the Purchase Street Church in Boston and found one of Transcendentalism's most visionary enterprises, the community experiment known as Brook Farm. Parker, just out of Harvard Divinity School in 1836 and with a congregation in West Roxbury, had already been drawn in his voracious studies to "the writings of the Mystics," "the voluptuaries of the soul." As Parker noted of the precious flora he had gathered from this literature during his student days, "I was much attracted to this class of men, who developed the element of piety, regardless of the theologic ritualism of the church." Emerson, Very, Ripley, and Parker were all well primed to take up the question of mysticism as they gathered at Stetson's home on High Street in Medford.

Perhaps the most expectant of all, though, was Amos Bronson Alcott (1799–1888), another key member present for this spirited meeting of the Transcendental Club. By turns vilified and celebrated — Emerson saw him as an almost unrivaled genius; many others thought he was insane — Alcott has had some of his quirks sanded down over the years through the culture's enduring fondness for his daughter, Louisa May Alcott, the author of *Little Women*. Even if many of his projects sputtered, including his vegetarian commune Fruitlands (which lasted all of six months in 1843), Alcott was a creative and compelling force, a down-on-his-luck Yankee peddler turned self-taught Transcendentalist with a mission to educate and inspire. He was, not surprisingly, effusive about the conversation the assembled intellectuals enjoyed that evening: "On the main topic of conversation, much was said," Alcott noted in his journal. "Was Jesus a mystic? Most deemed him such, in the widest sense. He was spiritual.... He used the universal tongue, and was intelligible to all men of simple soul." Here was one good measure of Alcott's excited and enduring preoccupation with the evening's topic: years later he would organize his own Mystic Club as the aptly named successor to this famed group of Transcendental associates.

Alcott was not one to curb impulsive utterances. He had already become a lightning rod for controversy because of his educational experiments at the Temple School in Boston in which he treated the spontaneity of children as a likely conduit of divine revelation. Rather than catechizing his young pupils, he led them in free-form conversations on the Gospels, confident that spiritual wisdom would well up naturally from their own unspoiled intuitions. Predictably, then, on the topic of mysticism Alcott proved voluble, even inspired. That night at Stetson's parsonage he even feared that he had "overstepped the bounds of true courtesy" by talking too much (certainly a danger to the well-being of any salon). Still, he was unbridled: "A vision was vouchsafed, and I could but declare it." Emerson, by contrast, was fearful that he had been "a bad associate" at the gathering, "since for all the wit & talent that was there, I had not one thought nor one aspiration." Trying to quiet this pang of intellectual insecurity, Emerson offered an excuse: "It is true I had not slept the night before." Alcott's

Ralph Waldo Emerson appears in this portrait in a pose for the lecture circuit, a main medium for him after he left the ministry. (Concord Free Public Library.)

ardor on that spring evening, rather than Emerson's sluggishness, was a better measure of the impact that this Transcendentalist turn to mysticism would have on American religious life.[7]

Two months later, on July 15, 1838, Emerson proved much more inspired when he addressed the graduating class of Harvard Divinity School. Having left the full-time ministry in 1832 over his inability to perform the sacrament of the Lord's Supper with sincere conviction, he had grown only more restive under the sleepy preaching of the New England pulpit over the next six years. Unitarian liberals were mired in doctrinal debates with traditional Calvinists—and often with each other as well—about everything from Original Sin to Christ's divinity to biblical miracles, and Emerson found the whole scene dispiriting. The address to the senior class of the divinity school provided him with the opportunity to declare the emancipation of human curiosity in the realm of religion, the freedom from dogmatic and canonical constrictions, and the awakening of spiritual intuition and individuality. "Truly speaking," Emerson exhorted, "it is not instruction, but provocation that I can receive from another soul. What he announces, I must find true in me, or wholly reject." Refuse the old path of imitative piety; throw off "secondary knowledge"; eschew "hollow, dry, creaking formality." "Yourself a newborn bard of the Holy Ghost," Emerson cajoled, "cast behind you all conformity, and acquaint men at first hand with Deity."[8]

Though his address ended on a cautious note in self-contradictory praise of breathing new life into the old institutions of the Sabbath and regular preaching, the oration nonetheless created a considerable stir. More controversy followed upon its publication the next month, and, since nothing vended quite so well in antebellum America as a religious hullabaloo, Emerson's goading of his alma mater quickly sold out. The rise of religious liberalism had many milestones and monuments in the first half of the nineteenth century: The election of Henry Ware, a theological liberal, as Hollis Professor at Harvard in 1805 pointed ahead to the movement's dominance over religious education there. William Ellery Channing's ringing defense in 1819 of a Unitarian conception of God against Trinitarian orthodoxy was another important sign of the times, as was his affirmation of the powers of self-cultivation against Calvinist notions of human depravity. Then there was the duo of September 1836—the organization of the Transcendental Club and the publication of Emerson's *Nature*. The latter included Emerson's famed moment of spiritual exhilaration, the experience of becoming a transparent eyeball at one with its surroundings, subsumed into God, all egotism gone. That episode helped earn him his enduring reputation as the movement's greatest mystic. The year 1838 represented another critical passage, and not only because of

Christopher Pearse Cranch, an artist within the Transcendentalist movement, was also its best in-house caricaturist. Here Emerson, the mystic, appears as transparent eyeball. (MS Am 1506 [3]. By permission of the Houghton Library, Harvard University.)

"Standing on the bare ground, — my head bathed by the blithe air, & uplifted into infinite space, — all mean egotism vanishes. I become a transparent Eyeball."

Nature, p. 13.

I expand and live in the warm day,
like corn & melons.
Nature, p. 73.

Cranch also pegged Emerson as among those Transcendentalists who relished all too much their spiritual absorption with nature. (MS Am 1506 [4]. By permission of the Houghton Library, Harvard University.)

Emerson's divinity school address, so deeply inspiring to other "heretics" of the period like the young Theodore Parker. The all but forgotten meeting of the Transcendental Club two months earlier to discuss mysticism was perhaps the most telling signal of change: Religious liberals intended nothing less than a redefinition of the spiritual life.

To see how innovative Transcendentalist discussions of mysticism were, to see why the birthday analogy is not too far-fetched, it is necessary to step back for a moment into the seventeenth and eighteenth centuries. That mysticism should come to stand, in the second third of the nineteenth century, as the pinnacle of a universal and timeless religious experience was anything but an obvious development. Through the early decades of the eighteenth century, the English category of "mysticism" did not exist. The prevailing notion instead was "mystical theology," and it signified a specific devotional branch within Christian divinity. In 1656, the lexicographer Thomas Blount, working off a Roman Catholic description of mystical theology from 1647, arrived at the following definition for his formative dictionary of "hard words": "*Mystical Theology,* is nothing else in general but certain Rules, by the practise whereof, a vertuous Christian may attain to a nearer, a more familiar, and beyond all expression comfortable conversation with God." Mystical theology, in other words, was a way of life that involved the Christian in a "constant exercise" of prayer, contemplation, and self-denial. And that was the heart of it: Blount's work contained no parallel entries for the nouns *mystic* and *mysticism.*[9]

Added to these theological dimensions were exegetical ones. From the first centuries of Christian history forward into the seventeenth and eighteenth centuries, among the most common associations for *mystical* were its connections to allegorical forms of biblical commentary. Scriptural texts, in this view, were not transparent, but contained hidden or spiritual senses behind the surface of the literal. To take a commonplace example from the eighteenth century: the passage in the book of Genesis saying "let there be light, and there was light" literally referred to the light of the sun but in its mystical senses pointed to the Messiah, grace, and the glory of God. These ancient forms of biblical commentary remained evident in as basic a compendium as Ephraim Chambers's *Cyclopædia* (1738), which still foregrounded "the *mystical sense* of Scripture" as central to understanding the term's religious significance. Like Blount, Chambers also stressed "MYSTIC *theology*" and did not employ "mysticism" per se as a category. Through the early eighteenth century, the meanings attached to *mystic* and *mystical* were inextricably woven into a larger system of Christian theology, linked at the level of practice to a recognizable set of devotional and exegetical habits.[10]

When "mysticism" emerged as an object of discussion in the middle of the eighteenth century, it was usually seen pejoratively. The concept initially crystallized within the eighteenth-century critique of Protestant enthusiasm—an attack aimed especially at taming the ecstatic extravagance that accompanied the rise of such high-flying movements as the Quakers, the French Prophets, and the Methodists. It was Henry Coventry (c. 1710–1752), a Cambridge wit and a relatively minor player in the larger world of the English Enlightenment, who first employed *mysticism* as part of a sustained critique of sectarian Protestant excitement. In a series of dialogues entitled *Philemon to Hydaspes; or, The History of False Religion,* the initial installment of which appeared in 1736, Coventry explicitly contrasted "the seraphic entertainments of mysticism and extasy" with the "true spirit of acceptable religion." By the latter, he meant a wholly reasonable commitment to civic virtue, cosmopolitan learning, public decorum, and aesthetic proportion. Religion, rightly practiced, was a "manly, rational, and social institution," and the "deluded votaries" of mystical Christianity had no place in that world of erudite conversations, moderated passions, and refined tastes. Coventry's understanding of mysticism was thus socially situated within debates about the fundamental comportment of religious people: were they to carry themselves with the genteel gravity of Cambridge divines and dons or the bumptious assurance of Quakers and Methodists?[11]

Coventry shared wider Enlightenment suspicions of false religion as a product of credulity, fraud, fear, and the ignorance of natural causes (for example, mistaking thunder for the angry voice of God or an earthquake for divine punishment). His dialogues tapped into all of those explanations at one point or another, and, in that sense, he was a secondary colleague of more famous and cutting *philosophes* such as Voltaire and David Hume. Still, his account of mysticism, though now completely forgotten, possessed its own edginess and originality. Probing for its erotic psychology, Coventry went further than the usual sexualizing of religious upstarts. That tack was epitomized in the prurience and wit of Jonathan Swift, who, in his *Discourse Concerning the Mechanical Operation of the Spirit* (1704), had richly satirized the "*ogling*" and "*orgasmus*" of Quaker spiritual exercises. Whereas Swift dwelled on the ease with which spiritual zeal fused with earthly lust,

Coventry developed a more explicit theory of sublimation and projection to explain the amorous qualities of "mystical dissoluteness." For Coventry, it was not the human emotions of fear and hope that explained the natural origins of religion—an explanation preferred especially by Hume. Instead, Coventry riveted attention on the unruly passion of love and the wildly illusory distortions that it produced.[12]

Coventry was nothing if not direct on this point: The great source of all mystical experience is "disappointed love." The frustrated passion is "transferred from mere mortals to a spiritual and divine object, and love ... is sublimated into devotion." That divine object is necessarily "an imaginary and artificial" contrivance, a mistaken substitute, a projection of the "wantonest appetites and wishes." In working from the perspective of the passions, which were understood to be stronger and more predominant in women, Coventry marked mysticism as primarily female, with a spirituality of sublimated sexuality making up "the far greatest part of female religion." He found such displacement of the sensual doubly sad; it was both a religious illusion and a loss of the genuine tactile pleasures of "connubial love." What devout women really suffered from, one of his male interlocutors winked to another, was "the want of timely application from our sex." Coventry's analysis fully anticipated the intellectual "fashion" that William James would later complain about in *The Varieties of Religious Experience:* namely, "criticising the religious emotions by showing a connection between them and the sexual life."[13]

Coventry helped bring *mysticism* into being in the Anglo-American world as a term laced with reproach. Misplaced sexuality, unintelligibility, pretension, and reason-be-damned piety were now among its chief associations. The Anglican bishop William Warburton (1698–1779), a contemporary of Coventry's, made those connections clear in his contemptuous conclusions about the ardent devotional writer William Law (1675–1752). Law's exposition of the rigors of piety, especially his *Serious Call to a Devout and Holy Life* (1728), had profoundly influenced such early evangelical luminaries as John Wesley and George Whitefield, and these dubious alliances already made him a marked man in Warburton's book. The perverse love that Law showed for mystical writers, particularly the German visionary Jacob Böhme (1575–1624), served to sharpen Warburton's suspicions to a knife's edge: "When I reflect on the wonderful infatuation of this ingenious man, who has spent a long life in hunting after, and, with an incredible appetite, devouring, the trash dropt from every species of Mysticism," Warburton declared, "it puts me in mind of what Travellers tell us of a horrid Fanaticism in the East, where the Devotee makes a solemn vow never to taste of other food than what has passed through the entrails of some impure or Savage Animal." Hard to put it more graphically than that: mysticism was seen as an excremental waste in the making of a learned, reasonable Christianity amenable to the forward march of the Enlightenment.[14]

Another noteworthy aspect of the understanding of mysticism before its Transcendentalist embrace was the way that the learned worked to narrow its signification rather than enlarge it. The mystics, though sometimes seen as part of a stream that flowed back to the ancient church, were commonly presented as a small camp with a few exemplary members. They were bearers, in this view, of a sectarian spirit, not a perennial philosophy. At the head of the sect was a controversial band of seventeenth-century French devotional writers—Jeanne Marie Guyon, Antoinette Bourignon, and François Fénelon—known for their supreme dedication to an inward life of prayer and utter abandonment of the self to God. In William Hurd's *New Universal History of the Religious Rites, Ceremonies, and Customs of the Whole World: or, A Complete and Impartial View of All Religions,* published in 1782, the "Account of the Mystics" was placed toward the end of his massive volume, tucked into accounts of other "smaller sects" such as the already defunct Muggletonians and French Prophets. Guilty of various excesses of piety, the mystics were, in Hurd's mind, clearly identifiable with a small group of French devotional writers and their misbegotten English successors like the unfortunate William Law.[15]

That factional understanding was encapsulated in the 1797 entry "Mystics" in the *Encyclopædia Britannica,* a multivolume project that epitomized the vast expansion and reorganization of knowledge in this century of light. "MYSTICS," the entry read, "a kind of religious sect, distinguished by their professing pure, sublime, and perfect devotion, with an entire disinterested love of God, free from all selfish considerations.... The principles of this sect were adopted by those called *Quietists* in the seventeenth century, and under different modifications, by the Quakers and Methodists." (The intensity of their withdrawal from the social world into the interior reaches of silent prayer had earned these "mystics" the disparaging sectarian label of "Quietists.") Enlightenment compilers and historians rarely followed Coventry's lead in universalizing "mystic" and "mysticism" as part of a sweeping critique of false religion. Instead, they preferred to keep the purview of the terms much more contained — and, in some sense, containable — by making them party labels for a singular brand of overwrought Christians.[16]

These British usages readily crossed the Atlantic to the new republic. Hannah Adams's compendious *Dictionary of All Religions and Religious Denominations,* which went through four editions in New England between 1784 and 1817, offered a more far-ranging account of mystics and mysticism than Hurd's parallel volume, but it nonetheless trotted out the same select club of "modern mystics." In the first edition of Noah Webster's *American Dictionary* in 1828, the narrow sectarian meaning was front and center: "MYSTICS, n. A religious sect who profess to have direct intercourse with the Spirit of God," and "mysticism" itself was still joined to seventeenth-century Quietist practices of prayer and submission. Through the 1820s and 1830s, sectarian and enthusiast understandings remained commonplace (indeed, through the sixth and seventh editions of the *Encyclopaedia Britannica,* which ran from 1823 to 1842, the entries on "mystics" closely followed the narrow eighteenth-century pedigree). These entrenched associations made mysticism an unlikely candidate for liberal absorption into their imagining of the universal religion. "The liberal mind is of no sect," Bronson Alcott proudly proclaimed. To give mysticism a sympathetic hearing, the Transcendental Club and its sundry successors would have to work against the grain of prevailing restrictions of the mystics to a minuscule sect of prayer-immersed, self-denying devotees.[17]

For a viable counterhistory to the received meanings from Catholic theology and Enlightenment critique, there were various waters for Transcendentalists, Unitarians, and fellow liberals to troll. Perhaps closest at hand were their own eighteenth-century forebears: above all, Joseph Priestley (1733–1804), a Unitarian apologist who, though often stammering in the pulpit, proved extremely fluent as a historian and natural philosopher. Like Benjamin Franklin's reputation, Priestley's fame was secured through experiments with electricity, but, unlike Franklin, Priestley was more than happy to lead a double life as a theologian. Abandoning England in 1794, which he had come to see as a wretched place of persecution, Priestley moved to postrevolutionary Pennsylvania, which he imagined as a blessed state of republican liberty. His *History of the Corruptions of Christianity* (1782) provided one common strategy for the rehabilitation of mysticism. Not that Priestley was particularly fond of the mystics; he said that he was "ashamed" as a Christian to see what kind of bodily "austerities" and scriptural "perversions" some of them had practiced in Christ's name. These horrid *"bodily exercises"* in which the flesh was tormented for the good of the soul were dismissed as Catholic vices.

Still, mysticism mattered for Priestley's Protestant Enlightenment as a flawed vessel of true interiority; it was the source of a Christian underground that managed to preserve at least the traces of true spirituality in the face of all the vulgar superstitions of pagans and Catholics. "For though the ideas of the Mystics were very confused," Priestley concluded, "they had a notion of the necessity of aiming at something of *inward purity*, distinct from all ritual observances." That proved a distinction that liberal reclaimers of the spiritual life could get their minds around, if not their bodies. The mystics contained within them the "sparks of real piety" and served, in effect, as clandestine prognosticators of pure religious interiority amid the dark ages of superstition. Nothing ascetic, nothing sacramental, nothing ritualistic, nothing bleeding or oozing—just unadulterated spiritual experience—that was a mysticism Priestley and his heirs could stomach, perhaps even savor.[18]

A little further afield, at least for most liberal Christians of the 1830s, were evangelical Protestant defenses of mysticism. Many in the evangelical movement were tired of getting beat up with the charge of enthusiasm and largely stayed clear of anything that would further associate them with such scorned sects as the Quakers and the French Prophets. But not all did. John Fletcher (1729–1785), one of John Wesley's ablest partners in Methodism's insurgency against England's Anglican establishment, wrote an explicit defense of "evangelical mysticism," by which he especially meant the unfolding of the spiritual senses of biblical passages. More than that, Fletcher had in mind a transformed mode of perception; "gospel mysticism" was a way of seeing the "invisible and spiritual" within things "gross and material." The natural world, like Scripture itself, was filled with hidden spiritual correspondences, and the reborn Christian lived in a world alive with poetic subtlety, symbolism, and grace.[19]

In a similar vein, Thomas Hartley (1708–1784), another Anglican with sympathies for the evangelical revival, was more than ready to defend mysticism, including William Law's perfectionist piety of ceaseless prayer. In 1764 he explicitly challenged the captious pigeonholing of the mystics in his *Short Defense of the Mystical Writers:* "Let it here be remarked, and constantly remembered, that the true Mystics are not to be taken for a sect or party in the church, or to be considered as separatists from it, for they renounce all such distinctions both in name and deed, being the only people that never formed a sect." By Hartley's account, *mystical* meant "nothing more nor less than spiritual," and the mystics were the "guardians" in all ages of "the spirituality of true religion." Fletcher, Hartley, and other defenders were part of wider counter-Enlightenment currents that were available for nineteenth-century projects of reclaiming mysticism as the essence of genuine spirituality. Evangelicals and Transcendentalists could both agree, for example, that devotional writers like Jeanne Marie Guyon and William Law led spiritual lives that were profoundly serious and could not be easily dismissed. They could agree, too, that the natural world was filled with divine encryptions awaiting those with the spiritual senses to decipher them.[20]

Births require parents, and, if the genealogy of the Transcendental Club meeting on mysticism in May 1838 is starting to sound complicated, it was. That lineage presented not so much a family tree, with stately branches, as a family thicket, dense with tangles. That complexity, not to say impenetrability, was clearly on display in Bronson Alcott's lifelong fascination with the subject, especially in his habits of book collecting. Emerson may have wanted active souls with fresh experiences rather than bookworms with blighted sight, but, in point of fact, reinventing mysticism required a lot of reading. Alcott's journey exemplified this. After his earnest contributions at that spring symposium on mysticism in 1838, he went on to amass a library of hundreds of volumes on "mystic and theosophic lore." If he could still talk your ear off about mysticism (he and Emerson had another long discussion of "this sublime school" on a December afternoon in 1839), that was in large part because he was an unabashed bibliophile.[21]

Alcott's collection ended up being immense. It included numerous seventeenth- and eighteenth-century editions of paragons Jacob Böhme, Antoinette Bourignon, and Jeanne Marie Guyon; several copies of William Law's works (including *The Spirit of Prayer; or, The Soul Rising Out of the Vanity of Time into the Riches of Eternity*); and a full selection of Neoplatonists from Plotinus to Thomas Taylor. There was a collection of revelations of divine love from the medieval visionary Julian of Norwich; and the venerable Thomas à Kempis, a perennial Catholic guide even for Protestants, was predictably still in the mix. These Catholic bearers of medieval mystical theology now shared shelf space, though, with such romantic works as Samuel Taylor Coleridge's *Aids to Reflection* (1825), a series of inward-looking meditations designed to help modern doubters move beyond the "uprightness" of the moral life to the "*godlikeness*" of the spiritual life. As such reading possibilities suggest, Transcendentalists and liberal Christians had many elements at their disposal to perform their alchemy of transforming mysticism from a sectarian affectation into a universal piety. Just as today's inquirers can do much of their seeking at Barnes and Noble or through Amazon.com, the nineteenth century's "New Spirituality" had a distinctly bookish feel, a communion of restless souls shaped as much through eclectic reading as through regular churchgoing.[22]

Beyond amassing an impressive library on the subject, Alcott long continued to be an arch-dreamer of mysticism. "Mysticism," he sweepingly concluded in *Concord Days* in 1872, "is the sacred spark that has lighted the piety and illuminated the philosophy of all places and times." In 1878, he enthused about the idea of starting a "Journal of Mysticism and Idealism," proposed to him in a letter from a young partisan in Osceola, Missouri. Alcott thought it would be a perfect outlet for anthologizing an array of mystical writings for the American public. His short-lived Mystic Club, essentially a reading group for corporate study and reflection organized in 1882, was an appropriate capstone to his proclamation of mysticism's global significance. Fittingly enough, Franklin Sanborn (1831–1917), as dedicated as anyone to the Transcendentalist movement and its memorialization, was also a founding member of this latest club of rapidly aging New England radicals. A biographer of Alcott, Thoreau, and Emerson, Sanborn would weave the connecting threads from the first-generation Transcendentalists through the third-generation progressives. A disciple of Theodore Parker and an abolitionist supporter of John Brown in the 1850s, Sanborn played a leading role in the Concord School of Philosophy in the 1880s and became a primary chronicler of

Sarah Farmer's Greenacre community to which Bjerregaard devoted himself. [23]

If Alcott's wide-ranging enthusiasm for the subject suggested the incorporation of a hodgepodge of materials into Transcendentalist aspirations, one source still stood above the rest: namely, Emanuel Swedenborg (1688–1772), mining expert turned mystic par excellence. In the mid-1740s, after long years of scientific inquiry, Swedenborg experienced a religious awakening that transformed him from natural philosopher to seer. Out of his newly opened spiritual sight came a vast array of writings: visionary commentaries opening up the spiritual sense of biblical texts as well as detailed reports on his grand tours of heaven and hell. Swedenborg took the Christian and occultist fascination with hidden correspondences to a new level of empirical exactness; everywhere Swedenborg turned he discovered mystical signs of the invisible world beyond the visible. The human ear, for example, corresponded to obedience to God; an odorous mouse to avarice; cats to inattentiveness to sermons. Even more mysterious was his self-reported ability to "converse with angels and spirits in the same manner as I speak with men," and it was his memorable relations of things seen and heard in the celestial world that especially garnered him a significant readership. By the 1840s, his posthumous fame had made him the most influential "mystic" in the United States, both a popular best seller and an intellectual with literary cachet. When the *Encyclopaedia Britannica* finally got around in 1858 to updating its entry on the subject, shifting from *mystics* and *mystical theology* to the increasingly universal *mysticism*, the essay paid Swedenborg an impossibly large tribute: "Nothing really new in the way of mysticism has been produced since the days of the northern seer." [24]

Almost as a matter of course Emerson chose Swedenborg, the "largest of all modern souls," to stand for his mystic of the ages in his *Representative Men* (1850). The appeal that Swedenborg held for Emerson and company was complex. As a symbolist of nature and

Scripture, his elaborate view of spiritual correspondences had resonance for Transcendentalists who held similarly arcane views of reality. Swedenborg was also a thorough anti-Calvinist, critiquing a variety of doctrines from predestination to infant damnation to the Trinity. (His rejection of John Calvin went deep: in one vision, the seer discovered that the spiritual shade of the Genevan divine was fond of frequenting otherworldly brothels.) A cosmopolitan universalist, Swedenborg saw heaven as open to all those, inside or outside the church, who sustained their love of God and active benevolence toward their neighbors. His dismissal of external miracles, while preserving room for direct internal experiences of the divine, jibed with Transcendentalist intuitions. Such theological convictions meshed well with the propensities of New England liberalism.[25]

For all those affinities, this was not a match made in heaven. In his essay enshrining Swedenborg as the representative mystic, Emerson often took away with one hand what he gave with the other. Swedenborg gained credit in Emerson's eyes for his versatility in prying into so many subjects, but there remained something strangely "scholastic" and "passionless" about him. The seer denoted whole "classes of souls as a botanist disposes of a carex," Emerson acidly remarked. Swedenborg's vast writings were without poetry; they lacked tremulous emotions and lustrous landscapes. Insufficient in his self-reliance, not ultimately rising to the level of creative genius, Swedenborg remained all too subservient to the Bible and Christian symbolism. For Emerson, the great mystic remained at last the faithful son of a Lutheran bishop, while the Concord sage was charting (so he believed) a more independent course far freer of such baggage. Swedenborg's angels, Emerson sniffed at one point, were "all country-parsons" on "an evangelical picnic." Differences aside, the larger Transcendentalist estimate of Swedenborg as mystical summit took the better measure of American fascinations with the seer. Whether for Walt Whitman, Julia Ward Howe, or Henry James Sr., no one surpassed Swedenborg as the archetype of mysticism's new possibilities in mid-nineteenth-century

America. He exemplified the potential for spiritual perception in everyday life and the renewed accessibility of angels.[26]

What mattered more than influences, even when as large and contradictory as Swedenborg's, were the distinct spiritual journeys that the growing love of mysticism made possible. Alcott and Emerson had numerous fellow travelers. Margaret Fuller (1810–1850), though not at the natal meeting for the new mysticism, joined enthusiastically in this dimension of the Transcendental Club's vision. Close to both Emerson and Alcott (she actually taught for a time with Alcott at the Temple School), Fuller served as editor of the movement's celebrated periodical, *The Dial*. Best known as a foundational thinker for the women's rights movement, she was also a self-confessed mystic. In October 1838, for example, she wrote a friend about a "heavenliest day of communion" in which "free to be alone" in "the meditative woods ... all the films seemed to drop from my existence." That

Margaret Fuller, a premier New England intellectual and a staunch advocate of women's rights, was also a self-avowed teacher of mysticism. (Firestone Library, Princeton University.)

evening, standing by herself outside a church and looking up at the crescent moon beyond the pointed spire, "a vision came upon my soul." In that moment Fuller made clear the extra-ecclesial character of her intensifying experience: "May my life be a church, full of devout thoughts." The real church was the inward life of solitary spiritual illumination, not the building, a relic of the external, whose very steeple pointed beyond itself.

Two years later Fuller was still immersed in these religious aspirations. She declared herself "more and more what they will call a mystic," even announcing that she was ready now to preach "mysticism." In her formidable work *Woman in the Nineteenth Century* (1845), Fuller imagined such religious exaltation as an essential vehicle for the progress and elevation of women, a primal source of "spiritual dignity." "Mysticism, which may be defined as the brooding soul of the world, cannot fail," she insisted, "of its oracular promise as to Woman." Fuller, like most of her compatriots, distanced mysticism from both its Catholic and its Enlightenment incarnations. It was neither an ancient form of Christian theology nor a predictable way of criticizing sectarian enthusiasm; instead, it was becoming part of an intuitive spiritual quest for originality, transcendence, and emancipation. For Fuller, laying claim to the democratic individuality at the heart of this romantic spirituality was especially important for women, so long defined in terms of their subordination to male relations. From Fuller's Transcendentalism through Annie Besant's Theosophy, "mysticism" and "spirituality," twinned nineteenth-century constructs pitting individual autonomy against ecclesial hierarchy, were often construed in radical circles as resources for the advance of women's rights.[27]

Other exemplars of the mystical turn were not hard to come by. The Transcendentalist reveries of Samuel Johnson (1822–1882) in "the serene, spiritual moonlight" of the early 1840s carried him through Harvard Divinity School and launched him on a lifelong study of Asian religions—an area in which he eventually emerged as a leading American authority. His three-volume, 2,559-page *Oriental Religions*

(1873–1885) still stands as a monument, even if now dust-gathering, to the kind of religious and historical inquiry that Transcendentalism authorized. Johnson's youthful meditations, by contrast, were more rapturous than erudite. As his friend Samuel Longfellow (1819–1882) remarked, Johnson "began soon to take on a *mystical* phase, which led him into some deep experiences." "This phase lasted but a short time," Johnson himself reported, "yet a very effervescent state it was while it lasted." An intuitionist, Johnson "sought spiritual truths by direct vision" and "by immediate inward experience." Caught up in "the rapture of devotion," Johnson asked in one rhetorical flight after another, what are the deepest longings, feelings, and aspirations at the heart of human existence? "What are the dreams of a pure spirit?"[28]

More audacious was Jones Very, a Harvard tutor of Greek and a poet of mantic insight. In attendance at the Transcendental Club meeting in May 1838, he was often seen as the most eccentric (and hence genuine) mystic of the whole crowd. In September of that year, Very had first awed Samuel Johnson, then an undergraduate at Harvard, but soon that impression turned to fright. In a letter home, the young Johnson reassured his father that Very's astonishing "absence of reason" and his wild declarations about being "a man of heaven" had not (yet) derailed his own "proper understanding of religious truth." With an increasing spiritual intensity, Very was evangelizing as much as he was teaching. He dumbfounded students and colleagues when he walked into the classroom one day and behaved like a rank enthusiast: "Flee to the mountains, for the end of all things is at hand!" he declared in a prophetic blaze that brought his days as a Harvard tutor to an abrupt end.

A nearly monthlong stay in the McLean Asylum followed, and Very gradually channeled more of his spiritual ardor and mental anguish into his identity as a poet. Eventually, he was even able to canalize his divine contemplations into brief Unitarian pastorates, but he remained far from that settled state in the fall of 1838 as he moved about the countryside as a latter-day John the Baptist. Emerson's support for Very stayed steadfast throughout this prophetic episode, even though many critics were more than willing to lay the blame for Very's "madness" on his intimacy with "Emerson & the other Spiritualists, or Supernaturalists, or whatever they are called." The journeys of Johnson and Very, like those of Alcott and Fuller, suggest the extent of mysticism's reconstruction in these liberal New England circles as a domain of individual insight and spiritual exploration. For the first time, Americans had a definable club of self-proclaimed mystics all their own, a group ready at a moment's notice, as Margaret Fuller's memoirists reported of her ecstasies, to "plunge into the sea" of "mystical trances."[29]

More sustained reflection soon emerged in this liberal religious world and even extended to those otherwise wary of the Transcendentalist ferment. Harvard's Henry Ware Jr. (1794–1843), writing for a wider liberal audience in the *Christian Examiner* in 1844, lifted up mysticism for the considered attention of all "rational Christians." "There is, perhaps, no one element of religion to which Ecclesiastical history has done so little justice," Ware suggested. Predictably cautious in his reclamation, he remained dismissive of "rude and unenlightened" forms of mysticism, including the "Fetichism" of devotions aimed at "outward objects" and the somatic tortures of "self-inflicted penance and scourgings." Ware, like Priestley before him, wanted a rarefied mysticism—one stripped of rituals and material symbols. "Now," he insisted, "as a higher stage in spiritual life has been reached, we find the mysticism of religious experience." That was a turn of phrase worthy of William James's work more than a half-century later. "We have used the word mysticism in a wider than its usual signification," Ware concluded, rightly highlighting the innovations of the era, "but what is mysticism but the striving of the soul after God, the longing of the finite for communion with the Infinite." For Ware, mysticism in the "good sense" was fundamentally about the reality of divine-human encounter, about the experiential realm of the soul that exceeded doctrinal statements, moral precepts, and worship forms.

Without mysticism, Ware insisted, there is nothing to "fill my soul's longing." "Without it there is, and there can be no religion."[30]

Robert Alfred Vaughan's two-volume compendium, *Hours with the Mystics,* first published in London in 1856 and often thereafter on both sides of the Atlantic, pushed nineteenth-century discussions of mysticism to the next level. An English Dissenter of a literary, meditative, and melancholy cast, Vaughan (1823–1857) had come around to the ministry by way of his father's example and "the lone dark room of the artist." He spent long hours wooing poetry as a youth, but he soon turned to writing theological essays, including one on Friedrich Schleiermacher, a German architect of religious liberalism, especially in his emphasis on experience as the essence of religion. Poetry and German theology were but preparation for Vaughan's work on his favored subject. "Mysticism is *the romance of religion,*" he bubbled at one point. And, like Bjerregaard after him, Vaughan was able to carry on that tryst throughout Christian history and just about anywhere else as well.

Amid his sweeping romantic vision, Vaughan still had moments of focus, and the Transcendental turn in the United States was one of them. None of his immediate contemporaries stood out more for him than "Mr. Emerson, the American essayist," whose writings possessed "in perfection the fantastic incoherence of the 'God-intoxicated' man." "Whether in prose or verse," Vaughan wrote, "he is chief singer of his time at the high court of Mysticism." Vaughan, who made comparing mysticisms an art, labeled Emerson a modern Sufi—a comparison that was not entirely an Orientalist chimera, since Emerson's eclecticism explicitly extended to the warm embrace of Persian religious poetry. Not all was similarity on this point, since Vaughan also drew a sharp contrast between what he saw as Emerson's realization of divinity through self-reliance and the Sufi's through self-conquest.[31]

Setting up his magnum opus as a series of genteel conversations among friends, Vaughan had his refined interlocutors leisurely pursue mysticism as it had found expression "among different nations and at different periods." Having produced a book with a mix of critical, appreciative, and diverting voices, Vaughan himself was hard to pin down. Sometimes he was sorting out the chaff; other times he was happily harvesting the wheat; always he was wary of appearing to endorse enthusiasm or fanaticism; quite often he simply lost his way in chatty nonchalance. That last quality especially raised the ire of Roman Catholic and High Church Anglican critics who found Vaughan's "mysticism" to be a terrible trivialization of "mystical theology." It was little more, in this view, than a shallow series of conversations "over port wine and walnuts," with the occasional "flirtation" thrown in. Those readers, of course, were hardly Vaughan's chosen audience, since he was exploring mysticism in intentionally expansive, woolly terms. Because of the very breadth and popularity of his compendia, Vaughan, more than anyone else, threw open the door for "mysticism" as a great conduit into "the highest form of spirituality."[32]

The availability of Vaughan's breezy collection made the expansion of interest in mysticism all that much easier. His volumes served as the basis for the next substantial exposition of Transcendental spirituality in the United States, a lengthy review essay by Octavius Frothingham (1822–1895), published in the *Christian Examiner* in 1861. An architect after the Civil War of the Free Religious Association, an organization that pursued (among other liberal projects) the distillation of a universal spirituality through the wide-ranging study of world religions, Frothingham helped tend the mystic flame in its transit from the first glimmering in the 1830s to the glare of fascination at the end of the century. The leading early chronicler of Transcendentalism's history, Frothingham imagined the future religion of the United States as a liberal, universal one of the spirit, not dogmatic, ecclesiastical, sacramental, or sectarian, post-Protestant as much as post-Catholic. "The mystic is only by rare exception," he insisted, "a ritualist or a sacramentalist." Above all, the mystic stands up for "the soul's light, right, and freedom against ecclesiastical authority." Offering a clearer endorsement of the mystics than Vaughan, Frothingham desired, above all, the rich interiority of their immediate insights: "We love the mystics for their inward, not for their outward life; because they lift us up above the world, not because they make us faithful in it," Frothingham avowed. "There are others, and enough of them, who will keep us up to that. We crave more mist and moonlight in America; and that the mystics give to us."[33]

The full development of "mysticism" as the basis of Bjerregaard's "New Spirituality" was all but complete when one last New England liberal, James Freeman Clarke (1810–1888), weighed in. A founding figure in the field of comparative religions at Harvard Divinity School and the author of a much heralded two-volume text called *Ten Great Religions*, Clarke delivered a lecture titled "The Mystics in All Religions" in 1880 and then published it a year later as part of his *Events and Epochs in Religious History*. Building on the tradition from Emerson and Alcott through Vaughan and Frothingham, Clarke grandly presented the mystic as one who "sees through the shows of things to their centre, becomes independent of time and space, master of his body and mind, ruler of nature by the sight of her inmost laws, and elevated above all partial religions into the Universal Religion. This is the essence of mysticism." Emerson and Jones Very took the lead as Clarke's "American Mystics"—in effect, a canonization of the first generation of Transcendentalists in which they were placed in the same company with everyone from Sufis to Swedenborg, from Buddhists to Böhme. With that lecture and essay, Clarke laid one last plank in the extensive platform that was in place for William James's exploration of mysticism in *The Varieties of Religious Experience*. "The everlasting and triumphant mystical tradition," James averred, is "hardly altered by differences of clime or creed. In Hinduism, in Neoplatonism, in Sufism, in Christian mysticism, in Whitmanism, we find the same recurring note."[34]

By 1902, when James published his great work on religious experience, the liberal reinvention of mysticism had reached its meridian. Between 1830 and 1900, American Transcendentalists and their like-minded heirs had created an ahistorical, poetic, essential, intuitive,

Harvard's James Freeman Clarke was one in a long line of nineteenth-century New England liberals who, in advance of William James, helped lift up the mystics as the bearers of a universal spirituality. (Firestone Library, Princeton University.)

universal, wildly rhapsodic mysticism. As Franklin Sanborn observed in 1900, "New England in its early days was no[t] very good soil for mysticism.... But for the past 70 years, mysticism has gained ground in New England." Sanborn, one of Transcendentalism's most devoted chroniclers, traced that development straight through from Emerson, Alcott, and Fuller to the "authors of the Greenacre school," lecturers like Carl H. A. Bjerregaard. The reinvention of mysticism that these religious liberals, radicals, and progressives effected between 1830 and 1900 would serve them well on many fronts.[35]

Of first importance was the deployment of the new mysticism in the intensifying conflicts between religion and science, which in some minds amounted to a warfare. On this minefield, the revamping of mysticism was intended as a shield against untrammeled naturalism, "the fierce onward current of purely scientific thought." "Never was there an age," one anonymous essayist insisted in 1878, "when what is true in Mysticism needed emphatic assertion more than it does to-day. The general drift of thought is antagonistic to the spiritual and the eternal. Science, and by this word is generally understood the material and economic province, absorbs in itself all thought and investigation." The very reality of the spiritual world was increasingly up for grabs in the second half of the nineteenth century, and mystics offered their own kind of empirical evidence for its existence. Not surprisingly, many of America's native-born mystics emulated Swedenborg in his ability to claim to occupy both religious and scientific domains. As the Concord seer Henry David Thoreau quipped in 1853, "The fact is I am a mystic—a transcendentalist—& a natural philosopher to boot."[36]

The cracks appearing in the once unified relationship between religion and science were bad enough, but more life-threatening were the ragged sectional divisions of the pre– and post–Civil War periods. The new mysticism had a modest place in these politics as Northern intellectuals sought a religious vision to serve the national cause of Union. Frothingham, for one, made it plain that the issues of disunion were crucial to his reflections on the future religion of the United States. These divisions whetted his desires to discern a transcendent spirit that would override knotted sectional differences, admittedly on the North's terms. Charles C. Everett (1829–1900), a Harvard professor of theology who took up James Freeman Clarke's mantle in comparative religions, wrote of mysticism in 1874 as having "to do with wholes," with the common and the unifying. "The word mysticism, whenever properly used," he said, "refers to the fact that all lives, however distinct they may appear, however varied may be their conditions and their ends, are at heart one." For Everett, no more sublime exemplar of this "mystical view of life" could be adduced than "our martyred president, Abraham Lincoln," a truly "tender and heroic soul" who understood "alike the glory and the terror" of his "great work" and who held firm for "the unity of all being" against "modern atomism." The growing liberal fascination with a globalized mysticism of universal brotherhood could serve a specific New England vision of capturing a holy union out of the rubble of rival nationalisms, North and South.[37]

Notwithstanding the interiority and solitude that these liberal Christians and post-Christians were championing, they were never far removed from the political and social realms. The suspicion that all this Transcendental talk of mysticism was isolating and self-absorbed is not borne out in these circles. Even Frothingham, who was as misty-eyed on mysticism as they came in his embrace of Vaughan's work, readily counseled that "genuine spirituality goes into the street" and does not seek the cloister. Indeed, much of the liberal writing on mysticism came to focus precisely on activism, on the "fusion of mystic communion with ethical passion." "Mysticism is the form of religion most radical and progressive," the Unitarian George W. Cooke wrote with complete confidence in 1894. William James himself was impatient with any equation of mysticism with a gospel of repose. His consistent measure of religious experience was its fruits, its production of saintliness and active habits—what he called "the moral fighting shape." James imagined mystical experience as a way to unleash energy, to find the hot place of human initiative and endeavor, and to encourage the heroic, the strenuous, the vital, and the socially transformative. Likewise, the Quaker Rufus Jones, who followed in James's footsteps and became one of the most prolific American writers on mysticism, characterized mystics as "tremendous transmitters of energy." He exemplified this through his own lifelong dedication to international relief work.[38]

Time and again, liberal religious leaders were adamant about the inseparability of mysticism and political activism, prayer and social progress. In his book *Mysticism and Modern Life*, published in 1915, the Methodist John Wright Buckham (1864–1945) made the connections between Christian spirituality and the tackling of the industrial crisis explicit with his category of "social mysticism." Buckham, a professor for more than thirty years at the Pacific School of Religion, drew a sharp line on this point: active service to others was actually a requirement to be considered under his tendentious heading of "Normal Mysticism." From the Unitarian Francis Greenwood Peabody (who developed social ethics as a distinct field at Harvard Divinity School in the 1880s) through the Quaker Howard H. Brinton (who was a guiding force in the Pendle Hill retreat center for contemplation and social action in the mid-twentieth century), the galvanizing concern for liberals was almost invariably "ethical mysticism." Those deep concerns for a spirituality of social vision and transformation would make Albert Schweitzer, Mohandas Gandhi, Dorothy Day, Martin Luther King Jr., and Howard Thurman patron saints for religious liberals. The convergence of political progressivism, socioeconomic justice, and mystical interiority was at the heart of the rise of a Spiritual Left in American culture.[39]

Finally, mysticism mattered existentially to all those wayfarers who invested so much in it. Spirituality in this new guise was embraced because of the distress it potentially assuaged, the questions of meaning it hoped to answer, the divided selves it tried to make whole, and the epiphanies it occasionally wrought. The dark question that James asked—"Is Life Worth Living?"—was hardly his alone, nor were his haunted feelings of meaninglessness, absurdity, and pointlessness. It was the sick soul in Leo Tolstoy's religious writings to which James was drawn as a worn and weary companion: "Why should I live? Why should I do anything? Is there in life any purpose which the inevitable death which awaits me does not undo and destroy?" James turned to the exploration of mysticism not out of any great optimism, but out of a profound sense of having stood all too often on a precipice of despair. His own experiences of melancholia and "quivering fear," he was convinced, "had a religious bearing." "I have no living sense of commerce with a God," James wrote. "I envy those who have, for I know that the addition of such a sense would help me greatly.... I have grown so out of Christianity that entanglement therewith on the part of a mystical utterance has to be abstracted from and overcome before I can listen. Call this, if you like, my mystical *germ.*" That experiential inkling was one James tried to safeguard from materialist suspicion, but he could never turn it for himself into more than a hedge or a hunch.[40]

Modern mysticism was always formed as much out of lacking and loss as it was out of epiphanic assurance. For many, it emerged out of an empty space of longing for "a heightened, intensified way of life" and represented a troubled quest for a unifying and integrative experience in an increasingly fragmented world of divided selves and lost souls. In his *Recollections* (1909) Washington Gladden (1836–1918), a titan among liberal Protestant thinkers and a bellwether activist as pastor of the First Congregational Church in Columbus, Ohio, tried to specify "the changes, which have taken place within the last sixty years in our conceptions of what is essential in religious experience." He recalled "so many nights, when the house was still, looking out through the casement upon the unpitying stars,... a soul in great perplexity and trouble because it could not find God." The loss of spiritual experience had become "my problem," he reported, as he increasingly lived with an ethical Christianity without raptures, without "marked and easily recognizable emotional experience." Likewise, Vida D. Scudder (1861–1954), an arch–Christian socialist and a much beloved professor of English literature at Wellesley, cultivated her mystical yearnings against a backdrop of religious loss, disorientation, and "inner misery." Turning to Episcopalian monasticism, medieval Catholic saints, and the Bhagavad Gita as contemplative anchors in her quest for interior stillness amid her exterior struggles on behalf of labor, Scudder was hardly at ease on her journey. The prayer that "punctuated my life for many years"—indeed, she said in old age, "it recurs to this day"—evoked doubt as much as hope: "O God, if there be a God, make me a real person."[41]

The turn to mysticism would have meant little if it had been primarily a species of nostalgia for lost faith, something people longed for, even as they got by without significant religious experiences. For many of these innovators, there clearly remained a living power to what they were describing as mysticism or spiritual consciousness. Take, for example, the manuscript account "My Creed So Far As I Have One," penned by the second-generation Transcendentalist and radical Thomas Wentworth Higginson (1823–1911):

> When the devout emotions come, says Emerson in substance—I have not the passage at hand—"yield to them; no matter what your theory, leave it as Joseph left his coat in the hands of the harlot, and flee." In the life of every thoughtful man, no matter how sunny his temperament, there are moments of care, sorrow, depression, perplexity when neither study nor action nor friends will clear the horizon: the tenderest love, the most heroic self-devotion leave the cloud still resting, the perplexity still there. It is at such times that the thought of an Unseen Power comes to help him; by no tradition of the churches, with no apparatus of mythology; but simply in the form that the mystics call "the flight of the Alone, to the Alone." It may be by the art of a prayerbook; it may equally well be in the depth of a personal experience to which all prayerbooks seem an intrusion. It may be in a church; it may equally well be in a solitary room or on a mountain's height.

Call these powerful experiences what you will, Higginson insisted— prayer, reverie, mystical flight, devout feeling—the critical point was "the genuineness and value of these occasional moments."[42]

Religion at its finest had become all about flashes of intensified feeling and transformed vision, about moments of direct experience, however ephemeral. "I had a revelation last Friday evening," the poet James Russell Lowell (1819–1891) wrote of one such moment. "The air seemed to waver to and fro with the presence of Something I knew not what." Likewise, in a poem he titled "The Mystic" David Atwood Wasson (1823–1887), another Transcendental preacher of the second generation and a brief successor to Theodore Parker as minister of Boston's Twenty-Eighth Congregational Society, imagined himself becoming "a leaf that quivers in God's joy," an experience of "pure participation" in the "Mystery of Being." At one of the early meetings of the Transcendental Club, in May 1837, the group had taken up the question of "what is the essence of *religion* as distinct from morality," and Emerson had responded by defining religion as "the emotion of shuddering delight and awe from perception of the infinite." The definition struck a resonant chord with his associates: Harvard's Convers Francis duly recorded Emerson's phrasing in his journal as representing the pith of the group's conversation.

A couple of years earlier, Orestes Brownson (1803–1876)—who eventually converted to Roman Catholicism, but who was then still in a liberal Protestant phase—had written a review essay titled "Spirituality of Religion" in which he portended much of the ensuing ferment. Feeling the chill of technological practicality all around him, Brownson lamented that "all our mysterious emotions, our interior cravings, [and] vague longings" are "allowed to count for nothing." He still used *spirituality* as a metaphysical term in opposition to philosophical materialism, but he also lamented "the want of spirituality" in the quietude of individual souls, the lack of the felt inspirations of the divine spirit. As weary as Emerson of religious formality, Brownson turned for warmth to "the poetry of the soul." But what, pray tell, were the rhythms and rhymes of that poetry? The awakening of spirituality was experienced, he claimed, as an intuition, an impulse, an energy, an enthusiasm, an inward breathing of God's spirit in the heart, a contemplative stillness, a waiting in silence, "a freedom of soul." It is hardly surprising that William James, a culminating figure in this New England lineage, imagined mysticism as "original and unborrowed experience" and fleeting "states of insight."[43]

If the Transcendentalists often seemed longer on excited prose than extended practice, their aspirations nonetheless carried the day. "Mysticism is an experience," C. H. A. Bjerregaard said assuredly in one of his lectures in 1896. "Learn to say with Thoreau: 'I hear beyond the range of sound, / I see beyond the range of sight.'" It would be almost impossible now to think of mysticism as only a wing of Christian theology and practice or as the domain of one small set of Catholic devotees and their few Protestant defenders. The efforts of Coventry and company to treat mysticism in terms of sexual pathology and psychological illusion still resonate, no doubt, with some diehard skeptics. In the early twentieth century, the notion of religion's "erotogenesis"—its origin in "sex mysticism"—gained a genuine intellectual vogue, but the appeal of that position, along with its ability to shock, has now long since dwindled. That kind of explanation hardly enjoys a fraction of the popularity of mysticism considered as a perennial philosophy, an ageless dimension of religious experience, or "a journey of ultimate discovery." The "mystic heart" beats vibrantly on as part of a "universal spirituality" gleaned from the religions of the world, a pulsing of interconnections still established through the timelessness of mystical states of consciousness.

Even a seemingly quintessential embodiment of the current New Age, the Zen-practicing basketball coach Phil Jackson, partakes as much of mysticism's nineteenth-century exaltation as more recent fads. In his spiritual memoir *Sacred Hoops* (1995), Jackson tells of his journey from a Pentecostal boyhood in North Dakota to a life of Buddhist meditation in the glamorous world of the National Basketball Association. The major catalyst for the shift in his spiritual sensibilities had actually occurred while he was on the road with the New York Knicks through a close reading of William James's *Varieties of Religious Experience,* "a book filled with firsthand accounts by Quakers, Shakers, and other Christian mystics." As Jackson related, "I couldn't put it down." The book led him to his own form of low-key "mystical experience," "a quiet feeling of inner peace" for which he had longed as a Pentecostal teenager, but which had always eluded him. Moving into the open air of Jamesian curiosity, Jackson read evermore widely on yoga, Sufism, and Buddhist meditation, even as he saw his quest as part of a fuller and more honest engagement with his Christian up-bringing and its principles of "selflessness and compassion." Having been exposed to James's club of mystics, Jackson could now "explore other traditions more fully without feeling as if I was committing a major sacrilege against God and family." The mystics, considered as an exalted fellowship of great souls free of history and bound together through firsthand experiences of the infinite, are clearly just as dear today with contemporary seekers as they were in the nineteenth century with religious liberals.[44]

CHAPTER TWO

SOLITUDE

I **SAT IN MY SUNNY DOORWAY** from sunrise till noon, rapt in a revery," Henry David Thoreau (1817–1862) wrote of an experience at Walden Pond in the mid–1840s, "amidst the pine and hickories and sumachs, in undisturbed solitude and stillness." Though "naturally no hermit" and happily entertaining various visitors in his makeshift home in the woods, Thoreau pronounced a distinct and enduring blessing upon isolation through his two-year experiment twenty miles outside Boston and a mile or so from the village of Concord. "I find it wholesome to be alone the greater part of the time," he confessed. "To be in company, even with the best, is soon wearisome and dissipating. I love to be alone. I never found the companion that was so companionable as solitude." His commitment to simplicity and seclusion hardly made for loneliness or melancholy. He said that only once during his sojourn, and only "for an hour" as a result of "a slight insanity in my mood," had he felt "the least oppressed by a sense of solitude." His was not a misanthropic withdrawal from friendship and society, but a spiritual retreat into a natural world of revelatory sounds and seasons. The question about solitude that

Thoreau put to himself and to his age was ultimately one of contemplative discernment: "What do we want most to dwell near to?"[1]

Beginning his sojourn in the woods on Independence Day in 1845, Thoreau gave practical embodiment to Transcendentalist self-reliance and religious aspiration, to "the solitude of soul" that his friend Emerson, fourteen years his senior, had already praised as a desideratum in his private journal and in his manifesto *Nature* (1836). "I got up early and bathed in the pond," Thoreau wrote of his morning ablutions. "That was a religious exercise, and one of the best things which I did." He reenacted in the glow of the sunrise his desire for casting off slumber and for awakening into "a poetic or divine life." "To be awake is to be alive. I have never yet met a man who was quite awake. How could I have looked him in the face?" His devout habits at Walden were anything but ethereal, enveloping his body, dress, food, and furnishings, which Thoreau imagined—loosely, to be sure—as a "Hindoo" discipline: "Nothing was too trivial for the Hindoo lawgiver, however offensive it may be to modern taste. He teaches how to eat, drink, cohabit, void excrement and urine, and the like, elevating what is mean, and does not falsely excuse himself by calling these things trifles.... We are all sculptors and painters, and our material is our own flesh and blood and bones." The angular hermit imagined an ascetic path of awakening; his exploration of the solitary life was a quest for a purity of soul and body.[2]

Thoreau devoted a distinct chapter to "Solitude" in *Walden* and at another point imagined a dialogue between a Hermit and a Poet, which allowed him to bring his spiritual and artistic sensibilities into a direct, if ironic, exchange. The Poet, rustling through the woods, interrupts the Hermit in the midst of "serious meditation" and tries to draw him off in a diversion. The Hermit initially resists and tries to recover his frame of mind and its "budding ecstasy," but finds that his thoughts have left no trail. "I was as near being resolved into the essence of things as ever I was in my life. I fear my thoughts will not come back to me," the Hermit laments. Resigning himself to his lost oppor-

Henry David Thoreau led
the way in the American
reevaluation of the spiritual
potential of solitude.
(Concord Free Public Library.)

tunity for heightened spiritual awareness, the Hermit goes off with
the Poet to fish. Confessedly, fishing in itself evoked mixed feelings
for Thoreau; it was, by turns, an instinctual means of subsistence and
sport, an offense to his "higher" inclinations to abstain from all "animal food," and an emblem of meditative retreat. Fishing was potentially redeemable from the uncleanness of killing when viewed as a
spiritual practice. It was for some, Thoreau surmised, "a sort of solemn
sacrament and withdrawal from the world, just as the aged read their
bibles."[3]

Thoreau's hermitage at Walden Pond constitutes no doubt the most
famous American exploration of solitude. "If any American," a contemporary commented a few years after Thoreau's death, "deserves to
stand as a representative of the experience of recluseness, Thoreau is

Walden, with its powerful evocation of Thoreau's pond-side hermitage, emerged as the classic text in the Transcendentalist reconfiguration of solitude. (Concord Free Public Library.)

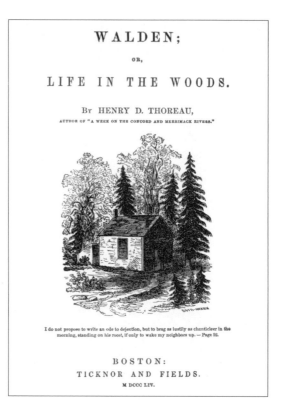

WALDEN;

OR,

LIFE IN THE WOODS.

By HENRY D. THOREAU,

AUTHOR OF "A WEEK ON THE CONCORD AND MERRIMACK RIVERS."

I do not propose to write an ode to dejection, but to brag as lustily as chanticleer in the morning, standing on his roost, if only to wake my neighbors up. — Page 92.

BOSTON:

TICKNOR AND FIELDS.

M DCCC LIV.

the man." Courting notoriety, the Concord hermit created religious controversy in seeking his inspiration primarily beyond the pale of the churches and its saints. He set up the Buddha especially as a sign of his desire to move beyond the usual ligatures of New England Protestantism and to question standing religious authorities: "I know that some will have hard thoughts of me, when they hear their Christ named beside my Buddha, yet I am sure that I am willing they should love their Christ more than my Buddha, for the love is the main thing, and I like him too." If Thoreau staked the originality of his religious journey upon the apparent confluence of the Concord and the Ganges, he still wrote in the shadow of the Bible and the church. His own solitude, however distinctive and celebrated, represented a wider cultural convergence and realignment, a crossing from Christian exemplars of holiness to more diffuse sources and inspirations. It took a lot of cultural work to get to Thoreau's Walden, let alone to produce William James's eccentric seeker for whom "at any time the word *hermit* was enough to transport him."[4]

Thoreau's experiment occupies a critical juncture in the long and rich history of the solitude of hermits, one of the romantic crossroads in the making of American spirituality. Transcendentalists were those strange philosophers, the historian Henry Adams wryly remarked in their wake, who "sought conspicuous solitudes" and who "looked out of windows and said, 'I am raining.'" Adams may have found Transcendentalism's attention-grabbing hermits "unutterably funny," but the movement's rise was crucial to the reconfiguring of the anchorite's practice. Thoreau and company revalued solitude, opening it outward from specifically Christian forms of retired devotion into more diffuse forms of aspiration, religious and artistic. "Spirituality did ever choose loneliness," the second-generation Transcendentalist William Rounseville Alger (1822–1905) declared in his formative work *The Solitudes of Nature and of Man* in 1866. "For there the far, the departed, the loved, the unseen, the divine, throng freely in, and there is no let or hindrance to the desires of our souls." Solitude, in effect, underwent a post-Protestant transformation in which the search for isolation and retreat became the spiritual motto for more than one generation of seekers. Thoreau and his circle managed to leave a lasting mark on American imaginings of spirituality, evident in a long train of figures from John Muir and John Burroughs to Thomas Merton and Annie Dillard who made the solitary life an object of meditation and desire. As Barbara Erakko Taylor cheerily explains of her "hunger for unbroken solitude" in *Silent Dwellers* (1999), "We all have idealized, even romantic, ideas of a hermit. Mine had a self-denying, Thoreau-like quality: a rustic cabin with wood furniture."[5]

The *Encyclopædia Britannica* of 1797 defined the hermit or eremite as "a devout person retired into solitude, to be more at leisure for prayer and contemplation." It took the early Christian history as its baseline, reckoning the story from fourth-century accounts of St. Paul the Hermit and St. Anthony; indeed, it had no other frame of reference beyond these desert fathers and their austere devotions. That starting point was hardly one of unambiguous faith and heroic asceticism for wary Protestants and equally wary philosophers of the Enlightenment. In his famed history, *The Decline and Fall of the Roman Empire* (1776–1788), Edward Gibbon portrayed the "perpetual solitude" of anchorites as the product of a "savage enthusiasm." "These unhappy exiles from social life were impelled by the dark and implacable genius of superstition," Gibbon wrote with horror of the spreading influence of these ascetic ideals throughout the empire and the peril they had posed to civil society and its manlier virtues. The solitary life of the hermit was a matter of "blind submission" to ecclesial tyranny and the very opposite of "the freedom of the mind" to which Enlightenment learning aspired. These supposed saints of the desert had their lives "consumed in penance and solitude, undisturbed by the various occupations which fill the time, and exercise the faculties, of reasonable, active, and social beings." The challenge that these Christian recluses posed to pagan virtues made them potentially ominous signs of decline and ruin. Gibbon's suspicion of hermits, in short, was akin to Henry Coventry's contempt for mystics.[6]

In a new nation steeped in the joined dicta of Protestantism and the Enlightenment, such fears of civic and religious deformity necessarily haunted American thinking on solitude. The entry on hermits and anchorites in the first edition of the *Encyclopedia Americana* (1829–1833) had some of Gibbon's vituperative tone: "the spirit of retirement and self-torment raged like an epidemic among the early Christians"; "the melancholy of solitude" had often degenerated into "fanatical excesses" and "moral insanity." In 1850 Henry Ruffner, one of a venerable troupe of Protestant college presidents in antebellum America, took up the history of "the primitive monks and hermits" as a cautionary tale in two volumes. Depicting the rise of early Christian asceticism as a descent into ever "deeper and drearier solitudes,"

Ruffner saw these "saintly savages" of the desert as men of wild superstitions about demons, angels, poverty, and sexuality. The hermits,
already perverse in their lewd chastity, gave way to the still greater depravity of monks who underwrote "the monstrous system of Popish
tyranny and persecution" and who served as a warning to any pro-
fessed Protestants for whom High Church Anglicanism or Roman
Catholicism offered even a remote temptation.[7]

In the nineteenth-century Protestant imagination, the ancient desert
fathers seemed at best exotic in their saintly warfare upon temptations
of flesh and spirit. In *Hours with the Mystics* (1856), one of Robert
Alfred Vaughan's interlocutors remarked that she had been "looking
at the pictures in Mrs. Jameson's *Sacred and Legendary Art,* of those
strange creatures, the hermit saints—the Fathers of the desert."
Vaughan's Protestant discussants were both appalled by the "wonder-
working pretensions" of these sanctified anchorites and yet drawn
into the tormenting visions of St. Anthony and the rest, which were
"not without grandeur." For refined Protestant audiences, the desert
hermits of Egypt remained present especially through their iconogra-
phy, an inherited part of nineteenth-century fine arts. The book that
inspired Vaughan's exchange, Anna Jameson's guide to sacred art, was
especially popular; it went through multiple editions after its initial
appearance in 1848 and contained numerous images of the hermit
saints in all their archaic difference. Their oddities, in other words,
were something to examine in well-illustrated books or on the walls
of museums, not an example to imitate.[8]

Even when not focused on the corruption of Christianity that the
perverse desire for the hermit's cell had precipitated, evaluations of solitude often remained admonitory. "In solitude the heart withers,—God
meant it for social life," the Reverend William Peabody preached in a
sermon published in 1831. An enemy of social benevolence and domestic happiness, solitude produced religious presumption, not mutual regard. "It is less a virtue than a sin," Peabody concluded. It was seen as
one more solvent that corroded civil society and highlighted the danger

of new democratic freedoms turning into self-loving vices. The American experiment with freedom and equality, Alexis de Tocqueville warned in his classic commentary *Democracy in America* (1835–1840), was begetting "a novel expression" of "*individualism*." The new democracy, however robust, remained vulnerable; it seemed to throw each citizen "back forever upon himself alone" and "to confine him entirely within the solitude of his own heart." From the vantage point of a fragile republic, solitude appeared the very antithesis of a religiously cohesive nation.[9]

The popular tales that circulated in the first half of the nineteenth century about more recent hermits reinforced the low and fearful standing of solitude as destitution. In the lore of contemporary wonders and marvels, hermits were known far more for lost love and

The woes of Robert Voorhis, a former slave turned solitary, exemplified the ways in which the hermit was presented as a tragic and forlorn figure in antebellum America. (Rare Books and Special Collections, Princeton University Library.)

ROBERT THE HERMIT.

unredeemed suffering than spiritual potential. Telling in this regard was *Life and Adventures of Robert Voorhis, the Hermit of Massachusetts, Who Has Lived 14 Years in a Cave, Secluded from Human Society* (1829), a narrative of a former slave from Princeton, New Jersey, who resided in a "solitary hermitage" close to Providence, Rhode Island. An object of local curiosity, Voorhis was thought by many to be a melancholy misanthrope, but the narrator revealed him to have been a cruelly mistreated slave, separated at age four from his mother and sister and as a young man from his wife and two children. The solitude of his "rude cell" was, Voorhis reported to his inquirer, a deliberate response to "the bitter cup of my afflictions!—afflictions which had more or less attended me through life!" To some, from the outside, the hilltop retreat might seem "a most romantic situation" as it supplied the hermit's simple wants from "the bountiful hand of nature," but the narrator quickly disposed of that idyll. Living in a dark, cold, cramped cave was not a resource for practical Christian faith; instead, only a hope for the ultimacy of divine justice sustained Voorhis, as did the principle "that human beings, whatever might be their complexion[,] were all created equally free." These were not religious and political convictions that he garnered from solitude, but ones he held on to despite his sorrow and separation. The life of Robert the Hermit was intended to inspire others not to devotional imitation, but to feelings of "sympathy for distress." His narrative was expressly published as a project of benevolence to raise funds to improve his condition and to further the antislavery cause.[10]

Other hermit narratives of the period told similarly forlorn stories of loss. John Conrad Shafford, whose tale of woe was published in 1841, spent his last fifty years living "a secluded and lonely life." He was driven to it through "being deprived of an only child, a beloved daughter," who was taken captive by Indians at age fifteen and who died "a wretched victim of their barbarity." Three months later he was "bereaved of my wife" as well, and so, like Robert, this "Dutch Hermit" had chosen "solitary retreat" as a result of "heavy afflictions."

Ruinous calamity also marked the life of Sarah Bishop, popularly known as the Hermitess. (Firestone Library, Princeton University.)

The Hermitess. Vol. 1, p. 24.

As one spiritual guide of the period put it, "The grieved heart, like the wounded deer, retreats into solitude to bleed."[11]

Similarly tragic was Sarah Bishop's story. During the American Revolution, British soldiers plundered her family's home on Long Island, and she "was made a victim of one of those demoniac acts, which in peace are compensated by the gibbet, but which, in war, embellish the life of the soldier." Bishop fled the shame of her rape and apparently lived in a desolate cave for most of the next three decades. Both Shafford and Bishop were reputed to take consolation in their gloom from reading precious (if tattered) copies of the Bible, and so both could be pictured as looking beyond this vale of tears to "a brighter and happier existence." In neither case was solitude thought to be the vehicle for spiritual attainment, however; instead, it was an isolated state of grief that was partially assuaged through the other-worldly vision of the Scriptures. When Walt Whitman actually met "a real hermit" in "one of my rambles," he projected only heartache upon him and his "lonesome spot," remarking that the man "did not unbosom his life, or story, or tragedy."[12]

The Protestant suspicion of monasticism and the pained commiseration of reform-minded benefactors were less than promising bases for Thoreau's revaluing of solitude. Pity and Protestant polemic, however, were not the only responses that hermits evoked in the early republic; they also attracted journalistic sensation and touristic attention. Hundreds had apparently sought out Robert the Hermit, hoping to penetrate the veil of his mysterious isolation and gratify their curiosity, and Sarah Bishop, likewise, attracted those looking for a good excursion, a double marvel as "a woman hermit." At the end of one pamphlet from 1815 titled "Remarkable Discovery of an American Hermit," Captain James Buckland even offered to provide "particular directions for any one to go and find the Hermit, and satisfy his own curiosity" about this mournful soul and his hidden cave. The architect Harriet Morrison Irwin in her fictional tale *The Hermit of Petræa* had her title character remark that if Yankee travelers were to get wind of "the charmed word *hermit* ...I should soon find myself driven out of this dear retreat of mine by sight-seers and sensation-mongers." Not surprisingly, one of Thoreau's visitors at Walden suggested that he needed to have on display in his cabin "a book in which visitors should write their names, as at the White Mountains." Would solitude be solitude without a log of witnesses, travelers, and guests? Would solitude be recognizable without intrusion and interruption?[13]

So travel, voyeurism, and curiosity provided a point of departure toward Thoreau's Transcendentalist crossroads. The hermit's cave or cabin was an attraction that carried the sensational appeal of secretiveness and mystery. One of the many nineteenth-century loners of the Adirondacks, a region rich in its interweaving of travel guides and hermit lore, doubled in the summer as a concessionaire for tourists. That did not disqualify Stewart Wilson from his reputation as the Hermit of Sacandaga Park—an embodiment of an aimless rusticity that only added to his allure for visitors. The Adirondacks, to be sure, became one of the great and lasting sources of tales about hermits and hermitages, and the park still retains that image. It is a place where hermits lurk on the edges of a visitor's peregrinations and imagination. As Sue Halpern writes at the opening of *Migrations to Solitude: The Quest for Privacy in a Crowded World* (1992), "Deep among the birch, some miles back from my house in the Adirondack Mountains, is a cabin where a man is said to have lived alone for a quarter century, maybe longer. Then one day, the story goes, he walked out of the woods and disappeared." In writing her own meditations on solitude, she looked for that man in prisons and monasteries to talk to him about his experience "as a physical fact," but, in a poetic deferral that only heightens the air of mystery and desire, she (of course) never finds him.[14]

Sensational tales of dark caves, heartbreak, meager diets, secret shame, unkempt bodies, and long years of isolation fed a popular fascination with hermits and seeking them out. Thoreau's visitors certainly participated in that romance of intrusion and discovery. Prying into a puzzle of eccentricity was alluring—why, an "extraordinary" narrative from 1839 asked, would one Amos Wilson, "usually termed 'the Pennsylvania Hermit,'" live in a cave for nineteen years and prefer a state of solitude to that of society? Wilson had been driven to seek refuge in a cave twelve miles from Harrisburg through the disgracing seduction, desperate infanticide, and spectacular execution of his only sister. Yet, unlike other hermit tales of unhappiness, Wilson's anonymous narrator insisted on finding religious redemption through "The Sweets of Solitude." The sister went to her death (despite a pardon from the governor arriving minutes late) with spiritual fortitude and peace. She left a letter to her brother, which contained as a "last request," that he "cherish religion" and promote it. And Wilson, accordingly, turned his dreary cave into a Protestant hermitage where he courted "only the company of the Divine Spirit" and escaped "the taunts of the children of pride." Spending his days in devotional reading and in making millstones to exchange for necessities, Wilson also wrote religious meditations on finding "true felicity" through withdrawal into "the blessing of Solitude." The Pennsylvania Hermit became, in the hands of his biographer, a spiritual guide who offered wisdom about overcoming worldly appetites, discontents, and vanities through renunciation and retirement, through "stricter intimacy with ourselves" and "closer communion with God."[15]

As the moralized life and writings of Amos Wilson suggest, Protestant guides, despite their anti-Catholic cautions, found ways to retain the value of solitude as a space for prayer, meditation, and self-examination. Ever alert to keeping Christian piety joined to the republican virtues of civic-mindedness, American Protestants usually found it necessary to perform a delicate balancing act in recovering solitude. Amos Wilson, however piously living out his life in a cave, could hardly be a model for that judicious moderation.

For the purposes of marrying "occasional retirement" and prudential social engagement, the work of the German physician Johann Zimmerman (1728–1795) was among the most useful. A genteel philosophical guide to virtue and self-knowledge, Zimmerman's *Solitude* became a standard in English translation between 1790 and 1850, with editions appearing in Boston, Brooklyn, Charleston, Philadelphia, and elsewhere. (Thoreau himself owned a copy of an early edition that had been published in Albany, New York, in 1796.) Against "the sterile tranquility of the cloister," Zimmerman pitted the serene self-awareness of the active and confident man of the world. His manual, with its careful calculation of the advantages and the dangers of solitude, was embraced as part of an eminently reasonable faith, especially valuable for the disciplining of youthful minds in the demands of tempered passions and civic duties. Zimmerman's solitude harmonized reason and the Reformation for didactic purposes that American Protestants could easily admire.[16]

Even in more devotional works, balance was critical. In his essay "Of Solitude," the seventeenth-century Oxford contemplative John Norris had struck a chord that remained typical for its moderation. He was careful not to commend the "*Eremetical* way of Living," "the undertaking of those *Ascetics*, that out of a pretence of keeping themselves *unspotted from the World*, take up their quarters in *Desarts*." At the same time, though, he praised solitude as "the proper opportunity of Contemplation, which is both the *Foundation* and the *Perfection* of a Religious Life." Jesus himself, withdrawing into the wilderness to pray, was taken as the great exemplar of vigilant solitude and underpinned Norris's advocacy of occasional retreat from secular and learned exchanges. In a similar vein, a popular Scottish devotional guide, making the transit across the Atlantic at the turn of the nineteenth century and thereafter frequently reissued, carried the title *Solitude Sweetened.* The sugars it offered were predictable enough: among them, meditations on the beauties of heaven, the excellencies of the Savior, and the mercies of God. Its larger practical point remained the value of frequent (but not too frequent) retirement for the cultivation of the spiritual life.[17]

American Protestants wanted the spiritual virtues of hermits without their supposed vices. The continuing circulation of a poem by the widely esteemed writer Thomas Parnell (1679–1718), a father to the protoromantic poets of melancholy and the graveyard, suggested the strain of this ambivalence. Parnell had embraced the figure of the solitary as a revered pilgrim who passed "a life of piety and peace," and his "Hermit" was considered so filled with fine sentiments that the New England Tract Society kept the poem in distribution a century later as an edifying moral and religious tale:

> Remote from man, with God he passed his days,
> Prayer all his business, all his pleasure praise.

In turn, in 1841 Parnell's poem appeared as an appendix to an unlikely Methodist devotional work, *The Life of Gregory Lopez, a Hermit in*

America, a religious biography of a Spanish Catholic monk who cultivated his austere calling in sixteenth-century Mexico. (John Wesley
had picked up Lopez's memoir for his library of Christian classics,
and American Methodists duly embraced it as a model of "perfect resignation" in the first half of the nineteenth century.) Here were two
hermit stories, Parnell's and Lopez's, happily packaged together for
American Protestant usage, and yet the editor, John Eyre, still felt the
need to disclaim his very paragons in the preface: "This narrative,
however, is not intended to excite any one to ... turn hermit." [18]

Eyre's blessing of the hermit's life was typically mixed. He confessed that those who had resorted to dens, deserts, and caves had
done so "probably from mistaken notions," but that they had nonetheless left some "worthy examples" of utter dedication to holiness. For
the Methodist editor, Lopez was an embodiment of the "perfect love"
of God, of the entirely sanctified life. Heroic in his denial of the flesh
and his scourging of vain self-assertion, Lopez lived on the sparest
diet, no meat at all, and, during Lent, his abstinence was even fiercer.
His exercise of prayer in his "little cell" was similarly dedicated and
systematic; it proceeded through three full years focused on the resignation of his will to God's, followed by a similar regimen around the
love of God, which ultimately led Lopez to a sense of union with
God. Humble, patient, ever careful of speech, Lopez was consumed
in prayer, so much so that he felt that the drawing of each breath returned him to God's presence. Perhaps the very extremity of Lopez's
example canceled the effect of Eyre's cautions, or perhaps it only redoubled the Protestant suspicion that "the life of a hermit is not the
life of a Christian." "Let us," the Methodist editor of this Catholic life
concluded, "practice his virtues at home, without retiring to the
desert." [19]

If a new love of solitude were to take flight, some of these standing
cautions—domestic, civic, moral, and religious—would have to be
thrown to the wind. The American wooing of the hermit was not going
anywhere if one arm kept pushing away what the other one embraced.

One counterpoint came, not surprisingly, from Roman Catholic writers, who increasingly weighed in on the side of the ancient hermits of the desert against the usual Protestant and Enlightenment dismissals. Through immigration especially, Roman Catholicism surged ahead in the mid-nineteenth century as America's largest denominational body. With that rapid growth, the lives of the first anchorites gained a new foothold and audience. Their visible holiness was a challenge to throw in the face of those Protestants who enjoyed consoling and titillating themselves with sensational tales of monastic depravity (grim stories about priests sexually assaulting imprisoned nuns were especially popular).

In 1853 Orestes Brownson, a onetime radical Transcendentalist now turned devoted Roman Catholic, aggressively reasserted the example of the early Christian hermits in lifting up the American publication of *The Lives of the Fathers of the Eastern Deserts,* a work by the English Catholic apologist Richard Challoner. These humble, self-macerating saints of solitude were seen as a rebuke to "the men and women of our material and luxurious age, which adores Mammon as God, and counts sensual pleasure heaven." Not coincidentally, within a decade, the first American edition of *Life of St. Anthony* appeared as a devotional exemplum. Likewise, the Trappist Abbey of Gethsemani in Kentucky, which the contemplative writer Thomas Merton later made famous, was slowly built from 1851 to 1866. (Challoner's book had carried particular praise for Trappist reforms and the wisdom they reflected about the soul's relish for "God in solitude" and silence.) Looking for a spiritual awakening through retreat houses and contemplative monastic orders rather than old-time Protestant revivals, Brownson wanted for his country more of "the spirit which led St. Anthony into the desert." He looked for less of Martha's bustling activity around Jesus and more of Mary's quiet listening to Him. Catholics like Brownson were intent on giving Protestants pause: "The saints of the desert, the religious of the cloisters, all the monastic orders" were "the pride and glory" of Christianity.

Brownson, the disaffected Transcendentalist, also made explicit that in his reading "these Oriental saints" did not offer a lesson about wilderness, wildness, and "natural beatitude," but an ascetic model for fathoming "God and heaven."[20]

Both Thoreau's embrace of solitude and Brownson's Catholic rebuttal suggested some of the abandon necessary to reclaim solitude from Protestant ambivalence. Another source was the budding romance that grew up in the nineteenth century around the memory of Johannes Kelpius (1673–1708) and the small band of German mystics whom he led into the Pennsylvania wilderness at the end of the seventeenth century. An ascetic, a celibate, an apocalypticist, and a contemplative, Kelpius embodied his spiritual purity and power through a hermit's life in a cave at some remove from Germantown. Thriving at the crowded intersection of multiple devotional traditions, including the exchange between Christian mystical theology and Jewish Kabbalah, Kelpius left a rich testimony to his own life of "inward prayer." His was a quest after a perpetual "Prayer of the Heart" through which "pure Love" and "the Presence of God" were drawn into him. "This Way," he said, "is called a mystical Way," and it moves the soul into an inward domain of silence and contemplation "without Thoughts, Words or Images." Every bit as strenuous as Lopez's, Kelpius's solitary life of uninterrupted prayer led into an experiential realm that he depicted as one of pure spirit, freedom, and love.[21]

Kelpius was part of a sectarian enclave, known as the Chapter of Perfection, small in number and inspired by a series of austere émigrés, including Johannes Seelig, Justus Falkner, and Conrad Matthai, all of whom lived as hermits at one point or another. Their influence was necessarily limited in colonial America, and they left little by way of an institutional legacy. That scant trace, however, in no way impeded these "Hermits of the Ridge" from growing in stature in wistful memory: Hermit Lane, Hermit Spring, Hermit's Glen, and Kelpius's "Anchorite Cell" all survived in the nineteenth-century topography of "the romantic Wissahickon." Wandering in that forest ravine and along its stream near the end of the nineteenth century, the leading remembrancer of these hermits experienced an enchanted landscape and imagined seeing in it "almost the same vast, silent and unmolested solitude" that Kelpius and his fellow recluses had found there two centuries before. This latter-day chronicler of the Hermits of the Wissahickon imagined a place of "mystic incantation" and "spiritual inspiration amidst the beauties of primeval nature." Some years earlier the poet John Greenleaf Whittier (1807–1892) had performed the same romantic alchemy with Kelpius's "hermit den" in his poem "The Pennsylvania Pilgrim." Imagining the mystic "deep in the woods" with visions vouchsafed to him alone, Whittier pictured Kelpius "weird as a wizard," the "maddest of good men." In nineteenth-century memory, the pious souls of this Chapter of Perfection became part of a larger dreamscape of mystic lore and solitude. Through the rosy lens of nostalgia, they became the Hermits of the Romantic Wissahickon. Mining this vein, lovers of solitude found their gold.[22]

John Greenleaf Whittier, a Quaker who late in life gave his blessing to Sarah Farmer and the landscape of Greenacre and who was remembered there as a spiritual seer, warmed also to Jean-Jacques Rousseau's heart-brimming experiences of solitude and nature. The French philosopher, especially through his *Confessions* and his *Reveries of a Solitary Walker,* provided valued sources for the consecration of lonely introspection, and Whittier expressly turned Rousseau's effusive feelings on the subject into poetry in "The Chapel of the Hermits." After picturing some hermits at their devotions in a secluded shrine in the woods, Whittier, always adept at the nostalgic touch, admitted that they may seem but "a morning dream, a tale that's told":

> *No Hermits now the wanderer sees,*
> *Nor chapel with its chestnut-trees.*

He insisted, though, on the freshness of their lesson as a check on creeds, institutions, and "clouds of doubt":

Henceforth my heart shall sigh no more
For olden time and holier shore;
God's love and blessing, then and there,
Are now and here and everywhere.

Remembering the solitude of hermits became a source of spirituality regained and transfigured. For Whittier—a poet of reform causes, especially antislavery—hermits became an invitation not to submit to churchly authority, but to "search thine own heart" and pursue Quakerism's "Inner Light" or "Christ within": "Make the truth thine own, for truth's own sake."[23]

Whittier's influence on the emerging cultus of solitude and interiority was important, if diffuse—a poem here, a memorial there. By the time of Whittier's seventieth birthday, Henry Wadsworth Longfellow was praising his fellow poet as the "Hermit of Amesbury" in "The Three Silences of Molinos," a piece that expressly joined Spanish Catholic mystical theology to Quaker practices of silence. Whittier was depicted as an American saint in whose daily life "the spiritual preponderates" and through whom "melodies beyond the gates" are heard. Shortly after the poet's death, Benjamin Orange Flower (1858–1918), a leading editor who had a hand in most of early progressivism's causes through his journal *The Arena,* hailed Whittier as "A Modern Apostle of Lofty Spirituality." In Flower's glowing estimate, the Quaker bard crucially rewrote New England piety in a liberalized form of love, intuition, optimism, social reform, and universal brotherhood. Whittier had led the way from the shadows of Calvinist theology into "the sunlight of spirituality," from orthodox narrowness to "largeness of spirit." Another commentator on "American Mysticism," the Unitarian George W. Cooke, lifted Whittier up in 1894 as the supreme embodiment of "a new type of devotional literature." "In the religious poems of Whittier," Cooke proclaimed, "we have the best interpretation of the devotional spirit this country has yet produced." "Altar, church, priest and ritual will pass away," Whittier had prophesied at one point of the end of organized religion, and in its place will be the devotion of the individual human heart, "the Holy of Holies."[24]

By comparison with Whittier's episodic contributions, William Rounseville Alger's lectures and writings on solitude were sustained and systematic. His book on the subject in 1866 came to constitute the fullest Transcendentalist statement on solitude's importance; it went through multiple editions and was partly serialized as well in the *Liberal Christian.* Attending Harvard Divinity School in the mid-1840s and joining in the meetings of the Hook and Ladder Club, another successor to the Transcendental Club as a gathering of liberal dissidents, Alger entered the Unitarian ministry in 1847 and served a church in Roxbury, Massachusetts. Unlike Emerson and George Ripley, but like his close friend and fellow abolitionist Theodore Parker, Alger spent his entire career in the ministry, mostly in and around Boston, but also in New York City and briefly as far west as Denver. At ease in the literary circles of first- and second-generation Transcendentalists, Alger first made a splash in 1856 with his anthology *The Poetry of the East,* later republished as *The Poetry of the Orient.* (Emerson himself welcomed it as a "brave sally into Orientalism" in a letter to Alger soon after its publication.) "Must not a spiritual contact between the enterprising young West and the meditative old East be a source of uncommon stimulus and culture?" Alger asked at the outset of his collection of translations. It was a loaded question, of course, typical in its Transcendentalist way of imagining a spiritualized Orient as offering a restored balance to a materialist Occident. Like his many coconspirators, Alger turned to "the mystic East" far more out of a desire to enrich Western religious traditions than to understand the complexities of Asian cultures.[25]

Roaming in his anthology from China to India to Persia, Alger found special inspiration in the "electric freedom" of the Sufi poet Jalal al-Din ar-Rumi (1207–1273) and his fellow mystics. (If one wants to fathom how the writer Coleman Barks has managed to turn

Rumi into a best-selling poet in contemporary America, one would do well to place Alger's *Poetry of the East* alongside Barks's *The Soul of Rumi* and see their common wellsprings.) "The Sufis are a sect of meditative devotees," Alger explained, "whose absorption in spiritual contemplations and hallowed raptures is unparalleled, whose piety penetrates, to a depth where the mind gropingly staggers among the bottomless roots of being, in mazes of wonder and delight, and reaches to a height, where the soul loses itself among the roofless immensities of glory in a bedazzled and boundless ecstasy." He even speculated that the Sufi "systems of means," "regular stages of initiation," and "diversified disciplines" could "scarcely fail of effect, if faithfully tried" among Christians in the West. Alger was ready, in other words, to make "the successful search" of the Sufis for God a practical part of his own universalized religious quest:

> We shall learn that all the world is Love's own dwelling,
> And but little care for Moslem mosque or Christian
> church.

Alger wanted to explore different "steps up to heaven," apart from the exclusive claims of traditional Christian institutions. For climbing that cosmopolitan spiritual ladder, he pinned many of his hopes on secluded retreat.[26]

Alger dedicated his work on "the genius of solitude" to James Martineau, a leading intellectual among religious liberals in England and a minister dedicated to reviving Protestant devotionalism in the face of what he saw as an increasingly secular society. Martineau's most popular work, *Endeavors after the Christian Life*, had carried ample emphasis on silence, meditation, and "the exercises of the solitary soul" as the way of renewing "earnest contact with the deep and silent God." Alger outstripped his model in this regard as well as his compatriots Emerson and Thoreau, both of whom influenced him, evident especially in his opening section, "The Solitudes of Nature." In seven parts, Alger offered meditations on the solitude of the desert,

THE

SOLITUDES

OF

NATURE AND OF MAN;

OR,

The Loneliness of Human Life.

BY

WILLIAM ROUNSEVILLE ALGER.

Hast du Begriff von Oed' und Einsamkeit?
GOETHE

BOSTON:
ROBERTS BROTHERS.
1867.

prairie, ocean, polar icescape, forest, mountain, and ruin in order to imbue the reader at the outset with proper feelings of immensity, brooding, lonesomeness, terror, and wonder. Alger's American forests, like Thoreau's Maine woods, were one of the environs of isolation and introspection. "The aboriginal woods of western North America," Alger dreamed of atomistic retreat, "seem as if they might harbor a million anchorites, not one of whom should be within a day's journey of any other."[27]

These scenes of the "wastes and wilds of outward nature" were but prelude to "the intenser inner deserts" of human consciousness. Solitude was reconfigured in psychological terms around the secrets and recesses of the true self, the loneliness of the individual in crowds, and the escape from anxieties of social emulation. The retreat into solitude was, in part, a formal recognition of "the fatal separateness and hiddenness of each individuality." "We hate or pity," Alger wrote poignantly of human alienation, "we strive or sleep, we laugh or bleed, we sigh and yearn; but still in impassable separation, like unvisiting isles here and there dotting the sea of life, with sounding straits between us. It is a solemn truth that, in spite of his manifold intercourses, and after all his gossip is done, every man, in what is most himself, and in what is deepest in his spiritual relationships, lives alone." Increasingly massed in cities, people experienced not affection for one another but indifference (most of Alger's life was spent in urban pastorates). "Souls, though crowded together in ranks," Alger said, feel all the while "as lonely as the rows of funeral urns in a columbarium." The studied alternation of solitude and society was imagined as a way of confronting these larger estrangements and imagining freer, more genuine forms of connection and attachment.[28]

Solitude emerged as a potential remedy for the diseases of self-absorption and self-reproach, which seemed, to Alger, newly magnified in the market-dominated world of go-getting success and failure that he inhabited. "The glare and stare of noisy society" turned life into an endless series of mirrors in which one's own self-image became "enslaved" to the reflections one obsessively imagined beholding in the eyes of others. "No other article of domestic furniture has been so multiplied in modern upholstery as the looking-glass," Alger complained. "Yes, this is the malady of the age,—an age of Narcissuses." The retreat into solitude, in Alger's view, would not magnify this "morbid consciousness of self," but would, in most cases, help relieve it: "Happy is he who, free from the iron visages that hurt him as they pass in the street, free from the vapid smiles and sneers of frivolous people, draws his sufficingness from inexhaustible sources always at his command when he is alone." These motifs—the fragility of self-esteem, the grind of competition, and the prevalence of social anxiety that modern glances and glares create—continue to inform contemporary meditations on solitude. "Before we are fully aware of it, we have sold our soul to the many grade-givers.... We are likeable because someone likes us," the Christian spiritual writer Henri Nouwen remarks in *Out of Solitude* (1974). "Somewhere we know that without a lonely place our lives are in danger."[29]

Alger, like Nouwen long after him, felt that people worried too much about what others thought of them, and, in that process of inspection, all too easily lost self-respect and sank into "self-idolatry" or narcissism. The "overtasked," the "weary, uneasy, ambitious," desperately needed a break from "a feverish and suspicious society" in order to take stock of who they really were apart from the layers of insincerity, affectation, and self-doubt that enveloped them through the social performance of the self. "One wishes to separate himself from all influences about him," the pulpit prince Henry Ward Beecher (1813–1887) noted in his own meditation on solitude, "and see just what is left of himself." "The quiet, the unquestioning silence, the absence of watching eyes, the subsidence of vigilance, guard, and circumspection, on our own part, the gentle rise of liberty in all things, the release of the nerves, the unvexed placidity of the disposition,—these are the first-fruits of solitude," Beecher claimed. Alger wholeheartedly agreed on these benefits with his illustrious contemporary.[30]

It would be easy perhaps to dismiss this new therapy of solitude as an expression of self-indulgence and individual freedom that came at the expense of ancient Christian emphases on self-denial and community discipline. Was not solitude lost as a spiritual regimen and made part of what Alger called "therapeutical instructions"? Was it not now designed primarily to soothe the "interior discords" and "baffled longings" of all those "restless and weary aspirants" that the nineteenth century seemed to be producing in superabundance? Had not solitude itself been transformed into a symptom of self-absorption and "moral liberty"? Maybe, but Alger certainly did not imagine it that way, as his own explicit critique of narcissism suggests. Even though he claimed that the hermit of Concord's sentiments remained vivid in his own soul and even though he reverently attended Thoreau's funeral, listening as the church bell "tolled the forty-four years he had numbered," Alger was brutal when it came to what he saw as Thoreau's "boundless pampering of egotism." "He is constantly," Alger said in scorning Thoreau's self-preoccupied prose, "feeling himself, reflecting himself, fondling himself, reverberating himself, exalting himself, incapable of escaping or forgetting himself." At minimum, Alger was a tough-minded therapist, ready to speak bluntly about the roots of the unhappiness of those he counseled. "The chief cause of failure to lead a blessed life," he wrote, "is the immodesty of our demands, and their fitfulness. Happiness cannot consist of orgasms.... And the constant effort to gratify exorbitant desires exhausts the soul into a chronic state of self-nauseated weariness incapable of enjoyment."[31]

Solitude was ultimately far more for Alger than a release from the gnawings of anxiety, embarrassment, envy, and emulation. Certainly Alger wanted, in practical ways, to help people feel better and to know themselves more fully, to ward off feelings of scatteredness, disintegration, emptiness, and despair. Still, he insisted that the "self must not be the conspicuous object of our contemplation"; solitude, Alger left little doubt, was about the spiritual life. "Solitude is God's closet," Alger exhorted. "It is the sacred auditorium of the secrets of the spiritual world." In matters of the soul, "in relation to what is deep and holy," "society is a concealer, solitude a revealer.... Society, full of multiplicity and change, is every way finite, wasting its force in incessant throbs; solitude, an unfaltering unity, is allied to the infinite." In the stillness of lonely retreat, Alger sought (and wanted others to seek) "the rejuvenation of the soul, the sentiments, the ideal faculties, when years have heaped their scars and burdens on us."

The scars and burdens, he knew them too well. Alger recalled at one point in *Solitudes* the death of his mother when he was still a youth: she died, he said, before "I knew to give her the love she needed." He remembered, too, the death of his "eldest born" and "youngest born"—his son Henry, age sixteen, and his daughter Annie, age three—"snatched away in the same week" in September 1864. In a pained letter that he wrote to his friend Frederic Henry Hedge shortly after Annie's death, but before his son's, Alger sank under the grief:

We have lost our darling little Annie, our youngest child, the sweet-est, brightest, dearest little creature that ever blessed a human house. We have always idolized her. She was so precocious, so affec-tionate and winsome, that her mother has a thousand times said that she was too bright and good to live.... And now as we sit in the room with her little marble form so cold and still the house seems awfully dark and silent. When my mother died, twenty three years ago, I longed to die and lie by her side, my heart ached and sunk so. And now the same old feeling comes again. Well, God's will be done. It is blows like these that detach the over strong ties of earth, and make life so much less dear that when its end comes we are quite ready.

However romanticized Alger's spirituality of solitude might have been, it was also filled with darkness, deep sadness, and debilitating heartache. "Solitude," Alger remarked, "is our trysting-place with the dead," and it was equally a preparation "for the lonely business of dying." "I am waiting on here in intense Solitude," he wrote in an-other letter to Hedge in 1882, this one reflecting on the recent death of their mutual friend Ralph Waldo Emerson, "but with entire patience and trust." In death's shadow solitude always left Alger haunted as much as soothed.[32]

Thoreau's *Walden* and Alger's *Solitudes of Nature and of Man* were telltale markers of the emergence of a spirituality of solitude and fugitive serenity in American culture. "Give me solitude, give me Na-ture," Whitman sang in 1865, "give me again / O Nature your primal sanities." (Fittingly, Alger had presented Whitman with a copy of his *Poetry of the East* when they met in Boston in 1860, a work that

Whitman claimed to have read "over & over again" and was still quoting from "with zest" at the end of his life thirty years later.) The spirituality of nature's solitudes found ever widening cultural expression in the next half-century. In 1869 Edmond Stuart Hotham, a divinity student, built a cabin "for solitude and economy" on Walden Pond not far from Thoreau's former retreat. Soon he was the toast of Concord's surviving Transcendentalists, including Emerson, Bronson Alcott, and Franklin B. Sanborn, all of whom were ready to see in him the second coming of the hermit of Walden. Even as he entertained notions of outdoing Thoreau's austerity, Hotham could not escape his predecessor's growing fame. Dogged by tourists and reporters who wanted to make their own comparisons, Hotham quickly despaired of the simple life at Walden and found solace instead in the Adirondacks. Two decades later, in 1889, the prolific nature writer John Burroughs, another dedicated admirer of Thoreau and Whitman, heralded the "extra virtue" of "those persons who voluntarily embrace solitude, who live alone in the country or in the woods, or in the mountains, and find life sweet." "The finer spirits," he claimed, "are not gregarious; they do not love a crowd." For that matter, Burroughs thought, they do not love church and creed, but instead experience religion through poetry and nature. Solitude is "necessary to insure deep and fast colors of the spirit. Those who are most alone are most like themselves."[33]

The most important extension of the insights of Thoreau, Alger, and their progeny came in the writings of the activist Elizabeth Cady Stanton (1815–1902). Her speech titled "Solitude of Self," delivered before two congressional committees as well as the National American Woman Suffrage Association in 1892, was a landmark in placing the highly masculinized ideal of the solitary individual within the reach of women. While white men could readily claim the rights of autonomy and "individual citizenship," Stanton knew all too well that women were routinely deprived of that independence. Social, religious, and political norms imagined the female self in terms of a series

The activist Elizabeth Cady Stanton extended the liberal estimate of the solitary individual to women as the equals of men. (Collection of the author.)

of relational subordinations—to fathers, husbands, ministers, and brothers. Given those structures, Stanton boldly embraced the ideals of "individual happiness and development" as equally applicable to women. With Susan B. Anthony and Matilda Joslyn Gage, her staunchest allies, Stanton imagined women becoming—through suffrage, education, and career—the arbiters of their own destiny.

In her famed speech in 1892 and in her notorious *Woman's Bible* (1895–1898), Stanton made her case for women's rights through a powerful invocation not only of democratic individuality and self-reliance, but also of the spiritualized solitude of each human soul. "The possibilities in one human soul will never be found in another," Stanton assured, and hence the desired outworking of political and religious liberty was to give full expression to the "infinite diversity in human character." Certain that institutional Christianity and the Scriptures underpinning that faith were a primary source of female oppression, she attacked those authorities for subjecting women to endless self-sacrifice rather than opening them to self-sovereignty. To spiritualize (and de-institutionalize) religion, to embrace the liberal notion that religion was chiefly a matter of the individual in solitude, was for many first-wave feminists and their allies an important move. Transcendentalist solitude was always much harder for women to claim than men—and hence it was all the more important that Stanton seized on "the immeasurable solitude of self" as both existential reality and political assertion. In doing so, Stanton was no sentimentalist of self-reliance, but an acquaintance of forlornness. Indeed, on Stanton's account, "the awful solitude of self" actually brought women into solidarity with Jesus' experiences of betrayal: the Last Supper, the Garden of Gethsemane, even the Cross. Women needed to recognize the forsakenness of their situation, the ease with which men deserted them, the agonizing costs of their dependency. Out of that self-recognition, they would muster the courage to face both the privation and the promise of individual responsibility and isolated interiority.[34]

The sheer aloneness of the solitary self in Stanton's work made her affirmations more haunting than most other incarnations of America's romantic cultus of solitude and self-reliance in the second half of the nineteenth century. While essayists like John Burroughs turned solitude into a virtual cliché of American nature writing, there was still plenty of room for more peculiar religious expressions. A fine example of that eccentricity was the posthumous enshrinement of John Chapman (1774–1845), better known as Johnny Appleseed, as archetypal wilderness hermit and holy man. Chapman had been born and raised in Massachusetts before migrating westward across the Alleghenies in the late 1790s. Eventually he amassed considerable land holdings and nurseries, but, despite these, Chapman became renowned through Ohio and Indiana as a fearless backwoodsman, itinerant

John Chapman, now known by American schoolchildren as the benignant Johnny Appleseed, was a religious eccentric, often romanticized for his ascetic remove from polite society. (Firestone Library, Princeton University.)

eccentric, and latter-day embodiment of "the faith of the apostles and martyrs."[35]

Johnny Appleseed's national canonization came in an article in *Harper's New Monthly Magazine* in 1871. Chapman had long been known for his zeal for reading and distributing the mystical writings of Emanuel Swedenborg (the first published notice of his activities actually appeared in Manchester, England, in 1817 among followers of the Swedish seer who saw Chapman as "a very extraordinary Missionary of the New Jerusalem"). It was those religious convictions that served as the springboard to transform him into a barefooted saint of the wilderness, an unkempt and highly ascetic pilgrim. As the *Harper's* essayist reported, "He was a most earnest disciple of the faith taught by Emanuel Swedenborg, and himself claimed to have frequent conversations with angels and spirits: two of the latter, of the feminine gender, he asserted, had revealed to him that they were to be his wives in a future state if he abstained from a matrimonial alliance on earth." Somehow such details of angelic conjugality have not made their way into the elementary school hagiography of Johnny Appleseed, the maker of orchards.

Pairing his visionary bent with bodily mortification (at least in this world), Chapman was said to be able to endure the pains of the flesh with heroic fortitude "in proof of which he would often thrust pins and needles into his flesh." "Homeless, solitary, and ragged," he also reputedly ate a meager vegetarian diet out of his close identification with God's creatures and refused even to harm a hornet that had stung him repeatedly: "No Brahmin could be more concerned for the preservation of insect life." The canonization proceeded apace from there. The poet Vachel Lindsay wrote of Chapman in 1909 that he was "a New England kind of saint, much like a Hindu saint, akin to Thoreau and Emerson" and imagined him progressing throughout his life on "The Mystical Johnny Appleseed Highway." By 1920, comparisons to St. Francis and St. Anthony were also common, and Johnny Appleseed had become America's "modern hermit of the wilderness," "a specter of the solitudes."[36]

The romance of the hermit kept moving farther west, and the trope soon inhabited the southwestern borderlands of cowboys, cattle herds, and wild expanses. The conventions of cowboy fiction developed between the 1860s and 1890s in dime novels of mystery, adventure, violence, and honor, and leading the way was William H. Bushnell's *The Hermit of the Colorado Hills: A Story of the Texan Pampas*. It opened with an evocation of cowboys (then still called herdsmen) who, mounted on "half-trained mustangs" and "careless of danger," embodied "the very picture of health, muscular beauty, daring and grace." They were part of a charged romantic landscape that in itself suggested a spiritual openness: "What a glorious dream of freedom are the Pampas! Where can mind, heart, lungs—ay, and the very soul, so drink in a realizing sense of freedom—so feel the perfect expansion that is typical of what we call the infinite?"

The Hermit of the Colorado Hills is not a herdsman himself, but a pastiche: a medicine man, a wizard, a tormented loner who, as in the earlier tales of woe, lives without human companionship because of love's disappointments. The demons of his past dwell with him in his cave, and there is no exorcism. "Sorrow is holy," the hermit tells a pair of intruders upon his solitude. "Gold is purified by fire, and the human heart by trial and crosses, and suffering." If the hermit espouses an ancient ascetic gospel, the reader is offered an easier redemption that comes through identification with the severe landscape and its taciturn inhabitants. Here in "these wild solitudes" is an escape from the overcivilization of the city, its social etiquette and effete luxury. The frustrated question that the hermit puts to his interlopers could equally be the question of bicoastal seekers as they look for tranquility now in the ranches of Montana or the reaches of New Mexico: "Can one never be alone, even in these barren hills?"[37]

If spiritual excursions into the infinite extended from Walden Pond and the Maine woods into the high deserts of the West, by the end of the century they had reached as far as the Himalayas. In 1893 Protap Chunder Mozoomdar (1840–1905), who represented "Liberal Hinduism" at the World's Parliament of Religions in Chicago that year to considerable acclaim, lectured in Boston on the "sublimity of the Himalayan regions," "the grandest range of mountains in the world." He already had captured the attention of an American audience through the publication of his *Oriental Christ* a decade earlier in 1883—a work in which, as a Hindu, he meditated on "the spirit of Christ" in relation to a universal religion of love, sympathy, self-surrender, and mystical experience. Mozoomdar built on that favorable reputation in the 1890s, preaching from various church pulpits that were open to him and publishing three spiritual guides, mostly aimed at liberal Protestant, Unitarian, and post-Protestant readers.[38]

If not as charismatic as Swami Vivekananda, his younger contemporary, Mozoomdar nonetheless awed liberals and latter-day Transcendentalists. The editor of the *Christian Register,* Samuel J. Barrows, was so impressed with him that he wrote a poetic tribute to "our mystic Mozoomdar" and the blending of "our rhythmic hearts," Christian and Hindu, American and Asian:

> *The mighty Ganges night and day*
> *Rolls onward to the sea;*
> *The Mississippi finds its way*
> *To kindred destiny.*

Mozoomdar heralded what he called the "mystic spiritualities of Asia," and the ranks of America's romantic inquirers warmed to "the mystic thrill and prophecy" of his work and his presence among them. Back in India, Mozoomdar corresponded with Barrows, fondly recalling his American sojourns as times of triumph and unbounded appreciation: "Now that America is so far away it seems I have left a glory in its light & sky, in its air and earth. My best work is there, my best success. God bless America & its people!"[39]

In the biographical sketch at the opening of *Heart-beats* (1894), a collection of short meditations on topics ranging from prayer to inspiration, it was noted that Mozoomdar divided his time in India between a "Peace Cottage" in Calcutta and a secluded retreat in the Himalayas, "five thousand feet above sea-level." The greater part of his spiritual guidebooks had been "written at this lofty height. Here, away from the distractions of Calcutta, he finds peace in communion with the spirit in nature and in man." His withdrawing into the mountains for six to eight months a year provided for his American biographer a stamp of authenticity. Mozoomdar knew solitude, and not just any solitude, but that of "the snow-world" of the Himalayas — "the transcendent heights, now seen, now unseen, now half-veiled, or faint, or dim, or ghostly, or fearful in their rugged reality." It was through prayer and meditation in these "untrodden regions of white" that Mozoomdar came to know "the great Immutable." Painting his picture of "Devout Loneliness" in the hues of multiple religious traditions — Moses on Sinai, Jesus in the wilderness, and the Buddha sitting for six years "on the banks of the Niranjana"—Mozoomdar swam in the waters of liberal universalism and Hindu reform. When he posed the question "What is Spirituality?" or "What is Self-surrender?" as he did in *Heart-beats,* Americans like Samuel Barrows listened attentively to his answers. Mozoomdar was one who knew "the difference between the passing and permanent," who knew "Godly Solitude," who knew "these Himalayas" as great mountains of spiritual discipline and communion. The American romance with solitude had gone global.[40]

It stayed that way. "I have found no mooring for my floating soul in any religious faith, in any philosophy," Paul Brunton wrote in *A Hermit in the Himalayas* (1937) "because I believe in the Spirit which, like the wind, bloweth where it listeth." Wanting nothing to do with "the mob with a Sunday religion," Brunton had headed to Tibet to further his search for secret paths (he had already been to India and Egypt). Among the lessons he learned in this long trek was the distinctly Emersonian one that a would-be preacher should submit to neither seminary professors nor orthodoxy, but should take Nature as his tutor: "I would compel him to go out to the lonely mountains and the unfrequented woods and stay there without books or friends to wrestle with his soul in that solitude until he either found God or found that the church was not his vocation." Brunton's epigraph announced his Transcendentalist affinities, a long excerpt from Emerson, which began: "Good-bye, proud world! I'm going home." Out to climb "the Himalaya of the soul" and reach "its white summit," Brunton drew on the nineteenth-century romance of the hermit and pushed it into still wider circles of seeking. "I am riding, not merely into Himalaya, but into heaven," Brunton effused. "The mountains are flushed with beauty that belongs, not to them, but to God. The entire journey has become a glorious poetic symbol.... [I]n these grand solitudes I may prepare myself for the sublimer solitude of God."[41]

In his diary in 1958 the celebrated Catholic contemplative Thomas Merton (1915–1968) noted that he had been reading "a remarkable though poorly written book" called *A Hermit in the Himalayas,* which he had picked up "by 'chance'" in a Louisville library. That note, if lukewarm in its praise, is a reminder that Merton, too, swam in these popular spiritual currents, that the romantic views of solitude remained pervasive and were not readily escaped even in the monastic life. More to the point than his fortuitous reading of Brunton, Merton had a clear affection for Thoreau. Along with Emily Dickinson, Thoreau was among a small handful of writers who helped Merton look favorably upon his identification as an American citizen. In his hermitage at the Gethsemani monastery in Kentucky, Merton more than once compared himself with Thoreau and had also invoked the Concord recluse's name at the outset of *Thoughts in Solitude* in 1958. Keenly aware that he was "living in the woods like Thoreau instead of living in the desert like St. John the Baptist," Merton remarked, "I must read *Walden* again, and see if Thoreau already guessed that he was part of what he thought he could escape.... Technology is here, even in the cabin." And, indeed, Merton, like Thoreau, imagined that his embrace of solitude was not "just a recipe for hermits," but had bearing on the very future of religion and the discovery of an "invulnerable inner reality."[42]

As American solitaries, separated by a century, Thoreau and Merton were vastly different—one a post-Christian individualist and the other a convert to Roman Catholicism and the monastic life. But that has hardly prevented them from being joined in the larger imagining of American spirituality. In one episode in *Migrations to Solitude,* Sue Halpern is visiting the Gethsemani monastery and invokes Thoreau's queries in *Walden:* "Why should I feel lonely?... What sort of space is that which separates a man from his fellows and makes him solitary?" And immediately she proceeds in her story on a walk to Thomas Merton's hermitage, which had been built for him on the abbey's property in 1959. "When we get there, I am disappointed that it looks more like a suburban California tract house than the cave of the Essenes or Thoreau's cottage at Walden Pond." For American seekers and retreatants, it was often hard not to measure Merton by Thoreau's Transcendentalist yardstick or simply to join the two at the hip (an ironic fate for hermits). As one writer in the 1970s claimed, "Thoreau and Merton ... found the best of life to be derived from solitude and to be born in silence. These men are America's 'Desert Fathers.'" It was not enough for Merton to be the obedient monastic living out his vocation; his spiritual cachet always depended on the way his decision to lead a hermit's life resonated with the desires of American romantics, bohemians, and seekers for the psychic spaces, artistic possibilities, and inward depths of solitude.[43]

The romantic imagining of solitude changed the way religion itself was conceived in many precincts in American culture, what it was in its essence and at its core, to what end and height it aspired. Religion, W. R. Alger had remarked in his study of solitude, "is essentially lonely and not social. The common notion to the contrary is vulgar fallacy; a fallacy, however, almost unavoidable from the intimate association of sociality with religious phenomena. The true and pure religious emotions are essentially solitary, and love only loneliness." In *The Varieties of Religious Experience,* William James offered as his working definition of religion "the feelings, acts, and experiences of individual men in their solitude, so far as they apprehend themselves to stand in relation to whatever they may consider the divine." Ecclesiastical structures, liturgical enactments, and formal theologies all paled when compared with the immediacy and extremity of individual religious experiences. What made religion still matter? What gave it force and energy? It was the inviolate experience of the solitary soul.[44]

The Harvard philosopher Alfred North Whitehead (1861–1947) was even more insistent on this point in his *Religion in the Making* in 1926. "Religion is what the individual does with his own solitariness," Whitehead declared. "Religion is solitariness; and if you are never solitary, you are never religious. Collective enthusiasms, revivals, institutions, churches, rituals, bibles, codes of behaviour, are the trappings of religion, its passing forms. They may be useful, or harmful;

The artist John Singer Sargent rendered the anchorite in explicitly post-Christian terms as a nature mystic in his painting *The Hermit*. (The Metropolitan Museum of Art, Rogers Fund, 1911 [11.31]. Photograph, all rights reserved, The Metropolitan Museum of Art.)

they may be authoritatively ordained, or merely temporary expedients. But the end of religion is beyond all this." So widespread and influential had the revised spirituality of solitude become that religion per se was said to be wholly identifiable with it. "The modern world has lost God and is seeking him," Whitehead exclaimed with another sweep of the arm, and apparently what was lost could be found only through solitude.[45]

In discussing the significance of one of his most admired paintings, *The Hermit* (1908), which the Metropolitan Museum of Art acquired in 1911, the American artist John Singer Sargent said that he wanted to move beyond "any Christian association" for the anchorite into a domain of "quietness or pantheism." Sargent's solitary, bearded and bare-skinned, blended into the subtle browns and beiges of the forest, a human chameleon at one with the deer, rocks, and bark. *The Hermit* rendered in a single canvas the modern transformation of solitude: here was the romance of Thoreau, Whittier, Alger, and James in all its speckled shades. American spirituality had moved beyond the walls of the churches and beyond Christianity itself, and it had done so through the exaltation of a universalized withdrawal of the individual into occasional solitude. As Roger Housden suggests in *Retreat: Time Apart for Silence and Solitude* (1995), the solitary way is a path to be learned simultaneously from Buddhist, Sufi, Christian, Hindu, and shamanic sources. It is "the way of the wilderness" and "the way of art"; it is Thomas Merton and Ram Dass; it is the American Southwest and the Himalayas; it is a quality of individual centeredness amid the noise, distraction, and dispersal of modern society. That depiction of spirituality is the progeny of Emerson, Thoreau, Alger, Stanton, and James; it first took flight on the Transcendentalist wing of nineteenth-century religious liberalism.[46]

CHAPTER THREE

——◆◆◆◆——

THE PIETY OF
THE WORLD

THE PHENOMENAL POET had a phenomenal funeral,"
Moncure Daniel Conway wrote of Walt Whitman's memorial service in early April 1892, little more than a week after
the poet's death in Camden, New Jersey. Conway, a Virginia Methodist
turned religious radical, had first sought out Whitman in the summer
of 1855 after Ralph Waldo Emerson had handed him a copy of the
newly published *Leaves of Grass* with the portentous pronouncement: "Unto us a man is born." Going on to produce his own *Sacred
Anthology* of the scriptures of the world in 1874 and a memoir in old
age called *My Pilgrimage to the Wise Men of the East,* Conway found
in Whitman an inspiration, a bearer of a "popular transcendentalism"
that brought together a heterogeneous mix of Quaker, Hindu, Buddhist, Sufi, and Zoroastrian elements. Whitman's untamed poetry
constituted, according to Conway, "a sort of New York Vedas"; it
was a fresh example of special revelation. Conway and friends presented Whitman in death, as in life, as the avatar of a new American
spirituality, "a spiritual pioneer" on an unremitting quest after a

transformed awareness of God. He was said to have anticipated that after death he would pass not into heaven, but into a blissful state of his own imagining—"some conscious Nirvana."[1]

About this much at least, Conway was right: Whitman's funeral was remarkable. On March 30, thousands filed through the poet's house on Mickle Street in Camden to get a final glimpse of his body, and thousands more were turned away. The funeral procession was similarly thronged as it wound its path out of Camden toward a hillside vault, which itself soon became a shrine attracting scores of visitors. The crowds may have been impressive, but that was not what made the graveside service particularly noteworthy. It was the liturgy. First, an excerpt from one of Whitman's most renowned poems, "When Lilacs Last in the Dooryard Bloom'd," was read. A memorial to Abraham Lincoln, it was "the carol of death," the "song of the bleeding throat," "the chant of my soul" for "the white skeletons of young men" and for "the dead I loved so well": "Prais'd be the fathomless universe." Next a friend offered an elegy in which he assured the assembly that Whitman's "views of religion have been misunderstood." It was not his negations of orthodox Christianity or conventional church membership but his affirmations and distillations that counted: He "recognized the good in all religious systems. His philosophy was without the limitation of creed, and included the best thought of every age and clime."[2]

The speaker's point was immediately underscored through the reading of three sacred texts. One came from "the words of Confucius" and another from "the words of Jesus the Christ." A third was supplied from "the words of Gautama": "The state that is peaceful, free from body, from passion and from fear, where birth or death is not,—that is Nirvana. It is a calm wherein no wind blows." Later in the service there were readings from the Koran, the prophet Isaiah, and the Gospel of John; still later came "the words of the Zend Avesta" and of Plato. It was an appropriately eclectic event for a poet who imagined the universe itself as so many roads for traveling souls and

This image of the poet Walt Whitman from the 1850s was called "The Christ Likeness" by one of his most devoted followers, the physician Richard Maurice Bucke, author of the spiritual manifesto *Cosmic Consciousness*. (Rare Books, Beeghly Library, Ohio Wesleyan University.)

who dreamed that soon there would be "no more priests" and only a ceaseless flux of poetry and prophecy. In *Walden*, Thoreau had lamented the provincial narrowness of Concord and his fellow Americans: "As for the sacred Scriptures, or Bibles of mankind, who in this town can tell me even their titles? Most men do not know that any nation but the Hebrews have had a scripture." By the time of Whitman's death four decades later, that sort of observation would have had less bite. His funeral, in the crowds of people it attracted and in its embrace of "all religions," seemed a token of Whitman's own vision of "a sublime and serious Religious Democracy."[3]

Whitman wished to contain multitudes, and in no realm more so than in that of religion. A Quaker by family background, a curious inquirer into clairvoyance and Spiritualism, and an admirer of Emanuel Swedenborg as Emersonian mystic, the poet fashioned himself a seer, a prophet of an all-encompassing piety. He was ready to accept all "the rough deific sketches" for what they were worth, for what they might tell him about himself, about the body and the soul, or about the universe:

> My faith is the greatest of faiths and the least of faiths,
> Enclosing worship ancient and modern and all between ancient
>   and modern,
> Believing I shall come again upon the earth after five thousand
>   years,
> Waiting responses from oracles, honoring the gods, saluting the
>   sun,
> Making a fetish of the first rock or stump, powwowing with sticks in
>   the circle of obis,
> Helping the lama or brahmin as he trims the lamps of the idols,
> Dancing yet through the streets in a phallic procession, rapt and
>   austere in the woods …
>   minding the Koran, …
> Accepting the Gospels, accepting him that was crucified, knowing
>   assuredly that he is divine,
> To the mass kneeling or the puritan's prayer rising, or sitting
>   patiently in a pew,
> Ranting and frothing in my insane crisis, or waiting dead-like till
>   my spirit arouses me

The list was wildly diverse, moving from ancient paganism through indigenous traditions of North America and Africa through Buddhism, Hinduism, Christianity, Islam, and Spiritualism. All were made part of Whitman's "perpetual journey," his religious tramping, and he invited others to join him on this open road. At the same time, Whitman advised his listeners to make their own way: "Not I, not any one else can travel that road for you, / You must travel it for yourself."[4]

By the time of Whitman's funeral in early 1892, a year and a half before the World's Parliament of Religions convened in Chicago, the cosmos of American religion had already expanded considerably beyond the usual spiritual fare. True, more orthodox Christians fought valiantly to limit the ill effects of "the Whitman cult." They tarred him with the same brush of dissipation, sensuality, and irreligion that had been used on Tom Paine. Fairly successful in marking Whitman as a dangerous renegade from Christian propriety, they only added to the thrill of his bohemian following and stoked the fervor of his disciples. Most were more than happy to identify with Whitman as poet of both body and soul, and a few were ready to see him in messianic terms, "the last and greatest of the prophets." The Whitmanites—a formal fellowship was actually inaugurated in 1894 and grew into a loose federation of chapters—were often exuberant in their religious aspirations and attested to an "uncontrollable, inconsolable yearning" for "a wider and fuller 'soul life.' " "Surely, in this widespread revival of mysticism," one celebrant effused in 1898, "Whitman has been among its most sincere and powerful teachers." In the poet's life the earthy and the commonplace converged with "the deepest and purest spirituality"; so remarked John Burroughs, the acclaimed nature writer, in the wake of witnessing Whitman's funeral. The spiritual drift into eclecticism, openness, and "rich soul experience" that Whitman embodied was as much a cultural trend of the 1890s as it was the 1990s.[5]

Many things beyond Whitman's sheer inventiveness made his new cosmopolitan gospel possible. The global reach of the market, the vastness of colonial empires, the heyday of Christian missions, and the achievements of Western philology—all of these helped bring more and more knowledge about comparative religions within the grasp of the poet and his contemporaries. The imperial politics, global economy, and world-combing scholarship that facilitated the assemblage of an eclectic spirituality are hardly to be gainsaid. It was not all a matter of knowledge-is-power politics, however. Crucial were the liberal sentiments that authorized a new kind of relationship to diverse scriptures and traditions. "He came into our generation a free, untrammeled spirit, with sympathy for all," the great agnostic

Robert G. Ingersoll said in his elegy at Whitman's graveside. "He was, above all I have known, the poet of humanity, of sympathy." As Whitman himself had declared in *Leaves of Grass*, "I am he attesting sympathy," and it would be hard to miss his near boundless identification with the suffering and oppression of others—prostitutes, slaves, the poor, the sick, the downtrodden. His collected letters to his mother at the time of the Civil War, during which he faithfully attended to the maimed and shell-shocked in Union hospitals, were issued under the simple title of *The Wound Dresser*. How nineteenth-century liberals and romantics thought about sympathy, especially "the sympathy of religions," provides a key to unlock the advent of a bracing eclecticism in spirituality. Whitman's funeral stands as an embodiment of the liberal principle of the sympathy of religions—a precept that became clearly enunciated between 1850 and 1900 and that has enjoyed a long afterlife.[6]

The story of this principle's impact on American spirituality is usefully brought into focus through the career of Thomas Wentworth Higginson (1823–1911), a minister and a man of letters who courted conflict as a fierce abolitionist, a colonel of a black regiment during the Civil War, and an activist for women's rights. Though Higginson had little regard for Whitman's poetry, which he characterized as prurient and formless—"a shower of bird-shot," "an accumulated directory of details," "proclamations of utter nudity"—he shared much of Whitman's spiritual expansiveness. In 1871, Higginson published his most influential religious essay, "The Sympathy of Religions," a subject he had first concentrated on during a six-month sojourn in the Portuguese islands of the Azores in the mid-1850s as part of an uncompleted book manuscript on "the Religious Aspects of the times." The subsequent essay soon began circulating as a tract for a New England club of garrulous radicals, the Free Religious Association, and met with much success. Its influence spread to Chicago, where it cropped up in the 1880s as a rallying call for religious unity put forth by heartland heirs of Emerson and Theodore Parker. Eventually it was republished as a philosophical standard-bearer for the World's Parliament of Religions in 1893, and Higginson himself journeyed to the gathering to give his latest rendition of what was by then a well-traveled manifesto. The essay, published in London in 1872 and translated into French in 1898, had international reach: when Higginson met the great scholar of comparative religions Max Müller on a trip to England, the latter immediately lit up over meeting the author of "The Sympathy of Religions" and promptly invited him to Oxford.[7]

Higginson's basic claim—that the foundation of religious unity and harmony lay in extending the notion of sympathy into the realm of comparative religions—set his essay within long-flowing discussions in Christian ethics and civic humanism. Sympathy was especially viewed as an ethic of compassion and benevolence, a fellow-feeling

Colonel Thomas Wentworth Higginson emerged after the Civil War as a primary architect of a cosmopolitan piety. (Firestone Library, Princeton University.)

with those in pain or distress, but it was more than that. Cultivating sympathy was a way of bridging differences and recognizing commonalities; it was a basis of overcoming isolation through affective connection, joining people in shared enterprises, and creating mutuality through identification with others. Higginson reworked that commonplace moral language, turning sympathy into a practical paradigm for dealing with the rapidly growing "knowledge of the religions of the world." In his hands, sympathy became an instrument for transforming Christian uniqueness into religious openness: "When we fully comprehend the sympathy of religions," he concluded, "we shall deal with other faiths on equal terms." Embracing this sympathy would release the liberal religionist into a global field of spiritual appreciation, cosmopolitan rapport, and eclectic insight.[8]

Attending Harvard Divinity School, the training ground for religious liberals, in the mid-1840s, Higginson rode the wake of the Transcendentalist movement, "the period of the Newness." Reading antislavery literature, celebrating Emerson and Samuel Taylor Coleridge, Higginson even rambled into Thomas De Quincey's *Confessions of an English Opium-Eater:* "I myself was led to try some guarded experiments in that direction. ...It seems, in looking back, a curious escapade for one who had a natural dislike of all stimulants and narcotics." Upon graduation in 1847 he took a Unitarian charge in Newburyport, Massachusetts. As a youthful radical, not only on questions of slavery but also on those of factory labor and women's rights, he proved too outspoken for his congregants and was soon removed from the pulpit. Eventually finding a religious society in Worcester more receptive to his tactless zeal, he moved to the Free Church there in 1852. From that venue, "a seething centre of all the reforms," as Higginson described it in his autobiography, he expanded his agitation and became "almost in fashion, at least with the unfashionable."[9]

In 1854, Higginson took more direct action. He helped lead a mutinous assault on the Boston Courthouse in an attempt to free Anthony Burns, a captured fugitive slave who was being held under armed guard and was threatened with a return to bondage. Even after he was clubbed by police and arrested in this failed rescue mission, Higginson's ardor did not cool. He recruited antislavery settlers for armed struggle with proslavery forces in Kansas and was among the "Secret Six," along with Theodore Parker and Franklin Sanborn, who helped back John Brown's slave insurrection at Harpers Ferry. Never wavering in his solidarity with arch-abolitionist William Lloyd Garrison and the *Liberator,* he was appointed in 1862 to lead the First South Carolina Volunteers. He served as commander of this African-American regiment until a war wound and disease forced him out of the army in 1864.[10]

Though remembered far less for it, Higginson was equally radical in theology. His efforts at a first book, a project he stopped midstream at the end of his Azores trip in 1856 to take up the Kansas struggle full-time, left him with a fragmentary manuscript on religion, "The Return of Faith and the Decline of the Churches." The abandoned book contained the seeds of his later sympathy essay, though his ideas on the subject were developing within more immediate theological frays, radical sticking points such as the rejection of the Lord's Supper and Jesus' divinity. The outlines of his larger argument were apparent in the scattered chapter drafts he did finish: Protestantism, in its sectarianism and half-baked revolt, was an embarrassing failure; Catholicism, while more attractive in its comprehensiveness and consistency than Protestantism, offered finally a faux universalism; and the alternative was "a Catholicism which is more than Roman," a universal religion in which Buddhism, Islam, Hinduism, and Christianity, among other traditions, "will disappear,... absorbed into something larger and grander." Higginson already discerned an astonishing equivalence of insight among sacred books, a shared profundity and ethical awareness across religions. Jesus and Buddha, for instance, were equal exemplars of noble and beautiful lives of "self-consecration." At the same time, he saw the churches as being in grave decline. The ministerial ranks were made up of all too many men who lived wretched lives of intellectual dishonesty and who failed to face squarely the new knowledge about the religions of the world and about Jesus and the scriptures. For the return of faith, a momentous transition was required, a shift from the outworn doctrines of Christianity to "the sublime sympathy of Universal Religion."[11]

Making that transition required a reinterpretation of religious authority. Higginson had published an initial discourse in 1854 on Protestant dependence on the Bible, a sixteen-page tract titled *Scripture Idolatry*, which he planned to turn into a central chapter in the book. In that piece, he sought to dismantle the Bible as a foundation of authority: "Of all the uncertain tribunals ever adopted by fallible mortals, the Bible appears to me the most uncertain," he wrote. On the crucial moral issues of the day—slavery, temperance, capital punishment, and polygamy, to name four—Higginson saw the Bible as akin to the Florida Everglades, a "wilderness of texts," a tangle that made sorting out the scriptural from the unscriptural fruitless, if not impossible. Higginson read Scripture, in part, as a man of reason, a latter-day Tom Paine who wanted to hack his way through the "utter indelicacy," "terrible cruelty," "entire improbability," and "strange miscellany" of the Bible in order to create a clearing for the light of "simple Natural Religion."[12]

In the place of biblical revelation, Higginson, like other liberals, turned inward into a domain of universal moral conscience and spiritual illumination more complexly experiential than the streamlined religion of Enlightenment deists. As the Bible's authority ostensibly tottered and crumbled, Higginson, like other Transcendentalists, strode in among the ruins to offer hope:

> *The soul needs some other support also; it must find this within;— in the cultivation of the Inward Light; in personal experience of Religion; in the life of God in the human soul; in faith in God and love to man; in the reverent study of the vast and simple laws of Nature.... [I]n these, and nowhere else, lies the real foundation*

of all authority; build your faith here, and churches and Bibles
may come or go, and leave it undisturbed.

Higginson's radical turn to experience as authoritative—a move characteristic of nineteenth-century liberal theology, already evident in the growing emphasis on mysticism—was at once hyper-Protestant and post-Christian. Or, in a distinction of his own devising, he was not "anti-Christian," but "extra-Christian," ultimately operating from a position "outside the Christian Church." [13]

Higginson, a Transcendentalist on an intellectual path similar to those of Emerson and Thoreau, was also deeply interested in Spiritualist phenomena—mediums, trance-speaking, and communication with the dead—throughout much of the 1850s. After abandoning "The Return of Faith," he found time to write two measured pamphlets in Spiritualism's defense and regularly sang its praises as a gospel of gladness and progress versus a Calvinist theology of terror and gloom. By 1859, he was ready to pin many of his hopes for a mighty religious transition on this movement, "destined to utterly transform religious denominations" through its expansive anticreedalism and experiential openness. In the years when Higginson made his initial forays into the sympathy of religions, his theological interests were appropriately eclectic: by turns Transcendentalist in his emphasis on soulful experiences, Spiritualist in his hands-on-table curiosity about mediums and the evidences of immortality, radical Unitarian in his doctrinal rejections and ethical commitments, and cosmopolitan universalist in his views of the religions of the world. [14]

According to his diary, Higginson "began on Sympathy of Religions" on January 24, 1870, and finished a thirty-page manuscript on February 4, 1870, having devoted at least nine of those days to working on it. Whether he drew directly on his earlier chapter drafts from the mid-1850s or simply started over with those ideas in the background is unclear. Certainly, the project was now substantially different; it was no longer part of a book, but was prepared as a lecture to be given at Horticultural Hall in Boston on February 6, 1870. Of the event, Higginson noted simply in his diary: "Read my lecture 'Sympathy of Religions' which seemed to please people very much." The event did go well enough that he immediately set out to revise the discourse for publication, which appeared early the next year in the *Radical,* an important nexus of liberal communications, clubs, and associations. The essay received favorable notice from several second-generation Transcendentalists and freethinking titans, including Octavius Brooks Frothingham, and from reform-minded media such as the Spiritualist newspaper *Banner of Light.* Though he dwelled often on religious topics, including a range of discourses on everything from "The Character of the Buddha" to "Greek Goddesses," Higginson always took special pride in the piece on sympathy as his "most learned" achievement. Late in life, in annotating a copy of his seven-volume collected works for his secretary, he placed this essay among "the very best things I ever wrote," "the most varied & labored piece of scholarship I ever produced."[15]

The essay's real home was with the Free Religious Association (FRA), founded in 1867 as a loose organization of religious radicals who intended both to further an incipient scientific study of religion and to explore the basis of a universal spirituality. Orthodox critics quickly impugned the FRA as a batch of infidels, but its members always saw that as a gross misrepresentation. The association aimed, one partisan explained, "to remove all dividing lines and to unite all religious men in bonds of pure spirituality." Its founding principles included ascribing to "all the religions of world ... an equality of origin and purpose" and seeing all confessions of faith "as achievements of the soul." Higginson was extremely active in the FRA; he served as a vice-president and then president of the group. By one in-house tabulation, over his four decades of involvement, he attended "more of its councils," presided over more of its social gatherings, and "delivered more addresses from its platform than any other person." Along with Emerson, Frothingham, Lydia Maria Child, and Felix Adler,

Higginson was among the FRA's leading literary figures (a fame garnered through his frequent contributions to the *Atlantic Monthly* and through his *Army Life in a Black Regiment*). The FRA made the sympathy essay its own, turning it into one of the charter documents of the organization and bundling it in 1876 as a tract—one hundred copies for three dollars. From there, it became a commonplace of "our Liberal Faith" and an intellectual prologue to the World's Parliament of Religions.[16]

"The Sympathy of Religions" opened at sea, passing "from island on to island," perhaps an imagistic legacy of the excursion to the Azores. "The human soul, like any other noble vessel, was not built to be anchored," Higginson emoted, "but to sail." The global web of commercial shipping, which so much facilitated the accumulation of knowledge that made Higginson's religious comparisons possible, was also present from the opening lines: "It would be a tragedy," he averred, "to see the shipping of the world whitening the seas no more, and idly riding at anchor in Atlantic ports; but it would be more tragic to see a world of souls fascinated into a fatal repose and renouncing their destiny of motion." It was an instructive image in which the market's unceasing transport of cargo paralleled the movement of religions from "stranded hulks" into the flux of endless exchange. In all that sparkling motion of ships and souls, in the twinned fluidity of religion and commerce, Christian devotions were no "more holy or more beautiful" than "one cry from a minaret" or the soft murmuring of "Oh! the gem in the lotus—oh! the gem in the lotus." All were equally symbols of spiritual aspiration.[17]

Higginson's essay was filled to bursting with optimism. The fast-growing knowledge of the religions of the world was not threatening, dispiriting, or fragmenting, but instead productive of progress, freedom, and concord: "There is a sympathy in religions.... [E]very step in knowledge brings out the sympathy between them. They all show the same aim, the same symbols, the same forms, the same weaknesses, the same aspirations." Certainly, Higginson acknowledged, there were "shades of difference" that emerged upon "closer analysis," but even those differences worked in symphonic harmony. And finally such nuances hardly mattered, for once the inquirer was alert to all "the startling points of similarity, where is the difference?" Religions took on the same forms from place to place, and it was the commonality of patterns (symbols, rituals, ethical precepts, holy days, sacred places, saints, saviors) and not sectarian "subdivisions" that mattered. Religion was not something to put under a microscope; it required instead a macroscopic vision in which all religions could be seen as facsimiles of one another. If difference continued to crowd into view, if particularity persisted, that was where religion failed, where it lapsed into creedal precision and lost sight of the universal, where it became a constraint rather than an inspiration for wayfaring souls.[18]

These points of unity, these universal sympathies, set the spirit free of any single institution, scripture, or tradition. From all religions and sacred books, from the Vedas and the Bible, from Chinese Buddhists and "Galla Negroes" will be "gathered hymns and prayers and maxims in which every soul may unite—the magnificent liturgy of the human race." The implications of such sympathies for liberal spirituality were manifest: the seeker of truth was not merely invited but enjoined to explore widely, to create a new composite scripture out of selected sheaves from the vast storehouse of religious inspiration. That might mean gathering the moral gems of Jesus or stringing together luminous passages from Emerson and Thoreau or pulling them all into the company of the Buddha. As Higginson grandly proclaimed, "I do not wish to belong to a religion only, but to *the* religion; it must not include less than the piety of the world."[19]

That vast expansion of piety was, to Higginson, spirit-enlarging and spelled the ultimate undoing of religious exclusion, partiality, and rivalry. No single faith could claim a monopoly on love, truth, devotion, forgiveness, prayer, equality, honesty, or mystical illumination; "all do something to exemplify, something to dishonor them"; "all show the same disparity between belief and practice, and each is safe till it tries to exclude the rest." Though Higginson still threw the occasional bone to Anglo-American Protestantism—in its production of "manners," "arts," and "energy"—that hardly made his argument more palatable to his orthodox brethren. Christian claims to uniqueness and superiority, the whole missionary enterprise, would yield the platform to the sympathy of religions, to meeting those of other faiths on common ground. As Higginson concluded bluntly of the exclusion of exclusion at the heart of liberal inclusion, "The one unpardonable sin is exclusiveness."[20]

Higginson's essay helped launch the idea of the sympathy of religions into prominence, and the notion became a commonplace in liberal religious venues from the 1870s through the 1890s and well beyond. Lydia Maria Child, Samuel Johnson, Samuel Longfellow, David Wasson, Cyrus Bartol, Ednah Dow Cheney, Martin K. Schermerhorn, John W. Chadwick, Minot Savage, and R. Heber Newton—all participated in this imagining of a universal religion of shared spiritual aspirations. Many of them directly echoed Higginson; all listened to the same poetic and prophetic voices: Emerson, Parker, and Whittier, especially. As John Chadwick predicted in 1894, the universal religion to come is "that Sympathy of Religions which already has possessed the mind and heart of many an individual thinker and explorer."[21]

Higginson had an especially important ally in the radical reformer Lydia Maria Child (1802–1880), a literary figure with a cachet as a poet, novelist, and editor that rivaled the colonel's. She is remembered today mostly for her Thanksgiving ditty about heading to grandmother's house "over the river and through the woods," but that is hardly a fair measure of her intellectual reach and achievement. A refugee from Calvinist orthodoxy in her youth, a restless admirer of Emanuel Swedenborg, a mentor of the young Margaret Fuller, and a zealous collaborator with the abolitionist William Lloyd Garrison, Child displayed a remarkable commitment to the burgeoning history of religions, producing a hefty set of three volumes titled *The Progress of Religious Ideas Through Successive Ages* in 1854. In *Aspirations of*

The abolitionist Lydia Maria Child joined Higginson in his commitment to the sympathy of religions. (The Schlesinger Library, Radcliffe Institute, Harvard University.)

the World: A Chain of Opals (1878), a volume much better adapted for a popular audience, Child explicitly sought to avoid the "endless mazes of theology," which divided one religion from another, and to concentrate instead on "the primeval impulses of the human soul," which "have been essentially the same everywhere." Like Higginson, she saw most Americans as being unfair in comparing the best in Christianity with the worst in other religions and wanted better translations of religious ideas from one culture to another—an immense undertaking that had thus far been done "very imperfectly." She even imagined an "Eclectic Church of the Future which shall gather forms of holy aspirations from all ages and nations." "Let not pious conservative souls be alarmed by this prophecy," she implored.[22]

Widespread liberal assent to the sympathy of religions did not mean that the construct went unchallenged among Higginson's peers. Francis Ellingwood Abbot and William J. Potter, two other leading participants in the FRA, found Higginson's formulations wanting and offered especially pithy critiques. The sympathy of religions, both claimed, was at best a partial account, and it required "a companion-picture" of "the 'Antagonisms of Religions.'" As Potter insisted, "What makes the special religions is not so much the things in which they agree as the things in which they differ—that is, the claims which are peculiar to each religion." Abbot and Potter matched Higginson's optimism about "a common ground-work of ethical and spiritual intelligence" with a frank emphasis on the conflicts that were constitutive of divergent religious perspectives. Joseph Henry Allen, another inside analyst, offered a still tougher reality check. Noting the religious animosities that circled the globe in the 1890s—from pogroms in eastern Europe to Muslim-Hindu strife in India—Allen deemed Higginson's concept to be naïve and bloodless: "We have not much encouragement ... for any signs of the 'sympathy of religions.' Each of them, so far as we can see, while it is a living force is far from sympathetic. Nay, it is antagonistic and aggressive." By 1897, William Wallace Fenn, another Harvard liberal who enjoyed dousing liberalism's ignes fatui, announced that the "idea of the sympathy of religions" had sometimes produced little more than "a huge cloud of thin but amiable sentiment." Again, the antagonisms of religions seemed the better, more realistic assessment of the global situation.[23]

Another, equally pressing accusation was that Higginson's whole drive for the "unification of religion" was at cross-purposes with the higher ideals within a liberal democracy of variety and individuality. In this view, insisting on the sympathy of religions was retrogressive, not progressive. Was not all this talk of religious commonality another way of fostering religious conformity, the unintended consequences of which would be a rolling back of Transcendentalist freedom, spontaneity, and eccentricity? How could liberals really expect to foster creative self-expression and spiritual independence under the banner of religious unanimity and sameness? Appropriately enough, that critique of "colorless cosmopolitanism" was expressed variously, but an especially astute version of it came from Solomon Schindler (1842–1915), a Reform rabbi, widely recognized as one of those "new-fashioned Jews" who were dedicated, like Higginson, to making "the liberal truly liberal."

At the annual meeting of the FRA in 1895, shortly after Higginson (then president of the society) had made another report on the forward march of liberalism's vision of the "one religion," Schindler rose to the lectern to speak on "The Present Tendencies in the Religious World." Arriving in New York as an impoverished German immigrant in 1871, Schindler peddled shoelaces and served a small synagogue in Hoboken before getting his big break in Boston at Temple Adath Israel in 1874, where he energetically engaged the city's liberal intelligentsia. Given Schindler's credentials as a long-standing defender of the FRA's radicalism and a leading ecumenist in Jewish-Christian relations, Higginson had good reason to expect one more ringing endorsement of the sympathy of religions. Schindler, however, took a different tack, immediately insisting that he spoke not for a class, denomination, nationality, or party, but as a free individual. In his view, all the chatter about unifying the religions was misguided; the realization of that vision would be "tantamount to mental stagnation or to mental misery." "The happiest state will come to pass," Schindler claimed, "when each individual will be allowed to formulate his own ideas regarding the universe and his position in and relation to it. Not one unified religion is the goal, but as many millions of religions as there will be individuals." Democratic individuality, not liberal universality, was the core spiritual value, Schindler was saying. Even as he remained a fervent critic of the economic individualism of laissez-faire capitalism, the rabbi insisted on autonomy in the realm of the human spirit: do not let the blithe pursuit of oneness impede the full expression of religious diversity and originality.[24]

Such cautions and corrections were part of the self-critical awareness that religious radicals relished, and most of Higginson's critics were on the side of refining his sympathies rather than repudiating them outright. William Potter and Francis Abbot, for example, continued to affirm Higginson's construct as a stepping-stone to a still greater rapprochement—that is, to a "sympathy of souls." In this view, the colonel's excessive commitment to the underlying sameness of religions provided an inadequate grounding for "an embrace of souls," for a "real fellowship" among people of different cultures and religions. His emphasis, the in-house critics suggested, put people on an endless chase of religious essences and did not help them much in the hard work of actual communication in settings of dense particularity. Would Higginson's discernment of abstract similarities, they wondered, really do any good at the level of face-to-face contact? Would his ideas produce any real practice of sympathy, any deeper communication and understanding? Would, in Abbot's phrase, "cosmopolitan relationships" be realized? Professions of sympathy were, indeed, turned into practice (as was evident in the eclecticism of Whitman's funeral), but those everyday translations and borrowings were anything but simple. Taking a closer look at how Higginson's ideas about the sympathy of religions actually fared on the ground in his own life suggests some of those complexities and perplexities.[25]

Higginson's essay, which had begun with the motion of the sea, ended with the sudden illumination of a "foreign cathedral" on an island in the Azores two thousand miles from Boston. That Higginson should return, fifteen years after his trip, to his experience of Portuguese Catholicism as the culminating episode for his lecture suggests that this excursion remained formative. When he and his wife, Mary, sailed for the Azores in October 1855, they did so mostly in hopes of improving her chronically poor health. For himself, Higginson looked forward to the trip as a break from the intense pressures of his reform efforts, even though he had a hard time parting with Worcester's "moral electricity" and could not let go of his habits of self-discipline. ("The disease of my life—the need of a few more hours in the 24, still haunts me here," he noted in his journal.) The islands, especially Fayal, were becoming, by the 1840s and 1850s, an increasingly popular place of resort for well-heeled New Englanders who were seeking a salubrious climate in which to convalesce and calm their nerves. Among Higginson's many causes was health reform, so his own report on his trip to Fayal, published in the *Atlantic Monthly* in 1860, underlined these associations. He emphasized flowers blooming all through the winter and songbirds that sang "without ceasing"—a climate so favorable to health and an "out-door life" that it made Boston feel like "a hospital for consumptives."[26]

Over the next three decades, the Anglo-American fantasy of the archipelago as "the sanitarium of the world," as "a perfect heaven for a neurasthenic," was established as a truism of the burgeoning tourist industry. As Alice Baker noted in her guidebook to the Azores in 1882, "The tired teacher finds here enforced rest with continual diversion; the nervous invalid, an engrossing change of scene, with absolute quiet, no temptation to hurry, and no excuse for worry." The languor of the islands was, of course, a kind of self-deception to which tourists were especially prone. Horta actually bustled as a commercial port and served as an important outpost for American whalers from New Bedford and Nantucket. New Englanders dominated this enterprise on Fayal, and the Charles Dabney family, with their commanding mansion and gardens overlooking Horta, served as the hub of American commercial and political interests in the islands.[27]

"There seem plenty of entertainments there," Higginson wrote in anticipation of the journey, "oranges, music, whaleships, Catholic priests, and a steep mountain 'Pico' half as high again as Mount Washington." As his inclusion of Catholic clergy in this list suggests, integral to his tourist expectations was the possibility of witnessing the "Moorish" Catholicism of Portugal. The arrival at Fayal on November 9 far exceeded his dreams of exoticism and sheer difference. "O wonderful, wonderful, & most wonderful, & again past all whooping!" he exclaimed:

Nobody ever told us, nobody ever prepared us, we knew nothing of it! They told us of the views & the mountains & the ocean, but that we should step suddenly into all the South of Europe at once, set our feet into Lisbon & Madrid & Naples all in one, a place where not a person looks as any person ever looked in America, not a sound but is new, not a square inch of surface that is like anything we ever saw before;—nobody ever prepared us for this. We have had the day that comes but once in a life—the first day in a foreign country. At Singapore or Batavia we should feel no farther from home.

Under "a bewildered spell" of the "picturesque and strange," Higginson at first did little more than stand agape at the window of his lodgings in Horta, transfixed by everything from caps to capes, from fruits to palm trees, from red-tiled roofs to basketwork, from robust and vigorous women (so unlike his invalid wife) to sun-basking children. A teetotaler, he giddily described his experience as one of utter intoxication.[28]

If Higginson was initially bedazzled with surprise in encountering the differences of the Azores, it was not for lack of Anglo-American travel accounts and guidebooks. As early as 1769, Thomas Hickling, a Boston merchant, deserted his wife and children and landed in the Azores or Western Islands, a commercial meeting point between Europe and the Americas of calculable consequence in Atlantic trade. Hickling rose to wealth on São Miguel through citrus exports, a business he came to dominate by 1800. When his children discovered his whereabouts, they journeyed to the islands to restore the broken bonds of "parental affection." His daughter Catherine kept an extensive journal about her visit in 1786–1787, and it offers an early glimpse of the encounter between New England Protestant travelers and the Catholic populace of the islands. The young woman especially "felt a great pity" for the nuns she met; "tho' they appeared happy, yet such a state of confinement must be repugnant." Hickling's pity was akin to Higginson's sympathy in its compassion for those denied liberty, but at a religious level their conceptions were far apart. With no Protestant services to frequent, Hickling found herself attending Catholic churches "from curiosity, not devotion." "I wish my God to be their God, but I can not let their God, b[e] my God, I can not worship Idols," Hickling concluded. "[B]less God, I was born of Christian Parents in a more enlightened land.... I rejoice every day, that I was not educated in the Catholic faith," she exulted with a thankfulness that held steady over her nearly two-year stay in the islands.[29]

The American account most contemporaneous with Higginson's was Silas Weston's *Visit to a Volcano; or, What I Saw at the Western Islands* (1856). Weston, who spent only eleven days touring the Azores, undertook the same two major hikes that Higginson did—one to Caldeira, a volcanic crater on Fayal, and the other to the top of Pico, the great peak across the harbor from Horta. There the similarities of these New England travelers ended. Weston, an adventurer who loved a tall tale, made unceasing fun of the locals, including a hearty round of mimicry of some beggars who annoyed him with their entreaties. The poor were turned into confidence men and rogues who elicited not sympathy but contempt: "The people beg for profit rather than from necessity," Weston quickly concluded. He and some of his traveling companions amused themselves "a short time by purchasing fruit and throwing it into the centre of the square, to see the beggars run and scramble for it." Difference—whether of architecture, conveyance, or farming—held his attention only as a matter of derision, not wonder and whooping. Of the way a boatman transported a local woman ashore atop his shoulders, Weston commented that the pair "much resembled a monkey perched upon a baboon."[30]

British travel accounts showed little more sympathy than those of Hickling and Weston and often more bellicosity. In 1810 Robert Steele, a lieutenant in the Royal Marines, experienced "a sensation of disgust" in encountering Catholic "ignorance and superstition" and felt keenly the superiority of British civil liberty to an absolutism in church and state. Such sentiments convinced him that the archipelago should be seized and placed under British rule: "When the abundance, beauty, and richness of these islands are considered, how natural it is to lament, they are not in the occupation of a people more calculated to improve and enjoy them!" Another observer in 1834, also far more interested in maximizing the economic and strategic utility of the islands for England, simply dismissed the religious practices of the people as vulgar, bigoted, priest-ridden, and immoral; the convents were "little better than public brothels." While the funeral procession of an infant riveted one British traveler in 1831, he was still at a loss in expressing his sense of how the ludicrous mixed with the solemn in these rites: "I am too much a friend to liberty of conscience, and universal toleration, to wish to treat them with levity and disrespect, and willingly forego those comments that I might otherwise be tempted to indulge in, though I could not avoid asking myself again and again, during the day, *Is this really the nineteenth century, and can such things be?*" Toleration did not mean acceptance, but forbearance; clearly, sympathy would demand much more of the liberal soul.[31]

Before Higginson's visit, Fayal had already become the occasional haunt of Transcendentalists and Unitarians. The United States consul, Charles Dabney, was noted for "his sympathy with free thought in religion," and he and his extended family helped make the island especially hospitable for Boston liberals in the mid-nineteenth century. In 1843, for example, the Dabneys hired Samuel Longfellow, the brother of Henry Wadsworth Longfellow, as a tutor for their children. Samuel, who had fallen under the sway of the Transcendentalist movement the year before as a student at Harvard Divinity School, enjoyed the stint. It improved his impaired health, and it afforded him time for pleasant rambles of isolated self-reflection. Following Longfellow's path to Fayal were such leading liberal ministers as Thomas Starr King (1848), John Weiss (1851), and Cyrus Bartol (1868). The Azores were in the spiritual geography of mid-nineteenth-century liberalism what New Mexico, Montana, or the Himalayas became to subsequent seekers.

Reclusive and spiritually restless, Samuel Longfellow resorted to the natural beauty of the Azores as Thoreau would soon to Walden Pond. "I have lived some beautiful hours and had some revelations from the world around me," Longfellow reported in a letter to his close friend Samuel Johnson, "revelations which have given peace to my soul and which I hope may prove nourishing dews to the germs of spiritual life within me." Through his "solitary walks" he was lifted out of moods of despondency and harsh self-criticism. At such times, "nature whispered" to him words of inner peace:

> Vex not thyself because thou art not as others! Be content to be that which thou art; manifest thyself according to the laws of thy individual being. The flower at thy feet hopes not to be a star, nor strives to be aught but a flower. Be calm, and fear not but thou wilt find thy place.... Such lessons did the trees and rocks and waters, the green hills and that calm, majestic mountain breathe into my heart. Nor were words of man wanting, and in the pages of Emerson I found strength and reassurance. I am content now to be silent when I have nothing to say. Indeed, I begin to think silence better than words.

A few years later, in 1849, an epigraph to Thoreau's *Week on the Concord and Merrimack Rivers* would read:

> I am bound, I am bound, for a distant shore,
> By a lonely isle, by a far Azore,
> There it is, there it is, the treasure I seek.

The consecration of the Azores was an integral part of the larger Transcendentalist project of conjuring inner serenity out of lonely, undisturbed places.[32]

Most New England visitors not only immersed themselves in the sunlit landscape of the islands, but also displayed considerable curiosity in witnessing Catholic processions and devotions. As Longfellow noted of his time on Fayal, he attended "Catholic mummeries with poetic faith." "There is," he wrote to a friend back home, "a sentiment of the poetic and a sentiment of the past hanging about them which appeals to my ideality and reverence." Still, he could not shake the predictable Protestant sadness at "how dead and lifeless a shell these forms have become." Woeful yet rapt gazing at Catholic ceremonies was a common practice of Protestant travelers, but Higginson took this staring to an especially high level of absorption, duly attending "all ecclesiastical festivals, grave or gay." In one paragraph alone in his *Atlantic Monthly* piece, he mentioned seven distinct solemnities from Carnival through Holy Week to Pentecost that he had ardently observed.[33]

Higginson recounted his experiences of Portuguese Catholicism in three successive places over a fifteen-year period: first in his journals and letters at the time, then in the *Atlantic Monthly* in 1860, and finally as the concluding episode in "The Sympathy of Religions" in 1871. During his travels in 1855 and 1856, he delighted in almost all aspects of Portuguese life, even as he kept his provincial love of New England safely intact: "They are indeed an attractive people," he remarked of the locals he met, "though I never for an instant prefer them to my earnest & resolute Yankees." Still, he threw himself into learning the language and was fearless in his pursuit of fluency; this helped earn him the respect of the people. "The Dabneys say that I am quite popular," Higginson noted with pride in his journal, "because of the pains I have taken to adapt myself to their ways." He styled himself a connoisseur of oranges and tangerines, participated in local dances, and laughed with Catholic acquaintances about the oddities of his identity as a Protestant "padre" (his being married and being a teetotaler were particularly puzzling, as was his lack of clerical garb and his inability to say Mass). Time and again, he commented on the beauty of a church service or the allure of a crowded procession. On Palm Sunday, he became a delighted souvenir seeker intent on locating one of the ornaments used in the festival, ears of corn decorated with ribbons and flowers, to bring home as a memento. The bells, the fireworks, the church decorations, the music, the candles, and the Carnival scenes all impressed him. His only disappointment was that Mardi Gras had not been even livelier and more mischievous.[34]

Throughout his journal, his chief impressions were favorable. Of the solemnities on Good Friday, he summarily remarked that these "were the most impressive we have seen." Of the rites of Hallelujah Saturday, "the best of Holy Week," he declared, "all was breathless anticipation," "all was joy." Again he became a devout souvenir seeker, and to his delight a Portuguese woman gave "Padre Thomas" one of the three flower-bedecked candlesticks that had blazed on the central altar and in procession. Though he did occasionally express anticlerical sentiments, even then he was mostly reassured that the Portuguese people themselves were every bit as suspicious of overbearing priests as he was. When he saw the laity in one church rise up against a cleric whom they charged with thievery, Higginson rejoiced that this "comes very near being a *Free Church,* after all!" At the time, on the ground, Portuguese Catholicism with its sundry "Orientalisms" occasioned in Higginson no revulsion or fear, no impulse to reform or purify; instead, it produced moments of wonder, curiosity, recognition, and gift giving. All in all, it was a remarkable display of liberal sympathy, especially given the fierceness of anti-Catholic agitation in Massachusetts politics in these very years—a cause that swept up one of Higginson's closest associates in the abolitionist movement, Theodore Parker. The Know-Nothing Party, supremely nativist in its attacks on the Catholic Church, was at its height of power in Higginson's home state in the mid-1850s.[35]

Even if remarkably expansive, the sympathetic feelings that Higginson mustered were hardly uncomplicated. He admitted that attending these festivals did not feel to him like a religious act, but remained instead a matter of aesthetic appreciation or artistic inspiration: "I suspect," he observed with a tinge of regret, "that I am beyond finding anything but *beauty* in any procession." At times,

Higginson seemed more a poet, voyeur, collector, and curiosity seeker than a sympathetic soul. In a series of emotion-laden experiences, each suggesting a tangle of observational relationships, sympathy was inevitably interlaced with other feelings. His ideas about the sympathy of religions were just emerging in "The Return of Faith" during this sojourn abroad, and in his everyday encounters that sentiment remained uneven and inconsistent. Travel, especially in Catholic climes, put liberal sympathy to the test through a flow of difficult cross-cultural meetings. Improving interreligious translations and exchanges in order to make Lydia Maria Child's Eclectic Church of the Future possible was never easy.[36]

In working back through his journals and turning them into publications, Higginson further compromised his sympathies; the tone of his observations now lurched toward critical disengagement. Four years later, in "Fayal and the Portuguese," he sniffed at the rituals as "acted charades" and at the churches as "vast baby-houses." "It must be owned," Higginson claimed in retrospect, "that these things, so unspeakably interesting at first, became a little threadbare before the end of winter; we grew tired of the tawdriness and shabbiness which pervaded them all, of the coarse faces of the priests, and the rank odor of the incense." Now, as a litterateur, he played openly to Protestant prejudices and made the religion of nature the singular source of inspiration that this land of health offered. With his proclivities to imitate Thoreau (he made a pilgrimage to Walden Pond, "that storied spot," shortly before embarking on his trip in 1855), Higginson held up immersion in the outdoors as the genuine spirituality that the Azores fostered. "The vapor in the atmosphere makes it the chosen land of rainbows," Higginson gushed about Fayal in December 1855. "[W]e have seen a great many, & one perfect one by moonlight." By 1860, that was the only piety he offered his readers in the *Atlantic Monthly:* "When over all this luxuriant exotic beauty the soft clouds furled away and the sun showed us Pico, we had no more to ask. And the soft, beautiful blue cone became an altar for our gratitude, and the thin mist of hot volcanic air that flickered above it seemed the rising incense of the world." The foul and artificial incense of the churches had given way to the purer and more authentic fragrance of nature.[37]

Higginson also rewrote his experience of the culminating rites of Holy Week, a revision evident already in 1860 and then made a capstone of his essay in 1871. Between 1856 and 1871, he moved from an engaged and glowing account of Holy Saturday to an increasingly distant, judgmental perspective. As he wrote in the last paragraph of "The Sympathy of Religions," the Portuguese church

> *looked dim and sad, with the innumerable windows closely curtained, since the moment when the symbolical bier of Jesus was borne to its symbolical tomb beneath the High Altar, while the three mystic candles blazed above it. There had been agony and beating of cheeks in the darkness, while ghostly processions moved through the aisles, and fearful transparencies were unrolled from the pulpit. The priests kneeled in gorgeous robes, chanting, with their heads resting on the altar steps; the multitude hung expectant on their words. Suddenly burst forth a new chant, "Gloria in Excelsis!" In that instant every curtain was rolled aside, the cathedral was bathed in glory, the organs clashed, the bells chimed, flowers were thrown from the galleries, little birds were let loose, friends embraced and greeted one another, and we looked down upon the tumultuous sea of faces, all floating in a sunlit haze.*

At various points, Higginson had edged into contradiction through the reinsertion of distance at the expense of sympathy. The tensions inherent in his perspective were at no point more apparent than in this concluding passage as he "looked down" upon the festive throng.[38]

His sympathy failed him in this closing scene in the Portuguese church. In the essay he now placed himself in a space grandly reconfigured as a "tumultuous sea" of Catholic otherness—dark, mystical, flagellating, ghostly: by what alchemy would he transform such feelings back into an expression of engagement? How would he move from distance to common ground, from difference to similarity? Suddenly, he claimed, his own illumination came: "The whole of this sublime transformation consisted in letting in the light of day! These priests and attendants, each stationed at his post, had only removed the darkness they themselves had made." If "this thought smote" him at the moment of his initial observation, as he subsequently maintained in redescribing the experience, that epiphany went unrecorded in his journal. Apparently, only upon further reflection did he take refuge in a simple natural religion that expunged his earlier feelings of attraction and connection. "Unveil these darkened windows, but remove also the darkening walls; the temple itself is but a lingering shadow of that gloom. Instead of its coarse and stifling incense, give us God's pure air, and teach us that the broadest religion is the best." In closing with this image, Higginson's liberal sympathies hardly seemed about bridging differences, but demolishing them.[39]

Higginson always had a lot of irons in the fire and roamed widely as a writer, and so it might be fair to allow him a lapse of memory and close reasoning in revising this episode. Yet, he had many opportunities to emend this essay, and he never tampered again with this concluding illustration of the pure universal religion rubbing out the particularities of local religious practices. In the moment of direct encounter in 1855–1856, Higginson was often able to practice a respectful understanding, but the more he actually speculated about the sympathy of religions, the less connected he became to the Portuguese Catholicism that had helped spark his initial reflections. Was the immediate journal somehow the "more real" or authentic account? As Higginson noted at one point in his *Army Life in a Black Regiment*, "I must resort to a scrap from the diary. Perhaps diaries are apt to be thought tedious; but I would rather read a page of one, whatever the events described, than any more deliberate narrative,—it gives glimpses so much more real and vivid." Or were the comparative abstractions of 1871 the better measure of the import of his principles?[40]

The contradictions within Higginson's ideas about the sympathy of religions mattered, but so did the testimony of his living example. After his trips to the Azores and through Kansas he went on to become a vociferous witness to African-American valor during the Civil War and remained an insistent champion of black soldiers and civil equality. From his days as a colonel, he also gained a sympathetic ear for slave spirituals and became an amateur folklorist of "negro-Methodist chants" and prayers. As with Portuguese Catholicism, he tended to turn religious expression into art: that is, to treat spirituals as folk ballads of great poetic beauty, relics in need of collecting and preservation. Still, there was no more influential transcriber of the spirituals in this period than Higginson, who described his feelings toward his "Gospel army" as that of "sympathetic admiration."[41]

Higginson, who was also a singular champion of Emily Dickinson's meditative verse, recognized the poetry of the spirituals as both a source of courage and "a tie to heaven," finally so sublime in expression that "history cannot afford to lose this portion of its record." Moved by the "religious spirit" of the soldiers in his command, he observed that their devotion "grows more beautiful to me in living longer with them." He even developed an appreciative understanding of the clapping, drumming, dancing, and ecstasy of the African-American "shout" tradition, insisting that such rites were "thoroughly identified" with the "most genuine religious emotions" of the soldiers. "The extremes of religious enthusiasm I did not venture to encourage, for I could not do it honestly," Higginson related, "neither did I discourage them, but simply treated them with respect, and let them have their way." Even some of the most dedicated abolitionists, including Sallie Holley and Lucretia Mott, expressed serious alienation from the singing and shouting of African-American revival meetings, making Higginson's respect on this count all the more noteworthy.[42]

In turning his Civil War journals into his famed book, he paid the black soldiers in his command his version of a supreme compliment in making two problematic comparisons: "Their philosophizing is often the highest form of mysticism; and our dear surgeon declares that they are all natural transcendentalists." Again, on the ground, his liberal sympathies served him better than his studied modes of comparison, which, in this case, turned the distinct religious experiences of African Americans into one more example of spontaneous Emersonian spirituality. The relational practice of sympathy remained more dynamic than the comparative theory of underlying sameness to which it was joined. "True sympathy teaches true largeness of soul," Higginson averred—one that opened him as much to African-American prayers and songs as it did to Buddhist chants and sutras.[43]

Higginson's deep love of the slave spirituals makes clear that his religious sympathies were not all sweetness and light or cheerful sentimentalism. These were Sorrow Songs, as the prophetic intellectual W. E. B. Du Bois so eloquently suggested in *The Souls of Black Folk* (1903), the music of "the children of disappointment." Du Bois himself built on Higginson's work in lifting up the slave songs as "the singular spiritual heritage of the nation" and shared an attraction with him to one haunting hymn in particular:

I walk through the churchyard
          To lay this body down;
I know moon-rise, I know star-rise;
I walk in the moonlight, I walk in the starlight;
I'll lie in the grave and stretch out my arms,
I'll go to judgment in the evening of the day,
And my soul and thy soul shall meet that day,
          When I lay this body down.

"Never, it seems to me, since man first lived and suffered was his infinite longing for peace uttered more plaintively," Du Bois approvingly quoted Higginson's praise and effectively joined arms with him through the universalism of religious liberalism and its "soul-hunger." "I believe in God who made of one blood all races that dwell on earth,"

W. E. B. Du Bois, pioneering civil rights activist, shared with Higginson an appreciation of the enduring importance of the slave spirituals. (Library of Congress, Prints & Photographs Division, LC-USZ62–36176.)

Du Bois related in his "Credo" in 1904. "I believe that all men, black and brown and white, are brothers, varying through Time and Opportunity, in form and gift and feature, but differing in no essential particular, and alike in soul and in the possibility of infinite development."[44]

These two Harvard-educated activists and intellectuals, Higginson (the genteel Bostonian with all the right connections) and Du Bois (the first African American to obtain a Harvard Ph.D.), were strangely connected through the Sorrow Songs. They were also bound together through a shared sense of the political and religious implications of sympathy. As Du Bois wrote,

The nineteenth was the first century of human sympathy,—the age when half wonderingly we began to descry in others that transfig-

ured spark of divinity which we call Myself; when clodhoppers and
peasants, and tramps and thieves, and millionaires and—some
times—Negroes, became throbbing souls whose warm pulsing life
touched us so nearly that we half gasped with surprise, crying,
"Thou too! Hast Thou seen Sorrow and the dull waters of Hope-
lessness? Hast Thou known Life?" And then all helplessly we
peered into those Other-worlds, and wailed, "O World of Worlds,
how shall man make you one?"

Du Bois's "Credo," though, was invariably far sharper than Higginson's "My Creed," especially in its keen sense of pervasive oppression and demonic racism. The common sympathies of the two men only stretched so far.

Higginson, having himself been a fiery abolitionist as a young man, should have been able to understand Du Bois's righteous anger, even if in his privilege he could not plumb its depths. Yet, in old age, Higginson's passionate immediacy for racial justice had taken on a far more patient, accommodating temper, and, in 1909, at age eighty-six, when asked to lend support to the founding vision of the National Association for the Advancement of Colored People (NAACP), the former radical balked. His hedging had the effect of betraying Du Bois's full-fledged civil rights activism in favor of a program of gradual race up-lift through education. Higginson never managed a cri de coeur on the order of Du Bois's "Litany," penned in the midst of massive violence against blacks in the streets of Atlanta in 1906: "Sit no longer blind, Lord God, deaf to our prayer and dumb to our dumb suffering. Surely Thou too are not white, O Lord, a pale, bloodless, heartless thing?... Thy silence is white terror to our hearts!" The sympathetic bond that Higginson and Du Bois shared in the Sorrow Songs bumped up against severe limits. A shared "soul hunger" did not erase the color line that divided their experiences and ultimately their politics.[45]

After the Civil War, Higginson had ceased any formal ministry and turned his religious energies to the Free Religious Association with its platform of religious inclusion and universality. That organization, he explained, is "no place for patronizing, nor even for toleration; it is a place of simple religious equality." If its successes seem rather modest in retrospect—for example, the alliance it formed among certain Unitarians, freethinkers, liberal Jews, progressive Friends, Universalists, Spiritualists, Transcendentalists, and Vedantists—its inclusive platform was seen as anything but tame at the time. To be sure, the FRA shared the larger liberal dilemma of whether to exclude the exclusive: "Into our kingdom of heaven no sectarian may enter," announced Octavius Brooks Frothingham, the society's first president. "Hold all opinions soluble, and you are one of us." That pluralistic dilemma hardly slowed them down in their desire to wake Americans from "the dream of exclusive revelation," and Higginson, like the rest, delighted in the challenge of this emancipation, the latest "war of liberalism." As Samuel Johnson rallied the gathering in May 1870, "I found myself democratic in my religious thought in the selfsame hour and from the same conviction that made me radical in my politics. A privileged race or sex cannot be more unnatural in the political order than the asserted absolutism of Christianity among religions is in the divine."[46]

With the sympathy essay in a kind of national syndication through the FRA, Higginson pressed on. He prodded Americans to cultivate more appreciative views of Buddhism and Islam and weighed in against sectarianism and creedalism at every opportunity. In 1877, he even chided his beloved FRA for its practice of tolerating "all but intolerance" and pressed now for ways to include the voices of those who otherwise spurned liberal principles. "Are we as large as our theory?" he asked. "Are we as ready to tolerate . . . the Evangelical man as the Mohammedan?" Unlike the position he took in his essay on sympathy, he now recognized the exclusion of those with exclusive religious claims as its own form of narrowness and a formidable "internal danger" to any liberal organization. Not that he ever resolved this issue to his satisfaction; he, like the rest of the FRA, remained terribly alienated from evangelicals and the old-time religion, even as more orthodox liberal Protestants (such as the Episcopalian Phillips Brooks) invariably responded negatively to invitations to participate in the organization.[47]

Three months shy of his seventieth birthday in 1893, Higginson headed to Chicago for the World's Parliament of Religions. As an éminence grise among religious representatives there, he participated in these events with characteristic aplomb and saw the Parliament as a grand fulfillment of the FRA's original platform. Though he made highly favorable remarks about the Roman Catholic delegation at the gathering, Higginson's voice lacked the Transcendentalist newness and prophetic edge that it had possessed in the late 1840s and 1850s. His public remarks offered no critique of the circus of Anglo-American condescension toward "primitive religions" on display on the Columbiad's Midway and left unnoticed the holes that remained in the Parliament's representation of the "great religions" (the near invisibility of Native American religions, for example). In lecturing one more time on liberal sympathies, Higginson gestured backwards toward the radical Transcendentalist ferment of the mid-nineteenth century more than he did forward into twentieth-century developments of

The World's Parliament of Religions, gathering in Chicago in September 1893, signaled that the long-accelerating interest in the study of comparative religions had reached a stage of practical application and highly structured performance. (Presbyterian Historical Society, Presbyterian Church [USA], Philadelphia.)

ecumenism and seeker spirituality. At this point, he chose to celebrate the distance already traveled rather than to emphasize the distance yet to go toward his vision of a cosmopolitan piety.[48]

By the turn of the century, Higginson's mantle had been passed to others. In 1899 the scholar Lewis G. Janes succeeded Higginson as president of the FRA and made the advancement of the "noble principles and sentiments" of "The Sympathy of Religions" a major part of his own agenda. At that time Janes was already directing the Monsalvat School for the Comparative Study of Religion, part of the Greenacre summer colony in Eliot, Maine, organized by Sarah Farmer as an embodiment of the ideals of the World's Parliament. With the Monsalvat School and the wider programs of Greenacre, Janes and Farmer opened up an annual forum for the exploration of comparative religions and created a highly visible public space for the enactment of liberal sympathies and eclectic affinities. Representatives came from Buddhism, Vedantism, Zoroastrianism, Jainism, liberal Protestantism, Reform Judaism, Transcendentalism, New Thought, and Theosophy; from Annie Besant to Swami Vivekananda to D. T. Suzuki, all converged there with a shared optimism about the realization of a new day in religious cosmopolitanism. "All religions are true," so an epigraph on the program book for 1897 declared. "[T]hey are like so many rivers, flowing towards the one ocean of Light and Love infinite." Sectarianism was finally to give way to a liberal millennium of international peace, religious harmony, racial amity, and gender equality.[49]

The grander dreams of Greenacre, needless to say, went unfulfilled, but the staying power of the sympathy of religions was left in no doubt. The example of two attendees at Greenacre suffices to demonstrate those ongoing allegiances: the Hindu Swami Saradananda and the Unitarian Alfred W. Martin. Saradananda, showing his familiarity with liberalism's theological vernacular, set the stage in May 1897 for his summer participation at Greenacre with a discourse in Boston expressly on "The Sympathy of Religions." (In turn, one of Greenacre's New Thought leaders, Horatio Dresser, published the paper in his

Journal of Practical Metaphysics.) "By sympathy," Saradananda related, "the Vedantist does not mean a kind of dull indifference, or haughty toleration, which seems to say, 'I know you are wrong and my religion is the only true one, yet I will let you follow it, and perhaps one day your eyes will be opened.' His sympathy is not a negative one, but it is of a direct, positive nature, which knows that all religions are true, they have the same goal." The devout Hindu, Saradananda insisted, did not reduce the "religious orchestra of the universe" to mere "monotones." The sympathy of religions (Saradananda was much clearer than Higginson on this point) would not be purchased at the price of particularity and variation: "The mission of Vedanta to the West is not to make Christians Hindus, but to make the Christian a better Christian, a Hindu a better Hindu, and a Mohammedan a better Mohammedan." Reaching God required specific paths, not a uniform one "in the place of the many."[50]

Alfred W. Martin, a Harvard-educated minister who went west to Tacoma to lead a church of like-minded liberals, made the trek back to Greenacre in 1897 to offer the season's closing lecture, "Universal Religion and the World's Religions." That topic became his life work. In one book after another, he strove to make people "more cosmopolitan" in their "sympathies" and "more responsive" to diverse scriptures. From *Great Religious Teachers of the East* (1911) to *Seven Great Bibles* (1930), Martin charted the progress of liberalism from mere toleration to the "cultivation of that modern virtue, appreciation." "Toward the Bibles of the great religions," he related, "appreciation takes the eclectic attitude, asking of each: What have you to offer? What can we borrow from your moral and spiritual thesaurus to increase our own sources of inspiration?" Martin's appreciation still echoed Higginson's sympathy at many points, but it also revealed how liberal theorists of an inchoate multiculturalism were shifting from an emphasis on "resemblances" toward an embrace of "differences." Sectarian narrowness was still the bugbear, but the peculiar teachings of distinct religions were to be "recognized" and "respected," not erased. The acknowledgment of difference was now "the indispensable condition upon which the only unity in religion worth having is to be attained—*unity in diversity.*" As Martin declared, his vision of a "fellowship of faiths" was in service of "the mutual enhancement of diversities." Perhaps the most telling augury of all in these shifting currents came in 1904, when the young Jewish intellectual Horace M. Kallen (1882–1974), not yet graduated from Harvard, signed the Greenacre guest book. A devoted student of William James, Kallen emerged in the next decade as the prototypical theorist of cultural pluralism against Anglo-Saxon homogeneity.[51]

In the half century after Higginson's formative exposition, sympathy and appreciation became bedrock virtues of the liberal character. No doubt those virtues were unevenly and inconsistently applied, as close attention to Higginson's own life has suggested. Still, the emphasis on cultivating those sentiments in relationship to people of other faiths remained momentous. Those ideals supported spiritual seeking across religious expanses hitherto little explored and helped create a liberal religious culture that opened outward into an eclectic spirituality. Entering appreciatively into that global religious exchange transformed American religious identities, but to what end? Certainly, liberal religionists deepened their understanding of unity and diversity (including the eventual celebration of difference), and yet they also ransacked other cultures for spiritual treasures; it was always a fine line between creative appropriation and naked thievery. They built their identity on cosmopolitan openness, but did breadth come at the expense of depth? Religious universalism could be thin and placeless; it could disorient as much as reorient lost pilgrims. Cultivating the sympathy of religions made for a restive, not restful posture; a fluid and relational precept, it supported the new flux and flow of modern religious identities. It was the métier of all those aspiring, audacious souls who declared themselves free to explore the piety of the world.

Pursuing the sympathy of religions created intractable puzzles about the solidity of Christian identity or any religious identity in a modern, pluralistic society. Yet it also provided answers to what a vital, mediating spirituality might look like amid that very diversity. William Norman Guthrie, a participant in the Whitman Fellowship and an Episcopal priest in New York City, exemplified the possibilities and perils of that new spirituality. Guthrie cut his literary teeth in the 1890s offering generous readings of Walt Whitman as "a religious teacher," a bearer of the "vital core" of Quakerism's Inner Light, and a poet-prophet who revealed "the mystic secret of religion." To Guthrie, Emerson was, by comparison, cold and abstract; Whitman "drives his ideas like wedges of live lightning into your soul." As pastor at St. Mark's in-the-Bouwerie, Guthrie was a liturgical innovator, especially open to the arts, including theater and dance. He was always on the lookout for ways to relieve the vast "religious boredom" that too many Americans were experiencing at church. Taking his cue directly from Whitman's embrace of "companions from lands and literatures strange to Christendom," he published *Leaves of the Greater Bible: A Spiritual Anthology* (1917), in which he sought to represent diverse "sources of perpetual refreshment and perpetual inspiration." In his collection he drew on Native American religions, American civil religion, Egyptian sun worship, Zoroastrian prayers, and Buddhist writings, as well as Jewish and Christian sources.[52]

To his critics, Guthrie looked like the worst kind of dabbler and crackpot, and yet, unlike Higginson, he insisted all along that he remained very much a member of the Christian church. "We are Christians, and what is more, Anglicans. Very well, let us start with the Prayer Book, and the Scriptures," Guthrie enjoined at the outset of his *Offices of Mystical Religion* (1927). Unwilling to stop there, though, he kept pressing on the outer bounds of liberal sympathies: "A good God must ... everywhere and in all times have answered His children's prayer for guidance and comfort. There cannot have been any exclusive monopoly granted to any race." Guthrie stumbled time and again in his codification of universalized scriptures, inclusive worship services, and fanciful pageants of comparative religion. What kind of leap was it to think that through an act of imaginative identification Christians could come to understand what it meant to be "a true Taoist" or "a true Buddhist"? How could Guthrie's wildly resilient faith in shared religious truths justify the collection of "separable lyrics" and "detachable ritual morsels" as if other cultures were curio shops at his artistic disposal? Guthrie wanted Americans to be open and teachable, filled with Whitman's democratic and cosmopolitan sympathies and imbued with his sense that the best religion transcended the confines of exclusive creeds. Creating that kind of open spirituality was never an innocent endeavor, rife, as it so often was, with class privilege, racial myopia, and cultural hierarchy. Yet Guthrie's failings, like Higginson's, do not lessen the importance of liberal attempts to appreciate diversity while simultaneously looking for ways to affirm religious unity across the bounds of difference. In decisive and enduring ways, these romantic souls confronted religious narrowness and bigotry with a positive vision of a cosmopolitan spirituality, the piety of the world.[53]

Those pioneering efforts have clearly left a lasting imprint on America's seeker culture and the spiritual journeys it fosters. Take just one instance—a current vogue borrowed ostensibly from the thirteenth century. Traveling eight centuries back in time, contemporary seekers rarely stop to extol the scholastic sophistication of Thomas Aquinas (1225–1274), the supremacy of his theological, philosophical, and moral system. Instead, what more often attracts notice now is the mystical universalism and essential wisdom of Sufi Jalal al-Din ar-Rumi (1207–1273): "Not Christian or Jew or Muslim, not Hindu, Buddhist, sufi, or zen. Not any religion or cultural system ... I belong to the beloved, have seen the two worlds as one." More to the point, it is less a thirteenth-century Rumi than a nineteenth-century

Rumi that draws admiration. Rumi refracted through Walt Whitman—that is how the Tennessee-reared, Berkeley-trained poet Coleman Barks has made the Persian mystic a best seller in America's seeker culture: "Listen to the presences inside poems, / Let them take you where they will." Quoting from Whitman's preface to *Leaves of Grass* in his own preface to Rumi—"re-examine all you have been told at school or church or in any book, dismiss whatever insults your own soul"— Barks lifts up the thirteenth-century mystic as a needed "bridge between religions and cultures," someone who knows the sparkling individuality of different religions but appreciates even more their common ground: "I say that the exclusivity of most of the organized religions *does* insult the soul," Barks powerfully exhorts. "We must be open enough to assimilate the insights of indigenous cultures as well as those of the Abrahamic religions, to glory in the clarity of Rinzai and Bodhidharma as well as that of the dreamtime drawings." Higginson, Child, Guthrie, or Whitman—all would have been right at home, or rather on the road, with Barks.[54]

CHAPTER FOUR

———◆◆◆◆◆———

MEDITATION FOR
AMERICANS

FELIX ADLER (1851–1933), a Reform Jew on his way to founding his own progressive religious organization known as the Society for Ethical Culture, had avidly digested the Transcendentalist writings of Theodore Parker and Ralph Waldo Emerson. Adler was among the coterie of intellectuals, alongside Thomas Wentworth Higginson and Octavius Brooks Frothingham, who energized the Free Religious Association during its salad days. At a meeting in 1876 he exhorted New England's religious radicals to make good on their expansive vision for the nation: "O America! America! that hast broken the bonds of despotism, and given political liberty to the world, if it were thine to break also those subtle bonds that fetter our spiritual life, and hamper the soul's free flight toward the Infinite!... Oh that we who yearn for free religion, as the thirsty man yearns for the living water-brooks, could feel and know, and make plain to all, that freedom is religion, and that religion is freedom!" Adler's credo brimmed with a moral intensity, a blend of his upbringing as the son of a prominent Reform rabbi and his own humanistic speculations within larger Enlightenment streams of ethical reasoning. Alarming many Jews and Christians alike, Adler appeared to be one of those liberals so committed to humanitarian reform and individual freedom that they are willing to slough off any and all religious practice in the name of progress. Yet, at the podium in Boston in June 1876, he insisted to his colleagues in the Free Religious Association that genuine social reform had to have its roots "deep down in the religious life." It had to be "undertaken in a spirit of *religious* devotion."[1]

That was not a theme that Adler let die in his long career as scholar, activist, lecturer, and writer. In 1905 he published *The Essentials of Spirituality*, a devotional book that made plain his conviction that work for social justice reached its "high mark" only when leavened with "spirituality," "a certain serene fervor which we may almost call saintliness." In what, besides saintliness or moral righteousness, did the essentials of spirituality consist? How was that vital spirituality to be attained, practiced, or cultivated, especially if it had no clear recourse to the historical particularities of Judaism or Christianity? "The first essential," Adler insisted, "is an awakening, a sense of the absence of spirituality, the realized need of giving to our lives a new and higher quality; first there must be the hunger before there can be the satisfaction." Once recognized, that hunger could potentially be satisfied through any number of religious channels, whether through pursuing "the Buddhist belief in Nirvana" or "the ideals of Ethical Culture." A student of comparative religions with sympathies akin to Higginson's, Adler claimed that "spirituality is not indissolubly associated with any one type of religion or philosophy; it is a quality of soul manifesting itself in a variety of activities and beliefs." Inspiration could come from the Bible; it could just as easily come from Emerson or Whitman.[2]

Adler's openness did not mean that anything goes. The spiritual life had "characteristic marks" beyond the quest for saintliness or "moral perfection," and these were serenity and inwardness. These

Felix Adler, founder of the Society for Ethical Culture and an active member of the Free Religious Association, championed an "essential spirituality" in which daily meditative practice featured prominently. (New York Society for Ethical Culture.)

soulful qualities were to be achieved through a daily practice of meditation and self-reflection. Adler's essential spirituality depended on acquiring "the habit of ever and anon detaching one's self from one's accustomed interests and pursuits, becoming, as it were, a spectator of one's self and one's doings, escaping from the sweeping current and standing on the shore. For this purpose it is advisable to consecrate certain times, preferably a certain time each day, to self-recollection; to dedicate an hour—or a half-hour, if no more can be spared—to seeing one's life in all its relations." He encouraged this practice both "on the ground of mental sanity" and "on the ground of spirituality." Even the most dedicated social reformer was likely to collapse in an exhaustion of mind and body without a due attentiveness to the inner life, without a spiritual discipline of "mental repose," "self-recollection," and "detachment." The inward calmness bred of daily meditation was no "moral luxury" or "an airy bauble of the fancy," but integral to living an ethical life, to "the identification of the self with others." Doing "justice to that inner self" was, Adler advised, critical for doing "justice to others." "Let us make daily provision for it," Adler concluded in his recommendation of this spiritual practice.[3]

Adler's endorsement of mental repose and serene inwardness was indicative of a wider turn toward a meditative spirituality during the late nineteenth and early twentieth centuries. How did a concentrated and calmed mind come to be seen in various circles as an essential of a devout life? It was not at all an obvious development. Throughout much of the nineteenth century, American identity had regularly been imagined through unrelieved pictures of bustling activity and outward movement. Philip Schaff, a Swiss churchman turned observer of American life, commented in 1854 that Americans were "uncommonly practical, energetic, and enterprising." American Christians, he said, with the Methodists in mind, were "more like busy Martha than like pensive Mary"; they lacked "German depth, and inwardness, the contemplative turn for the mystical." Americans, he concluded, "are a people of the boldest enterprise and untiring progress—Restlessness and Agitation personified. Even when seated, they push themselves to and fro on their rockingchairs; they live in a state of perpetual excitement in their business, their politics and their religion." By one account after another, the culture's religious trademark was not devotional quietude and serene meditation, but evangelical fervor and anxiety-ridden conversion. The hoopla of the Methodist camp meeting seemed to mirror perfectly the commotion of the American marketplace and the rough-and-tumble of American politics.[4]

There was, of course, more contemplative interiority to American religious life than Schaff was ready to acknowledge. Meditation had long been an important feature of American Christian practice, Catholic and Protestant, particularly meditation on the life and sufferings of Jesus. It was interwoven with the commonplace habits of Scripture reading, prayer, and self-examination. Many nineteenth-century devotional guides, as had their seventeenth- and eighteenth-century counterparts, offered collections of scriptural texts for daily meditation on core Christian themes ranging from the wages of sin to the joys of heaven. Others offered meditative techniques for preparing for the Lord's Supper, for a penitential encounter with Christ's Passion in which contemplatives were instructed to imagine themselves on Calvary with the cleansing blood of Jesus dripping down upon them. In 1868 a Catholic publisher in Philadelphia issued a tract titled *The Practice of Meditation,* which simply consisted of venerable excerpts from St. Alphonsus Maria de Liguori (1696–1787) and St. Teresa of Avila (1515–1582) on contemplative practice as an aid to vanquishing fleshly temptations and valiantly pursuing the holy life. For their part, Episcopalians, keeping the liturgical rhythms of the Christian year in view, often published guides to meditation for the church seasons of Advent and Lent; these devotional books aimed at an annual reenactment of Jesus' life, death, and resurrection through the inward reflections of pious souls.[5]

As Adler's *The Essentials of Spirituality* suggested, the practice of meditation was in the midst of an overhaul by 1905. A few years earlier, in *The Varieties of Religious Experience,* William James registered an awareness of this shifting terrain: "It is odd that Protestantism, especially evangelical Protestantism, would seemingly have abandoned everything methodical in this line.... It has been left to our mind-curers to reintroduce methodical meditation into our religious life." James overstated the extent to which Christians, including evangelical Protestants, had relinquished these practices, but he was right to sense that the familiar associations were rapidly losing ground to new movements and methods. The practice of meditation mutated in American culture after 1880 through the spread of various mind-cure gospels of health and happiness, which, under the banner of New Thought, were regularly made a constitutive part of "a Liberal Faith" in divine immanence, Inner Light mysticism, social service, and cosmopolitan openness to "many roads." Several New Thought leaders, including the luminaries Horatio Dresser and Ralph Waldo Trine, happily melded Christian emphases with their growing knowledge of comparative religions. That cognizance came not only through texts, but also through personal encounters with practitioners of yoga and Buddhist meditation, notably at the Greenacre community in Maine. A changed set of purposes governed most of the new practices of meditation as they found expression in late Victorian America and afterward: sustained concentration, self-integration, repose, serenity, silence, introspection, cosmopolitanism, and social reform.[6]

The New Thought movement was never tidy. Some early proponents, such as Warren Felt Evans, read the mystic Emanuel Swedenborg with particular assiduity in seeking out spiritual correspondences behind the material semblances of the body. Most of the initial advocates had pored over Emerson as a philosophical source for their popular transcendentalism, and many of them heralded the Concord sage as their spiritual father, "the illumined one so far in advance of his time."[7] Few contemporaries would have missed the substantial debt to mesmerism, to the discovery of the hidden powers of the mind in trance or under hypnosis. Mesmerists, animal magnetizers, and somnambulists had in the middle decades of the nineteenth century electrified American audiences with vivid demonstrations of clairvoyance, healing, and hypnotic suggestion. The mind, rightly concentrated, seemed to have tremendous influence over the body and appeared a causative force all its own in curing disease. It was in this context that Phineas P. Quimby (1802–1866), a mental healer in Portland, Maine, came to the attention of Mary Baker Eddy, the subsequent founder of Christian Science. A patient of Quimby's, Eddy turned his mind-cure philosophy into a body of authoritative scripture in *Science and Health* (1875). That book, in turn, served as the revelatory basis of a new religious movement with her at the helm and with Boston as its headquarters.[8]

Mary Baker Eddy's canonical rendering of mind-cure in *Science and Health* did not clean up the messiness of New Thought. Lecturers, teachers, healers, and metaphysicians proliferated rapidly in the 1880s and 1890s, bringing to naught Eddy's desire to control the movement and shield her followers from the "malicious animal magnetism" of innumerable competitors. One author, in advising would-be followers of mental healing, tweaked in typical fashion Eddy's desire for "strong outward organization" and suggested that prevailing religious currents favored instead the "free and individualistic spirit" of New Thought: "Be your real self, and you will be original.... Truth follows no rut. It is better to search for it than to walk in the groove of some leader's estimate of it.... You must have *your own* New Thought, rather than that which belongs to someone else."[9]

With a movement this decentralized, fluid, and enterprising, alliances of vastly different kinds were possible. One of the most important, though, was with New England's religious liberalism. Horatio Dresser (1866–1954), the son of two devoted patients of Quimby's, had grown up in a household that served as a storm center for controversies over the power of mental therapeutics in the treatment of sickness and in the production of health and happiness. While the son made many of his parents' causes his own (including upholding Quimby's originality over Eddy's inspiration), he also went his own way. In helping to found the Metaphysical Club in Boston in 1895, the Harvard-educated son made clear that he looked as much to the Transcendental Club and the Radical Club for models as he did to Quimby's healing practice in Maine. A Unitarian minister, L. B. McDonald, served as the group's first president, and Frederick Reed, active in the Greenacre summer conferences, was appointed secretary. Julia Ward Howe, the famed author of "The Battle Hymn of the Republic" and about as prominent a liberal Protestant as the country boasted, delivered the new club's initial public lecture. Sarah Farmer, the bright light of New England religious ecumenism, was on the executive committee and became a lifelong ally of Dresser's through the joined projects of Greenacre and the Metaphysical Club. Given such convergences and alliances, Dresser was right to see much of New

Thought as "the liberal wing of the therapeutic movement" or as part of the "more spiritual phase of liberalism."[10]

Also among the founders of this Metaphysical Club was Henry Wood (1834–1908), one of the more prolific and influential early New Thought writers. (This long-lived Metaphysical Club, by the way, should not be confused with the short-lived one of 1872, which included Charles Peirce, William James, and Oliver Wendell Holmes Jr., among others. Though James had a considerable interest in New Thought and knew Dresser well at Harvard, these were quite different groups of metaphysicians.)[11] For Wood, as for most of his fellows in this Boston circle, more was at stake in the mind-cure movement than a gospel of healing for the sick. One clue to his larger interests in the spiritual life was his financial support for the establishment of a "Silence Room, for quiet and meditation" within the Metaphysical Club.[12] Not coincidentally, Dresser's early work *The Power of Silence,* published in the very year the club was founded, built on the same foundation of meditative practice. Contemplative habits were every bit as important to the New Thought movement as was spiritual healing, which was derived from the mental powers accessed through disciplines of concentration and silence. Mind over Matter was the metaphysical motto, but a more precise rendering would have been The Meditative Mind over Matter.

The author of a half dozen advice books as well as two New Thought novels published between 1890 and 1908, Henry Wood insisted that he was "*not* a professional healer" but a "student of Truth." Turning to this spiritual path relatively late in life, Wood was old enough to have personally witnessed the rise of hypnotic suggestion as a sensational practice among animal magnetists. He wanted nothing to do, though, with those theatrics or with the miracles of faith healers, their anointing hands and demonic expulsions. His program of "ideal suggestion" and "mental photography" was, by contrast, a meditative technique of concentration, visualization, and self-awareness. "Many shrink from such a searching inward reconstruction," he wrote in 1893, "because they instinctively feel that it will reveal them to themselves. They are willing to look outward, but cannot abide introspection." Embracing a typically evolutionary and progressive view of human consciousness, Wood imagined an ascent to new intuitive levels of insight, culminating in union with "the Christ spirit" or in attainment of "illuminated spiritual consciousness."[13]

The "how to" questions were central to Wood's enterprise: How was "a weary traveler on the highway of life" to get to that next level of spiritual consciousness? How were "harmony and illumination" to be realized in practice? "The key which unlocks spiritual storehouses of strength and attainment" was "thought discipline and control." In "quiet leisure moments by day" and "wakeful hours by night," the aimless mind was to be sharpened through a regimen of meditations and affirmations. "At such favorable seasons the outside world, with all its current of daily events, is barred out," Wood related, "and one goes into the silent sanctuary of the inner temple of soul to commune and aspire." The Transcendentalist inflections of spiritual aspiration were distinctly audible, and Wood invoked not only the Christ spirit, but also Emerson's self-reliance.[14]

Wood recommended a daily practice of meditation and concentration, performed in solitude and silence in a seated and restful posture. The mind was first riveted on a short devotional passage or "meditation" through repeated reading, and terseness was of the essence: "I am now filled with the divine energy. I open my soul to it and let it possess me. It overflows so that I give it out to those around me." Already absorbed in these clipped truths, practitioners were then to fasten their eyes upon one compact saying or "suggestion"—"GOD IS HERE" or "I AM FREE" or "DIVINE LOVE FILLS ME" or "CHRIST IS WITHIN" or "I MAKE HARMONY"—for "ten to twenty minutes." (Wood included bold full-page renderings of each of these suggestions, and twenty more besides, to hold up as visual aids for these daily exercises.) After aspirants had gazed upon the motto with open eyes, Wood instructed, they were to "close the eyes for twenty to thirty minutes more," continuing to behold the same words with "the mind's eye" and thus further photographing them onto their consciousness. Wood offered no quick fixes. This practice took practice, much of it; only slowly would "the power to focalize the mind" grow into a fully formed capacity that allowed for both "intensive concentration" and "perfect rest and receptivity." Whatever else its fruits, Wood's "mental photography" was a pioneering technique of self-help through visualization. He saw it as having innumerable practical applications, including particular potential as "an efficient remedy for the slavery of intoxicants"—not a bad foreshadowing of Alcoholics Anonymous, which got its start in 1935 and helped launch a whole raft of self-help programs.[15]

Wood was certainly well liked in his day, but for popularity and durability he could not hold a candle to Ralph Waldo Trine (1866–

The New Thought leader Henry Wood was especially convinced of the value of concentrating the mind on distinct mottoes, including these two, which appeared as visual aids in one of his advice books. (Collection of the author.)

DIVINE LOVE

FILLS ME.

I AM

NOT BODY.

1958), a Boston-based activist and metaphysician who later in life settled in southern California. A year after publishing *What All the World's A-Seeking* in 1896, he released *In Tune with the Infinite,* a blockbuster that sold over 1.5 million copies in the next half century. In terms of sales for books of religious inspiration, it had no rival until the appearance of Norman Vincent Peale's *The Power of Positive Thinking* in 1952.[16] Though easy to dismiss at first glance as the promoter of a shallow gospel of health and wealth, Trine was a complex figure of at least occasional subtlety. A religious radical and a socialist with a good education from Knox College, the University of Wisconsin, and Johns Hopkins University, Trine mingled easily with Whitmanites, Vedantists, New Thought healers, and Christian social gospelers. As a reform advocate and committed vegetarian, he took an especially active role in the Massachusetts Society for the Prevention of Cruelty to Animals and the American Humane Education Society: "Glory to God, Peace on Earth, Kindness, Justice and Mercy to Every Living Creature" was the latter group's motto. (Trine would actually spend much of his literary capital on such unpopular causes as outlawing the "brutal" amusements of sportsmen clubs, including the use of live pigeons for target practice.) Writing *In Tune with the Infinite* while in residence at the Greenacre retreat, he was extremely well acquainted through Sarah Farmer's ingenious leadership with several of the most renowned inquirers into comparative religions of the day. That Maine community offered an appropriately eclectic religious environment in which to produce what Trine imagined as a newly universalized practice of the concentrated mind.[17]

Trine began with God or the divine principle, what he often called the Spirit of Infinite Life, but which he could just as easily refer to as Omnipotence, Kindly Light, or the Over-Soul. This transcendent spirit was likened to a reservoir of superhuman power ever brimming over and pouring itself out as an immanent presence in the world; it was always poised to flow into the lives of those who were prepared to receive it. Being open to this "divine inflow" and being in harmony

The social reformer Ralph Waldo Trine (seated on the ground in the center of the photograph with his face turned toward the camera) wrote his best seller, *In Tune with the Infinite,* on the grounds at Greenacre amid the numerous visitors there. (Eliot Bahá'í Archives, Eliot, Maine.)

with "the thought energies of God" became integral to realizing the creative powers of "the real self." One of the signs of that divine presence in day-to-day life was a focused mind full of cheer and confidence. "Thoughts are forces," Trine averred, "subtle, vital, creative, continually building and shaping our lives according to their nature." Despondent, pessimistic thoughts made for stunted lives and revealed souls that were out of sync with the Infinite Source. "A mind always hopeful, confident, courageous, and determined on its set purpose, and keeping itself to that purpose," Trine claimed, "attracts to itself out of the elements things and powers favorable to that purpose." Worrying minds and disordered emotions—fear, anger, jealousy, sorrow, or malice—wreaked havoc on people's bodies. This was a very basic correspondence for New Thought: the turmoil of the mind became manifest in the body.[18]

The restoration of physical health was at the heart of this gospel of soothed minds, but it was not all renewed bodily vigor all the time. Trine took on that subject in an early chapter of *In Tune with the Infinite* and then moved on quickly to "the secrets, power, and effects of love." The physical and mental health that came from the realization of oneness with the Spirit of Infinite Life was a preparation for the recognition of the Spirit of Infinite Love in which the interrelationship between self and others—"the oneness of all life"—was acknowledged. "We find," Trine insisted, "that we are all members of the one great body, and that no portion of the body can be harmed without all the other portions suffering thereby." As was evident in his dedication to the cause of animal welfare, Trine was constantly trying to train people's hearts in the ethics of love and compassion, the moral imperative "to protect and care for the weak and defenseless." If this spirit of sympathy sufficiently suffused the heart and mind, prejudices and hatreds would be relinquished, and selfishness would be recognized as "at the root of all error, sin, and crime."

Trine was hardly inviting his readers into a narcissistic piety. Instead, he was enjoining them to lose their "small, personal, self-centered, self-seeking nature" through "the service of others." To be sure, he wanted people to have peaceful, empowered, and fulfilled lives, but his care of souls was not simply a therapeutic gospel of health and wealth. Capitalist materialism was as misbegotten as scientific materialism: "When we come into the realization of the higher powers, we will then be able to give more attention to the real life, instead of giving so much to the piling up of vast possessions that hamper rather than help it." For Trine, it was still hard for a rich man to enter into the kingdom of heaven. The divine life remained the Christ life of a servant to the sick, the brokenhearted, the weak, the faltering, and the afflicted. That is certainly how Trine imagined the purpose of his own ministry.[19]

Less interested in the "how-to" questions than Wood was, Trine regularly announced that his teachings could not be reduced to a method or a formula. There was enough of Emerson and Whitman in Trine that he always insisted that each individual had to make "practical application of these truths" on his or her own, that "one person cannot well make this for another." In 1908 he did manage to articulate "A Creed of the Open Road," but only with the proviso that it was "to be observed to-day, to be changed to-morrow, or abandoned, according to tomorrow's light." Still, he managed to slip makeshift suggestions for various meditative techniques into his work. Like Wood, Trine recommended retreating into "the quiet of your own interior self" and holding certain thoughts in mind in a sustained, repetitive way. The examples Trine gave could sound silly and feathery — "I am one with the Infinite Spirit of Life" or "Dear everybody, I love you" — but he offered them as tentative suggestions, not magical dicta. The use of constant prayers and recurring resolutions focused the mind, but it was all the more important, by Trine's lights, to open the mind to intuition and inspiration. Receptivity was crucial, and here Trine suggested as "an aid" the everyday cultivation of a calmed yet expectant mind. This state of silence, reminiscent of Quaker devotion, he saw as conducive to discerning the voice of interior Wisdom or the Christ within. Trine did not care what such practices were called — a form of "meditation, realization, treatment, or whatever term" — as long as they helped prompt people in the here and now to seek the kingdom of heaven within and beyond themselves.[20]

Trine also made clear that his work, though most influenced by his Christian roots and context, was not to be bound by those confessional limits. *In Tune with the Infinite* was, among other things, a brave manifesto for a cosmopolitan spirituality, and Trine's endorsement of vaguely defined methods of concentration, meditation, and prayer fit well within that universalizing impulse. "Patriotism is a beautiful thing;" Trine noted in his chapter titled "The Basic Principle of All Religions." "It is well for me to love my country, but why should I love my own country more than I love all others?" If nationalism was a dangerous form of partiality, so was religious particularity in Trine's view. When religion was viewed in its essentials rather than inessentials, the impermanent would give way to the permanent. "We shall find," Trine naively prophesied, "that minor differences, narrow prejudices, and all these laughable absurdities will so fall away by virtue of their very insignificance that a Jew can worship equally as well in a Catholic cathedral, a Catholic in a Jewish synagogue, a Buddhist in a Christian church, a Christian in a Buddhist temple. Or all can worship equally well about their own hearth-stones, or out on the hillside.... For true worship, only God and the human soul are necessary." In a revealing testimony to Trine's place in this world of cosmopolitan spirituality, the leading scholar of comparative religions at the time, F. Max Müller, wrote him from Oxford in 1898, telling of his "delight" in reading Trine's work and offering him detailed advice on further insights to be garnered from Müller's own *Sacred Books of the East:* "You teach what I have tried to teach all my life."

Like Müller, Emerson, Child, and Higginson, Trine happily heralded the wisdom of other scriptures and traditions—at least insofar as they supported "the universal religion": " 'Whatever road I take joins the highway that leads to Thee,' says the inspired writer in the Persian scriptures. 'Broad is the carpet God has spread, and beautiful the colors He has given it.' " "Let our Churches grasp these great truths," Trine implored at a time when most American Christians still deeply hallowed the triumph of empire and evangelization. Trine may have pushed further toward liberal universalism than most New Thought leaders did, but this emphasis was hardly uncommon in these circles. When ten thousand members of the International New Thought Alliance assembled in New York in 1926, they hastened to stage their own "Parliament of Religions." Trine was prominently featured, but innumerable other New Thought leaders joined him in this congress, which included Hindu, Jewish, Muslim, Bahá'í, Buddhist, and (for good measure) Baptist representatives.[21]

In the open fields that Trine and company walked, the meditative practices of mind-cure intersected with a larger series of religious exchanges with Asian traditions. These convergences were embodied especially in the Theosophical Society, founded in New York in 1875 and rising to prominence at the same time that the Free Religious Association flourished and New Thought grew in stature. Organized by the Russian occultist Helena Petrovna Blavatsky (1831–1891) and the American lawyer and Civil War veteran Henry Steel Olcott (1832–1907), the Theosophical Society originated within a Spiritualist milieu of séances, mediums, and table-rapping. Both Blavatsky and Olcott were Spiritualists before they were Theosophists; they actually met in 1874 in Chittenden, Vermont, where both had traveled to investigate the latest sensation in spirit manifestations. Over the course of the next year, the two became close friends and together began to add more esoteric elements to their Spiritualist practices, including resort to the occultist essentials of alchemy and ancient magic. In September 1875, a small fellowship of sixteen members signed on for a society dedicated to further study of such secret wisdom and, ironically, to the wide diffusion of knowledge about those underground mysteries. A month later Olcott was elected as the first president of the new Theosophical Society—a role that would eventually help turn him into a global figure in religious reform movements.[22]

The teachings of the Theosophical Society, especially as they were embodied in the writings of Blavatsky, were a hodgepodge. They included: (1) an imaginative compilation of esoteric and Spiritualist lore; (2) a grand synthesis of religion and science in an era when the two were widely seen as in the midst of an acrimonious divorce; (3) a reassertion of Neoplatonist yearnings for the spiritual ascent of the soul out of its earthly prison; (4) a universalistic faith that all religions contain at their core the same truths and that these truths are available to all earnest seekers without regard to caste, creed, sex, or race; and (5) an insistence that certain mahatmas or masters (among them, Jesus and the Buddha and also lesser-known ones such as Koot Hoomi) attend to the growing illumination of an individual's spiritual consciousness. If all that creativity was not enough, the Theosophical Society was also an important bridge for the addition of Asian religious symbolism and texts to American understandings of spirituality. Karma, a cosmic law of reward and punishment in which people reap what they sow, was integral to Theosophical belief, and so was the concept of reincarnation, which was presented as a series of rebirths leading to gradual spiritual elevation. Both concepts gained their initial American currency through the auspices of the Theosophical Society. Already in 1876, Olcott was in the vanguard as well of advocating cremation over burial as a funerary practice to Americans, heralding its spiritual purity as a sacred Hindu rite as well as a modern sanitary reform.[23]

In 1878 Olcott and Blavatsky left the United States and headed for India and Ceylon (now Sri Lanka), leaving the fledgling American wing of the Theosophical Society to the attention (and inattention) of others. Over the next decade Olcott especially emerged as a pivotal player in his support for an anticolonial revival of Buddhism in Ceylon and even produced his own *Buddhist Catechism* for use in schools there and elsewhere. His catechism—by 1897, it had been "published in twenty languages, mainly by Buddhists, for Buddhists"—was a strange mix. On the one hand, it showed Olcott's immersion in the life and teachings of the Buddha and displayed his considerable sympathy with basic Buddhist precepts. On the other hand, it could easily have been read as a primer on Transcendentalist spirituality in its evocation of wise and dignified hermits in their forest solitude and its emphasis on mystical experience, a sudden moment of enlightenment in which the mind "entirely opened, like the full-blown lotus flower." Buddhism was presented not as a "religion," but as a spiritual "approach" to life; it did not offer "salvation," but "emancipation"—from, among other things, selfishness, sensuality, intoxicating liquors, and gender inequality. Its highest truths came not through "reason" or "ceremonialism," but through "intuition—a mental state in which any desired truth is instantaneously grasped." Olcott's Buddhism was, in sum, largely compatible with religious liberalism—"a religion of noble tolerance, of universal brotherhood, of righteousness and justice."[24]

Among the clearest points of affinity between Olcott's Transcendentalism and Olcott's Buddhism was the way in which "progress in spirituality" was charted through practices of "deep meditation." The American colonel posed a catechetical question: "What plan of discipline did [the Buddha] adopt to open his mind to know the whole truth?" And he answered, "He sat and meditated, concentrating his mind upon the higher problems of life, and shutting out from his sight and hearing all that was likely to interrupt his inward reflections." The concentrated mind was at the bottom of it all; it was the basis for the attainment of the holy life of pure compassion and the "supernormal wisdom" that accompanied that life. "Right Meditation," Olcott summarized, "leads to spiritual enlightenment, or the development of the Buddha-like faculty, which is latent in every man." Some have been quick to label Olcott's formulations as a kind of Protestant Buddhism, but that misses the most dynamic interface—the overlapping emphasis on meditative concentration among Theosophists, latter-day Transcendentalists, and New Thought metaphysicians.[25]

Through the 1880s Theosophists like Olcott were more of a curious anomaly than a notable presence on the American scene, but the period from 1890 to 1910 proved one of growth and proliferation for them just as it did for their New Thought counterparts. Madame Blavatsky herself had been more concerned with the elaboration of secret teachings and with Spiritualist phenomena than with developing the devotional lives of her disciples. Near the end of her life she did produce *The Voice of the Silence,* published in New York in 1889, which offered something akin to a spiritual guide for the Theosophical quest and showed some affinities with emergent New Thought emphases. "Thou hast to reach that fixity of mind in which no breeze, however strong, can waft an earthly thought within," Blavatsky ad-

vised in her little book of occasionally garbled fragments. "Thus purified, the shrine must of all action, sound, or earthly light be void; e'en
as the butterfly o'ertaken by the frost, falls lifeless at the threshold—
so must all earthly thoughts fall dead."[26]

In the same year that Blavatsky published *The Voice of the Silence*,
the Theosophical Society gained one of its most important followers,
Annie Besant (1847–1933), a minister's wife who, through the anguish
of Christian doubt, had turned into a liberal religionist, freethinking
radical, and energetic reformer in the cause of women's emancipation
(among many other causes). Besant took up the mantle of the founders,
and her numerous writings decisively shaped the movement's course
in India, England, and the United States. Devotional practices—from
prayer to the Christian sacraments to yoga—held her attention at numerous points, and she searched them all with a "reverent sympathy
for every expression of man's longing after God." Meditation, not
surprisingly, was among the leading devotions in Besant's picturing of
the "eternal quest" for divine knowledge and love. "Anyone who de-
termines to lead a spiritual life," she instructed, "must daily devote
some time to meditation. As soon may the physical life be sustained
without food as the spiritual without meditation. Those who cannot
spare half an hour a day during which the world may be shut out and
the mind may receive from the spiritual planes a current of life cannot
lead the spiritual life. Only to the mind concentrated, steady, shut out
from the world, can the Divine reveal itself."[27]

The intersection of New Thought and Theosophy was again evident in Besant's endorsement of the concentrated mind, especially in
her little book titled *Thought Power: Its Control and Culture* (1908).
The mind was seen as an "unbroken horse" over which the rider must
learn to assert control through developing the habit of fixed attention.
According to Besant, concentration was an exercise to be systemati-
cally cultivated, and that could be done in either devotionally concrete or abstractly intellectualized forms. As a devotional discipline, it
benefited from an incarnate object of contemplation, "a beloved

image" of "the Beloved." For the Christian, that could be a real or imagined picture of Christ, the Virgin Mary, or a patron saint; for the Buddhist, it could be an image of the Buddha or a bodhisattva; for the Hindu, a picture of Vishnu or Krishna; and so on. For those questing souls who were not "attracted to a personality as an object of devotion," attention could instead be riveted on moral ideals or virtues (as was the case with meditation in Felix Adler's essential spirituality). For Besant, developing the "one-pointedness" of the concentrated mind was important whether it flowed from "a devotional temperament" or from "an act of self-creation." Whichever the case, bringing meditative focus to a wandering mind was never easy; it required great patience and "regularity of practice." As Besant warned, "When the mind loses hold of its object, whether devotional or intellectual — as it will do, time after time — it must be brought back, and again directed to the object."[28]

Among Besant's many works was *An Introduction to Yoga* (1908), and there, too, she recommended the practice of meditation as a means of bringing quietude to the "restless, storm-tossed mind." The embrace of yoga as one more method of concentration points to another important crisscrossing force in the remaking of meditation in American culture. Not an innovator in this regard, Besant followed the example of various Hindu gurus, especially Swami Vivekananda (1863–1902). A follower in India of the ascetic reformer Ramakrishna (1836–1886), Vivekananda was a charismatic figure in his own right, with considerable gifts as a cultural go-between. A defender of India's religious life against Western ethnocentrism and an ally of liberal universalists at home and abroad, Vivekananda proved a crucial broker of a Hindu-inspired "practical spirituality" in the United States.

Vivekananda first emerged as a forceful presence on the American lecture circuit after his headline-grabbing performances at the World's Parliament of Religions in Chicago in 1893. There he managed to turn the tables on the era's more conventional Protestants who thought the whole "heathen" gathering should be imbued with a Christian mis-

Swami Vivekananda, a luminary at the World's Parliament of Religions, stimulated the growth of the Vedanta Society in the United States and, through that group, the practice of meditation. (Eliot Bahá'í Archives, Eliot, Maine.)

sionary logic: "If anybody dreams of the exclusive survival of his own religion and the destruction of the others," Vivekananda related in his closing address, "I pity him from the bottom of my heart." In the three years following the World's Parliament and on a subsequent return visit, Vivekananda toured the country from Maine to California, effectively putting the Vedanta Society (as his emergent fellowship was called) on the American religious map. At Greenacre, at Harvard, in San Francisco and Los Angeles, Vivekananda attracted the considerable admiration and financial support of numerous liberal Protestants and post-Protestants, forging alliances in the wider milieu of Transcendental Unitarianism, Theosophy, and New Thought metaphysics.[29]

The vivacious swami quickly adapted himself to the American fondness for lectures, and most of his published writings ended up being transcriptions of talks and classes. With a handful of well-honed themes to draw on, Vivekananda could easily launch into a discussion of the social realities in India, the ills of missionary and colonial hubris, or the universal religion discovered through studying comparative religions. Among his favored topics, though, were the techniques of the spiritual life. Already in 1895, he had set aside six weeks to hold a retreat on an island in the St. Lawrence River for a small group of American disciples to train them in Raja-Yoga, a formal path of concentration and meditation. There and elsewhere Vivekananda offered detailed instructions on breathing exercises, on the right bodily postures (sitting with the spinal column "left free"), and on "holding the mind in certain spots." "The greatest help to spiritual life is meditation," he noted summarily in his "Hints on Practical Spirituality"—a talk he gave to an eclectic audience of seekers in Los Angeles in 1900. "In meditation we divest ourselves of all material conditions and feel our divine nature."[30]

Vivekananda had various successors as a teacher of yoga and meditation at the turn of the twentieth century, among them Swami Paramananda (1884–1940), who presided over Boston's Vedanta Centre. To be sure, Paramananda carried on the specific teachings of Raja-Yoga, but he also highlighted how easily that practice flowed into the wider religious currents of the day. The author of various devotional books on the powers of meditation, including *Vedanta in Practice* (1908) and *Concentration and Illumination* (1912), Paramananda published a lecture series expressly focused on the essential affinities between New England Transcendentalism and Indian philosophy entitled *Emerson and Vedanta* (1918). Moving back and forth between the "Hindu classics" and Emerson as a spiritual genius, Paramananda happily endorsed the religious experientialism of the free individual: "Spiritual verities can never be matters of tradition. We can never believe in things until we become acquainted with them through our own direct perception."[31]

Illumination came, according to Paramananda, as it did for Vivekananda, through the disciplines of the concentrated mind. "Through meditation we feel the nearness of Divinity," Paramananda instructed. "There is no other way to reach Him. No external power can give us the vision of God." In his *Book of Daily Thoughts and Prayers,* his reflection for April 18 put it this way: "Meditation means a finer province of thought.... Only when our whole nature becomes silent, free from pretense, free from demand and discontent, can we have the steadiness of mind necessary for communion with the Ideal." In his long and vigorous career as a religious intermediary, Paramananda presented his joined message of Ramakrishna devotionalism and religious liberalism not only in Vedanta centers from Boston to Los Angeles, but also in Unitarian churches, local Theosophical societies, and sundry New Thought venues, including the Metaphysical Club of Dresser, Wood, and company. By 1910, as the careers of Vivekananda and Paramananda clearly suggest, the cultural mixture that would make meditation a critical practice among American seekers was already being stirred. As one fearful commentator expressed her alarm about the growing American clientele for "the turbaned teachers of the East," "The yoga class is becoming as popular as the Browning class or the Shakespeare class."[32]

The final ingredients in the recipe for the American concoction of meditation came from various strands of Buddhism, often in much more direct forms than Olcott's loose Theosophical translations. Particularly prominent early on was a South Asian monk, Anagarika Dharmapala (1864–1933), and the American dimensions of his career can be taken as an epitome of these larger confluences. Even as he had maintained a strong sense of Sinhalese Buddhist identity within his family and home village, Dharmapala had been educated at three different Christian mission schools in Ceylon—Catholic, Methodist, and Anglican—and often felt shamed for surreptitiously keeping up study of Buddhist texts alongside the prescribed Bible lessons. He continued to associate with the "meek and abstemious" Buddhist monks whom he knew as a youth against those he saw as "my wine-drinking, meat-eating and pleasure-loving missionary teachers."

It was through Buddhist monks interested in reviving the native religion in the face of colonial and proselytizing pressures that Dharmapala became associated with Anglo-American Theosophists, particularly Olcott, Blavatsky, and Besant. The Theosophical Society proved the mediating space for him to identify with the cause of Buddhist revival, resist the cultural negations of boarding-school Christianity, and yet still engage Westernized notions of religion and reform. Of his first meeting with Olcott and Blavatsky at age sixteen in Colombo, he remarked: "I remember going up to greet them. The moment I touched their hands, I felt overjoyed. The desire for universal brotherhood, for all the things they wanted for humanity, struck a responsive chord in me." In the 1880s, he worked six years on behalf of the Theosophical Society before going on to found the Maha Bodhi Society in 1891 for the revival and defense of Buddhism in India and

The Sinhalese monk Anagarika Dharmapala modeled Buddhist devotional practices, including meditation, for America's sundry seekers at the end of the nineteenth century. (Collection of the author.)

Ceylon. He started publishing a journal for that new society in 1892, and it was that magazine that brought him to the attention of organizers of the World's Parliament of Religions and an invitation to come to the shores of Lake Michigan.[33]

Like Vivekananda, Dharmapala made a considerable impression on American audiences during visits surrounding the World's Parliament and its aftermath. In Chicago, several of liberalism's luminaries warmly embraced him; among those who proved especially welcoming were Charles Bonney, one of the parliament's chief architects; William Rainey Harper, the bold president of the University of Chicago; Jenkin Lloyd Jones, a major Unitarian heir of Parker and Emerson in the Midwest; and Paul Carus, a pioneering editor from LaSalle, Illinois, who would work also with D. T. Suzuki. Of a visit with Harper in 1896, Dharmapala noted in his diary with typical pleasure, "We parted like two old friends." With Carus, he enjoyed a "perfect sympathy," traveling widely with him and helping extensively with Carus's own writings on Buddhism. In the case of Jones, Dharmapala attended his church to hear him preach and, in turn, took to the same pulpit himself; his summary diary entry on that reciprocity simply read: "Holy alliance." Other coalitions were equally engaging, if culturally more problematic, such as the warm relationship he developed with the head of Chicago's Vegetarian Society and the consequent "Message of Peace and Love" that he offered to the American people to "abstain from destroying life" on Thanksgiving Day.[34]

From Maine to California, Dharmapala moved with ease from one liberal religious setting to another. Dozens of Unitarian and Universalist congregations received him and opened their halls for his lectures; Theosophists in Toledo and elsewhere held celebratory meetings with him, as did Spiritualists encamped in upstate New York; a "Lady's Club" in Fargo, headed by a woman "very liberal in her ways of thinking," warmly welcomed him, as did a progressive church in town; a group of "all German Liberals" convened to hear him in New Ulm, Minnesota; and a Jewish Club in San Francisco presented another appreciative audience. As a matter of course, the Free Religious Association offered a "very sympathetic" convention, and Dharmapala mingled happily with Thomas Wentworth Higginson, Lewis Janes, and the rest.

His reception at the Procopeia Club, one of the first New Thought groups to organize in Boston and a favorite haunt of Ralph Waldo Trine, was especially revealing in its warmth. Members picnicked with him in Salem, where they commiserated together over religious intolerance and the execution of innocent "witches" in the same town two centuries earlier. They capped the day off with a pilgrimage to the home of the recently deceased poet of Inner Light liberalism, John Greenleaf Whittier, and then all joined in a ribbon-laced circle as Dharmapala chanted Buddhist verses on compassion. Clearly, his American trips constituted a full immersion in the emergent networks of a liberal spirituality, and Dharmapala thrived within them. He often marveled in his diary at the sympathetic reception of the Americans he encountered, but the surprise became the familiar: "Mr. Nash is an episcopalean clergyman, his wife is a Radical. In his presence she said that she is one like myself and she had the boldness to say that Buddhism will spread in America like wild fire. The women in America are a daring lot." It was repeated encouragement like this that informed the adulatory good-bye that Dharmapala penned in his diary in September 1897: "America, land of freedom. I love thy people. I will come back and work for thy people and establish Buddha's Dharma."[35]

Unlike Vivekananda, Dharmapala did not enjoy a faithful scribe in his travels and so offered up little by way of published lectures and devotional directions for his American listeners. But he did model the practice of meditation for them in a way that many found alluring. In the pages of his diary from his American sojourns, Dharmapala made plain that he was intensively practicing what he was preaching, even while keeping up a vigorous schedule of public appearances and social engagements. Spending the month of August 1897 at Greenacre, he held classes under the pines, lectured, studied, chanted, and meditated. "Last night I gazed attentively at the candle from 9 to 10; again from 11 to 2," he wrote in his diary for August 5. "Passed the night in the tent," he noted on August 9. "The bliss of solitude. All classes and men of all creeds in search of wealth and gold and selfish power risk their lives. I want neither gold nor power but only Truth and Holiness. I am alone and I will find out Truth even at the sacrifice of my life." On the 11th, he offered a talk on the "Holy Life" and then immediately took in a lecture by the illustrious Franklin Sanborn, one of the last of the surviving Transcendentalists, on Emerson. On the 15th, he was up at 4:30 in the morning, sitting, concentrating on the steady back-and-forth of inhaling and exhaling: "Began counting 1 to 10 at each breath and it was successful. Then the new experience began. The counting should never be stopped; but must be carried on all through until the appearance of the mental picture. Then the counting should be made so as to solidify the vague picture and then the picture will remain. Peace to all the world."[36]

The effects of Dharmapala's sojourn at Greenacre on spiritual practice flowed in two directions. On the one side, he offered specific instructions to various adepts on how "to cultivate peace," on the postures and practices of meditation, and on such worship ceremonies as offering flowers and reciting the Buddha's words. Dharmapala's connections with Ralph Waldo Trine were perhaps most telling. Trine heard him lecture several times, joined in his zeal for the compassionate treatment of animals, and observed his devotional practices at close hand at Greenacre—all in the same years that Trine himself was producing his initial and most popular New Thought guides. After one talk Dharmapala gave under the pines on the "Development of Consciousness," he met one-on-one with Trine: "I gave him hints on 'Buddhist Nirvana.'" What these hints were exactly is unknown, but the advice was likely to have been demanding, anything but an easygoing lesson on popular psychology. In a paper on the subject of "supreme enlightenment," Dharmapala explained: "Nirvana is a state of positive realization free from ignorance, ignoble desires, hatred, ill-will, pride, covetousness, false beliefs, and full of faith, energy, vigilance, peace and wisdom." "The emancipation from the idea of Self is the real bliss," he underlined in his American diary. "It is ignorance that makes one think that there is bliss in the idea of 'I am I.' ... People talk of spirituality and yet how few they are who know of the immense sacrifice they are expected to make." Dharmapala's very strenuousness resonated with Trine's own spiritual idealism, and his practical hints answered to New Thought desires to open people out of their "self-seeking nature" through an intuitive enlightenment that came in meditative silence and solitude.[37]

The influences flowed in the reverse direction as well: Dharmapala, ever busy in his American travels, found his monthlong retreat at Greenacre personally rejuvenating, if not transformative. "I stayed here," he noted in his diary near the end of the month, "to experiment on my self whether the religious life could be practiced." Living alongside and listening to Vedantist, New Thought, Jewish, Christian, Quaker, Buddhist, Zoroastrian, Unitarian, Transcendentalist, Spiritualist, and Ethical Culture representatives, Dharmapala was both shaken and moved (at one interfaith meeting, he confessed, "tears ran down from my eyes"). Greenacre he dubbed "a Centre of spirituality" and rhapsodized on his last day there: "Blessed Greenacre. The future Home of Truth. Under the shade of the trees I enjoyed for nearly 28 days the ecstasy of Renunciation. Miss Farmer, the angelic sweet woman, helped me to realize the truth of the Buddha's Dharma." However rare, this was the sort of practical mutuality to which America's religious liberals at their best aspired. This was a two-way street in which they received instruction from Dharmapala and he, in turn, flourished during his time with them.[38]

At the turn of the twentieth century, the new sources of meditation for Americans were diverse: New Thought, Unitarianism, liberal Judaism, Theosophy, Vedanta, and South Asian Buddhism crisscrossed one another in an intensive series of encounters and innovations. How-

An unidentified participant at the Greenacre summer conferences, most likely the Jain lecturer Virchand Gandhi, meditates under the pines there (as did Vivekananda and Dharmapala, among other visiting teachers). (Eliot Bahá'í Archives, Eliot, Maine.)

ever distinct the metaphysical starting points of the various movements were, they all shared an absorbing concern with the concentrated mind—a curiosity that flowed from overlapping impulses, desires, and anxieties. These exchanges were global in reach, but the larger dynamic that held them together—or, at minimum, made possible productive alliances—was religious liberalism's imagining of an essential, universal, and practical spirituality in which meditation would serve as a technique held in common. The historian Robert Sharf has observed in his study of modern forms of Buddhism that the emphasis on meditation and the mystical experience of enlightenment as the defining features of Buddhist practice are largely "of recent provenance, a product of twentieth-century reforms inspired in part by Occidental models." Meditation centers, he points out, have proved leading embodiments of these distinctly modern innovations within Westernized configurations of Buddhism.[39]

Whether in the form of Dharmapala's theosophical Buddhism, D. T. Suzuki's Zen, or Vivekananda's Raja-Yoga, meditation was reimagined as a cosmopolitan, inclusive practice that blended the spiritual and the scientific in perfect harmony. It was seen as productive of flashes of pure intuition and immediate experience that transcended the bounds of ceremony, monastic rule, and narrow particularity and that opened into a universal knowledge. An "intensity of thought," Vivekananda claimed, characterized practitioners of meditation; they "churn up their own souls. Great truths come to the surface and become manifest. Therefore the practice of meditation is the great scientific method of knowledge." The practice of meditation, so conceived, helped make it possible to speak of a variety of religious experiences— whether Hindu, Buddhist, New Thought, or Christian—under the catchall of *spirituality,* a term that took on new significance through the shared practice of meditation and the enlightening experiences that flowed from it.[40]

Putting meditation at the center of the new spirituality served more than the rhetorical purposes of a universalized religious liberalism and its cosmopolitan dreams. If there was an overriding desire in all of these sources and appropriations, it was a longing for repose and calm, for Dharmapala's bliss of solitude. In *Power through Repose* (1891), another pioneering New Thought work that issued from Boston's metaphysical frontier, Annie Payson Call was completely absorbed with American nervousness, unrest, and overexertion. "Nervous disorders, resulting from over-work, are all about us," she commented. "Extreme nervous tension seems to be so peculiarly American, that a German physician coming to this country to practise became puzzled by the variety of nervous disorders he was called upon to help, and finally announced his discovery of a new disease which he chose to call 'Americanitis.' And now we suffer from 'Americanitis' in all its unlimited varieties." Call wanted to compose and relax Americans, to heal them of their enervating worries and fears, through "mind training" or "true concentration." Her program was premised on a daily quieting of the body and mind—the release of contracted muscles, the counting of slow breaths, the elimination of distracting thoughts. Those routines would, in turn, lead to a calm yet focused state of mental equilibrium—one in which work and rest, productivity and peace, power and repose were held in unwavering balance. The contemporary fascination with meditation as a form of stress reduction is, to be sure, anything but new.[41]

Annie Besant, likewise, was especially interested in eradicating worry through acquiring "the *habit* of steady thought." As she advised in *Thought Power,*

> *Perhaps the best way to get rid of a "worry-channel" is to dig another, of an exactly opposite character.... Let, then, a person, who is suffering from worry, give three or four minutes in the morning, on first rising, to some noble and encouraging thought: "The Self is Peace; that Self am I. The Self is Strength; that Self am I." Let him think how, in his innermost nature, he is one with the Supreme Father; how in that nature he is undying, unchanging, fearless, free, serene, strong; how he is clothed in perishable vestures that feel the sting of pain, the gnawing of anxiety; how he mistakenly regards these as himself. As he thus broods, the Peace will enfold him.*

Across the board, meditation was heralded as a salve for anxiety and as an unrivaled source of serenity. As Dhan Gopal Mukerji, another Hindu go-between in the footsteps of Vivekananda, advised his American audiences in his own riff on the practice of repose in the early 1930s, "We should all meditate every day at a given hour in order to charge ourselves with serenity."[42]

In the same way that Reinhold Niebuhr's "Serenity Prayer" became a great motto of Twelve-Step groups, meditation merged with a therapeutic culture in which peace of mind often seemed to be the ultimate measure and ambition. Teaching the powers of the concentrated mind was a ministry to the worried and the anxiety ridden, and it was a therapy for the scattered and fragmented as well. Meditation became a critical practice of self-integration in a culture in which the problem of divided selves and a unified personal identity had become, as William James observed, "the most puzzling puzzle with which psychology has to deal." The serial qualities of the self, the wholesale conversions of the twice born, and the irregular streams of human consciousness fascinated James, and he was far from alone in seeing the modern self as protean, fragmented, and discontinuous. How to recenter the decentered or reintegrate the disintegrating was at the heart of the modern turn to meditation. "To live undisturbed by passing occurrences," Trine insistently advised, "you must first find your own center. You must then be firm in your own center.... Find your center and live in it." The appeal of meditation depended on the anxieties of the dispersed and distracted self and the desire to recover (or, rather, discover) a core sense of identity through the centering and calming effects of the concentrated mind.[43]

In his best-selling *Peace of Mind* (1946) Rabbi Joshua L. Liebman made this diagnosis plain. "Another new truth about man that religion must emphasize now is the truth of pluralism. Man is not a single self," he observed matter-of-factly. "He carries within him many selves—a happy self, a frightened self, an angry self. Man is like an omnibus with many little egos jostling each other as the vehicle of life hurtles down the highway.... The understanding that life is inescapably pluralistic does not mean that we should permit ourselves to become a disorganized chaos, a wild landscape without any organizing principle at work. Every man has the task of arranging his life into a pattern of unity." It was against this psychological backdrop that meditation became popular as a therapy of integration for unfocused minds and scattered selves. For those Americans who felt increasingly burdened with lives of multiple tasks and many hats, they were offered the coping mechanism of the stilled mind in which repose and resolve were mystically united.[44]

By now, it goes without saying that the turn to meditation as a spiritual resource was, in part, therapeutic. It was promoted and embraced for the fostering of inward calm, self-awareness, self-help, and self-improvement. For many critics of contemporary American life, those associations would be enough to indict the rise of meditation as one more example of the culture's narcissism and self-absorption. From this perspective, meditation for Americans led not on a journey beyond the self but to a pampered and aggrandized self in which petty anxieties and neuroses were overcome and success and business efficiency blossomed in their place. The guru Dhan Gopal Mukerji, for example, instructed his American audiences that in India "meditation is an essential part of our religion," yet "it is not its religious aspect to which I want to call attention. Leaving religion out of the question, the practice of repose applies to everyday secular living." He then pictured a man on a business trip in a noisy city who needs a good night's sleep in order to have his "best concentration" to do his work well the next day. Owing a debt to Trine and Call as much as to Vivekananda, Mukerji then guided his readers through a series of exercises for "going into the silence" and for removing themselves from "all noises and every worry" in order to better accomplish their secular labors. All too clearly, the concentrated mind could be as much about capitalist discipline and corporate growth as spiritual aspiration. The title of one little guide from 1909 put that displacement in a nutshell—*Concentration: The Secret of Success.*[45]

The new teachers of meditation often simply left theological questions open, focusing instead on a pragmatic program, on what works, on effectiveness. Raja-Yoga, Vivekananda observed during a talk in San Francisco in 1900, "proposes no faith, no belief, no God.... Practise a few days, and if you do not find any benefit; then come and curse me." For an emergent professional class that made its living behind desks and through intellectual labor, through brain-work, the message of the mind's fertile and barely tapped resources seemed especially well suited. "Who put a limit to the power of the mind?" Vivekananda exhorted. Surely, there was a kind of will to power on display in a fair number of the reflections on the benefits of meditation. Annie Besant made this as apparent as anyone in her joining of the concentrated mind to the persona of a superhero: "The concentrated intelligence, the power of withdrawing outside the turmoil, mean immensely increased energy in work, mean steadiness, self-control, serenity; the man of meditation is the man who wastes no time, scatters no energy, misses no opportunity. Such a man governs events, because within him is the power whereof events are only the outer expression; he shares the divine life, and therefore shares the divine power." Were these the gifts that the bliss of solitude brought? If so, it would be hard to tell the enlightenment of the New Thought contemplative from the acumen of the wide-awake business executive or the success of the Zen-talking basketball coach.[46]

It would be little more than a caricature to stop there or to accept the usual hue and cry about the ills of possessive individualism and the obsessive pursuit of self-realization. Besant, for example, went on to make clear that "peace is not to be found in the continual seeking for the gratification of the separated self. . . . It is found in renouncing the separated self. . . . Even in ordinary life the unselfish people are the happiest—those who work to make others happy, and who forget themselves. The dissatisfied people are those who are ever seeking happiness for themselves." Trine's "Spirit of Infinite Plenty," in particular, has easily been mistaken for a new god of desire for an expanding consumer culture, but he essentially endorsed a spiritual economy in which those who fathom the kingdom of God freely receive and freely give. Equally critical of an ascetic poverty and a misguided wealth, Trine in his practical advice centered on how to overcome the adversities of unemployment or unsatisfying work through confessedly simplistic affirmations. Those tidbits on positive thinking were not to be confused with Trine's sharper message on "the real riches of the inner life" and the "stunted and dwarfed" lives of those who focused on "temporary material accumulations." The desire for vast wealth and possessions was "a species of insanity," a "loathsome disease," and a terrible hindrance to a higher life. The Master, Trine said, expected stewardship, not accumulation; generosity, not hoarding: "The time will come when it will be regarded as a disgrace for a man to die and leave vast accumulations behind him."[47]

Just as liberals sought an ethical mysticism, they sought a moral practice of meditation that focused on love, sympathetic connection, emancipation, self-giving, and serene resolve. If the active and contemplative lives were classically counterpoised to one another, the practical spirituality of religious liberalism wanted nothing to do with that opposition. That was evident in the social reform energies of Adler, Olcott, Dharmapala, Farmer, Trine, Besant, and Vivekananda, and it was true as well of many who followed in their wake. "One of the most important questions we come to in spiritual practice is how to reconcile service and responsible action in the world with a meditative life," Jack Kornfield writes in *Seeking the Heart of Wisdom: The Path of Insight Meditation,* a text he coauthored with Joseph Goldstein in 1987. "Are the values we hold that lead us to giving and serving and caring for one another different from the values that lead us deep within ourselves on the journey of liberation and awakening?"[48]

The answer for Kornfield and Goldstein, who together founded the Insight Meditation Center in Barre, Massachusetts, is an integration of broadly Buddhist spiritual exercises with social compassion, connectedness, and "sympathetic joy." The aim is a balance of equanimity with engagement, a composed concentration with a lively openness to others. "True spirituality is not a removal or escape from life. It is an opening, a seeing of the world with a deeper vision that is less self-centered" and that highlights "interconnectedness" over exclusion, separation, and withdrawal. Through the sustained practice of meditation, the aspirant seeks a wider understanding of "us"—a liberal, pluralistic "us" that is keenly aware of the baneful process of diminishing "others" based on "race, nationality, age, sex, ideology, [or] religion." One of the ideals Goldstein and Kornfield hold up is a "meditation master" who is also involved in "direct action" and "development work" with the homeless: "If there are people who are hungry for food, my response is to help feed them. If there are people who are hungry for truth, my response is to help them to discover it. I make no distinction."[49]

By 1920, the religious brew that transformed meditation in American culture was simmering, and, as the work of Joseph Goldstein and Jack Kornfield suggests, it has very much continued to bubble. On the New Thought side, Joel Sol Goldsmith, a nonobservant Jew turned Christian Scientist turned independent mystic of the Infinite Way, showed the enduring emphasis on the powers and practice of concentration in such popular works as *The Art of Meditation* (1956) and *Practicing the Presence* (1958). Among Theosophists, Clara M. Codd kept up the spiritual direction of Olcott and Besant in little devotional works such as *Meditation: Its Practice and Result* (1952). The Eastern influences, evident in Theosophy and through the missions of Vivekananda and Dharmapala, came to exercise all the more sway: Aldous Huxley, master anthologizer in *The Perennial Philosophy* (1944), was closely associated with a Vedantist community in southern California; Shunryu Suzuki, founder of the Zen Center in San Francisco, arrived in America in 1959, offering instruction in meditation and eventually publishing his talks as *Zen Mind, Beginner's Mind* (1970); and Ram Dass underwent a "journey of awakening" that led from psychedelic experiments as a Harvard faculty member to various yogic practices and the production of the still very popular *Meditator's Guidebook* (1978). The search has remained as open, eclectic, and cosmopolitan as it was in the days of Dharmapala's retreat at Greenacre. Take but two examples from the new millennium: David A. Cooper's *Three Gates to Meditation: A Personal Journey into Sufism, Buddhism, and Judaism* (2000) and Mary Rose O'Reilly's *The Barn at the End of the World: The Apprenticeship of a Quaker, Buddhist Shepherd* (2000).

One of the better compendia of the ongoing ferment, Daniel Goleman's *The Varieties of the Meditative Experience*, first published in 1977, lifts up meditation as something still "new to the West." The title, though, straightforwardly echoes William James's *Varieties of Religious Experience* and serves, in effect, as an invitation to explore altered states of consciousness that James had already made famous. History, not newness, was the better guide to the book's concerns and contours, and that was evident from the foreword. Ram Dass prefaced his own prefatory words to Goleman's work with an epigraph from Walt Whitman's *Leaves of Grass* and closed with a coda from Aldous Huxley on "the universality of the spiritual journey." That intertextual play—Whitman, James, Huxley, Ram Dass—was already whirling before Goleman uttered his own introductory words that dated the book's birth (predictably enough) from a recent sojourn in a Himalayan village rather than from the more extended parentage of religious liberalism.[50] Whether it be Jiddu Krishnamurti's debt to Theosophy or Maharishi Mahesh Yogi's invoking of Whitmanite "cosmic consciousness" within Transcendental Meditation, Goleman's version of the *Varieties* reveals this much at least: that practical spirituality, imagined at the end of the nineteenth century and embodied in the heightened power accorded meditation, has been reincarnated again and again in American culture, and that cycle of rebirth shows no signs of being extinguished.

CHAPTER FIVE

FREEDOM AND
SELF-SURRENDER

ALEXANDER RUSSELL WEBB (1846–1916) was one of the more unusual pilgrims that nineteenth-century America produced. Born in Hudson, New York, and "reared 'under the drippings' of an orthodox Presbyterian pulpit," Webb worked as a journalist and editor in Missouri for many years before becoming the U.S. consul to the Philippines under President Grover Cleveland in 1887. For six years prior to taking up his diplomatic post in Manila, Webb had been "earnestly engaged in the study of Oriental religions and spiritual philosophies" and imagined the consulate as "an opportunity to read, study, and experiment along these lines." Arriving as a religious wayfarer, Webb was within the year knee-deep in "the works of Mohammedan authors"; he dealt summarily with his official duties while maximizing his time for studying Islam and other religions. Soon he had managed to make connections to Muslims in India and Burma as well as the Philippines. In 1892 he resigned from his government position and headed back to the United States as a convinced convert to Islam and as the leader of a Muslim mission to America.

181

The next year, sporting a changed name and a dapper red fez, Mohammed Alexander Russell Webb lectured to large and demonstrative audiences on his acquired faith at the World's Parliament of Religions in Chicago. Some hissed this Yankee turned Muslim, but he also won applause for his sympathetic portrayal of the Prophet Muhammad.[1]

Webb's journey was unusual, but it had familiar sources. As he explained in *Islam in America* (1893), "The almost universal disposition, among liberal-minded Americans, to know more of the Oriental religions than their ancestors knew, has been productive of at least one good result, viz.,... the development of an independent, fearless spirit of thought and investigation, which is gradually becoming the aggressive and relentless enemy of the mental slavery of creeds." Webb claimed that his mission was not one of making "proselytes for Islam," but instead of furthering "among English-speaking Christians a spirit of calm, persistent and unprejudiced investigation" into "their own as well as other systems of religion." In other words, Webb was another apologist for liberal sympathy, learned inquiry, and spiritual independence. American Christians, he exhorted, needed to approach religious systems without the assumption of "the falsity of all others" and the lone truth of their own beliefs. He saw his mission as one of jarring his fellow Americans out of the complacency of their prejudices and their very limited knowledge about "the Arabian prophet" and Islamic history. In starting a monthly journal in New York called the *Moslem World,* he recommended it to "Mussulmans, Unitarians, and Non-Sectarians," to "every independent thinker" and "every investigator of spiritual philosophy." He knew who his audience was: the same broad swath of liberal religionists to whom Swami Vivekananda, Felix Adler, or Thomas Wentworth Higginson also spoke.[2]

Webb's stance, of course, was more complicated than an advocacy of open-mindedness and free inquiry, though he began with those values and remained committed to them. One more liberal refugee from

Calvinist orthodoxy, he had become a generously eclectic truth seeker only to settle into a new and well-bounded religious identity. Like Emerson and Thoreau, he had found that abstruse expositions of Christian doctrines—whether the Atonement, the Trinity, or the Virgin Birth—left him cold, and he had come to prefer "the glad sunshine," "the murmuring brooks," and "the gorgeous flowers" as "more satisfying sermons" than those he heard in church. Failing to find in Christianity the balm for "the longings of my soul," he drifted for a time into scientific materialism and a bare-bones social ethics. And then he kept drifting through the close study of Buddhism, Theosophy, and finally Islam. Ultimately, for Webb, the global search across religious traditions was not open-ended. It was not seeking for the sake of seeking; it was seeking for the sake of truth and a clearly anchored identity. "I began to compare the various religions, in order to ascertain which was the best and most efficacious as a means of securing happiness in the next life," he observed. Just as he had left Presbyterianism behind as a young man, he moved beyond Transcendentalism, unbelief, and Theosophy through choosing to become a Muslim.[3]

Webb's search flowed out of the increasing liquidity of liberal religious identities, but it ended in a discovery of the limits of those spiritual fluctuations. Even as he continued to refract Islam through the combined lens of liberal religion and late Victorian culture—he praised it for its "personal and moral cleanliness," its fraternalism, its teetotalism, its Unitarian monotheism, and its lack of a priesthood, for example—Webb nonetheless adopted a particular religious path with particular scriptures to study and particular practices to habituate: prayer, fasting, almsgiving, and pilgrimage among them. Indeed, one of his first publications upon his return to the United States was an exposition of daily devotional practices, "a complete and explicit guide to prayer," including pictorial depictions and detailed descriptions of bodily postures. His "aspiring soul" had found in Islam a specific path "out of the darkness of materialism," a way of life as

"Resignation to the will of God." Webb's journey is an important reminder that when Americans looked East, it was not to India alone that they turned their eyes. Persia especially exercised its own fascination in the forms of Zoroastrian, Islamic (especially Sufi), and Bahá'í faiths.[4]

The struggle at the heart of liberal spirituality, including Webb's quest, was over the firmness and fragility of religious identity in the modern world. Was being a Christian something that remained neatly bounded by authority, tradition, and liturgy—by unreserved affirmation of the Nicene Creed or the Westminster Confession, by the Bible's utter sufficiency or the pope's infallibility, by the sacraments or strict Sabbath observance? Or were religious identities much more fluid and unbounded than orthodoxies of whatever kind imagined? And if they were indeed readily adjustable to modern forms of freedom, where were the outer limits of their flexibility? How much, for example, could Reform Jews relinquish or rearrange before they ceased to be identifiable as Jews? How much could Unitarians alter the Christian faith or add to it before they ceased to be identifiable as Christians? In cutting loose from tradition—Jewish or Christian—how could a religious identity be resecured or stabilized? Was Whitman's open road about ceaseless and adventuresome questing, about exploring many paths rather than settling on one, about the intuitive and artistic openness of the individual to inspiration come where it may? Was the point precisely the *freedom* of spiritual seeking? Or was the real point to find a well-marked path and to submit to the disciplines of a new religious authority in order to submerge the self in a larger relationship to God and community? And if one submitted to that kind of regulation, did one forfeit the very liberties—religious and intellectual—to which modern liberal democracy had pledged itself?

Those sorts of questions about identity, freedom, tradition, authority, and obedience haunted religious liberalism and modern forms of spirituality at nearly every turn—and still do. However vast and abstract they sound, they were deeply particular and personal as they played themselves out in people's lives. Esther Davis, a Jewish inquirer in New Jersey around 1900, crystallized these dilemmas in two contending thoughts that gripped her as a young woman: on the one hand, she told herself, "Study your own religion. It will teach you many things"; on the other, she asked herself, "Why not look into other faiths, go into other churches, make comparisons?" The best way to appreciate the wrenching struggles that such competing impulses provoked is to get up close to the scuffling. The place Esther Davis turned—"by some fortunate chance or destiny"—to resolve her own nagging questions about "spirituality" was Sarah Farmer's Greenacre community in Eliot, Maine.* Between its founding in 1894 and Farmer's death in 1916, Greenacre was among the greatest sources of religious innovation anywhere in the country. It was the last great bastion of Transcendentalism, a school of philosophy and art for Emersonians and Whitmanites; it was a New Thought proving ground for such leaders as Ralph Waldo Trine, Henry Wood, and Horatio Dresser; it was a hub for representatives of the Society of Ethical Culture, Theosophy, Buddhism, Reform Judaism, Vedanta, Zoroastrianism, Islam, and the Bahá'í faith. It was the World's Parliament of Religions brought to its grandest fruition, attracting the curious and the questing—like Esther Davis—by the hundreds and even thousands in these years. At Greenacre, the dream of a cosmopolitan spirituality found its flesh and blood.[5]

And, yet, Greenacre was also a divided place where Transcendentalist eclecticism confronted the reassertion of more particularistic religious identities. Farmer's eventual acceptance of the Bahá'í faith or "the

---

* "Greenacre" was the preferred form for the community's name in its first decade, but it regularly appeared also as "Green-Acre" and "Green Acre." Eventually, " Green Acre" became the settled form, but that shift in itself, as we will see, got bound up in the heart of the community's conflicts. I use "Greenacre" to signal my particular concern with the early period of the retreat's history rather than its subsequent redefinition and ongoing embodiment.

Sarah Farmer was the visionary behind the grand cosmopolitan venture in Eliot, Maine, where so much of the emergent spirituality came together. (Eliot Bahá'í Archives, Eliot, Maine.)

Persian Revelation"—a movement originating in mid-nineteenth-century Iran and inspired especially by the prophet Bahá'u'lláh (1817–1892)—discomfited her liberal, universalistic friends, many of whom preferred ongoing inquiry to actually finding one path to follow. For Farmer (1847–1916), the vision that she found in the Bahá'í faith of a new age of religious unity, racial reconciliation, gender equality, and global peace was the fulfillment of Transcendentalism's reform impulses and progressivism's millennial dreams. To her skeptical associates, her turn to the Persian Revelation represented a betrayal of their deepest ideals as free-ranging seekers whose vision of a cosmopolitan piety dimmed at the prospect of one movement serving as a singular focus for the universal religion. How open and fluid could the new spirituality be? Was any religious authority that preached resignation and submission an anathema, even one that had an uncanny resemblance to religious liberalism, especially in its fantastic hope that people of diverse faiths were on the verge of universal peace, brotherhood, and unity? For Farmer, the conflicts that erupted among her friends over the Bahá'í faith proved almost unbearable, and she eventually fell into severe mental anguish, with competing parties battling over her sanity and her need for hospitalization. To her Bahá'í friends, she was an exalted mystic who had seen the light; to her more eclectic companions, she was a good-hearted woman who had gone off the deep end.[6]

In clearing out a clutter of papers from one of the cottages at Greenacre in 1914, a woman came across Sarah Farmer's old address book for 1895 and dutifully preserved it, one more piece of memorabilia from the frail and ailing founder of the summer colony. The address book provides a good indication of the intellectual and religious strands that Farmer was trying to pull together in Eliot, Maine,

Sara Bull, a leading acolyte of Swami Vivekananda and a serious practitioner of yoga, was among Farmer's most important allies and backers. (Eliot Bahá'í Archives, Eliot, Maine.)

just across the river from Portsmouth, New Hampshire. There was C. H. A. Bjerregaard, the expositor of mysticism from the Astor Library; William Rounseville Alger, the Unitarian minister who had offered the most extensive Transcendentalist commentary on solitude; John Burroughs, the successor of Thoreau as an American nature writer; Felix Adler and Lewis Janes, leaders of the Free Religious Association and exemplary scholars in the nascent science of religions; Henry Wood, Alice B. Stockham, Helen Van-Anderson, Annetta Dresser, and Ursula Gestefeld, luminaries of the late-nineteenth-century metaphysical and mental healing movements; Swami Vivekananda and his leading American disciple, Sara Bull, an intimate associate of Farmer's, a socialite to be reckoned with in Cambridge, and a bellwether in embracing yoga as a spiritual practice.

Included as well in Farmer's address book was the Chicago reformer Jane Addams, whom Farmer met with at Hull House in 1896 and whose name pointed to Farmer's express desire to turn part of the Greenacre community into a settlement for impoverished mothers. A dyed-in-the-wool progressive, Farmer also made peace activism a rallying cry at Greenacre—a cause that brought her a tangible role in international affairs when she played host to the Japanese envoys in 1905 during the negotiation of the Treaty of Portsmouth, which ended the massively bloody war between Russia and Japan. Along with Thomas Wentworth Higginson and a half dozen college presidents, Farmer served on the advisory board of the National Union for Practical Progress, which advanced such causes as Christian socialism and the abolition of capital punishment. For all of Farmer's openness to new religious movements, there always remained a substantial liberal Protestant and social-gospel constituency. That was evident, for example, in the number of prominent Unitarian reformers in her little book of associates. These included the ministers Jenkin Lloyd Jones and Edward Everett Hale as well as the women's rights activist Matilda Joslyn Gage.

Farmer had a knack for building bridges between liberal New Englanders and international emissaries of various religious traditions. Here she poses with the Unitarian clergyman Edward Everett Hale (seated in the chair) and Swami Vivekananda (seated on the ground), as well as an ambassador from Armenia. (Eliot Bahá'í Archives, Eliot, Maine.)

Perhaps the clearest marker of Farmer's voracious appetite for a variety of spiritualities and inexplicable experiences was the neatly printed address of Professor William James of Harvard. In November 1894 and again in April 1895 she corresponded with James about an episode of Spiritualist trance-speaking (a precursor to today's channeling) that had occurred at Greenacre the previous summer. A visitor, "suddenly psychologized in some way," had begun to speak in "various tongues," including the spirit voice of Farmer's own deceased mother with such uncanny similitude that the family's aging St. Bernard dog, "a special pet of my mother," seemingly recognized the voice and began lapping the man's hands. James found the account so extraordinary that he sought out his own opportunity to witness this man's "vocal automatism" and then presented the whole case to the Society of Psychical Research, an organization dedicated to researching the paranormal. Though James was more the hard-nosed scientist and skeptical seeker than Farmer ever was, they were in many ways kindred spirits. As late as 1910, Sara Bull sought James's advice on the best physician to treat Farmer in her mental collapse, which Bull saw, somewhat ironically given her own penchant for strenuous devotions, as a result of "too much psychic indulgence." (Bull, after all, kept a space in her house that she called "the Meditation Room," where she displayed portraits of Emerson and Vivekananda, burned incense, and practiced yoga.) James, with a fond concern for Farmer, recommended "our best Massachusetts Asylum, the McLean Hospital at Waverly." To James's satisfaction, Farmer was placed there for care and soon showed good progress toward recovery.[7]

That initial list of contacts—from Adler to James—begins to suggest the intricate religious tapestry Farmer was trying to weave. There were also, though, numerous other names in the address book that carried no particular notoriety or fame, but that wound up being quite influential in Farmer's spiritual journey and in the course of her larger religious experiment. Among those was Josephine Locke of Chicago, one of the first Americans to undertake a pilgrimage to 'Akká to meet 'Abdu'l-Bahá (1844–1921), the eldest son of and successor to the prophetic messenger Bahá'u'lláh. That excursion in February 1900 ended up including Farmer, who was on a restorative vacation when she fortuitously reconnected on board ship with Locke. Ever the ready religious inquirer, Farmer changed plans midstream and headed to Ottoman Syria, where in late March she met 'Abdu'l-Bahá face-to-face—a religious teacher whom she would embrace as the Master, the divinely authorized expositor of Bahá'u'lláh, the culminating Manifestation of God. At the time of Farmer's conversion about seven hundred American seekers had joined this new religious movement, with visible communities having developed in about a dozen cities and towns across the country. Many of these pilgrims shared Farmer's eclectic religious background in liberal Protestantism, Transcendentalism, Theosophy, and New Thought. Not atypical was the fellow wayfarer who became Bahá'í after explorations of the teachings of Emerson, Madame Blavatsky, the Buddha, Vivekananda, and Marcus Aurelius—one more aspirant after the religious peace, finality, and unity that the movement preached.[8]

Sarah grew up as an only child in a devout and well-educated Protestant household. Her mother, Hannah Tobey Farmer (1823–1891), had found spiritual assurance as a young woman in the early 1840s through the fervent prayers and intimate testimonials of a Methodist meeting, though she subsequently felt quite comfortable cultivating a mix of ministers—Congregational, Unitarian, Presbyterian, and Episcopal—as friends and associates. Hannah's youthful love of Christ carried her into one benevolent society after another, particularly in service of the abolitionist cause, even as her dedication to raising a godly daughter soon became a consuming responsibility. She also had an infant son die shortly after birth, and that loss provoked, as such grief did for Mary Todd Lincoln and innumerable others of the era, a sustained fascination with Spiritualism. In addition then to a strong Christian formation, Sarah grew up in a home with all the preternatural curiosities that the Spiritualist movement implied: its interest in trance states, communication with the dead, and mesmeric healing. And those fascinations, evident in the episode reported to William James, clearly followed her through the rest of her life. In his diary of his American visit in 1897 the Buddhist monk Anagarika Dharmapala even noted hearing about a séance at Greenacre in which "Miss Farmer was wedded to a spirit bridegroom." It sounded farfetched to him, but "Miss Farmer is angelic in her appearance and so it is possible that she is in touch with the spirits."[9]

Hannah's maternal commitment paid off in turning Sarah into a devout schoolgirl who could toss off a letter of encouragement to a homesick soldier during the Civil War and lace it with all the expected marks of serious piety: "My dear father and mother are Christians; and I have been religiously educated, and, I trust, have given my heart to the Saviour. I have tried to. Every morning and night when I pray I unite with my prayer a petition for our brave soldiers." Years after her religious world had become far more eclectic—through her relationships with the Zoroastrian emissary Jehanghier Cola and the Jain lecturer Virchand Gandhi, to name but two acquaintances—Farmer remained a churchgoer with a biblical text always at hand to give expression to her most devout feelings. "I waited patiently for the Lord; & He inclined unto me & heard my cry," Farmer jotted in her diary in April 1898 in an echo of the Psalms. And it was the Lord's assurance to the Apostle Paul from II Corinthians 12:9—"My Grace shall be sufficient unto you"—that reverberated in her mind in late 1893 as she felt called to her new work at Greenacre. Even after her conversion to the Bahá'í faith, she still listened to "the voice of Jesus" alongside "the voice of Beha'u'lláh." Like her friend Emma Thursby, who found the preaching of the Reverend Henry Ward Beecher and the lectures of Swami Vivekananda equally inspiring, Farmer's identity as a Christian was simultaneously robust and porous. The very permeability of her Christian faith was a sign of spiritual seriousness, not indifference.[10]

Sarah's father, Moses Gerrish Farmer (1820–1893), was in fundamental harmony with the faith of his wife, and the daughter saw him as a similarly devout Christian and dedicated parent. A Dartmouth graduate, he emerged as a prominent inventor who performed experiments that were crucial to the expansion of the telegraph and who pioneered electrically linked fire-alarm systems for American cities. Never marrying, Sarah remained closely associated with her father in his professional life, keeping records for him and managing his correspondence. In late 1892 Sarah would journey with her father to Chicago's Columbian Exposition, where he displayed some of his latest electrical inventions and where she caught sight of her life's work through meetings with Charles Bonney, a Swedenborgian who was the visionary behind the soon-to-open World's Parliament of Religions. Her father died that spring, and Sarah only got back to Chicago in October 1893, not in time to participate in the parliament itself, but soon enough to make a round of further connections in its wake.

With the father's success, the family's fortunes had risen, and their circle of friends had become similarly high achieving and well placed. They were close, for example, to the young artist Arthur Wesley Dow and the old poet John Greenleaf Whittier, both of whom would consecrate the landscape of the family's hometown-turned-summer-resort through brush and pen. They knew, too, the Transcendentalist poet Jones Very, whose mystical flights as a young man had cost him his job at Harvard. More important, the daughter, always comfortable in public, was able to enlist as supporters of her project the likes of Edward Filene, the Boston department-store magnate, and Phoebe Hearst, a leading member of California's dynastic family. The wife of a U.S. senator and a benefactor of the University of California, Hearst emerged as the most important financial backer of Greenacre (Farmer idolized her as the "Beloved Mother of the Faithful"). Coming from a family at home with America's social, intellectual, and religious elites, Farmer had the indispensable asset of access.[11]

Early in 1894, with the parliament having generated huge press coverage and the high hopes of religious liberals everywhere, Farmer stormed ahead with the planning of her own experiment in comparative religions. Her first summer conference opened that July on the grounds of the Greenacre Inn in Eliot. At the inaugural ceremony, during which Farmer preached her ideal of spiritual harmony, "a great white flag," inscribed in block green lettering with the word "PEACE," was raised above the assembled throng. "Harmonious may your efforts be," Farmer intoned, "and harmonious your thoughts and hearts, so that beauteous Peace may dwell in your midst." All she required of participants was a commitment to spiritual openness and respectful engagement rather than sectarian rivalry and judgmental exclusion. That meant, first and foremost, a sincere attentiveness to the presentation of alien perspectives. Invidious comparisons were to be a matter of private reflection, not public pronouncement; points of agreement were to be conscientiously privileged over marks of difference. As Farmer summarily explained her principles, "The spirit of criticism will be absolutely laid down—if it comes in it will be gently laid aside; each will contribute his best and listen sympathetically to those who present different ideals. The comparison will be made by the audience, not by the teachers." Finding a way to cut through religious hatred and intolerance was her grandest ideal, and Farmer pursued that dream with both impossible optimism and splendid dedication. The "PEACE" flag became a fixture at Greenacre, but it inevitably proved easier to raise the banner than realize the message.[12]

Farmer's principle of harmony extended to a genuine receptivity to participating in the practices that various speakers introduced and demonstrated. Dharmapala's candlelit processions, chants, and meditation techniques were among the possibilities, for example, as were practical introductions to the devotional disciplines of yoga. Also popular, at least for a season or two, were barefoot walks on the dew-drenched grass, a practice recommended by the health reformer Sebastian Kneipp (1821–1897), who promoted various forms of hydrotherapy—such as cold-water baths and face "gushes"—as a way of toughening up the body and invigorating it. (Those barefoot strolls proved so memorable to Emma Thursby that thirty-five years later, unable to walk now without assistance, she sweetly recalled in a letter to Ralph Waldo Trine "the days at dear Greenacre when I had my first kneipping with you in the early mornings.") The sincerity, high-spirited freedom, and sheer nerve with which the congregants approached new spiritual practices struck Swami Vivekananda in the fellowship's first season: "I teach them Shivo'ham, Shivo'ham, and they all repeat it, innocent and pure as they are and brave beyond all bounds." Many of the different classes were held in the woods, and specific trees quickly took on storied associations and distinct names: the "Swami Pine," the "Emerson tree," the "Persian Pine," and "the Bodhi tree"—the last referred to the legendary spot where the Buddha had received enlightenment. "It is a queer gathering," Vivekananda confessed in a letter from Greenacre in July 1894. Still, Farmer and the rest were "very good and pure people," "quite free and happy," only "a little erratic and that is all."[13]

Over the next decade or so Farmer recorded one success after another. The summer conferences received wide press coverage, some of it bemused, but most of it favorable, including celebratory coverage in the *New York Times Illustrated Magazine, Harper's, Outlook,* and *Progress Magazine.* "Years ago intellectual Boston would have gone out to Concord for spiritual regeneration at the feet of the good, sweet poets and philosophers who lived there," the *Boston Sunday Journal* opined in 1903. "Today the inner circle of intellectual Boston goes to Green Acre to sit at the feet of the gentle and wonderful prophetess-priestess, Sarah J. Farmer." The slate of lecturers Farmer pulled together from one summer to the next was a who's who of liberal religion at its meridian: Annie Besant, the emergent leader in Theosophy circles; Henry Berkowitz, Solomon Schindler, Charles Fleischer, and Joseph Silverman, premier Reform rabbis of the era, all leading advocates of a cosmopolitan, liberal Judaism; Paul Carus, go-between publisher of journals and books on Asian religions, as well as D. T. Suzuki, the emergent ambassador of Zen Buddhism to the West; George D. Herron, controversial prophet of the social gospel in Protestant circles; and W. E. B. Du Bois, guiding light of the National Association for the Advancement of Colored People and celebrated author of *The Souls of Black Folk.* From 1894 to 1915, the Greenacre conferences presented a diverse, challenging, often brilliant platform of speakers.[14]

Under Farmer's leadership a variety of programs in the arts and social sciences flourished, the most distinctive of which was the Monsalvat School for the Comparative Study of Religion. Incorporated as an entity of its own in 1896, the school was placed in the hands of Lewis Janes, the founder of the Brooklyn Ethical Association. A cosmopolitan idealist critical of America's imperialist policies from Cuba to the Philippines, Janes saw the advancement of the Kingdom of God as revolving around the "peaceful federation" of nations, the sympathy of religions, the extension of self-government, and the relinquishing of colonial possessions. Janes, at least by comparison to Farmer and many of her other deputies, was the restrained intellectual; he cared a lot about establishing the scientific bona fides of the Monsalvat School, whereas Farmer's purposes were "wholly constructive." Though she paid due obeisance to the internationally renowned scholar of comparative religions Max Müller and frequently courted his less accomplished American counterparts, she was in this endeavor "to quicken the spiritual life" far more than to sharpen "critical methods."[15]

Control over the roster of speakers was only one source of tension between Janes and Farmer. Even more discouraging to Janes was Farmer's strong preference for trust-in-the-Lord financial arrangements, which made him crazy with frustration. Here the lines were drawn sharply, often in gendered terms, between her "faith" in voluntary contributions and his techniques of "sound business management." "This difference of understanding," Janes remarked in one letter to Farmer in late 1899, "could never have occurred between two men accustomed to business methods." By the next year, the breach was so severe that the disharmony came close to shutting this school of harmony down; only through Janes's timely death in 1901 was a complete rupture avoided. His memorial service, held that September in Eliot, struck a more concordant note and soared on the same wings that had made Whitman's funeral so eclectic. Even the local Congregational minister, otherwise solidly orthodox, rose to the occasion, quoting in his brief homily various world scriptures in addition to the Christian Bible. Despite the fond adieu the Greenacre community paid the deceased director of Monsalvat, the bickering between Farmer and Janes was a bad omen for spiritual unity.[16]

To Farmer, the Monsalvat School was not primarily a laboratory in which the emergent science of religions could display its scholarly powers, and it was most definitely not a venture to be sullied with good business sense. Flush with excitement about her flagship, she imagined the school as an American residence for visiting teachers such as Vivekananda and Dharmapala as well as a place for Christians to come into "a fuller realization" of a larger religious unity. As she detailed her vision in 1898, "I would have in this school the most consecrated Christians whom I could find—men and women who can live the life of a child of God and do the work which Jesus did. I would have the most devout Catholic I could find; the most simple, learned Jew; the most devoted Swami. I would like as many representatives of the great faiths of Persia, Turkey, India, China, Japan, as can be brought to us." That expansiveness hardly made Greenacre a divine deli or gluttonous smorgasbord for the indulgence of the appetites. It was, instead, more of a holiness camp for religious liberals: Here they would all join together, Farmer exhorted, in "the conquest of Self—the most important requirement of all."[17]

Greenacre was a patchwork. One of the prevailing patterns revealed strong Emersonian and Whitmanite colors. Transcendentalists had long kept their movement alive through various clubs and associations, one of which, the Concord School of Philosophy, opened as an annual summer symposium in July 1879 with Bronson Alcott, still a garrulous lecturer on mysticism, as its guiding light. The school attracted the participation of such old stalwarts as Thomas Wentworth Higginson, David Wasson, Cyrus Bartol, Frederic Henry Hedge (the original convener of the Transcendental Club), and even Emerson himself. Alcott suffered a debilitating stroke in 1882, and Emerson died the same year, giving some credence to the remark of one satirist who called the graying assembly the Conquered School of Philosophy. Still, the association hung together through 1887 and managed to gather many of America's leading intellectuals for its conversations. Farmer's experiment was in part a reproduction of Alcott's Transcendentalist curriculum, but hers would be a summer school less for philosophy than for the comparative study of religion. It would be, in effect, a testing ground for eclectic spiritualities or, as one newspaper headline proclaimed in 1899, the "HOME OF SOUL CULTURE."[18]

The most important bridge between the Concord School and Greenacre was Franklin Benjamin Sanborn (1831–1917), among the most productive and resilient of the Transcendentalists. A youthful admirer of Emerson and Thoreau, an abolitionist partner-in-arms with Theodore Parker and Thomas Wentworth Higginson, and an exhaustless reformer of prisons and asylums after the Civil War, Sanborn also emerged as the diehard remembrancer of his Concord neighbors. Publishing biographical studies of Emerson, Thoreau, and Bronson Alcott, he heralded their American genius and burnished their reputations at every turn. He tended especially to Thoreau's manuscripts, publishing letters and journals and helping in crucial ways to turn "our Concord hermit" into "an American classic." For dramatic effect, Sanborn sometimes showed up to give lectures on his

Franklin B. Sanborn and Charles Malloy, both of whom imagined Greenacre as a latter-day Transcendentalist enclave, were bitterly aggrieved when Farmer's religious journey went well beyond the Concord school. (Eliot Bahá'í Archives, Eliot, Maine.)

beloved philosophers with autographed manuscripts in hand. Indeed, he actually circulated some of Emerson's original letters at Greenacre, providing the frisson of the relic for the faithful.

As an impresario for public commemorations, Sanborn staged "Emerson Day" celebrations for Farmer for more than a decade. The first, held in August 1896, was followed the next day by a formal Reunion of the Concord School of Philosophy on the grounds in Eliot. Sanborn's "favorite spot" for holding the Emerson fetes was deep in the pines in front of "a gigantic boulder known as The Mystic Rock." Sanborn and his colleague Charles Malloy (1823–1914) sometimes stood on top of it when offering their "tender intimate touches" about the sage's life. Malloy, as founder and president of the Boston Emerson Society, was one of the few other New Englanders who could actually give Sanborn a run for his money as an Emerson enthusiast, not to say cultist. Malloy, like Sanborn, had become devoted to the Concord sage early in life, and, for his part, Emerson had taken a direct interest in the young man's intellectual and spiritual development, loaning him his own copy of the *Bhagavad Gita,* which Malloy in his youthful enthusiasm proceeded to copy out in longhand. Malloy, in turn, gave four lectures on Emerson's indebtedness to the *Bhagavad Gita* at Greenacre in 1899, and, when he helped orchestrate the dedication of the Emerson Pine on Emerson Day in 1907, the opening scripture was, not surprisingly, a selection from this Sanskrit text of religious knowledge, self-restraint, sequestered meditation, and blissful discernment. Besides these doting rites that Sanborn and Malloy conducted at The Mystic Rock, there was another neat symmetry involving that spot. Ralph Waldo Trine, by one account, built "a willow-woven hut" near the huge boulder and withdrew there to compose *In Tune with the Infinite.*[19]

Sanborn reported tirelessly on the Greenacre meetings for the *Springfield Republican,* doing all he could to shape Farmer's experiment into a renascent Transcendentalist community and to bring it to public prominence. The point seems to have been for Sanborn less a revival of dysfunctional utopias like Brook Farm or Fruitlands than the creation of a new shrine. In July 1904, a year after he had helped stage a string of centenary celebrations of Emerson's birth, Sanborn noted that as usual the Concord sage had been featured at the Greenacre meetings: "Indeed, Emerson may be said to have been for the 10 years since these conferences began in 1894, the chief patron saint of the varying throng of visitors." Emerson may well have been the focus of the shrine's devotions, but Thoreau occupied far from a peripheral niche. In 1908 Sanborn reported (in the third person, no less) on how well one of his own lectures at Greenacre had gone; it was a talk on Thoreau's religion, presented under "a giant pine which would have delighted the sylvan soul of Thoreau." Sanborn was more invested than anyone else in Greenacre as a late Transcendentalist enclave. In his mind, every day there was Emerson Day or Thoreau Day, and, not surprisingly, he would be among the most critical of Farmer's turn to the Bahá'í faith as a derailing of his own designs.[20]

Whitman's memory, perhaps even more than Emerson's or Thoreau's, was alive and well at the encampment on the Piscataqua. The poet's spirit was so apparent that Greenacre sometimes appeared to be the Whitman Fellowship on holiday: Horace Logo Traubel, a liberal Jew turned Whitman's Boswell, was involved, and so were such devoted followers as William Norman Guthrie, Gustav Percival Wiksell, and Thomas Bird Mosher. The Whitmanites, not surprisingly, thought that they were the source of Greenacre's real vigor and offbeat energy, that without them the place would quickly sink into old-fashioned religious asceticism. As Traubel wrote to one of his fellow Whitmanites in 1907,

> I hate Greenacre & I love it. God made it magnificent. ... I shall never be sorry to remember that Greenacre is a fact. There are the best of reasons for thinking the worst of it. And there are also the best of reasons for cherishing its sacred intimations. I do not go much for the pale saviors. I like my saviors to have red faces &

passions. To walk about on strong feet. To have appetites & to be proud of their bodies. A few of you at Greenacre save the place. But for you it would wash out in the first storm.

It would not be the last time that Farmer's experiment was pictured as having an unresolved conflict at its heart: a struggle between robust appetites and wan sacrifices, Promethean creativity and feeble submission.[21]

The Whitmanite engagement with Farmer's experiment was indicative of the larger mingling of religion and the arts in the Greenacre fellowship. Take a typical convergence in the 1896 program: Mary Hicks gave a lecture on Whitman on August 15, two days after Emerson Day and three days before a lecture titled "Mysticism in

MODEL FOR A MEMORIAL
"THE WAY OF THE REDEEMED"

Greenacre, also something of an art colony, attracted the sculptor William Ordway Partridge, whose model for *The Way of the Redeemed* evokes the religious yearnings of the journeyers. (Firestone Library, Princeton University.)

Marsden Hartley got his first break as an artist with a solo exhibition at Greenacre in 1907. His *Musical Theme,* 1912–1913, suggests his continuing interest in the spiritual eclecticism that he imbibed from reading Emerson and knowing Farmer. (The Rose Art Museum, Brandeis University, Waltham, MA; gift of Mr. Samuel Lustgarten, Sherman Oaks, California.)

Modern Art," which was, in turn, followed by Bjerregaard's week-long class called "The Mystic Life." The place attracted established artists of national renown: the poet Edwin Markham, the sculptor William Ordway Partridge, the vocalist Emma Thursby, the stage actor Joseph Jefferson, and the novelist William Dean Howells, among them. The connections to the art world—epitomized in the appearance of Ernest Fenollosa, curator of Oriental art at the Boston Museum of Fine Arts—only reinforced the larger spiritual aspirations of the sojourners. Fenollosa, a convert to Buddhism in 1885 when studying in Japan, praised the Buddhist abbot who mentored him as "my most inspired and devoutly liberal teacher in matters religious." Like Farmer, Fenollosa imagined a grand "marriage" of East and West, a culminating synthesis of "Spiritual Wisdom," a theme he pursued as both a cognoscente of East Asian art and a poet.[22]

The artist Marsden Hartley (1877–1943) was among the leading exemplars of the ways in which Transcendentalist spirituality and art converged under Farmer's scheme. Hartley, who put on his first solo exhibition under the patronage of the wealthy Vedantist Sara Bull at Greenacre, had a "conversion experience" in his early twenties when first reading Emerson's *Essays*—a copy of which "I was to carry in my pocket for... at least five ensuing years, reading it on all occasions, as a priest reads his Latin breviary on all occasions." If Emerson was his "holy script"—the author responsible for bringing "the religious element [into] my experience"—it was the Whitmanites who drew him to Greenacre. Mosher, a publisher of Whitman, introduced Hartley to Horace Traubel, to whom he listened eagerly for "nice touches of the daily life" of the storied poet. It was Mosher, too, who urged Hartley to attend the "Congress of Religions" at Eliot and meet Sarah Farmer, "a frail wisp of a woman who was all fire in spirit and a bundle of energy." "God has breathed heavily on these acres," Hartley wrote Traubel of his time in Eliot, "and we want the Godbreath to stay." Hartley, in his art and life, would thereafter long evince an interest in "mysticism" and the coming of "the universal religion," a harmonious spirituality that he pictured in such canvases as *Musical Theme*, also called *Oriental Symphony* (1912–13). Not coincidentally, he produced that painting at the same time he was reading Richard Maurice Bucke's *Cosmic Consciousness*, the ultimate manifesto of Whitmanite mysticism. By then, Hartley had moved on to Paris, an American expatriate who had joined the avant-garde and who thrilled now at Wassily Kandinsky's *On the Spiritual in Art*.[23]

That was one wing of Farmer's constituency: the Emersonians, Whitmanites, and various seekers of spirituality through poetry, art, and music. Another equally prominent and often overlapping section was New Thought, one of the movements crucial for legitimating meditation as a practice for Americans. It was among the leading religious influences on Farmer in the 1890s beyond her natal Christianity, though she would hardly have distinguished between the "newness" in New Thought and the "newness of life" in Christ. One of Farmer's few publications was an address titled "The Abundant Life," which she gave at the International Metaphysical League in Boston in 1899 and in which she commended prayer, meditation, and silence as pathways to God and drew on eclectic religious sources to make her point—from St. Augustine to the Buddha.

The networks of Boston New Thought were Farmer's own: Ralph Waldo Trine served as a publicity agent for Greenacre, even as he was turning his attention to metaphysical writing; Horatio Dresser started up his own School for Applied Metaphysics at the summer retreat in 1897; Helen Van-Anderson, among Farmer's closest associates at the time Greenacre was launched, held healing services there as well as offering lessons on Emerson's "Over-Soul." (Van-Anderson, ordained to the ministry in Boston in 1894, headed the Church of the Higher Life, newly formed "to aid all individuals to attain their own best development, regardless of creed, sect, or dogma.") So prominent were mental healers at Eliot that Swami Vivekananda upon arriving at Greenacre in 1894 initially thought he had fallen in with Christian Scientists. He took note of various practitioners—Henry Wood, in particular, whom he referred to quizzically as "a mental healer of metaphysico-chemico-physico-religioso what not!"[24]

New Thought currents were as sweepingly diverse and free-spirited as the Whitmanite stream. Dresser, for example, praised Greenacre not only as an outpost for the metaphysical movement, but also more broadly as a center of religious liberalism and progressivism, a place where one could live "the ideal of the fullest spiritual life":

The two months spent there in camp, at the Inn, or at some farmhouse nearby, have been the turning-point in life for many people, and many return year after year because of the great help they receive in daily living.... Early and late there is some lover of nature ready to call you up to see the sunrise, to study insect or plant life, or sit in silence with you while the sun sets across the river. It is indeed a unique experience to be one of a throng of people gathered on the hill at sunset, while the Parsee chants a native hymn, or some one reads from one of our own poets. And after one has heard Emerson expounded underneath the pines, or listened to the Swami setting forth in his quiet way the venerable doctrines of Vedanta, one is ready to exclaim that there are no such woods anywhere outside of Greenacre.

There were few airtight compartments or creeds in New Thought, at least as Dresser and his friends in the Metaphysical Club articulated their mission. They seemed as bound and determined as any Whitmanite to pursue self-reliant individuality and boundary-crossing cosmopolitanism.[25]

One of the implications of that openness was that the New Thought contingent at Greenacre formed a natural alliance with the Transcendentalist wing, Horatio Dresser's Applied Metaphysics with Franklin Sanborn's Concord School. New Thought leaders were as charged with a heady sense of emancipation from authority and tradition as ever Emerson was in addressing his audience at Harvard Divinity School. "We affirm the freedom of each soul as to choice and as to belief," the International New Thought Alliance proclaimed. "The essence of the New Thought is Truth, and each individual must be loyal to the Truth he sees. The windows of his soul must be kept open at each moment for the higher light, and his mind must be always hospitable to each new inspiration." Religious identity, in this light, was free-form and improvisatory, not fixed or ascribed. By definition, people were supposed to keep seeking, to remain open to new perspectives and insights, not to settle on one path alone among the many. A generous dose of open-mindedness was at the heart of the spiritual quest.[26]

It is no wonder that Dresser and Sanborn did not know what to make of Farmer after her pilgrimage to Ottoman Syria and her enthusiastic embrace of the Persian Revelation as the culmination of her grand vision of the unity of all religions. The rift that opened up after 1901 between the Transcendentalist–New Thought wing and Farmer's new Bahá'í associates made the earlier squabbles between Janes and Farmer pale in comparison. Farmer crystallized the misunderstanding in a provocative letter that she wrote to Dresser in March 1902:

> Thank you dear Brother, for your clear and kind letter, but it shows me that you cannot realize my point of view. My joy in the Persian Revelation is not that it reveals one of the streams flowing to the great Ocean of Life, Light and Love, but that it is a perfect mirror of that Ocean. What, in Green Acre, was a vision and a hope becomes, through it a blessed reality now. It has illuminated for me every other expression of Truth which I had hitherto known and placed my feet on a Rock from which they cannot be moved. And it is the Manifestation of the Fatherhood—Behá'u'lláh—who has taught me to look away from even the Greatest and find within the One, 'Powerful, Mighty and Supreme' who is to be the Redeemer of my life. It is a Revelation of Unity such as I had never before found. By means of its Light, as shown in the life of the Master Abbas Abdul Behá, I have entered into a joy greater than any I have hitherto known. Green Acre was established as a means to that end and in proportion as we lay aside all spirit of criticism of others and seek only to live the Unity we find, shall we be able to help others to the same divine realization.

Surely, it would have been of little consolation for Dresser to learn that Farmer was now praying for him to see "the full Light." "I beg of God to manifest His Lights in the heart of Horatio so that he may apprehend that which he has never before apprehended," Farmer beseeched in one hand-written prayer.[27]

In light of the new revelation, Greenacre became, in Farmer's mind, less about an open door than a final realization, less about a quest than a fulfillment. Fittingly, the place even took on a subtle change of name in her mind from Greenacre to Green Acre, the latter suggesting to her an exchange—at the level of a homonym—between Acre and 'Akká, the Syrian abode of 'Abdu'l-Bahá. That shift, in turn, riled her critics. As one New Thought backer of the summer colony fumed, "Cannot we drop the name of Greenacre[?] [I]t is now Green-Acre—the home of *the Master*—it is entirely too suggestive of fanaticism." Farmer wanted to maintain the inclusive ideals of her experiment, but now with a sense that there was an ultimate capstone in place under which all the other religious representatives would be enveloped in unity. "Green Acre people fear that its open free platform is to be swallowed up and narrowed to an 'ism,' " Farmer confessed in 1903. "It must be taught that only now is its freedom being assured.... We are never free until we have felt the *Rock* under our feet."[28]

Though Farmer clearly felt she had a new foundation for her message of religious unity, her evangelism for the cause was rarely heavy-handed. She hoped to exude a radiance—a kind of spiritual beauty—that would draw others at Greenacre to ask her about her newfound source of joy. Throughout, she showed little interest in lording the Persian Revelation over the assembly; she agreed in 1905, for example, to keep the study of Bahá'u'lláh's writings separate from the rest of the programs of the Monsalvat School in order to relieve "other Green-Acre workers" of any "embarrassment" and to prevent misunderstanding. She hoped her associates, like Dresser and Sanborn, would see the light, but she also wanted to preserve her original ideals for Greenacre as a great congress of religions. Indeed, many of the initial American admirers of the Bahá'í faith saw it not as a replacement of their prior religious affiliation, but as something of a cosmic score that would hold all of the different religions together in symphonic harmony. Several seekers were happy to embrace the Persian Revelation without giving up their church membership, and Farmer accepted this mixing. She herself never attempted to foreclose the flux and flow of religious identities that had become a defining feature of Greenacre.[29]

Sadly, though, Farmer was caught between a rock and a soft place. How was she going to stand firmly upon the rock of Truth while embracing a generous cosmopolitanism that disclaimed all sectarian partiality? How was she going to maintain peaceful relations with her Transcendentalist, New Thought, Buddhist, and Vedantist friends now that, deep in her heart, she viewed their prior work together as but preparation for the spiritual fulfillment she had discovered? The pressures were intense from all sides. While the Bahá'í movement lined up extremely well with many progressive causes—from internationalism to interracialism to women's equality—it remained highly conflicted on the nuts and bolts of religious unity, at least in its nascent stage. If Moses, Jesus, and Muhammad were all true prophets and pointed to the same God, Bahá'u'lláh was nonetheless seen as the exalted successor. The son of the prophet, 'Abdu'l-Bahá, breathed both an all-inclusive love and the supreme wisdom of the divinely led. When a young woman approached him at Greenacre on his visit there in August 1912, she asked him for assistance in identifying her life's work. "Be a perfect Bahá'í," he advised. "Associate with Bahá'ís. Study the teachings of Bahá'u'lláh." She protested, "I am a good Jewess." And the Master replied, "A good Jew can also become a Bahá'í. The truth of the religion of Moses and of Bahá'u'lláh is one. Turn toward Bahá'u'lláh and you will acquire peace and tranquility ... and you will attain the highest degree of perfection." Here was the core tension: the liberal idealization of cosmopolitan variety in the expression of religious truth was paired with the ultimacy of the Bahá'í version of that truth.[30]

When dealing with Farmer's own penchant for eclecticism, 'Abdu'l-Bahá was often less discreet than he was with this Jewish inquirer. Though he exalted Farmer as a maidservant of God and repeatedly blessed and confirmed her vision of Greenacre, he also exerted heavy pressure on her to follow the straight path of the Bahá'í faith. In his frequent correspondence with Farmer and as a visitor to Eliot, 'Abdu'l-Bahá made his own vision clear: "If one looks for praiseworthy results and wishes to produce eternal effects, let him make exceeding effort, in order that Green Acre may become an Assemblage for the Word of God and a gathering place for the spiritual ones of the Heavenly World. The mouldered, two thousand years old superstitions of the heedless, ignorant peoples, whether of Asia or Europe, should not be spread in that revered gathering place." The Hindu swamis were apparently particular targets for rebuke; one acquaintance insisted that Farmer was under specific instructions from her Persian teachers to "gently close the door in their faces." 'Abdu'l-Bahá wanted Farmer to be an emissary for the Divine Kingdom, not a moderator of plural faiths; he also wanted Greenacre to be under the clear administration of "the Beloved of Baha" and wished there to be "no influence" from the "spurious[,] decayed and unproductive trees" of the "old sects." Only with that purification would Greenacre be turned into "the Empire of the Greatest Spirituality." Or, as one of Farmer's leading American Bahá'í associates, Charles Mason Remey, put the matter in 1916: "The period of seeking along many divergent channels" was over at Greenacre; now the school was to be devoted to the glad tidings of the Persian Revelation.[31]

The pressures that Farmer faced from the Transcendentalist wing were just as intense. Sanborn loathed her new religious turn and insistently characterized the change in the community's fortunes as a Bahá'í "take-over." He missed few opportunities to lament the loss of "the Greenacre spirit of its best years" and the debasement of a "free parliament of religions" through the machinations of "a proselyting sect." The conflict often got ugly, mean-spirited, and downright illiberal. One woman reported to Lewis Janes that Charles Malloy, Sanborn's esteemed partner in the Emerson extravaganzas, had bravely proclaimed that he was "not afraid of Babs [an early label for the Bahá'ís] or Babboons—they have no terrors for him." Another of Sanborn's allies, Nathaniel Schmidt, a professor at Cornell University, was readily enlisted in the failed campaign to hold off Bahá'í influence and leadership; angrier than ever, he was barred from speaking in the hallowed pines in 1914, but he still defiantly gave a lecture on the roadside nearby. Paul Carus, another warm supporter turned chagrined critic, published in the pages of the *Open Court* some of the hardest-hitting commentaries on Greenacre's transformation into "a sectarian institution." As one letter to the editor from "a friend of Miss Farmer" proclaimed in 1915, "When the *true* history of Miss Farmer's work at Greenacre is written, as it must be some day, the history of the untold good to the untold numbers that it has accomplished and still might be accomplishing if that fatal, mentally unbalancing disease, Bahaism, had not crept in, the world will wonder with regret at the magnitude and beauty of that which it permitted to be destroyed."[32]

Through 1907, despite mounting tensions and recurrent financial pressures, Farmer effectively maintained Greenacre's high repute, but in March of that year, she suffered severe injuries when she fell from an elevated train in Boston. Even with months of rehabilitation, she was never really at full speed again. With Farmer sidelined from the day-to-day work of the summer community, the factions became all the more apparent: Bull's Vedantists, Sanborn's Transcendentalist and New Thought alliance, and Farmer's Bahá'í associates. The 1908 and 1909 seasons were successful, but fractious; the debilitated Farmer made one of her last appearances at the summer gathering in 1909. It was a disaster. The physician Fillmore Moore—an advocate of the simple life, a longtime associate at Greenacre after a stint with the Concord School of Philosophy, and a successor to Janes as director of the Monsalvat School—criticized her publicly for her ostensibly sectarian turn. By the next summer, Farmer was not only physically frail, but also emotionally strained to the breaking point. Sara Bull and other close friends had her committed to an insane asylum in Waverly, Massachusetts, in July 1910. Slowly recovering her bearings, she was relocated from that setting to a more recuperative venue, the Psychotherapeutic Sanitarium in Portsmouth, where she spent most of the last five years of her life. The presiding physician, protective of his new patient, wanted as much as possible to shield Farmer from the turmoil of the politics at Greenacre. He did permit her, though, to visit Greenacre again in August 1912 for the visit of 'Abdu'l-Bahá, which proved, for both Farmer and the Master, a culminating moment of encounter and reunion.[33]

From that point, the divisions at Greenacre descended into tragicomedy—messy battles over the disposition of an estate, the composition of the trustee board, and the shape of the ongoing programs. The *Boston Post* and the *Portsmouth Herald,* among other newspapers, relished the controversy and ran reports on it with banner headlines: "War Between Bahaists and 'Antis' May End in Court" or "Greenacre Factions Line Up in Battle Array." The Bahá'ís won most of these scuffles, and by 1914 only Horatio Dresser remained among the leadership as a token of the institution's wider metaphysical roots. The saddest, and most farcical, battle was over Sarah Farmer's fate. Meeting with Farmer on his visit in 1912, 'Abdu'l-Bahá insisted that Farmer, far from suffering from "insanity," was undergoing a period of mystical "exaltation." He urged his followers to find the legal means to get her out of the clutches of the sanitarium, return her home to Maine, and allow her to preside again—at least symbolically—over the Greenacre community. Her friends in Eliot gladly took up the prophetic commission, offering up "ceaseless prayers" for Farmer's "release from the prison Sanitorium."[34]

The plot thickened when various secret schemes were hatched to "rescue" Farmer. Urban J. Ledoux, later known by the code name of Mr. Zero in his work with the homeless and unemployed in Boston and New York, was the chief operator in the first mission. A flamboyant social reformer, Ledoux always relished the theatrical dimensions of righting wrong: he subsequently staged mock "slave auctions" of the jobless on Boston Commons, donned sackcloth and ashes for a meeting with President Warren Harding, and marched an army of ill-clad hobos into the midst of New York's fashionable Easter Parade to highlight the gap between rich and poor. Even as he explicitly strove to get "in tune with the Infinite" and to achieve "Brahmic Peace,"

Ledoux also cultivated his connections with American Bahá'ís and was heralded in those circles as a social prophet who shared the faith's mission to combat "Prejudice, Religious, Racial and Class." If Mr. Zero's radical religious profile seemed to fit to a tee the part of Farmer's rescuer, he nonetheless failed miserably in acting this role. Entering the sanitarium in the guise of a patient, Ledoux tried to use the arrival of the circus in town as the necessary distraction to spring Farmer, but the staff quickly foiled him. Eventually slipping away from the Greenacre scene, Mr. Zero reemerged in Boston a couple of years later as the nettlesome leader of the "Church of the Unemployed." For his part, Ledoux viewed his mission—particularly his efforts to shelter the homeless, feed the hungry, and cross the color line—as an appropriate expression of Jesus' imperatives and also an outworking, in expressly Whitmanite terms, of his "cosmic-conscious self."[35]

Undeterred by his initial failure, Ledoux reconnoitered with some of Farmer's Bahá'í friends and Maine relatives who sought the assistance of the chief of police in Portsmouth. Even with that official cooperation, dubious and disputed as it was, a small band of liberators still felt the need for a surprise invasion of the Psychotherapeutic Sanitarium, which they undertook late in the evening on August 3, 1916. Bundling the frail Farmer into a waiting car, they whisked her back to Eliot under the cover of darkness. Of course, Sanborn and company hardly saw these exploits as a courageous jailbreak and quickly characterized them instead as the "Kidnapping of Miss Farmer." The press, not surprisingly, ate up the latest turn of events, playing up the hostage-taking versus hostage-freeing debate to great effect. Before the issue could be settled one way or another, Farmer died in late November of that year, her "WEIRD ADVENTUROUS LIFE," as the *Boston American* had it in one headline, coming to an end amid continuing conflict, not harmony. For all intents and purposes, her death marked the end of the old Greenacre fellowship and the close of an era. Soon the National Spiritual Assembly of Bahá'ís formally acquired the inn and cottages, which they continue to use as a school and retreat center and through which they teach "the spiritual principles of the New Day."[36]

Upon her death one newspaper ran an obituary that announced that Farmer had "lived one of the strangest lives ever granted to a woman"—a religious visionary and "a prophet of liberalism" who had managed to draw "many great minds as well as many small ones" to her Greenacre conferences. Another posthumous appraisal of her life performed an apotheosis with a distinct New England twang: "The significance of Miss Farmer in the history of American progress is she stands as the actual fulfiller of Emerson in terms of applied influence. Miss Farmer can be considered the feminine counterpart of Emerson." Her practical abilities, this eulogist claimed, had managed to turn Transcendentalism's "abstract formulas" into "tangible results." Her experiment, from this perspective, represented "well nigh the flower of modern liberal thought."

Other epitaphs were less generous and more biting. The *Open Court* published the most wide-ranging postmortem: Even as it called for "a new summer Parliament of Religions" built on the principles of Greenacre's founding in the glory days of the 1890s, it buried Farmer with contempt for having lost her senses in succumbing to a new religious authoritarianism. Instead of Farmer as prophet of religious liberalism and implement of Transcendentalism's promise, the *Open Court* pegged her as one more symbol of an old tyranny:

> *A seeker after a new creed, a person who after liberation from the bonds of the old dogmatism is uneasy until he has shackled himself anew to a cult and again entered into spiritual bondage, is simply a natural born slave in search of a master, and such a person is no asset to a liberal movement.*

By this account, her spiritual experiment had ended in failure; "a particular sectarian herd" had overrun "broadmindedness and appreciation of the blessings of diversity." Greenacre stood finally for narrowed sympathies, not widened ones; for obedience, not autonomy. By one script, Farmer had struggled mightily and with considerable success to push a progressive spirituality forward; by the other, she had betrayed religious liberalism through a retrograde form of submission.[37]

The conflict over Farmer's legacy cut to the heart of the debate over modern religious seeking. Was the quest open-ended, fluid, and uncontainable? Could the new spirituality brook feelings of acquiescence, submission, and obedience? Farmer, at the end point of her seeking, had found her footing through "Resignation to the Will of God" and the revelatory power that she discerned in the very presence of 'Abdu'l-Bahá as an authoritative teacher. In one letter written in 1907, addressed to her as "the attracted Maid-servant of God," the Master praised her directly for her "humility and submission of heart and spiritual emotions." In another letter written the same year, 'Ab-

When 'Abdu'l-Bahá, the leader of the Bahá'í faith, toured the United States in 1912, Farmer had the deep satisfaction of joining him at Greenacre for various events, including this car ride, at the end of which he leaned over and kissed her on the cheek as one more sign of his blessing. (Eliot Bahá'í Archives, Eliot, Maine.)

du'l-Bahá responded to an exegetical question from Farmer about a passage from his father's *Hidden Words* (1857–58), explaining to her how the "splendor of the Being of the True One" would illumine those who pursued "the station of renunciation" and who entirely lost their "I-hood." Farmer, for her part, displayed her profound deference publicly in 1912 when 'Abdu'l-Bahá visited the Greenacre gathering; she "fell at His feet weeping and received from the Master His infinite favor and utmost kindness." The very memory of "the face of our Master as it shone upon me" could transport her in body and soul with "warm currents" of joy and bring the words "God is all glorious" to her lips.[38]

Spirituality, as a construct and a living practice, mattered deeply in the emergence of the American Bahá'í movement. Among its first organizations was a gathering of the faithful that took the name the Chicago House of Spirituality in 1902 at 'Abdu'l-Bahá's urging. On his visit to Greenacre in 1912 the Master had blessed this "delightful spot" as a place in which "an atmosphere of spirituality haloes everything"; while there, he had also specifically exhorted some ascetics in the community to worry less about dietary restrictions and more about the importance of "acquir[ing] spirituality." As Farmer's experience suggests, though, the Bahá'í version of a universalized spirituality often mattered in a way that confounded one of the primary emphases of religious liberalism: namely, it challenged the notion of the self-reliant quest—or what the Transcendentalist John Weiss had called "sacred independence." In *The Varieties of Religious Experience,* William James puzzled repeatedly over the tensions between self-assertion and self-surrender, independence and passivity in the spiritual life:

> *Obedience. The secular life of our twentieth century opens with this virtue held in no high esteem. The duty of the individual to determine his own conduct and profit or suffer by the consequences seems, on the contrary, to be one of our best rooted contemporary*

Protestant social ideals. So much so that it is difficult even imagina-
tively to comprehend how men possessed of an inner life of their
own could ever have come to think the subjection of its will to that
of other finite creatures recommendable. I confess that to myself
it seems something of a mystery.

How could a woman like Farmer—active, vigorous, reform minded, independent in spirit—find salvation through resignation of her own will not only to God, but also to one of God's mortal representatives, a white-bearded holy man residing in a compound near Haifa? That seemed, to her detractors, slavish. What kind of sick soul would find so much joy in spiritual bondage?[39]

Farmer was far from the only seeker at Greenacre to find spiritual rest through self-surrender. Two of her coworkers at Greenacre and friends in the new faith, Ellen Beecher (1840–1932) and Stanwood Cobb (1881–1982), produced more extensive narratives about their own religious experiences, and their stories help supplement the sparer record that Farmer left of her inner life after 1901. In a four-page manuscript account of a spiritual experience in February 1905, Ellen Virginia Beecher (distantly related through marriage to the famed New England clan of Lyman Beecher, Harriet Beecher Stowe, and Henry Ward Beecher) recalled how she awoke at dawn one morning to pray and meditate, two of the main devotional practices in the Bahá'í faith:

> *All at once I heard the rustle, as it were, of a garment, and realized*
> *a* presence *beside my bed, but supposing it to be a member of the*
> *family who had come to enquire after my health, I kept my eyes*
> *closed for some minutes, wishing to continue my meditations undis-*
> *turbed; but the person so persistantly remained standing at the bed-*
> *side that at last I opened my eyes and beheld that Benign Face and*
> *Form which I had seen twice before at different intervals, and*
> *which the Blessed Master had written me was that of Baha'u'llah.*

He stood looking down into my eyes until my whole frame shook with emotion.

The envisioned prophet then worked with "tender Hands" on her body and spirit as "a Panorama of the Potter and the Clay passed before my eyes."

With great skill and subtle probing Bahá'ulláh extracted from Beecher's body, much to her own "astonishment," "my *Ego*." At that moment she was able to see how her life had been "ruled more or less by this Ego" and how it had "encouraged pride, self-sufficiency and independence." Beecher's experience turned on self-surrender and the vanquishing of self-will. "How I loathed that Ego!" she exclaimed. "I saw that it had been my devil, which had so often possessed me. I shrank from it as if it had been a viper.... My heart seemed broken, as the realization of my nothingness and powerlessness dawned upon me." Turning to the Bahá'í faith allowed Beecher, in effect, to recover a Calvinist sensibility that had become increasingly foreign to the liberal Protestant world she had hitherto inhabited. Her dramatic vision issued in a feeling of being chosen and not choosing, a recognition of God's utter sovereignty and her own sinfulness, an experience of self-emptying and not self-realization.

Beecher's mystical experience was not only of God as Father, but also of God as Lover and Bridegroom: "In an instant I was in His embrace, lost to all things else. I had attained to the Meeting—and Glory be to GOD! my soul was clothed with the 'Wedding Garment' such as mortal could never create or conceive of." In that mystical turn Beecher's experience resonated with long-standing Christian forms of piety that had been infused with the love poetry of the Song of Songs and New Testament images of Jesus as bridegroom. It also corresponded to the heady emphases of Bahá'u'lláh's Sufi-inspired text, *The Seven Valleys*, which American Bahá'ís made available in translation in 1906 and which chronicled the passionate journey of the soul after "the Desired One": "O friend! Be alien to the self, that thou may'st find thy way to the Incomparable One.... *Nothingness* is needed until thou mayst kindle the fire of existence and become acceptable in the path of love.... The veils of the satanic ego must needs be consumed with the fire of love." Beecher's own visionary encounter with Bahá'u'lláh fittingly culminated not in feelings of self-mastery or empowerment, but instead in a sense of envelopment in submission. She heard again and again in her soul: "The Holy Spirit dominates My limbs." Ecstatic, to be sure, Beecher nonetheless was hardly traveling the wide-open, self-doting expanses of Whitman's open road.[40]

Stanwood Cobb's experience was more muted, but it struck similar themes. He had made "a pilgrimage" to Greenacre in August 1906, his curiosity whetted by the weekly coverage of the gathering in the *Boston Transcript.* A student at Harvard Divinity School studying for the Unitarian ministry, Cobb had already been exploring comparative religions and had shown considerable interest in mysticism, Theosophy, New Thought, and Reform Judaism. (Earlier in 1906 he had visited at length with the rabbi Charles Fleischer, and they enjoyed a far-ranging exchange about "esoteric experiences" and "the *coming religion.*" Fleischer, too, was involved in Greenacre, and the pair made a good conversational match.) Cobb had already met Farmer at one of Sara Bull's salons in Cambridge and was clearly impressed by her "warm spiritual glow." He later dubbed her, on more than one occasion, "a spiritual genius."

Approaching Farmer at the Greenacre meeting for a reintroduction, Cobb found himself transfixed. She took his hand in hers and "looked into my eyes and asked, 'Have you heard of the Persian Revelation?... I know by your eyes that you are ready for it.' " Within a half hour, Cobb reported later, he had abandoned his plans to enter the Unitarian ministry and had become "a confirmed Bahá'í" at the ripe old age of twenty-four. A youthful social reformer, often downtrodden in spirit, having suffered from "nervous depression" as a student at both Dartmouth and Harvard, Cobb had been looking for a new impetus for the realization of the Kingdom of God. He was longing for someone "with more than human authority" to sustain his flagging idealism and to pull him out of the hole of his own dark moods. And he found what he had been seeking in "the spirit of 'Abdu'l-Bahá," first communicated to him that day at Greenacre. By December 1906 he was in correspondence with the Master, and in February 1908 he journeyed to 'Akká to meet him in person—a radiant encounter that Cobb claimed left him "permanently relieved" of his melancholy.[41]

Cobb wound up spending most of his professional life in prepschool teaching and in promoting pedagogic reforms through the Progressive Education Association. Good schooling, from Cobb's perspective as with like-minded reformers of the era, was not about drills, rote learning, and grades, but about releasing the gifts and creativity of each child. Not surprisingly, as a youth Cobb had adored the essays of Emerson and the poetry of Whitman. His educational dreams conjured up in a new guise the Transcendentalist world that had produced such experiments as Ripley's Brook Farm and Alcott's Temple School. Besides his work in education, though, Cobb led another life as a sagely writer of spiritual books, including *The Essential Mysticism* (1918) and kindred essays, all of which breathed Whitman's religious eclecticism even as they explored a counterpoint to Transcendentalist freedom and individual inspiration.

Cobb was keenly aware of the religious and intellectual tensions within his own heart and mind. These strains were evident in a diary entry he penned in October 1909, while teaching English and Latin at Robert College in Constantinople and studying in his off-hours with two "native Bahais" there: "Self-assertion as opposed to self-sacrifice— self-expression as opposed to self-restraint & asceticism.... The old problem, that has been on my mind and heart for months. Can religion win me, or must faith give way to a pagan naturalism & rational philosophy?" The thorough conversion that he imagined having occurred at Greenacre was obviously not so neat and clean, but he nonetheless tried to keep his head from buzzing too much with readings of

Nietzsche on power, self-will, and the subversion of Christian ethics. Writing an article titled "The Spirituality of the East and the West" for *Open Court* in 1913, Cobb displayed an Orientalist vision as he imagined the vanquishing of "Western" self-assertion through "Eastern" self-surrender: "It is from the East that there have come the ideas of renunciation, submission to God, and the absence of all desire save his will—which I take to be the essence of spirituality; without these qualities no individual can be called spiritual."[42]

Paul Carus (1852–1919), the colorful and eclectic editor of *Open Court* who once described himself as "a religious parliament incarnate," opened the pages of his journal to Cobb's musings on spirituality. He did so, though, mostly for the sake of argument, for the

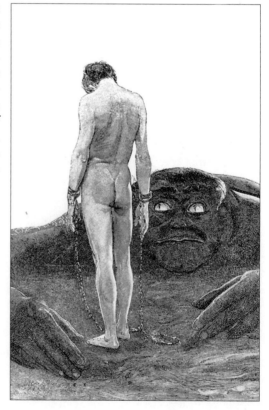

The editor Paul Carus used the pages of his journal *Open Court* as a forum for religious exploration as well as critique. His suspicions of pious self-surrender were embodied in this frontispiece, Sasha Schneider's *The Feeling of Dependence* (1899). (Firestone Library, Princeton University.)

opportunity it provided him to take up the cudgels against religious dependency and the "passive Oriental piety" that Cobb was defending. The stalwart American friend of the Zen Buddhist expositor D. T. Suzuki as well as of Suzuki's teacher Shaku Soyen, Carus expressed at least grudging respect for the "advantages" that Cobb's piety possessed. After all, Carus had been known to endorse the notions that "the existence of the self is an illusion" and that true religion consisted in the extinguishing of "egotistical desire." He was perfectly happy to praise Christianity and Buddhism together as religions of "resignation," dedicated to "the surrender of self." Yet in this case Carus made plain his offense at Cobb's praise of submission and renunciation as the essence of spirituality. (Perhaps Cobb was the chosen target because Carus took him to be an embodiment of the growing Bahá'í presence at Greenacre and the eclipse of his own eclectic ideals there.) Whatever the reason for his personal disagreement with Cobb, Carus saw clearly now that a childlike piety deprived of "manly vigor" was not what Americans or the rest of the world needed to move forward into the future. Instead, "a higher spirituality" was called for—one that "does not consist in a submission to God or the powers that dominate destiny, but a courageous effort to build up a nobler life through a deeper comprehension of the laws of nature."

Carus's object was far larger than the ridicule of Cobb's spirituality. In another piece, called "Is Religion a Feeling of Dependence?" Carus had overtly taken on one of the fathers of liberal Protestant theology, Friedrich Schleiermacher (1768–1834), for having defined religion in these acquiescent terms. American admirers of Schleiermacher had long recognized that his appeal to feelings of absolute dependence seemed strikingly gendered. One reviewer even praised him in 1862 for having been "wonderfully gifted with … womanly qualities": "Women could comprehend him best." In Carus's view, that strain of effeminate piety had left liberals, in spite of their own professions to the contrary, in a terribly unprogressive posture of weak-kneed submission: "To the lovers of freedom the feeling of dependence is a curse.... Truly if we cannot have a religion which makes us free and independent, let us discard religion!" Carus felt so strongly about this that he printed a frontispiece alongside his article picturing "The Feeling of Dependence" as a naked man, bound in shackles, who is being leered at by "a terrible monster whose prey are the weak—those whose religion is absolute submissiveness." Now, far from wanting to embrace a religion of resignation, Carus seemed intent on defending a self-determining spirituality even through lurid images of psychosexual fear and vulnerability. He, in effect, attacked Cobb's manhood—and that of all liberals who had somehow lapsed in their spiritual life into womanly feelings of dependence and submission.[43]

Cobb very much felt these tensions in his own body. When he first met 'Abdu'l-Bahá, he did not know how to display his reverence. Should he fall to his knees and kiss the hem of the Master's robe as the female pilgrim he was traveling with did "with the devotion of a Mary Magdalene"? Or could he get away with a more masculine gesture and "merely shake hands with Him"? Fortunately, the Master sensed Cobb's awkwardness and quickly threw his arms around him in an embrace. Clearly, even for Cobb, a spirituality of hem-kissing deference was easier for him to get his mind and body around if it involved a woman rather than himself. Still, that clumsy hug notwithstanding, Cobb was on the side of a spirituality of self-surrender, even as he long remained committed to progressive education and its concomitant, creative self-expression. How that might all come together for him was evident one day in 1910 as he read Whitman in a serene, withdrawn lull: "I love Whitman more than ever now," he wrote in his journal in January of that year. Loafing is "my only hope. In order to accomplish anything, I must be anxious to accomplish nothing. No strain, no eagerness, no hurry, no worry, no crowding—the readiness to drop all—fold the hands, retire—let others do the work."[44]

Carus's critique of Cobb and company resonated with William James's sense that religious subjection and obedience had become mysteriously alien to liberal Protestant ideals by the turn of the twentieth century. "The moods of piety are all reversed," Octavius Froth-ingham had happily proclaimed as early as 1872. "For self-distrust, self-abnegation, self-depreciation, we have self-reliance, self-respect, self-culture, self-development." Yet, Cobb's desire for resignation got a lot closer to James's own religious yearning than did Carus's bluster or Frothingham's self-congratulation. Elsewhere in the *Varieties* James spoke in terms that hallowed the very kinds of experiences to which Cobb, Beecher, and Farmer gave expression. "The athletic attitude" of will power and self-improvement, which James saw as so prevalent on the contemporary scene, tends inevitably "to break down":

> *To suggest personal will and effort to one all sicklied o'er with the sense of irremediable impotence is to suggest the most impossible of things. What he craves is to be consoled in his very powerlessness, to feel that the spirit of the universe recognizes and secures him, all decaying and failing as he is. Well, we are all such helpless failures in the last resort.*

In this recognition of absolute dependence and unalterable human limitation, only religious experience can come to "our rescue"; only then can "the will to assert ourselves and hold our own" be "displaced by a willingness to close our mouths and be as nothing in the floods and waterspouts of God." This ability to annul annihilation through self-annihilation was "religion's secret." Ask me not, James said in one of his many resorts to ineffability, to "explain the matter."[45]

Deep in the heart of the new spirituality was an exploration of fini-tude alongside freedom, resignation alongside autonomy, submission alongside assertion. "For when all is said and done," James lectured, "we are in the end absolutely dependent on the universe; and into sac-rifices and surrenders of some sort, deliberately looked at and ac-cepted, we are drawn and pressed as into our only permanent positions of repose." Cobb, Beecher, and Farmer, as well as Alexander Russell Webb, for that matter, wanted more from their seeking than a perpet-ual tramping of many roads, and that resting place came for them through surrender to new religious authorities. Perhaps that turning was a betrayal of both their liberal and their Christian identities. Perhaps. Yet, the "spirituality" that they claimed against their former "religiosity"—to use another of Stanwood Cobb's distinctions—was a clearly recognizable riff on religious liberalism's own highest aspirations to develop "a deeper spiritual life." As James suggested, the crisis of self-surrender remained "the vital turning-point" in the religious experience of many nineteenth-century liberals and Transcendentalists, just as it did for more-orthodox Christians. The point for many seekers was to put down roots elsewhere in order to exchange homeless wandering for protective shelter. Often when they moved beyond their own religious upbringings, it was to rediscover the meaning of self-sacrifice and God's overpowering grace.[46]

The struggle at the heart of Farmer's spiritual journey and James's religious psychology—the tension between autonomy and self-surrender—has hardly disappeared from America's contemporary seeker culture. In *At the Root of This Longing* (1998), the feminist spiritual writer Carol Lee Flinders, for example, examines the strains that she has experienced in her simultaneous embrace of the freedoms of the women's movement and the disciplines of meditative practice. A teacher of writing and mystical literature at Berkeley as well as a longtime member of a Vedantist community, Flinders increasingly sensed dangerous currents running back and forth between her spiritual commitments and her feminism: "I felt sometimes as if I were picking up two raw ends of electric cable and drawing them very tentatively toward each other. In one hand I held everything I'd gleaned from my teacher and my practice. In the other was everything I knew as a woman living in a male-centered culture."

The sparks flew about her in the flash and flicker of hard-to-resolve questions. Was the feminist vision of full emancipation and equality compatible with the religious desire to "unseat the ego"? In a culture that often still enshrines male authority at the expense of female "voice," how could she possibly accept religious enjoinders to silence and selflessness? Had not women's desires been demonized for too long to submit to contemplative practices that hallowed the concentrated mind over the sensuous body? A century after Farmer's own self-division between her first-wave feminism and her renewed submission to male religious authority, Flinders is perhaps in a better position to arrive at a synthesis of the seeker's curiosity and the finder's clarity. Yet, her effort to join the two worlds together—spiritual disciplines and modern freedoms—is hardly any easier; it still requires dedicated pursuit of the contradictions between self-expression and "self-naughting" to a point of profound convergence. Flinders has gathered sustenance for her journey from cross-cultural study of the mystics, especially medieval women mystics like Julian of Norwich, but there hovers behind her a more proximate (yet unseen) communion of seekers and saints, not least in that company Sarah Farmer herself.[47]

CHAPTER SIX

SEEKERS

OCTAVIUS FROTHINGHAM (1822–1895), the matchless chronicler of New England Transcendentalism, remarked in *The Radical* in 1870 that for inquirers of his generation the big question had become "What is religion?" It was not enough to gather adequate descriptions of specific religions, whether Unitarianism or Mormonism, in order to make sense of the religious world. Rather, the issues at hand cut deeper: What was the nature of religion itself? Did it still matter? Was it of "vital, practical, daily use to anybody"? These problems were entangled with the meaning of religion itself. It was a term, in Frothingham's view, that carried all too much baggage; it was sinking under the weight of those who for too long had defined it as "a thing of tradition" or a "set of rules." With an erudite flourish he returned to two Latin derivations of *religion* to suggest its fundamental limitations: *relegere*, "to repeat, to travel over and over again"; and *religare*, "to bind, to bind closely, to bind back." Tedium and coercion: now those two connotations were not going to lift romantic spirits.

Insisting that "earnest seekers" wanted "to push the quest much further," Frothingham claimed that only when religion came to be seen as meaning "to *unbind*"—that is, to have a "dissolving significance," to be "the spirit that loosens, the emancipating spirit"—did it speak to that larger search. "Hold all opinions soluble," he exhorted. "Drop the polemic[ist], the controversialist, the apologist, and be a seeker, willing to stay or to go, whithersoever the spirit of truth leads." The spiritual life could be reclaimed from all the perceived shortcomings of religions past and present through recognition of religion's essence. That core, to borrow a phrase from one of Frothingham's colleagues in the Free Religious Association, was "man's search for the secret of life." Out of the depths—and the shallows—of religious liberalism came a new answer to the question "What is religion?" as well as a new standard-bearer for its redefinition: religion was the universal human search for meaning, and its archetype was the individual seeker. Religion, in effect, could be saved only if it became spirituality.[1]

The idea of the spiritual seeker received stimulus through the rise and spread of Transcendentalism. In his essay "Circles" in 1841, Emerson had famously called himself "an endless seeker" with "no past" at his back. "We can never see Christianity from the catechism," he warned in the same piece, but there was at least some chance of recognizing it "from a boat in the pond." The high enthusiasm of that essay for "newness" and "the way onward" was another Emersonian benchmark, and the sobriquet of the "endless seeker" was one that the next generation, including Frothingham and James Freeman Clarke, happily reiterated. Despite Emerson's fondness for the "energizing spirit" of the unsettled and the experimental over the burdensome checks of precedent and convention, the very idea of the religious seeker had a specific history that was ultimately reinvented rather than shed. That history would serve to give greater cultural resonance and legitimacy to the tradition-be-damned stance of the Emersonian seeker as a deep-seated affirmation of America's spiritual democracy (and, yes, the irony of the appeal to history in this context was usually missed). In "Circles" Emerson had grandly imagined the past being swallowed up and forgotten, but history turned out to be all too serviceable in authorizing the American embrace of what is now routinely referred to as seeker spirituality.[2]

When Emerson and then Frothingham chose to employ "seeker" as a religious category, they were hardly engaged in original wordplay. Instead, they were discounting some of the more prevalent associations the term had come to carry through clearing a little of the dust off its history. Though nineteenth-century America could boast a multitude of "seekers," there was one small problem for the transcendentally inclined: namely, only a minority of those seekers would have thought of their quest in spiritual terms. The most prominent use of the term in Emerson's day was in connection with California's gold rush, the flood of "gold seekers" streaming westward after 1849. That, in turn, was a variation on the notion of "treasure seekers," the vagrant hunters who wandered the antebellum American landscape looking for buried fortunes. (Not that religion was entirely out of view here: it had been the restless treasure seeking of the Mormon prophet Joseph Smith that had helped prepare him for the discovery of the golden plates of new revelation.) In the second half of the nineteenth century, old-fashioned pleasure seekers also enjoyed a whole lot more modish, self-seeking company—health seekers, sight seekers, and notoriety seekers, among them. Radical freethinkers had also commandeered the term for their purposes as "truth seekers," the bold debunkers of popular superstitions. One of the few promising counterpoints to these prevailing associations came predictably from the Quaker poet John Greenleaf Whittier, whose poem "The Prayer-Seeker" enjoyed popular circulation after 1870.

There was, though, a historical precedent that, if properly tweaked, had possibilities. In its religious usage, *seeker* had actually emerged in the seventeenth century as an orthodox Christian designation for a particular type of heresy. Ephraim Pagitt (1574–1646), an Anglican rector trying to classify and thereby bring some order to the profusion of "false Prophets" and "seducing Spirits" who were pushing

England to the brink of revolution, first gave the term currency in his *Heresiography; or, A Description of the Hereticks and Sectaries of These Latter Times* (1645). Pagitt clearly had his work cut out for him in this heyday of Protestant enthusiasm as he labeled and defined such separatist upstarts as Adamites, Brownists, Familists, Grindletonians, and Soule-Sleepers, among a few dozen others. On page 141 of his chronicle of "the plague of heresie" and its spreading infection, he finally got to "the Seekers, or Expecters." Garnering all of a paragraph of Pagitt's attention, the Seekers were identified as those wayfarers who had wrangled so long about the nature of the true Church that they had finally given up on all its current institutional forms, ministers, and sacraments. Still hoping to find the true Church through their seeking, they refused to "returne againe to the bosome of that Church, from which they have, to the great dishonour of God, and the scandalizing of the Gospell made so fearfull a defection." As suggested by Pagitt's thin description, the Seekers were of relatively minor significance in the wider whirl of English dissent, pretty easy to lose sight of in a sea of millenarian sects. After the Restoration of Charles II and the Anglican Church's reconsolidation of power, the "heresy" was of small consequence even as a sectarian label, having none of the polemical reach of terms like *Antinomian, Enthusiast,* or *Quaker*.[3]

In one of the odder stories of rebirth in American religious history (and there is, safe to say, a lot of competition on that score), Pagitt's seventeenth-century "Seekers" enjoyed a new life in writings on spirituality among liberals and modernists in the early twentieth century. The decisive turn came in the writings of Rufus M. Jones (1863–1948), a Quaker who emerged as one of the most influential American writers on mysticism and the inner life in the half century after 1900. His highly spiritualized version of the Society of Friends (indeed, of Christianity across the board) was sweepingly influential. Almost single-handedly, he transformed his small denomination into a great purveyor of devotional wisdom for aspirants from various religious backgrounds. Through historical romances and mystical surveys Jones managed to exalt the Society of Friends as the consummate community of seekers.

The force of Jones's muse was evident in various locales. It was given material expression in the development of Pendle Hill, a retreat center founded outside Philadelphia in 1930 and a notable indicator of the direction spiritual seeking was heading in American culture. Jones's reach was also evident in the range of his students and admirers: it stretched from the well-regarded Quaker writers Douglas Steere and Elton Trueblood to the famed émigré authors Aldous Huxley, Christopher Isherwood, and Gerald Heard to the visionary Howard Thurman, founder of the interracial Church for the Fellowship of All Peoples in San Francisco. Thurman, in particular, saw in Jones a kindred soul; after graduating from Morehouse College and Rochester Divinity School, he came to study one-on-one with Jones at Haverford in 1929, making liberal religion's charge of "Mysticism and Social Change" distinctly his own. Jones's legacy would be especially apparent in the impact he had on the spiritual quest of Thomas R. Kelly, a fellow Quaker whose *Testament of Devotion* (1941) became a hallmark text for his own generation of seekers.[4]

Born on a farm in South China, Maine, in 1863, Rufus Jones was a Quaker through and through in his upbringing. Several relatives were itinerant Quaker ministers, including his aunts Peace and Sybil as well as his uncle Eli; years later, in 1889, his first book would be a biographical homage to the religious example of Sybil and Eli. His cousin Augustine was headmaster of the Friends School in Providence, Rhode Island, which Rufus attended before matriculating at another Quaker school, Haverford College, in 1882. By his senior year at Haverford he was already deeply drawn to mysticism, making it the subject of both his thesis work and his commencement address. Soon he headed off to Germany for a year of further study, including attention to such medieval Christian luminaries as Johannes Tauler and Meister Eckhart. He later capped off his education in the Department of Philosophy at Harvard, where he encountered the venerable idealist

Josiah Royce—in Jones's estimate, "one of the oddest-looking men since Socrates"—and where he regretted missing out on courses with William James, who was on leave writing and convalescing. That did not prevent Jones from consulting with James and accruing a strong sense of indebtedness to him: "It was always amazing the way this busy man welcomed a young quester," Jones marveled later. For his part, James was more than ready to support Jones's own idealizing of the Quaker faith. As a religion of "liberality" and "spiritual inwardness," the Society of Friends, James claimed, was "impossible to overpraise" (though that hardly kept him from trying).[5]

After a six-year stint teaching at two different Friends schools, Jones returned to Haverford in 1893 to teach philosophy and to serve as editor of *Friends Review* (later *American Friend*). That personal advancement in his career was hardly news in liberal Protestant circles in a year headlined by the World's Parliament of Religions, but it signaled an important watershed all the same. Over the next forty years Jones would turn Haverford into a focal point for the elaboration of modern mysticism and spirituality, gathering Thomas Kelly and Douglas Steere into the fold as colleagues in philosophy and lending his vision of Quakerism and the inner life to the nearby Pendle Hill community in Wallingford, Pennsylvania. The latter quickly emerged as an important publisher of tracts on spirituality and social justice, two of Jones's dearest themes. A tireless writer, Jones cranked out more than a book a year on average for the rest of his life—*Studies in Mystical Religion* (1909), *The Church's Debt to Heretics* (1924), and *George Fox: Seeker and Friend* (1930), to name three of the more than fifty volumes. Also a popular lecturer, Jones made the rounds on the university circuit in the 1920s and 1930s: Princeton, Yale, Stanford, Harvard, the University of Southern California, and the Pacific School of Religion, among numerous other campus visits. Hardly confined to his vocation as scholar and lecturer, Jones led the relief work of the American Friends Service Committee from its founding in 1917. The agency was awarded the Nobel Peace Prize in 1947, the year before

Jones's death. He was as close as American Protestants came to having a mystic and a saint in this era.

Jones obviously accomplished many things in his long and intensely productive life—one of which was his popularization of the notion of the spiritual seeker. Tellingly, he had initially discovered his "life work" on mysticism not through seventeenth-century Quaker testimonies, but through more immediate romantic sources, particularly Emerson's *Essays* and Robert Alfred Vaughan's *Hours with the Mystics.* It was George Fox (1624–1691) and the rise of the Society of Friends as seen through the prism of nineteenth-century writers such as Emerson, Vaughan, Thomas Carlyle, George Bancroft, and John Greenleaf Whittier that redirected Jones's life. "My studies in Emerson led on into an extensive reading of Carlyle and both these men

Rufus M. Jones spent much of his working life in his study at Haverford, surrounded by his massive library on mysticism and by images of those who most inspired him, including one of the poet John Greenleaf Whittier above his desk. (Haverford College Library, Haverford, Pennsylvania: Quaker Collection, Rufus M. Jones Papers, Coll. no. 1130.)

planted in me a new idea in reference to the significance of the Quakerism in which I had been nurtured," Jones recalled. "They both treated it not as the religion of a small Protestant sect, but rather as a *spiritual movement* of the mystical type." That intellectual transformation was perfectly materialized on the walls of Jones's study at Haverford. Prominently displayed above his desk was a portrait of Whittier; nearby, to Jones's right-hand side, was a smaller profile print of Charles C. Everett, Harvard professor of theology and one of the minor architects of the liberal turn to mysticism; above Whittier and Everett were a paired set of Emerson and Carlyle prints. Although Jones did have two portraits of Fox in his office as well, the most eye-catching, mantel-grabbing piece was a large, gilt-framed print of Emerson in which the Concord philosopher appeared as a younger, more vigorous man than in the sagelike image above Jones's desk.[6]

Beyond those New England idols, Jones would also identify closely with the Quaker elements in Walt Whitman's life and writings. These linkages certainly included the poet's own hallowing of George Fox's seventeenth-century soul-searching, but more important were Whitman's rosy memories of the "very mystical and radical" preaching of the American Friend Elias Hicks (1748–1830). One of Whitman's most extensive pieces of religious writing had been an encomium in 1888 to "the irrepressible devotional aspirations" and "naked theology" of Hicks, whom Whitman had heard as a boy and whom he boldly romanticized as a fellow "tramp" of the open road. Whitman's rendering of Hicks, "the most *democratic* of the religionists," was resonant with Jones's own spiritualized view of Quakerism: "The true Christian religion, (such was the teaching of Elias Hicks,)," Whitman wrote, "consists neither in rites or Bibles or sermons or Sundays—but in noiseless secret ecstasy and unremitted aspiration, in purity, in a good practical life, in charity to the poor and toleration to all." So, even as Jones continued to uphold Emerson as "America's foremost mystic," he came to hear in Whitman's prose and poetry "the Quaker hush and quiet and the whisper of the Infinite Presence." On the shelves in his study, for example, was Henry Bryan Binns's *Life of Walt Whitman* (1905), with a chapter on Whitman "The Mystic." Jones duly made marks in the margins of those passages that emphasized the affinities of Whitman with Fox and Hicks.[7]

The expansive Transcendentalist rendering of Quakerism's spiritual significance allowed Jones to reimagine his own religious identity in grandly universal terms. He came to see himself not as part of "a peculiar and provincial sect," a family clan in and around South China, Maine, but as part of a questing movement that pursued the pure mystical core of religion itself. Thus situated within "an unbroken line" of spiritual seekers, he could see his family, especially his supremely intuitive aunt Peace, as possessing an "unconscious mystical propensity," though "the word 'mystical' was never spoken and of course had never been heard in our circle." (The Quaker vernacular for experiences of direct divine promptings would have been "openings" or "leadings.") The self-conscious change of diction proved crucial to Jones. His beloved Quakers—all appearances to the contrary—were not quirky sectarians, mired in doctrinal debates about what distinguished one band of Friends from another, Hicksites from Wilburites from Gurneyites, quietists from evangelicals. Instead, Jones claimed, the Society of Friends stood for an "inward, mystical religion"; it was an exemplar of the universal "religion of first-hand experience." That perspective, deeply indebted to wider currents in religious liberalism, was intended to override all the schismatic factionalism plaguing nineteenth-century Quaker meetings and to lift Jones into the company of a timeless band of spiritual reformers intent on finding "a direct way to God." Religion, he claimed again and again with utter clarity, is "at heart, the personal meeting of the soul with God."[8]

Important to Jones's vision was the historical recovery of that otherwise obscure group of English sectaries the Seekers. In his *Studies in Mystical Religion*, Jones moved from apostolic Christianity to the eve of the Reformation and then brought the whole to conclusion with four chapters on Protestant radicalism in sixteenth- and seventeenth-century England. That emphasis was, to put it mildly, disproportionate. It clearly reflected Jones's lifelong desire to make sense of the religious world out of which his own Society of Friends emerged. Stranger still, though, was that one of those four chapters was on the Seekers, and, perhaps strangest of all, was that group's representation as the personifying spirit of mystical religion: "As soon as faith in the authority of the Church grows faint, and the sufficiency of established forms and rituals is seriously questioned, the primal right of the soul to find God Himself is sure to be asserted. 'Seekers,' under different names, we have found at every period of this history." Jones had to admit he had "very slender" evidence for actually linking up the sundry groups in his study to the English Seekers, but that was not as important as the suggestiveness of this handle for thinking about religion as a quest. The term morphed in Jones's hands into a general attitude, a searching and unsettled disposition that had relevance far beyond seventeenth-century England. "There are 'seekers' today in all lands," Jones asserted in 1931, "who are keen and eager for fresh truth and new light on mysticism."⁹

The Seekers would have made lousy seekers on Jones's liberal religious terms. Fervently expecting the restoration of apostolic Christianity, these straying souls condemned the apostasy of all the churches and ministers that stood in the way of the purity of New Testament patterns. They prayed and waited for the renewed gifts of the Holy Spirit and in the meantime looked with fright at what passed for sermons and sacraments in the Church of England as well as the vast majority of Puritan assemblies (not even to mention the Church of Rome). There were, at the extreme of this sectarian reading, no genuine ministers of Christ or acceptable church bodies currently on the scene, and yet Jones slid right over the uncharitable separatism of those claims. One juxtaposition suffices to suggest Jones's rhetorical posture: First, Jones quoted John Jackson, as close to a bona fide seventeenth-century Seeker as he could find, to the effect that "persons called by the name of Seekers having compared the present ministry with the Word of God, and not finding it to conform thereto dare not join ... in the present practice of it." Then, Jones offered this commentary on Jackson's claim that no one was currently entitled to call himself a minister of Christ: "The real pith of the Seeker movement is thus clear. It was at heart a mystical movement; a genuine spiritual quest for something deeper than the empty show of religion." That bold-faced generalization easily eclipsed Jones's more judicious Quaker history in which the Seekers figured as a nucleus for the emergence of the Society of Friends in the 1650s.[10]

The Seekers fascinated Jones most of all as a trope for the modern religious quest, an English antitype for an emergent American cultural type. As such, they seemed too good to be true. By Jones's account, they were a "quiet, devout people who never attended church and who nevertheless were intensely religious." If one wanted a prescription for an anti-institutional piety, "the Seeker attitude" as conjured up by Jones provided it in spades. Tucked into the English countryside and the side streets of London, the Seekers of the 1640s and 1650s, Jones related, "set themselves to a valiant quest for a nobler type of church—the Church of the Spirit." Remembering their search was to recall America to its own quest for a sublime religious democracy in the spirit of Emerson and Whitman. For the post–World War I period—an era that Jones described as one of "disillusionment" and slumping "faith in democracy"—he discerned in the example of the Seekers a testimony to the inseparability of "spiritual mysticism" and "the democratic experiment." Hence the Seekers floated free of their mid-seventeenth-century context in all its violent unrest and apocalyptic specificity, and, with Jones working the billows, they wafted their way right into the heart of America's spiritual-but-not-religious culture. Such currency even allowed the great Progressive-era historian Vernon L. Parrington to invoke the notion of Seekers in his *Main Currents in American Thought* (1927) as an eponym for the "full stature" of Transcendentalism's "romantic revolution." Finally, noted

Parrington with a sigh of relief, the repressive legacy of the Puritans—those who would "close all roads to heaven but one"—had lost sway to the "mystical aspirations" of religious liberalism's uncooped seekers.[11]

In 1940 one of Rufus Jones's chief acolytes, Thomas R. Kelly (1893–1941), offered a short meditation on the "Secret Seekers" within contemporary churches who were at a loss to satisfy their "deep, deep hunger of the soul." The piece made clear that Jones's peculiar history was working its way into wider reflections on spirituality. Kelly opened his reflections, first published posthumously in a Methodist student-movement magazine in 1944, with an invocation of Jones's history of the Seekers that simultaneously gestured toward its larger figurative use as a token of modern spiritual longings: "We know that Quakerism arose in a time when England was full of seekers, men and women who hungered desperately for the last deeps of reality." Despite the materialistic absorptions of Americans with "automobiles and financial security and social recognition," Kelly sensed a profound spiritual urgency, the "perennial God-hunger of the human soul." "For today, here in America, and here in this meeting, and here in your meeting on Sunday morning, are *seekers*," Kelly remarked. "The land is full of seekers, the church is full of seekers," he said almost as a refrain. "To you in this room who are seekers, to you, young and old who have toiled all night and caught nothing, but who want to launch out into deeps and let down your nets for a draught, I want to speak, as simply, as tenderly, as clearly as I can." As Kelly's meditations suggest, the trope of the spiritual seeker had become both insistent and expansive. "We are all seekers," Kelly concluded with a summary sweep that would have made Jones proud. "The world is full of seekers ... baffled, confused, hardheaded, discouraged seekers, yet seekers nonetheless."[12]

By the time Kelly himself joined the Haverford faculty in 1936, his association with Rufus Jones went back more than twenty years. Born on a farm near Chillicothe, Ohio, Kelly had grown up in a devout Quaker family; raised mostly by his mother, he was only four years old when his father died in 1897. His mother retooled herself through some business courses and found employment as a secretary. A hardworking single mother, she managed to put both her son and his sister Mary through Wilmington College. Kelly, throwing himself into the demands and opportunities of student life, won a scholarship for a postgraduate year at Haverford in 1913. Already having been active in the reigning youth ministries of the day—Christian Endeavor, the YMCA, and the Student Volunteer Movement, as well as the local Young Friends group—Kelly arrived at Haverford ripe for the spiritual intensity of Jones. Thinking of himself in college as a budding chemist, Kelly began to shift gears under Jones's tutelage toward philosophy. Jones also pointed him toward his first teaching job at a Quaker school in Newmarket, Ontario, and helped inspire his relief work in prisoner-of-war camps in England during World War I. Two

Thomas R. Kelly's family photographs included this portrait of his mentor and spiritual exemplar Rufus Jones. (Haverford College Library, Haverford, Pennsylvania: Quaker Collection, Thomas R. Kelly Papers, Coll. no. 1135.)

years into his professorship at Haverford in 1938, Kelly wrote Jones of his enduring appreciation for his support and wisdom: "I never forget your large part in opening the way to this the richest period of [my] life. But the debt is deeper than that. For there is a richness and vitality in what one might call the Rufus Jones tradition in the phil[osophy] department, which surrounds us and gives a warmth and vigor to the quest for the deepest Real, and to the expectation that the Real will come to seek us."[13]

Jones was also a critical supporter of Kelly's in his decision to go to Harvard for further graduate work in philosophy—a decision that would ultimately lead Kelly, through failure, into a period of spiritual renewal that resulted in his most important work, *A Testament of Devotion*. Kelly had started his graduate education at Hartford Theological Seminary in 1916, but his decision to do civilian service after the United States entered the war cut his time there short. Upon his return from England he married Lael Macy, the daughter of a Congregational minister, and took a teaching job back in Ohio at Wilmington College, both in 1919. He soon found that going home again had not been the best decision; in the heartland he felt unfulfilled in his smoldering intellectual ambitions. Kelly returned to Hartford, sure that church work was not for him, to complete his Ph.D. Finishing his degree in 1924, he accepted a job at Earlham College in Richmond, Indiana, but first went to Germany for fifteen more months of relief work, this time with a food program for children in Berlin, sponsored by the American Friends Service Committee.

Once at Earlham he loved his work, but his academic aspirations still seemed somehow unrequited. Within a few years he was pushing for a leave of absence so that he could pursue further study and finally make his scholarly mark. Hobnobbing at a meeting of the American Philosophical Association in New York in 1929, he felt that he lacked the ticket for professional success: "Harvard, Columbia, Chicago and Johns Hopkins furnish practically all the philosophy professors [in] the country. I see that in going to Hartford I have not been in the stream at all, and that there is only one regular way to get in. So it looks as if we will go to Harvard!" Arriving in Cambridge, Kelly seemed to relish how "merciless" the professors were in matters of scholarly excellence: "I'm a man of few strong convictions," Kelly reported one professor of symbolic logic announcing at the first class meeting. "But get this through your heads right away. I can't stand intellectual mediocrity. If you can't keep up the pace, get out of here!" (That course, Kelly reported later, ended abruptly when the professor perversely "decided to go into seclusion to write a book.") This much seems evident: Kelly was drawn to such intellectual brusqueness and unyielding meritocracy, even as it made him intensely anxious and self-doubting.[14]

Kelly soon wanted more from Harvard's Department of Philosophy than the faculty was ready to give: namely, he ceased to be satisfied with a little postdoctoral course work; he became determined (almost maniacally so) to complete another Ph.D. Surely, a Harvard doctorate would get him out of small-town, church-related schools in the Midwest and into the established East Coast intelligentsia he so much wished to emulate. But, with his Harvard mentors dragging their feet and with his wife wondering why he had become so obsessed with the scholarly life, Kelly returned to Earlham after a two-year absence, the Crimson degree still up in the air rather than in

These three interlinked snapshots suggest the many faces of Thomas Kelly as a young man. (Haverford College Library, Haverford, Pennsylvania: Quaker Collection, Thomas R. Kelly Papers, Coll. no. 1135.)

hand. Out of money and a little shamefaced, he went "back to the sticks" full of regret at not having secured "a foothold in the New England educational world." He had hardly lost the fire, though; he made a vow "to spend every minute of spare time writing" in order to strengthen his publication record. He agreed with one of his professors back at Hartford that all the stress on publishing in "technical journals" was "a very poor way to judge men," but, alas, "that is the most decisive factor in the minds of most universities." Professionalization is a bit of jargon, an abstracted process, but the very real costs of internalizing the standards of credentialing, productivity, and networking were quite apparent in Kelly's anxious quest for validation as "a 'Harvard man' in my field."[15]

After positions at Wellesley and Dartmouth failed to come his way, Kelly's academic restlessness was finally rewarded with a job offer from the University of Hawaii in 1934. Accepting the post as the next stepping-stone—in coldly calculating terms he called it an opportunity "to be used now, to be exhausted and then left, if possible"—Kelly continued to labor feverishly on his "philosophical scholarship." Ever driven to prove himself, he finally suffered a breakdown "as a result of the usual American foolishness of working too much." Largely confined to bed, yet wanting desperately to bring his Harvard research on the epistemology of the French philosopher Émile Meyerson to fruition, he looked every bit a man who was trying to publish *and* perish. He seemed, indeed, ready to mortgage his family's financial security to get a book out with Princeton University Press, borrowing against his life insurance to cover the $545 in permission costs for which the press was billing him. His wife worried explicitly about his self-absorption; if he was ever going to be happy, she thought, he needed to control his "selfishly acquisitive" attitude toward academia and become more self-giving. Suffering "terrible waves of depression and melancholy," Kelly was finally reduced to reading "detective stories all the time" and making "little or no preparation for classes." Despite the physical and psychic toll, he was in no mood to let up; he was sure that "I can't be anything but this kind of person."[16]

The latest crisis stemmed, in fair measure, from his need to compensate for a career move that looked like it had only taken him further away from the world of elite liberal arts colleges. He assured one of his Harvard mentors, for example, that it was certainly not "the lure of palm trees and tropical moons that takes us there"; he had no intention of being "lulled to intellectual sleep" or escaping "the keen competition" that the profession demanded. Likewise, he found himself defending his choice of Honolulu to Jones from the appearance that he had withdrawn to "a very restrictive little field." In actuality, he reported in a letter in May 1936, "the reverse has been the case." Having wanted for some time to study Asian religions, Kelly found Hawaii to be a place where old religious horizons could be "broken" and "new and wonderful vistas" could be opened in their stead. Of course, he was more than ready to move again when he finally got the East Coast offer at Haverford that he had long wanted. Still, his studies at the University of Hawaii (those he managed when not confined to bed and crime fiction) left an enduring imprint. Once back at Haverford, he promptly introduced courses on Buddhist and Hindu philosophy, including lecturing on the devotional disciplines of yoga such as the regulation of breathing, sensory withdrawal, concentration, meditation, and bodily postures (to be "carried through," he told his students, "not in [the] spirit of gym exercises").[17]

Finally settled in at Haverford—"one of the slickest small men's colleges in the East," he crowed, with "blisteringly high" standards— Kelly showed again his penchant for vainglorious academic decisions. Resolving to make a final push to get the Harvard Ph.D. in the summer of 1937, he returned to Cambridge that fall for an oral defense of the thesis. Once he was face-to-face with his examiners, who were still dubious about the wisdom of a second Ph.D., Kelly's own dragons of anxiety seized him. He completely froze (he had previously suffered sudden bouts of wooziness on at least two other occasions, once in an oral examination at Hartford). In what, by all accounts, was a bewildering display of incoherence and blankness, Kelly failed the oral and was denied any chance of sitting for the degree again. For someone always anxious about his standing in the academy, this was a body blow. It sent Kelly spiraling downward again into depression; it was so bad this time that his wife feared he would commit suicide. One of his colleagues, Douglas Steere (1901–1995), stayed up with him late into the night trying to convince him that this setback had no bearing on his standing at Haverford. Steere was a loving, pastoral figure—a spiritual seeker as much as an academic philosopher himself, whose first book, *Prayer and Worship,* was about to appear. But he was also Phi Beta Kappa, a Harvard Ph.D., and a Rhodes Scholar, so it is hard to know how Kelly could have taken too much heart in his presence at this moment of crisis. Only after several weeks did Kelly reemerge from the dense fog of shame and despair.[18]

The philosopher Alfred North Whitehead, his most highly esteemed mentor at Harvard, had apparently confided to Kelly's wife that he thought her husband's academic energies had been "misdirected" and that, in his view, his real interests were in religion, not philosophy. Perhaps the remark was mere hindsight or perhaps it was offered as a way of lessening the blow, but it was almost certainly not meant to be patronizing. (Whitehead had been warmly encouraging of Kelly's philosophical work at various points along the way.) In any case, Kelly did redirect his energies through a heightened dedication to spiritual discipline and devotional writing; in effect, he recovered some of the religious fervor that he had long harbored, though carefully dampened and qualified. As a young man growing up in the revivalistic wing of midwestern Quakerism, Kelly had sometimes bubbled with evangelistic exuberance, red-hot to win souls to Jesus. Largely through Jones's influence, Kelly had gradually moved away from his evangelical roots, expressly repudiating any camp-meeting style of worship with its shouts of hallelujah and amen. He increasingly embraced instead a liberal understanding of the significance of the Society of Friends as a mystical leaven rather than a tiny denominational organization. "The Religion of the Spirit runs through all history," Kelly remarked, specifically summoning Jones's *Studies in Mystical Religion* to his side. Lecture notes he prepared between 1925 and 1930 for use in a class called "The Mystic's Experience" already placed him squarely in the camp of William James and company.[19]

Kelly's shift from youthful evangelicalism to spiritualized liberalism was well expressed in a "little spiritual autobiography" that he prepared in March 1928, a copy of which he then sent to Jones the next month. In that unpublished piece he wrote movingly of his changed experience of God:

> *I found within myself that Quakerism is essentially a mystical fellowship, which transcends the ordinary barriers of religious organizations. The meaning of the universal presence of the Inner Light, the Logos, in every man, the essential Christ in all peoples, glowed out, suddenly.... I saw the whole world of men, and all religious faiths, as a striving mass of people in whom the divine Light, the Logos, dwelt, all reaching out, by that leading, to the Source, the Indwelling God, who moved them to Himself. I suddenly felt a great nearness to people of all religions who "lifted hands of prayer."*

In a moment of exquisite illumination, Kelly felt he had embraced "a very different Jesus" than the "Church-Jesus" he had grown up with. Wondering "if Jesus ever wanted to found a church," he discerned Him now as "a laboring, struggling, seeking man,... knocking at the hearts of his fellow-men and saying 'Wake up to who you are! Discover that your life contains the divine life.'" Through the immediacy of that experience Kelly believed that he had moved beyond "a narrower 'Christianity'" into a global kinship with all those "who are led by the Light toward the Light."[20]

His shift toward a more open, cosmopolitan religious identity was given clear expression in an unpublished sermon from this period of liberal awakening, entitled "Master, Where Dwellest Thou?" Insistently asking his auditors "Where do *you* live?" Kelly pressed home his larger point: "Some live just in their own country, some live just in one nation, America. The struggles of Europe, the economic exploitation of Africa,—these just aren't in their world." But American society cried out "for people who are world-minded,... whose horizons are not bounded by narrow loyalties.... Inadequate patriotisms are making some of our good people far less than ...*citizens of the world.*" Kelly then quickly made clear that this was a religious matter as much as it was political:

> *Do you live just inside the Society of Friends? Or do you have your vision turned upon all Christendom? Do you feel at one with many denominations, and faiths, or is your world shrunk down to one little sect, one little group, one pet idea ...? I would even call you to live in a larger world than Christendom, to enlarge your horizon to include in sympathy all true Buddhists and Mohammedans and Confucianists and Taoists and Shintoists, and see that they, too, are struggling toward the light of Truth.... Too long has Christianity been unchristian by scornfully excluding other people and faiths from their sympathetic fellowship.*

Sounding like the scion of Thomas Wentworth Higginson as much as Rufus Jones, Kelly proclaimed "a world of sympathy" over "a world of disillusionment."[21]

"Do you live with the artists, the dreamers, the poets, the sensitive souls of all time?" he asked his midwestern audience in the same sermon. The answer, he came sadly to believe, was mostly negative, and, thus, his longing for a "mystical fellowship" of sympathetic seekers increasingly left his "liberal soul" feeling all the more isolated in Indiana. "A great loneliness" had set in before his return to Haverford, and he felt more and more tempted "to withdraw into myself" and give up on saving the Quaker meeting in particular and the church in general as institutions. That religious alienation certainly fed his restless careerism (and vice versa); his need to be constantly moving on to the bigger gig—from Wilmington to Earlham to Hawaii to Haverford. But that unsettledness also reinforced his sense of himself as a spiritual seeker. In that same "short spiritual biography of myself" that he sent Jones, he wrote: "There are isolated, and semi-isolated souls all over the country, in all the churches and faiths.... Here at Earlham I find a very few, but some, who feel as we do. But I usually keep all this to myself, and tell no one." Rightly or wrongly, he thought he would have a better chance of finding those stray seekers, ready for "the real Society of Mystical Brethren," in the Northeast rather than the Midwest. But, of course, he would take their fellowship wherever he found them—from Boston to Berlin, from Honolulu to Philadelphia. When his academic ambitions blew up at Harvard in the fall of 1937, he was already primed through professional mobility and liberal sympathy to identify with the "Secret Seekers" of the land and offer them the light of his own redirected mysticism.[22]

Kelly had been torn about his vocation as a scholar for a long time, seeing it, by turns, as integral to his religious life and in sharp opposition to it. He assured Jones in a letter in 1935 that he was not about to become "so enamoured of rigid scholarship" as to lose "all concern for the warm, human, personal, and religious." Yet, in a letter the same year to his first Ph.D. adviser back at Hartford he claimed to be pulled irresistibly "toward the pole of pure scholarship and research" and unable to pursue a life of practical service with any of the same passion. He moved back and forth between worlds in the mid-1930s, one day speaking at Pendle Hill to seekers on retreat and another still cajoling Harvard philosophers for their blessing. Kelly claimed he wanted a "balance" between his life of piety and "the abstruse and technical sides of philosophy," but his supposed equilibrium looked at best like ambivalence. Between 1938 and 1941 he finally appeared to find a genuine steadiness through the "Holy Obedience" he witnessed to in his *Testament of Devotion*.[23]

One of the wisest moves he made in the months following his disillusioning Harvard experience was a return to the work of the American Friends Service Committee. Heading to Germany in the summer of 1938, this time traveling in Quaker faith networks both repressed by and resistant to the Nazis, Kelly gave up the self-deception of his balancing act. In Germany he met with numerous Christians and Jews, including a memorable encounter with Abraham Joshua Heschel (1907–1972) before the rabbi's escape to the United States and his work at Hebrew Union College and Jewish Theological Seminary as a distinguished writer on prayer and mysticism. Kelly, indeed, intuited an interfaith kinship with the "young rabbi, a mystic who would be profoundly at home in a Quaker meeting." However naive it was for Kelly to turn Heschel's witness into something instantly recognizable, there was more than a grain of truth in his observation on Heschel's crossover ability as a spiritual guide. Heschel's meditations in *God in Search of Man* (1952) and *Man's Quest for God* (1954) would soon migrate from the world of Orthodox Judaism into the thick of America's seeker culture. "The goal of religion is not primarily to help us to express ourselves, but to bring us closer to God," Heschel once reminded in a critique of "the myth of self-expression," and Kelly was now coming to see the search for God and God's search for him with some of Heschel's own *"radical amazement."*[24]

As Kelly worshiped with Friends across Germany, the testimony of those who were living in faith under the pall of Nazi violence and surveillance deeply affected him. "It is not merely heroism," he wrote from Nuremberg in August 1938. "It is depth of consecration, simplicity of faith, beauty in the midst of poverty or suffering that *shames* us. I have met some *giant* souls.... [O]ne *can't* be the same again." In a letter to Rufus Jones that September, he exuded a dramatically changed spirit through the fellowship and solidarity he had experienced in Germany: "I have had this summer, and still have, such a *sweeping* experience of 'refreshment of the spirit,' so amazing, so sweet, and so prolonged as to go clear down to the roots of my being." The spiritual light came through an identification "with the oppressed and the despairing" and an overwhelming recognition of "the meaning of suffering." In the face of secret police and raging race hatred, in the face of all those "clubbed, beaten, dragged over briars," Kelly felt a call to minister in his "blind way" to those suffering in body and soul: "Dear people, how I love them. Dear people, how they suffer."[25]

In the winter of his depression, sometime before leaving for Germany, Kelly had already begun to experience a new sense of divine "Presence—something that I did not seek, but that *sought me.*" It was his time in Germany, though, that really brought the experience home. "*In the midst* of the work here this summer," Kelly wrote his wife in a safe moment from France, "has come an increased sense of *being laid hold on* by a Power, a gentle loving but awful Power":

> *And it takes away the old self-seeking, self-centered self, from which selfishness I have laid heavy burdens on you, dear one. Help me, sweetheart, to become more like a little child—not proud of learning, not ambitious for self, but* emptied *of these things, and guided by that amazing Power, which is so gentle.... We have been so hardened, so* crusted, *so worldly-wise. I have been so self-seeking.... I see my way now to a richer life of serenity and childlike faith and joy.... I have been far from this way. Now I feel I must come home.*

Kelly had been severely humbled at Harvard the previous fall, but he now saw the triviality of his own ambitions and anxieties. And his scrambling was not a to-each-his-own trifle in the sardonic sense that one of his poet friends saw it: "I can't really understand your ambition, for to me an academic career is a dreary misery, and I like teaching only as a not too onerous way of winning [leisure] for life and creation. But (as Kipling says) 'To each his dream and vision.'" Instead, and Kelly finally saw this with absolute clarity, his intellectual pride was trivial in the light of the self-forgetfulness of Jesus as suffering servant. What did his professional life count compared to the command to bear one another's burdens?[26]

God-seeking replaced self-seeking for Kelly with all the intensity he had formerly mustered for his philosophical scholarship. Upon his return to Haverford he continued his association with the American Friends Service Committee and had to fight feelings of estrangement from the American churches for their seeming complacency in the face of the grim realities he had witnessed in Europe. He also started a student group to read devotional books together and serve as a token of his long-imagined mystical fellowship, "a little religious order" of seekers after God, a tiny cell of "creative, heaven-led souls." Not all the undergraduates appreciated his intensified devotion or the fervor he inspired in his gung-ho band of apostles; some took to disparaging him as St. Thomas, and one even telephoned him with a crank call from "the Inner Light." Fran Bacon, another college student and a distant relative, read one of Kelly's postawakening meditations and thought he was dangerously close to lunacy, perhaps guilty in his rapturous turn of "spiritual mast[u]rbation." "If you have a narciss[is]tic tendency," she advised, "don't make a sap of yourself; go to a psychoanal[y]st and let him straighten you out in a reasonably respectable way." His "abnormality," she feared, might be worse than mere foolishness: in an era that knew fascism all too well, wasn't an "over balanced emphasis on submission" dangerously totalitarian? His resurgent spirituality was unappealing to many, and the majority, even at Haverford, turned a jaded eye on the changed Kelly.

Still, several youthful seekers gravitated to him in his remaining years at Haverford. Together they pored over texts ranging from St. Augustine's *Confessions* from the fourth century to the Protestant missionary Frank Laubach's *Letters by a Modern Mystic,* hot off the press in 1937. They also had a special penchant for the French Carmelite Brother Lawrence of the Resurrection (1611–1691) whose *Practice of the Presence of God* inculcated habits of unceasing prayer. Brother Lawrence—like St. Francis, whom Kelly also extolled—was enjoying a renewed vogue as a universal Christian model in these decades, and Protestants happily embraced his spiritual maxims as their own and saw his discipline of adoring God even in the most routine actions of the day as a way to find a sense of divine presence in their own quotidian schedules. With a nod toward his college audience, Kelly specifically exalted youthful striving in his meditation titled "Holy Obedience": "Young people, you who have in you the stirrings of perfection, the sweet, sweet rapture of God Himself within you, be faithful to Him until the last lingering bit of self is surrendered and you are wholly God-possessed." Even as members of the group grandly imagined lives entirely consecrated to God in the spirit of Brother Lawrence and St. Francis, they also found time to listen to Kelly's "recently purchased records of 'Gregorian Chants.'" (There was no need to wait for the 1994 release of *Chant* on Angel Records for the "serene spirit" of Gregorian chant to pique the curiosity of seekers unlikely to frequent the Catholic Mass.) [27]

Though the small group he gathered around him was a kind of bellwether, the source of Kelly's wider emergence as a spiritual paragon was his *Testament of Devotion*. In the outpouring of new books on spirituality between 1930 and 1950, it proved one of the most successful and enduring, regularly praised as among the few perennials on devotional practice produced in the twentieth century. Rufus Jones, with keen affection for his protégé, set the tone in lifting Kelly into "the order of true mystics." "He had been *there* with the key that opens, and he knew experimentally," Jones averred. Given Jones's venerable standing as the dean among American Protestant writers on the spiritual life (he was then closing in on his eightieth birthday), his word counted for a lot. Here was a devotional book, Jones said, that ranked among "the great ones," and Kelly was a genuine peer of the ancient "spiritual guides." [28]

Other commentators soon fell into line. That included the reviewer for the *Christian Century*, who predicted the volume would come to stand "among the few great and undying books of devotion."

And the garish praise lingered. Kelly was already placed, alongside Jones, in the canon of Protestant mystics (stretching all the way back to Martin Luther and John Donne) in a popular collection introduced by the poet W. H. Auden in 1964. A decade later in his autobiography Elton Trueblood, a prodigiously productive writer on the Christian life, hailed Kelly's volume as a "devotional masterpiece"; another Harvard-trained and Haverford-connected Quaker, Trueblood had begun his long and distinguished career with *The Essence of Spiritual Religion* (1936), dedicated to none other than Rufus Matthew Jones. ("We are using spiritual as roughly opposed to *formal, literal, legal, ceremonial, hierarchical, sacerdotal, creedal, material, external, traditional,*" Trueblood explained at the outset of that book in a revealing series of antitheses.) Kelly's impact on the devotional writer Richard J. Foster, whose *Celebration of Discipline* (1978) remains a best-selling title, was similarly pronounced. Kelly's work, Foster claimed in 1992, had "set me free from my own inner clamoring for attention and recognition and applause." A lost soul after the Harvard debacle in 1937, Kelly became—in the eyes of many, at least— "a giant soul," a timeless master of devotional practice, "a Brother Lawrence for our Time."[29]

There were no doubt ageless qualities to Kelly's *Testament of Devotion*, evocative ways in which the spiritual life it presented was resonant with the seventeenth-century Carmelite Brother Lawrence and his practice of continual prayer amid the humdrum labors of a monastery's kitchen. Certainly Douglas Steere, Kelly's initial biographer, and Rufus Jones, his proud teacher, thought it was most important to see Kelly's quest in the light of eternity rather than, say, the immediate crises that engulfed the United States during the Great Depression and World War II. Devotional books and their admirers are always prone to minimizing cultural context, to the downplaying of time and place in order to lay claim to the eternal. Kelly was as given to that gesture as anyone, invariably imagining himself as grasping for the timelessly Real beyond the minutely particular. Those calling his book a "classic" were, in effect, diverting attention from the present in order to establish capital-P Presence, a theological ploy (or affirmation) designed to lift devotional books—and spirituality generally—above the limits of culture and history. *A Testament of Devotion* was taken to be compelling as a witness to everlasting practices of piety, a simple reiteration of tried and true methods of prayer, at the very heart of Christianity or even religion *tout court*.

Kelly's little book, though, is better read with his immediate world left in rather than left out. He was all too clearly a frail and flailing man of his time, a spiritual seeker speaking to other similarly situated seekers about what they lacked and hoped to find. Repeatedly there are passages that sound differently, more sharply edged, when Kelly's own recently relinquished aspirations are kept in mind. "Positions of prominence, eminences of social recognition which we once meant to attain—how puny and trifling they become!" Kelly wrote near the end of the first meditation, employing the deceptive indirection of the first-person plural. "Our old ambitions and heroic dreams—what years we have wasted in feeding our own insatiable self-pride.... Again, we have quailed and been tormented in our obscurity, we have fretted and been anxious because of our limitations, set by our own nature and by our surroundings.... What needless anguishes we have suffered because *our* little selves were defeated, were not flattered, were not cozened and petted." Kelly wanted to help other seekers pry themselves loose from their own false attachments, but he was still hammering on the nails of his own self-renunciation.[30]

In his speaking and writing Kelly had a definite picture of his intended audience—not monks or solitaries, but hurried, well-educated professionals living in the "here and now, in industrial America." Offering no fanciful dreams, but "a serious, concrete program of life," Kelly called for very specific "internal practices and habits of the mind" that allowed for the spiritual life to flourish, even "while we are also very busy in the world of daily affairs." He imagined a perpetual return to the Light Within, to the "Divine Center" of silence and peace, within the workaday world of committees, fitful social engagements, and incessant appointments. "There is a way of ordering our mental life on more than one level at once," he claimed. "On one level we may be thinking, discussing, seeing, calculating, meeting all the demands of external affairs. But deep within, behind the scenes, at a profounder level, we may also be in prayer and adoration, song and worship." Too much about contemporary life, he said, was shallow, clipped, dispersed, and fragmentary: "Each of us tends to be, not a single self, but a whole committee of selves. There is the civic self, the parental self, the financial self, the religious self, the society self, the professional self, the literary self. And each of our selves is in turn a rank individualist," Kelly said, sounding a lot like William James on the problem of serial identities. Given such hectic, divided, complex lives, spiritual techniques of integration were desperately needed. The decentered had to "*center down.*"[31]

Kelly imagined cultivating habits of inward prayer that would create an underlying sense of continuity in lives filled with alternations, lapses, interruptions, and distractions. Required, in his view, was a spiritual discipline that allowed for "serenity, unshakableness, firmness of life-orientation" without encouraging withdrawal from the day-to-day world. "Walk and talk and work and laugh with your friends," Kelly specified. "But behind the scenes, keep up the life of simple prayer and inward worship. Keep it up throughout the day." Kelly, in effect, shifted away from the Transcendentalist emphasis on ephemeral moments of spiritual awareness—"the flickering of our psychic states"—to sustained "inward practices of the mind." Not transient states of mystical consciousness, but continuous, day-to-day habits of devotion—these were Kelly's chief pursuit: "Practice comes first in religion."

Practice was the heart of Kelly's testimony, but how was this "internal continuous prayer life" to be achieved? Like the affirmations popular in New Thought, the mantras available through the Vedanta Society, or the Jesus Prayer increasingly in circulation from Eastern

Orthodox Christianity, Kelly relied especially on the repetition of a single phrase or sentence as a centering technique: "Be Thou my will. Be Thou my will"; "I open all before Thee. I open all before Thee"; "Take all of me, take all of me, take all of me"; or even a line of adoration borrowed from the Upanishads, "O Wonderful, O Wonderful, O Wonderful." Through regular return to the same words of prayer even after hours of forgetting, the discipline would gradually take greater hold of the mind. Slowly the gaps of failing attention would narrow; the alternations would give way to a profound sense of simultaneity and continuity in consciousness. In surrendering the scattered self to this practice one would come ultimately to an experience of being prayed through as much as actively praying. "Learn to live in the passive voice," Kelly advised, "a hard saying for Americans." Then, stillness would replace striving; focus would replace fluctuation; "whole selves" would replace divided ones. All the "agitated, half-committed, wistful, self-placating seekers" would finally discover that "God is the Seeker, and not we alone."[32]

Kelly's newfound emphasis on a spirituality of obedience and self-abnegation looked, at one level, like a challenge to the spiritualized liberalism that he had previously embraced — in much the same way that Sarah Farmer's submission to the Bahá'í faith had a generation earlier. Like Farmer, though, Kelly was not renouncing his liberal ideals as much as critically engaging their own internal tensions. Liberal religion cherished the quest for autonomy *and* feelings of dependence upon God; it simultaneously valued mystical experience *and* social reform, a spirituality of individual epiphanies *and* a progressive gospel of institutional transformation, solitude *and* society. Playing upon such tensions, working back and forth between them, worrying that one or the other had the upper hand, was a major part of what it meant to be a religious progressive in the first half of the twentieth century. Come hell or high water, the double affirmation of the Inner Light within each individual and the obligations of the beloved community had to be maintained.

Always sensitive to "fevered strain," Kelly displayed a good intuitive grasp of such pressure points. "Our religious heroes of these social gospel days," he remarked, "sit before a battery of telephones, with full office equipment, with telegraph lines to Washington and London and Tokyo and Berlin. And this is needed, desperately needed." Active in the American Friends Service Committee—indeed, transformed by that engagement—Kelly was hardly going to disavow the social gospel in "an epoch of tragic sorrows." But he also knew the rhetorical power of sharply contrasting the bustling extroversion of social activists and church bureaucrats with the other side of liberalism, its "glorious yearning" to cultivate the inward life of the spirit. Spiritual growth meant entering through prayer into the depths of "serene, unhurried calm"—a psychic space that, in turn, provided the needed counterweight to the "intolerable scramble," "absurdly crowded calendars," and undue "busyness for the Kingdom of God." "Has the Nietzschean ideal of the superman, with heroic, world-striding power, hypnotized the church into an over-activistic attitude?" Kelly queried. Yet, like Rufus Jones, Howard Thurman, and just about every other liberal Protestant writer on the spiritual life, Kelly continued to insist on a larger coherence: "The straightest road to [the] social gospel runs through profound mystical experience. The paradox of true mysticism is that individual experience leads to social passion.... If we seek a social gospel, we must find it most deeply rooted in the mystic way."[33]

Kelly was only one seeker in a world, as he liked to say, now filled with seekers, and his work, posthumously at least, would be joined to a much more eclectic band of aspirants. In early 1941, at age forty-seven, Kelly suffered a sudden and massive heart attack one evening at home while doing the dishes, orphaning his young children as well as his student disciples. Despite the shock of his death, Kelly's little order at Haverford kept meeting in Lael Kelly's home. It was later that year that the recently immigrated novelist, screenwriter, and autobiographer Christopher Isherwood (1904–1986) frequently joined

Thomas Kelly poses with his family not long before his death in 1941. The novelist and religious seeker Christopher Isherwood, who wound up at Haverford shortly after Kelly died, found life in the suburbs with the Quakers too much centered on home and family. (Haverford College Library, Haverford, Pennsylvania: Quaker Collection, Thomas R. Kelly Papers, Coll. no. 1135.)

the group. A close friend of W. H. Auden and Aldous Huxley, Isherwood had already published *Mr. Norris Changes Trains* (1935) and *Goodbye to Berlin* (1939), stories that had brought him critical acclaim and subsequently gave him popular fame through the musical adaptation *Cabaret*.

A spiritual seeker as much as a literary savant, Isherwood was a follower of Swami Prabhavananda (1893–1976), founder of the Vedanta Society of Southern California in Hollywood in 1929. Prabhavananda had formally initiated Isherwood into Vedanta—with practices of meditation, prayer, and floral offerings—in a ceremony in November 1940. The next October Isherwood headed to Haverford to work for a year with a Quaker-led refugee program, the Cooperative College Workshop, devoted especially to resettling German Jews. Just before heading East, he had participated in a freewheeling summer seminar, sponsored by the American Friends Service Committee in La Verne, California, twenty miles east of Los Angeles, on "the relative merits of the two ways of life, 'active' and 'contemplative.'" Along with three sessions daily of meditation and silence, the monthlong seminar featured group discussions of various medieval and modern guides to the spiritual life. On the docket was Kelly's just published *Testament of Devotion*.[34]

Though Isherwood closely identified with the social vision, pacifist witness, and seeker spirituality within the Society of Friends, he never felt fully at home among the comparatively demure Quakers. Openly gay, he had found religious acceptance among fellow Vedantists in Southern California, especially from Swami Prabhavananda, who effectively provided Isherwood with "a brand-new vocabulary" for the spiritual life distant from the Christian sexual taboos familiar from his British upbringing. When stammering out the question to the Swami—"Can I lead a spiritual life as long as I'm having a sexual relationship with a young man?"—Isherwood had "feared a blast of icy puritanism." Instead, he experienced reassurance and loving guidance. "From that moment on," Isherwood wrote, "I began to understand that the Swami did not think in terms of sins, as most Christians do. Certainly, he regarded my lust for Vernon as an obstacle to my spiritual progress—but no more and no less of an obstacle than lust for a woman, even for a lawfully wedded wife, would have been."

In his time at Haverford, by contrast, Isherwood felt compelled to closet his homosexuality, though he still occasionally hooked up at a safe remove from suburban "Quakerdom" at bars in downtown Philadelphia. Having corresponded with the Swami about the possibility of being a follower of both Ramakrishna and George Fox, he soon dispensed with that idea mostly on the grounds of Quaker propriety and "provincialism." "I can't belong to a religious group," he concluded, "which would be shocked by even many comparatively innocent features of my private life—by my novels, by the conversation of my friends, by my literary and artistic tastes." Isherwood came to have special disdain for Kelly's colleague Douglas Steere as an embodiment of the prim, middle-class, heterosexual piety he had long ago rejected. Granted Steere is "a good speaker, and awfully glib about Christ's love, passion, death, etc.," Isherwood confided to his diary, "but it just doesn't have any teeth in it. One looks at his wife and his job and his nice little house, and says, 'Oh yeah?'" After one lunch meeting with Steere, Isherwood was even more caustic about the twinned blessing of spiritual dedication and heterosexual desire, the blending of mystical transcendence and tame monogamy, that he found among the Quakers: "There's something greasy about him," Isherwood groused about Steere. "He acts so monklike, and all the time one knows he's having sex with his wife hard — but somehow not quite hard enough."[35]

The Quaker devotion to "the values of family life" notwithstanding, Isherwood made his way into Kelly's tiny fellowship of would-be mystics as well as to the Pendle Hill retreat center. Later he would famously chronicle his journey into Vedanta and his own dedication to Swami Prabhavananda in *My Guru and His Disciple* (1980), but in 1941 he ironically saw the college students as a little too devoted to Kelly — as if he had given them "the exclusive lowdown on the spiritual life" and Rufus Jones was just "an old dope." (Isherwood, who admired Jones as a speaker and writer, felt some defensiveness for the aged Quaker's reputation — as surely Kelly would have, too; Jones, having previously met Isherwood, warmly received him at Haverford "like an old friend.") Despite the students' hallowing of Kelly at the expense of Jones, Isherwood found this little order of Quaker mystics congenial to his own seeking. "We bring books with us, sit silent for quite long spells, then read aloud, discuss a little. I quite enjoy it," he wrote in his diary. In a flourish that suggested again how easy it was for spiritual seekers to dwell on similarity at the expense of difference, Isherwood concluded of his meditations in Kelly's group: "There is no reason why you can't equate the Quaker Inner Light with the Hindu Atman."[36]

The spread of an eclectic, seeking spirituality was borne outward through those sorts of rippling effects that connected Jones to Kelly to Isherwood. The same circulatory patterns were evident in the word getting around about Kelly's turn to devotional writing after his spiritual awakening. With a series of overlapping contacts—Douglas Steere, Rufus Jones, and Elton Trueblood among them—the religion editor at Harper and Row, Eugene Exman, soon caught wind of Kelly's latest meditations and wrote to solicit them. When Kelly submitted drafts of the religious talks that would form the basis of *A Testament of Devotion,* he got a different kind of response from Exman than he had expected: "I have been moved much by what you have written here," Exman wrote. "I've been [led] recently to enlarge my own spirituality so you were speaking not to an editor, perhaps, as much as to a fellow seeker.... A few of us who have lighted a torch from Gerald Heard are to meet in N.Y. regularly—a kind of 'Beloved Community.'" The self-description Exman provided Kelly was both evocative and appropriate—one seeker responding to another seeker. A publisher of a raft of books on spirituality, Exman had been one of the participants, with Isherwood, in the La Verne seminar. He would later help put together, with Steere and others, a small chronicle called *Search for Meaning,* done in honor of Louise Mendenhall, a prominent member of the very group of seekers whom Exman had commended to Kelly as a blessed fellowship. A convert to Jones's mystical version of the Society of Friends and herself a careful reader of Kelly's *Testament of Devotion,* Mendenhall was "best described," Exman said in his opening line, "as a seeker."[37]

The immediate inspiration for the group in which Mendenhall and Exman participated was the hybrid Quaker-Vedantist Gerald Heard (1889–1971), a Cambridge-educated intellectual renowned for his grand speculations on the social and psychological evolution of humanity. Joining Huxley in migrating to Southern California and followed there by Isherwood, Heard came to see practices of concentration and meditation as integral techniques for the forward development of a higher human consciousness. Engaged in "his own drastic program of self-preparation," as Isherwood described it, Heard meditated for six hours a day in three two-hour blocks, morning, noon, and evening, and also practiced celibacy. A participant at Pendle Hill as pilgrim and lecturer in the late 1930s, Heard served for several years on the editorial board of its devotional magazine, *Inward Light,* a compendium of how-to advice on the spiritual disciplines of prayer, meditation, silence, study, and retreat. Heard also knew about Kelly's quest and spoke excitedly about him with both Isherwood and Steere; he shared with Kelly a deep affection for Brother Lawrence, whose *Practice of the Presence of God* Heard lifted up at length in the pages of *Vedanta and the West.* Another of Exman's authors, Heard explicitly presented his pieces on devotional practice, including *Training for the Life of the Spirit* (1941) and *Prayers and Meditations* (1949), as "hints to other seekers."[38]

Heard's writings on religion attracted many inquirers in this period, one of whom carried especially large consequence for the further development of the literature on the spiritual quest: namely, the scholar Huston Smith, a primary architect of the twentieth century's own version of transcendental cosmopolitanism. Born in China in 1919 to American missionary parents, Huston Smith landed at Central Methodist College in Missouri before ending up in graduate school at the University of Chicago in the early 1940s. Spending a year at Berkeley in 1944–1945, still laboring on his dissertation, working within the intellectual bounds of scientific naturalism, Smith happened on one of Heard's volumes, "the first book on mysticism I had ever encountered." It occasioned an "unforgettable night" of intellectual transformation (he whimsically compared the event, in one autobiographical fragment, to his wedding night):

From its opening page, that book took me over, and I found that from the soles of my feet all the way up, I was saying "Yes! This is the way things are!" As for my scientific worldview, which I had

been so gung-ho for, it collapsed that night like a house of cards.
So I crossed the frontier into mysticism.

After that revelatory night in which Heard "converted me," Smith pledged "to read everything this man had written. I kept that vow— about twenty-five books." Soon deciding he had to meet Heard in person, he hitchhiked to Southern California, and the two sat together in silent meditation. Heard also put him in touch with Huxley, who, in turn, directed him to the Vedanta Society. In particular, Huxley pointed him to Swami Satprakashananda, a guru in St. Louis, where Smith, then in his late twenties, was about to start his own career teaching classes on "World Religions" at Washington University.

So began Smith's spiritual search, first augmenting his Methodist Christianity with a decade of instruction in Vedanta, then journeying on to D. T. Suzuki's Zen Buddhism, and from there to Rumi's Sufism, "each adding immeasurably to my religious understanding." Also through the influence of Heard and Huxley, Smith came to experiment with "psychedelic substances" as potential pathways to religious experience, becoming a pioneer in that area of inquiry at MIT in the early 1960s (alongside Timothy Leary at Harvard). Like Huxley as well, Smith "crossed the frontier to the tribal, indigenous peoples and their religious outlook," eventually emerging as an arch-defender of Native American religious freedom. Long before Smith ended up on PBS with Bill Moyers in the 1990s and emerged as an archetype of the American scholar as seer of the infinite, he was a youthful member of the seeker culture of the 1940s, which Heard, Huxley, Isherwood, Jones, and Kelly had helped build. Through these diffuse yet ever widening religious and literary circles, the self-conscious seeker as a modern religious type came into its own.[39]

The social networks, publishing ventures, conference gatherings, and community-building efforts were all coming together to support a wider culture of spiritual seeking by the 1930s and 1940s. That was particularly evident in a handful of experimental retreats, designed, as

Greenacre had been in the 1890s, more for religious wayfarers than devout communicants of a given denominational tradition. In 1939 Gerald Heard had glimpsed in the Quaker example of Pendle Hill a "mutation" in education and spiritual development that was worth emulating and spreading. Two years later he founded his own parallel retreat, known as Trabuco, on three hundred acres in a canyon sixty miles south of Los Angeles. Though it is hard now to imagine any part of California between San Diego and Los Angeles as isolated, Trabuco was intentionally remote. "There is something weird about the emptiness of these south California uplands," Isherwood observed. "Those creeks are uncontaminated by human nostalgia, unviolated by Longfellow's pen or Thoreau's boot," he continued. "Trabuco is not a place on the map. It is a hole in it."

For Heard, Huxley, Isherwood, and other wayfarers involved in founding this latest "club for mystics," Trabuco was imagined as an experimental "college of the spiritual life." Meditation and prayer

Christopher Isherwood, pictured here about 1950, was among a formative group of spiritual inquirers in Los Angeles that included Gerald Heard and Aldous Huxley. (Bill Caskey, Photo of C. Isherwood, CI 3145. Reproduced by permission of The Huntington Library, San Marino, California.)

were to form its core curriculum, and practice was to predominate over theory. Not a monastery or ashram, Isherwood insisted, Trabuco was instead an "organically democratic" gathering of colleagues dedicated to "the hardest work there is," "a deliberately rationed life" in the pursuit of mystical awakening. No free-riders, no idlers, no gossip-mongering journalists, no children, but also no masters or dogmatists—only the seriously absorbed could join this association of seekers. "Perhaps," Isherwood wrote playfully in September 1942, "we should have done best to call the place: 'The Southern California Branch of the Non-Sectarian Society for the Practice and Study of Mysticism.'"

Eclectic in its design, Trabuco breathed Heard's cosmopolitan interests in mysticism, yoga, and meditation as well as Huxley's *Perennial Philosophy* (1944). An enduringly popular anthology that mapped the contours of a universal and timeless spirituality, Huxley's book joined Heard's retreat as a leading emblem of the spiritual ferment that these émigré writers were helping create in and around Los Angeles. "A small resident community at Trabuco has been almost constantly host to a procession of earnest seekers," Douglas Steere reported in *Time to Spare* (1949), a book designed to codify the new-fangled retreat movement of the 1930s and 1940s. It had been to Trabuco that the young Huston Smith hitchhiked in 1947 to meditate with Heard in the seclusion of his canyon hideout. And it had been there, too, that Steere headed for inspiration. A major architect of the Quaker renewal at Haverford and Pendle Hill, Steere went to California in 1942 to explore Heard's contemplative methods firsthand. Returning to lead a retreat at Trabuco in 1944, Steere came to see the eclectic, bohemian, intellectually voracious Heard as one of his most important spiritual advisers. Typically, the two men joined as well in another Quaker-inspired venture in these years, the Conference on the Nature and Laws of Our Spiritual Life, an association that met annually to explore, among other things, the interplay between the psychology of Carl Jung and the modern quest for spiritual meaning.[40]

Heard's mystic club proved a relatively short-lived experiment—

at least, as an independent college of prayer. Trabuco's buildings soon passed into the hands of the Vedanta Society and eventually formed the basis of a thriving monastery for that group. The Quaker mutation that had helped inspire Trabuco, though, hewed a steadier course. Through the decades the Pendle Hill retreat center in Wallingford, Pennsylvania, has remained a connecting thread in the weaving of an ecumenical and activist spirituality—one that has pulled together, among other strands, the mystical Quakerism of Rufus Jones, the contemplative Catholicism of Thomas Merton, and the prophetic witness of Mohandas Gandhi. A leading contemporary writer on contemplative practice, Parker J. Palmer recently remarked that Pendle Hill has served over the years as "a commune, an ashram, a monastery, a zendo, a kibbutz," all in one. (Palmer himself presents a fascinating biography not unlike Kelly's as an alienated academic turned Quaker seeker, a Berkeley-trained sociologist turned community organizer and spiritual guide. Like Kelly, too, he is preoccupied with bringing wholeness to divided lives, his own and others, through integrating practices of prayer and meditation.) After abandoning professional sociology, Palmer spent a formative decade at Pendle Hill as its dean of studies: "Whatever one calls it, Pendle Hill was a life unlike anything I had ever known." Pendle Hill, a cooperative venture of the 1930s to which Jones, Kelly, Heard, and Steere each devoted their time, stands as an enduring bridge, directly connecting contemporary seekers to their early-twentieth-century counterparts.[41]

A spirituality of seeking grew luxuriantly in American culture in the century after Emerson's self-portrait as an "endless seeker." By the time of his death in 1948, Rufus Jones had lived long enough to see his outlandish reveries on seventeenth-century "Seekers" as paragons of the modern quest for God open up many unanticipated paths. Self-proclaimed seekers were cropping up all over the place—often far beyond the reach of Jones's own Society of Friends. In *My Guru and His Disciple,* Christopher Isherwood wrote of the abounding number of "Seekers" whom he met in the 1940s:

There was also an assortment of men and women whom I will call "Seekers," because many of them would have so described themselves. I met them through Gerald [Heard], who had now become a central figure in their circles, not only in Los Angeles, but throughout the country.... [H]is mail was enormous and urgent. "It's funny," I once said to him, "how these people invariably write to you airmail special delivery, when all their questions are about eternity."

Some of the Seekers had unquestionable integrity and courage—even perhaps saintliness: a man who had become a clergyman because he had had a vision of Christ when he was fighting in World War I, a Japanese who had been persecuted by his countrymen for his pacifism, an ex-burglar who had practiced mental nonviolence while being beaten up by prison guards. As for the rest, many might have been called cranks but almost none of them fakes.

"What was I looking for, amidst these people? What made me sit through their lectures and join them in hours of earnest discussion?" Isherwood asked himself. It was, above all, his kinship with them as a fellow seeker.[42]

That fellowship of seekers, as Kelly had dreamed, could make for good company and even beloved community. Growing up under segregationist rule in Florida, Howard Thurman (1900–1981) went on to Atlanta, Rochester, and Oberlin before his "watershed" experience at Haverford. Having happened upon one of Rufus Jones's books at a church sale in Oberlin for a dime, Thurman was transfixed and resolved that "if this man were alive, I wanted to study with him." Finding out that Jones was still actively teaching, Thurman wrote him to see if some kind of independent work would be possible, and Jones immediately welcomed the idea. Once at Haverford, Thurman came to love Jones for his informality, whimsy, and lack of presumption, his ability to open "before my mind a stretch of road down which I was invited but never urged to travel." Sharing Jones's twin passions for mysticism and social activism, Thurman set out to enact his teacher's "vital religion"—one that "knew no boundaries of nation, race, denomination, or religion." Years later, writing in his autobiography, he still considered it "an enigma" how Jones had "transcended race" in their relationship and allowed him to be an equal as a philosophical seeker in the "field of mystical religion." That was no mean feat. As Kelly confessed at one point of his own inadequacies as a white liberal, he was "distressed" at how "few real personal friends" he had "among the Negroes." Only when genuine interracial solidarity was achieved—and it seemed a long way off in 1940, even for most Quakers—could American Christians speak with any integrity of the leveling love of the gospel: "Then Christ walks on the streets again."[43]

Always eloquent about the disciplines of the spirit, Thurman invoked a "Divine Presence" in which "there is neither male nor female, White nor Black, Gentile nor Jew, Protestant nor Catholic, Hindu,

Howard Thurman, cofounder of the Church for the Fellowship of All Peoples in San Francisco, was a leading visionary of an Inner Light spirituality of racial inclusion and social justice. (Boston University Photo Services.)

Buddhist, nor Moslem, but a human spirit stripped to the literal substance of itself." Working out his interreligious and interracial vision as pastor of the Church for the Fellowship of All Peoples in San Francisco in the 1940s, Thurman helped give consummate form to the grandest dreams of liberalism's cosmopolitan spirituality. Invariably pressing hard on the distinction between the religion of Jesus and institutionalized Christianity, Thurman had emerged by the end of the decade as a leading prophet of a justice-delivering, segregation-ending, dignity-advancing spirituality. That standing was embodied especially in his *Jesus and the Disinherited* (1949), a book that served as an inspiration to Martin Luther King Jr. and the larger civil rights movement. Like Higginson and Du Bois before him, Thurman knew the slave spirituals, the Sorrow Songs, as the timbrels of suffering, resistance, and hope: "I know moon-rise, I know star-rise, / I lay this body down. / ...I lie in the grave and stretch out my arms, / To lay this body down."

All along, too, there remained a strong Quaker element of prayer, silence, meditation, and nonviolence in Thurman's work. He would provide, in many ways, the fullest expression of a progressive spirituality that combined work and contemplation, solitary retreat and thriving community, spiritual seeking and social reconciliation. On matters of race especially, but certainly not only on matters of the color line, Thurman represented a crucial advance on the liberal, democratic spiritualities of Walt Whitman and Rufus Jones. "If there was a metaphor that was central to Howard Thurman's being it was The Journey," the writer Sam Keen said in memorializing him. "The human spirit is a pilgrim; it is only at home on the road. When we met and talked we swapped lore, tales of the road, descriptions of the territories of the spirit we had passed through since our last meeting. And we wondered what was ahead." Most seekers fell well short of Thurman's vision of the journey—or of Thomas Kelly's, for that matter. Still, if there were plenty of cranks, as Isherwood suggested, there were few fakes and, every once in a while, a saint.[44]

EPILOGUE

BE GENTLE WITH
YOURSELF

N *Habits of the Heart* (1985), a national best seller on how
American individualism had "grown cancerous" and was laying waste to the country's civic institutions and religious traditions, the sociologist Robert Bellah and his coauthors famously
lamented "liberalized versions" of morality and spirituality. The over-
blown ideals of self-reliance and self-expression were seriously under-
mining the welfare of community, family, and congregation. "Finding
oneself" and "leaving church," from their perspective as public philosophers, had increasingly become complementary processes in contemporary American culture. They pointed to the self-accepting credo of
"one ecology activist," the Unitarian Cassie Cromwell, as a leading
exhibit of "liberalized religion's relaxed sense of duty, authority, and
virtue":

> *BE GENTLE WITH YOURSELF. You are a child of the Universe*
> *no less than the trees and the stars.... [B]e at peace with God,*
> *whatever you conceive Him to be. And whatever your labors and*

aspirations, in the noisy confusion of life, keep peace in your soul.
With all its sham, drudgery and broken dreams, it is still a beautiful
world.

"Here," Bellah and his collaborators chided, "the self as metaphoric child echoes ecology, aestheticism, and nature mysticism, not biblical revelation." Thanks to Emerson, Whitman, and their too numerous progeny, religion in American culture had slowly been narrowed to little more than "a frame of reference for the self."[1]

Cassie Cromwell, environmentalist and Unitarian, was bad enough, but then there was that truly unfortunate "young nurse," Sheila Larson, who had (the reader is told up front) "received a good deal of therapy." In a moment of misplaced trust and whimsy, Larson had revealed to the researchers that she had named her faith after herself: "It's Sheilaism. Just my own little voice." No one in the book became a more oft-cited example of what had gone wrong with American religion and culture than Larson, and *Sheilaism* quickly emerged as a byword in conservative commentaries for modern self-doting run amok, "the dead end of radical individualism." The Bellah group, made up of clearheaded academics of high repute, suddenly mutated into an ecclesial court, even closing the discussion of Larson with an over-the-top gesture of thinly veiled aggression: "How did we get from the point where Anne Hutchinson, a seventeenth-century precursor of Sheila Larson's, could be run out of the Massachusetts Bay Colony to a situation where Anne Hutchinson is close to the norm?"

What was the spiritual dissent that Bellah and company wanted so much to redirect, if not chill? "It's just try to love yourself and be gentle with yourself," Larson explains of her faith. "You know, I guess, take care of each other. I think He would want us to take care of each other." Surely, the problem here is not the vocational ethic of service and compassion that Larson articulates. One of her most important religious experiences is an intimation of seeing Jesus in the mirror when she is caring for a dying woman whose husband is unable himself to deal with the suffering of his wife's last hours. And, surely, the problem is not her avowal of religious tolerance or the strength that she has drawn from her spirituality: "I'm not a religious fanatic.... My faith has carried me a long way," Larson relates. The harsh criticism must have been directed instead at those little words that had already been capitalized in Cassie Cromwell's indicted and unidentified credo: "Be gentle with yourself."[2]

Strange how much concern the faith of these two women caused these public-minded scholars. Who would have thought that the "cosmic mysticism," "nature pantheism," and "expressive individualism" of Emerson, the Transcendentalists, and their heirs could have become this corrosive and threatening? Strange as well that two of the leading embodiments of "liberalized religion" in *Habits of the Heart* were caught with the same spiritual motto upon their lips: "Be gentle with yourself." The authors, as public philosophers rather than historians, did not explore the source of that self-soothing dictum or any framework for it beyond the triumph of therapeutic individualism. Placing that affirmation (and, by extension, the piety of Cassie Cromwell and Sheila Larson) in a larger context reveals the stunted quality of so much cultural criticism of contemporary American spirituality—as if the only reason to examine it is to have our worst fears about American religious and civic life confirmed. It should be clear by now that the nexus of spirituality and liberalism made for social and religious worlds far more creative than such thin readings of "romantic individualism," "the mystical quest," "solitude without community," and "Sheilaism" allow.[3]

The little credo to which Cassie Cromwell referred in full and Sheila Larson in a one-line snippet comes from the poetry of Max Ehrmann (1872–1945), specifically a small piece of his called "Desiderata," which he first published in 1927. Like the Quaker seeker Thomas Kelly, Ehrmann was a midwestern youth from a small church-affiliated college who had headed to Harvard as a graduate student to study philosophy. Arriving in Cambridge in the heady days of the 1890s,

Ehrmann enjoyed late-night, pipe-smoking bull sessions with his fellow students and recast himself as something of a literary bohemian. With a youthful zest for the life of the mind, he worked with such luminaries as William James, Josiah Royce, and the young George Santayana, a philosopher whose artistic ambitions helped fuel Ehrmann's own. Through the New England world of metaphysical clubs and literary salons, he even struck up an acquaintance with the elderly Thomas Wentworth Higginson, who was flattered that this energetic young man took such an interest in "us oldsters in Cambridge" and who subsequently praised Ehrmann's poems as "strong sermons" that "ought to live."[4]

After Harvard, Ehrmann dutifully returned home to Terre Haute, Indiana, where he often held court with the professors at the state university and tried to eke out a precarious living as a writer. His early literary efforts, two novels issued at the turn of the century, quickly fizzled, and his three plays published in the 1910s—one of them a Passion play "stripped of supernatural embellishment"—did little better. A bachelor struggling to keep financially afloat, he decided to grind out a career in law and business, even as his love of poetry kept him from flagging. As he wrote in his journal in March 1931, "For ten years I worked in the office of a large factory, where, had it not been for some enterprise of the mind in leisure hours, I could not have lived. During these years I wrote a book of poems out of the thoughts and feelings of my experience. Each night I washed my soul." His two-year stint as a deputy state's attorney was not much better: "Often after closing the office at night, I opened all the windows, burned incense, and read Emerson," he commented on how he saved himself from feelings of quiet desperation. Far from providing evidence for the vapidity of therapeutic piety and the emptiness of "liberalized" religion, Ehrmann's pursuit of the spiritual life bring the critics of Sheilaism up short. His example is a good condensation—an illuminating way to move toward a final estimate of this American-made spirituality of losing, seeking, and occasionally finding.[5]

Admittedly, Ehrmann did his reputation no favors in producing a fair amount of saccharine poetry and blithe religious verse. His reputation as a reassuring poet-priest was actually established early on through a chance crime in 1904. A "daring souvenir 'fiend'" stole a framed copy of his prose poem "A Prayer" from the display in the Indiana building of the St. Louis World's Fair, and the national press (as well as Ehrmann's publisher) ran with the story: of all things, a thief who would steal a prayer! The text of "The Stolen Prayer" was then widely reprinted and gave Ehrmann an unusual break into pop-culture circulation. With its gentle tones of encouragement, Ehrmann's "Prayer" proved his biggest hit before the "Desiderata":

> *If the darkened hours of despair overcome me, may I not forget*
> *the strength that comforted me in the desolation of other times.*
> *May I still remember the bright hours that found me walking over*
> *the silent hills of my childhood, or dreaming on the margin of the*
> *quiet river, when a light glowed within me, and I promised my*
> *early God to have courage amid the tempests of the changing*
> *years.... May I not forget that poverty and riches are of the spirit,*
> *though the world know me not.*

Hardly the route to literary recognition that Ehrmann would have chosen, he was launched to some renown on the wings of "A Prayer"—and a petty theft.[6]

Trying to make his way in a middlebrow literary culture and desperate to save himself from the factory and the law office, Ehrmann was eager to earn some money where he could with his poetry. He happily turned "A Prayer" as well as some other pieces into decorative cards and ornamental wall hangings (advertisements for both kinds of trinkets already appeared in an early collection of his poems in 1906). He also struck up a relationship with the Dodge Publishing Company in New York, which proved a particularly assiduous promoter of Ehrmann as an inspirational writer, "a soul that seeks to scatter sunshine." It was not long before some of his religious writing, especially "A Prayer" and "Desiderata," entered a netherworld of ceaseless reproduction similar to the fate of the theologian Reinhold Niebuhr's "Serenity Prayer": "God, give us grace to accept with serenity the things that cannot be changed, courage to change the things that should be changed, and the wisdom to distinguish the one from the other." As with Niebuhr's equally famous prayer, spurious legends about origins and authorship soon began circulating about Ehrmann's "Desiderata," especially an attribution of it to a seventeenth-century Anglican source. And, like Niebuhr's prayer, Ehrmann's prose poem appeared on posters, plaques, and samplers as a venerable embodiment of wisdom about spiritual peace, calm, and fortitude.[7]

In the early 1960s the "Desiderata" got an added boost of acclaim when journalistic word spread of the statesman Adlai Stevenson's affection for it at the end of his life, and then its popularity really took

The Dodge Publishing Company produced various flyers like this one to promote Max Ehrmann as an inspirational writer early in the twentieth century. (Archives and Special Collections, DePauw University, Greencastle, Indiana.)

off in the 1970s. It was made the sole subject of a Protestant book of sermons and meditations in 1975, a pretty good indication that it had taken on the aura of a homespun American scripture. It also became popular music through Les Crane's Grammy-winning album of the same name, sharing the limelight with songs inspired by Thoreau's *Walden* as well as by Native American poetry. With its pop-culture cachet mounting, the poem-turned-song invited satire as well, which it richly received through the *National Lampoon.* Tony Hendra, later of *Spinal Tap* fame, skewered it in his piece "Deteriorata" in 1972 with the chorus "You are a fluke of the universe." (Though Hendra has recently tried his own hand at spiritual consolation with his soul-saving memoir *Father Joe,* he countered the "Desiderata" only with sardonic disillusionment: "Be assured a walk through the ocean of most souls would scarcely get your feet wet.") By the 1990s, Ehrmann's poems were circulating primarily in mass-market editions — *The Desiderata of Love, The Desiderata of Faith,* and the like. These curios now even included winsome little drawings of bouquets, clouds, feathers, and hearts stenciled around his words to set the mood. Under auspices like these Ehrmann's poems continue to offer solace and wisdom; as one of the latest incarnations of the "Desiderata" puts it, Ehrmann provides a "survival guide for life" in the twenty-first century. He reassures more people now than he ever did in his own lifetime.[8]

Ehrmann was certainly a poet of consolation and self-composure, but that singular promotional rendering nonetheless constituted a narrow reduction of his spiritual life. "Do not think I am one who would cover with sweet speech the tragedies of life," he wrote in an early series of poems he grouped under the title "Confessional." "Hope has died in me a thousand times. I walked out in youth with Christ in my soul and was crucified at the first crossing." Just as Cassie Cromwell and Sheila Larson appeared more serious about their religious faith than Bellah and company allowed, Ehrmann's spirituality was not fluff. His journey was one of lost faith, prolonged introspection, fleeting religious experience, and abiding civic engagement.[9]

Max Ehrmann posed with wall-mounted copies of "A Prayer" and "Desiderata" at his alma mater in 1945. (Archives and Special Collections, DePauw University, Greencastle, Indiana.)

Ehrmann grew up in a German Methodist family, the son of first-generation immigrants who were refugees from the revolutionary convulsions that shook Europe in 1848. His parents were regular churchgoers, and he remembered family prayer, Sunday school, and his childhood minister with affection—and nostalgia. Recalling the earnest words of the pastor—"I want you boys to think of Jesus every day—this week, next week, next month, all your lives!"—Ehrmann remarked that he had long tried "to obey the minister's words." He closed this diary recollection, though, with a distancing, ironic query: "I wonder—are there still little boys who try to please Jesus?" He began journaling at the height of World War I, and it was, in large part, an effort to console himself in a universe that seemed increasingly brutish, soulless, and chaotic. In 1918, he confided: "Some of the fundamental beliefs of my life have been shattered by the war. Now I know that the God of my youth—the romantic, all-powerful, loving-father God, sitting in the heavens like a huge plaster cast of Michelangelo's Moses, sending rewards to the good and punishing the evil—now we know that such a god never lived."[10]

Like the journeys of Emerson, Higginson, and Farmer, Ehrmann's search began with a deepening alienation from Protestant Christianity that led him to seek a ground for religion beyond the institutional church. His estrangement carried him into a spirituality that, by now, should sound familiar in its contours: the yearning for mystical experience (especially through immersion in the outdoors), the longing for solitude and serene meditation, the open-minded eclecticism that invited both questioning and questing, the joining of artistic creativity and religious exploration, and the ethical earnestness that pushed for progressive social reforms. "Mysticism," Ehrmann intuited in a passage in his diary from 1933 that could just as easily have been uttered at the Transcendental Club in the 1830s, "might have better standing, if it could divorce itself from all the world-wide, theological paraphernalia.... The Absolute—the absolute truth—still is hidden behind a thousand walls."[11]

Ehrmann's own experience of the transcendent buzzed with William James's indefinite mystical aspirations. A feeling of spiritual connection came through the "quiet voice" discerned in Quaker silence or the solitary Thoreau-like epiphany of "God painting on the sky-curtain of the softening dark." "I need no bibles of old revelation," he wrote with a typically Whitmanesque flourish. The experiential dimensions of Ehrmann's spirituality were evident in his diary entry for April 5, 1927:

> *I have just returned from a long, solitary walk and am ravished by the infinite beauty of the starry night. Astronomy can explain this and that, but what has it to say of this diffused, indefinite exaltation that now floods the centers of my mental life? These strange emotions come to me less frequently as the years pass. What is this indescribable beauty of the night, this diamond-studded, tender*

gauze stretched over the heavens? If all the world is illusion, yet
surely what I now feel may have some reality, some otherworldly
significance.

Ehrmann held to a spiritual perspective on the world through a mysticism of natural beauty, deep feeling, lonely repose, and resurrected enchantment. Fleeting moments of awe and serenity kept meaninglessness and alienation from dominating him, though they hardly eliminated his nihilistic suspicions.[12]

Through the steadying practices of journal writing, meditation, and solitary walks, Ehrmann was looking for inner quietude and self-knowledge. His "Desiderata," which he actually wrote as a personal guide to "those virtues I felt myself most in need of," opened with the imperative: "Go placidly amid the noise and haste, and remember what peace there may be in silence." The distracting din of machinery and marketplace caused recurrent alarm in his diary: "Noise is making city dwellers a race of maniacs. Even the rural districts are not wholly exempt, for motors and tractors plow and reap, and airships help to murder silence. The bronze paperweight Buddha on my table sits with sweet unconcern." Leaving the poet's desk with its bronze Buddha and the "mob-life" of the city, Ehrmann would often spend several days in a nearby forest in a small cabin at Turkey Run; there he could escape "talk of investments" and "academic theorizings" and cultivate instead the "shelterhouse" of the inner life. The search for "inner silence" was not a matter of caprice, but of disciplined effort to overcome "the incessant hurly-burly" and to take "an inventory of the chamber of my soul." The eighteenth-century Quaker John Woolman, who was nothing if not exacting in his pursuit of purity of conscience, served as an exemplar; Ehrmann lifted up Woolman's labors for "an inner Stillness" as a transforming testimony to "the dignity of silence." The poet's twenty years of journaling stands itself as a sustained witness to his own hungering for "soul-calm."[13]

Ehrmann's spiritual seeking led him not only into solitude and silence, but also into an abiding sense of connectedness to place. However diffuse his religious feelings were, they remained decidedly local. As he observed in his journal in March 1922 of his commitment to Terre Haute, Indiana: "It seems good to be here on this spot of earth, not far from where I was born, where I have lived and worked nearly all my life.... I would that all persons might find some such loved spot of earth. It is a spiritual possession no less valuable than solid masonry. To belong somewhere, to be known somewhere, to labor somewhere, to have ties somewhere that the years have endeared—these are not the least among the durable satisfactions of life." Ehrmann hardly offered a spirituality of rootlessness and restlessness, but instead conjured up the solid social ties of the local community and the specific geography of the Wabash. A similar emphasis on place is certainly as noteworthy as unmoored individualism in contemporary American spiritual seeking. It has been evident, time and again, from Gary Snyder's grounding in the Sierra Nevada foothills to Kathleen Norris's dwelling in *Dakota*; it has appeared as well in distinctly local places of a global spirituality such as Sanctuary House in Crestone, Colorado, and the Omega Institute in Rhinebeck, New York. The open road has repeatedly looped back to living communities, revisited shrines, and familiar retreats, grounding wayfarers more than isolating them. Certainly, Ehrmann's own journey led to belonging, not disconnection—to the "spiritual possession" of place.[14]

Bellah and company worried deeply that following out the mystical strain of liberalized spirituality ended in an asocial absorption with nature rather than engagement with the social world, that indeed Cassie Cromwell's ecological activism was part of a flight from social responsibility rather than an indication of virtue and discipline. Cromwell's citing of Ehrmann's "Desiderata" as a summary credo had occasioned not a few of those qualms, but reading even a little bit of Ehrmann's journal would have been a good therapy for those anxieties. Ehrmann was a diehard progressive whose passion for metaphysics was always balanced by critical engagement in political life. For all his spiritual seeking, much of his social vision remained firmly anchored in the Jesus of liberal Protestantism and "the ethical teachings of love, brotherhood, and service." As World War I came to an end, he still dreamed of Jesus overcoming Nietzsche, "the WILL TO SERVICE" ultimately withstanding "the WILL TO POWER." Ehrmann's political commitments were hardly unimpeachable, of course; his pen ran hot with prophetic rage on some issues and sat cold on others. Like so many white progressives of the era, he was far more attuned to economic injustice, corporate corruption, and gender inequity than racism. "In my time I have fought for socialism, woman's suffrage, birth control, and minor forward-looking movements," he noted with due accuracy in 1931, suggesting both the range of his causes and his blind spots.[15]

Of the issues that engaged him, Ehrmann was especially concerned with the improvement of sex education, composing a number of pieces for the cause in the late 1910s and 1920s. With a highly idealized view of sexuality as "a beautiful, spiritual thing," Ehrmann—like Walt Whitman before him—was opposed equally to license and prudery: "Youth wishes the happiness that comprises a full realization of the sex-life. Let us not permit youth to stumble in the dark. Let us light the way, even with our imperfect light. Let us teach youth that the love-life, with all that it comprises, sex included, should be satisfying, beautiful, and sacred." Not that the promotion of progressive views on sex education and birth control was unproblematic: Ehrmann, like other sex reformers of the day, dallied with eugenicist notions of improving the human lot through a more carefully regulated system of "selection." In this era the defense of contraception often ended up being joined to such misbegotten causes as the forced sterilization of criminals and other "defectives." Also, it was easy to catch a whiff of Ehrmann's Methodist upbringing in his vehemence about venereal diseases, prostitution, and "scarlet women," though he actually turned much of that moralism against his natal faith. Christianity, in his view, had "darkened man's love life for nineteen hundred years," perversely substituting "the love of Christ" for "the love for a woman.... We wait for the apotheosis of *human* love." All along, Ehrmann's express allegiance was to the radicals Havelock Ellis (1859–1939) and Margaret Sanger (1879–1966) against the sundry crusaders opposed to obscenity and free speech.[16]

On the economic front, Ehrmann's position was similarly complicated, if no less passionate for social equity and justice. A friend of the socialist hero and union organizer Eugene V. Debs (1855–1926), a neighbor in Terre Haute, Ehrmann repeatedly eulogized him in the press. He saw a profound moral heroism in Debs's work as agitator on behalf of labor and celebrated this "ex-coal shoveler" and "jail bird presidential candidate." "I have seen the scars that the teeth of greed have left upon your flesh. But I have never seen you cringe," Ehrmann wrote of Debs in the pages of the *American Socialist* in 1916. Yet, even in his considerable admiration, Ehrmann distanced himself from some of Debs's radical oratory and admitted to a divergent pair of voices clamoring in his own head—one socialist, one bourgeois. "Write something that will teach economic justice," the one voice insisted, only to be taunted by the other: "Bah! Write something that will pay." Like most of us, Ehrmann was not as consistent or as resolute as he would like to have been.[17]

In his political engagements, the Terre Haute poet always had a double mission. He wanted to stand for social justice, but he also hoped to offer spiritual resources for those who were ready to despair over the slow gains of progressive causes:

> *In the course of these battles, I met some fighters whom life had embittered. But our hatred of injustice ought to be sweetened by the love of justice. One ought not to be fighting all the time. A few miles away from us the fields are green with corn and the wheat is ripening. I have seen sunsets that took all the fight out of me. What is the business of man compared to the affairs of the cosmos! We*

should struggle for the right but there should be hours of respite,
when we cast from our souls the debris and rancor of the world and
receive some mystical calm that, though inarticulate, satisfies.... We
ought not to give up the soap box; but on our way home it is good to
look up at the stars.

Serenity was always fugitive for Ehrmann. The "brutality" of the market, the law office, and the factory ground him down, and he spewed venom at the "mesozoic reptilian economics" that dominated American life. Should Bellah and company have wanted a companion voice for their own critique of America's neocapitalist oligarchy, they would have found one in Ehrmann. No less than they, he was devoted to contemplating "the nature of success, the meaning of freedom, and the requirements of justice in the modern world." Yet, Ehrmann also required practices of unperturbed calm to restore his spirit and maintain a tincture of humanitarian idealism in a chaotic world that demanded tough realism and tempted utter pessimism.[18]

"Be gentle with yourself." Placed within a fuller biographical and historical context, the "Desiderata" hardly seems like a take-it-easy gospel of no worries and no responsibilities. "Today we celebrate again this Fourth of July," Ehrmann commented in his journal in 1933. "True freedom is the fruit of social and individual discipline.... A strong, happy, useful nation is a disciplined nation; disciplined not in the interest of groups, but in the interest of all citizens." Even the "Desiderata" itself fronted the imperative of gentleness with the necessity of discipline. "Be yourself"—Ehrmann's advice was not to lose your inhibitions and forget everyone else, but to cultivate enough self-reflection and interiority that you had an off chance of distinguishing a purposeful and virtuous life from one without genuine affections and high ideals. "Self-reliance is good," Ehrmann told a young artist in a discussion of Emerson's famed essay, "if the *Self* to be relied on is worthy to be relied on." Ehrmann combined romantic individualism with civic virtue, "the colorful multifariousness of the inner life" with a politics of the Left, "the love of the body" with "the love of the soul," art with mysticism, liberty with community. In those confluences Ehrmann represented what was by the 1920s and 1930s a long tradition in which a cosmopolitan spirituality and modern liberalism were mutually sustaining. Though Cassie Cromwell and Sheila Larson spoke in the diction of that long-standing convergence, Bellah and his colleagues only occasionally had the ears to hear its subtler resonances.[19]

The withering critique of "liberalized" spirituality constitutes, by now, its own rich tradition. Already in 1934 Ehrmann had noted with some puzzlement that "an editor in Kansas criticizes my *Desiderata* because it is not socially-minded nor interested in any *cause.*" Twenty years later a critic of the "new look" in American piety found "religious narcissism" everywhere on the horizon, especially evident in the supposed limiting of "religion to 'spiritual' concerns": "The individual and his psycho-spiritual state occupy the center of the religious stage. Here is piety concentrating on its own navel." In *Protestant-Catholic-Jew* (1955), a much heralded sociological analysis of American religion in its own day, Will Herberg worried about the "almost lascivious preoccupation with self" in the feel-good spirituality of the time. That self-centeredness produced a piety "so empty and contentless," "so utilitarian, so sentimental, so individualistic," as to be "poles apart from authentic Jewish-Christian spirituality." Herberg drank deeply at the well of neoorthodox critiques of Protestant liberalism, and the least whiff of "divine-human chumminess" made him retch. Good religion shattered self-regard and underscored "the nothingness of man."[20]

That theological lament was only redoubled in the wake of the 1960s as one commentator after another stepped forward to save America from the disintegrating spiritual effects of the counterculture, including its experiments with altered states of consciousness and its exploration of new religious identities. The critique has, if anything, become more pervasive in the first years of the new millennium, acting, in effect, as the superego of the current spirituality boom. The conservative *New York Times* columnist David Brooks, who had already deflated the latest "Soul Rush" in *Bobos in Paradise* (2000), claimed in March 2004 that the nation need not fear Mel Gibson's zealous Christian orthodoxy but should instead worry more about "the soft-core spirituality that is its opposite." The country is being overrun by "schmaltzy shamans," "psychobabble," and "easygoing narcissism," Brooks maintains. The widely esteemed Protestant observer Martin E. Marty reached the same conclusion as recently as January 2005, calling the "spirituality" versus "religion" debate "a defining conflict of our time" and making clear his preference for the old-time religion over the homegrown spirituality. With the singer Melissa Etheridge standing in for Sheila Larson, Marty dismisses "religionless spirituality" as "banal" and "solipsistic." Typical of the knee-jerk qualities that this critique has taken on, Marty fails even to consider why Etheridge, as a pioneering lesbian vocalist, might well have some good reasons to prefer the freedoms of spiritual seeking to the exclusions that are still a common part of American church life. If anything about this debate has become banal, it is the hackneyed familiarity of the male pundit's jeremiad against Sheilaism—America's self-made spirituality of me, myself, and I.[21]

No doubt there are good reasons to worry about the corrosive effects of therapeutic values on American civic and religious life, but what resources should be drawn upon to counterbalance those deficiencies remains a high-stakes question. Clearly, many Christians see a return to orthodoxy as the sole remedy for self-loving pieties. In *The Making of the New Spirituality: The Eclipse of the Western Religious Tradition* (2003), the evangelical author James A. Herrick neatly divides the contemporary religious sphere between the Revealed Word and the Other Spirituality, the latter a usurper that is threatening to turn the religious inheritance of the West on its head. For Herrick and other evangelicals, real spirituality is anchored in the supreme authority of the Christian scriptures, the uniqueness of Jesus

Christ as the incarnate redeemer of sinful humanity, and the once-and-for-all finality of the Last Judgment. The Other Spirituality is, well, other. It is self-aggrandizing, pluralistic, mystical, Gnostic, evolutionary, and nature loving. It includes everything from Ralph Waldo Emerson to UFO abductees, from the Mormon prophet Joseph Smith to the mythologist Joseph Campbell. The Other Spirituality is, in this rendering, everything orthodox Christianity is not; it is, by definition, freakishly incoherent and without resources of self-critique. Just as a historian of late antiquity would be unlikely to trust the church fathers as unbiased sources on heretics—whether Montanists, Arians, or Gnostics—it seems ill-advised to accept uncritically the parameters of the Other Spirituality as they are being drawn by today's arbiters of orthodoxy.

In the latest round of social and religious criticism, the desire to personify—or demonize—the "new spirituality" has found an outlet in particularly harsh castigations of Oprah Winfrey and the so-called Church of O. Born-again Protestants and traditional Catholics both offer salvation from what they refer to as the "Oprahfication" of American religion and culture: that is, the spread of the feel-good spirituality that Winfrey urges upon her fans through her massive media empire. Herrick actually opens his book with a sharp-edged description of how Winfrey's show has helped popularize the Other Spirituality of Gary Zukav, a best-selling author on the emergent religious consciousness. For good measure, another evangelical author explicitly links "the Oprah Winfrey phenomenon" to the "moral/spiritual vacuum" of Bellah's Sheila Larson: "Sheila is the woman that Winfrey woos.... Winfrey provides the Sheilas of the world with an unhealthy dose of New Age deception." Or, as one Catholic writer in *Our Sunday Visitor* claimed, "Here's what Oprah's spirituality is about: a higher power, spirit, soul, 'authentic power,' meaning, healing, affirmation, helping, miracles, meditation, journaling and angels. An unremarkable New Age hodgepodge. Here's what Oprah's spirituality is not about: sin, redemption, sacrifice, conversion, humility, worship, holiness and Jesus Christ." Saving the nation from this Other Spirituality requires a return to the good news of orthodox Christianity, including submission to church authority and the uniqueness of biblical revelation.[22]

The point here is not to defend the media-made Church of O (Winfrey has a sufficiently large platform from which she can offer her own defenses—or confirm her critics' worst fears). Rather, the aim is to question the wisdom of all-or-nothing critiques of the "new spirituality" and to emphasize the alternative evident from the long history made visible in the foregoing chapters of this book. Here a tradition emerges—call it transcendental cosmopolitanism, Inner-Light liberalism, Whitman's sublime religious democracy, or the Spiritual Left—in which the primacy of individual experience is joined to a whole web of spiritual practices and social commitments. That progressive tradition, worked out within Christianity and Judaism as well as beyond them, has a depth and coherence that the capacious category of the Other Spirituality necessarily obscures in an effort to sharpen the choice between rock-solid orthodoxy and muddled heresy. The open-minded eclecticism of this liberal tradition seems, indeed, to resonate deeply with many Christians who also imagine their faith as a form of seeking and questioning, as something beyond belief. After all, Christian progressivism itself has long been more interested in bridging differences and forging alliances than enforcing boundaries, whether of creed, caste, race, class, gender, or sexual orientation.

By now, this much should be clear: the "new spirituality" is old and not other. The Spiritual Left goes deep in the grain of American culture; it is here for the long haul. Not that this recognition will lessen the criticisms or quiet the alarms. What can happen, though, is a greater sense of ownership of this cosmopolitan spirituality as an inheritance in American religious life among those most likely to be attracted to it: affiliated and unaffiliated seekers, mainline Protestants, Reform Jews, liberal Catholics, Quakers, Unitarians, Vedantists, Bahá'ís, spiritually minded feminists, members of meditation centers, social activists, tamed cynics, and intractable progressives among them. Here, too, is one of Bellah's "communities of memory," constituted not by individual selves empty of commitment or unencumbered by history, but instead by people of diverse faiths who share in the piebald tradition of America's spiritual democracy.

A good sense of the living public memory of the Spiritual Left comes from the newly elected Democratic senator from Illinois, Barack Obama. Despite the results of the 2004 election, Obama comments that it "shouldn't be hard" to reconnect progressive politics with religious vision: "Martin Luther King did it. The abolitionists did it. Dorothy Day did it.... We don't have to start from scratch." Perhaps, though, his most telling remark about the deeper ties that bind those on the Spiritual Left, even in their oft-criticized defection from organized religion, appears in his observations about his mother's faith: "My mother saw religion as an impediment to broader values, like tolerance and racial inclusivity. She remembered churchgoing folks who also called people nigger. But she was a deeply spiritual person, and when I moved to Chicago and worked with church-based community organizations I kept hearing her values expressed." Obama's careful invocation of the "spiritual" as an inclusive term, inextricably interwoven with the "broader values" of American democracy, suggests the grounds for hope, however audacious. The return of a more progressive political order goes hand in hand with the vitality and integrity of religious liberalism.[23]

Spotted with its own failed inclusions, dubious appropriations, and misguided causes, the Spiritual Left must also know itself as a tradition of mixed blessings. To keep today's seekers from repeating the old errors of cultural presumption and pointless consumerism, it must know its own contradictory urges: How many white wannabe Indians can there be before Native Americans lose the claim to speak for their own traditions? How many Peace of Mind® gum balls from Origins, one of any number of companies now offering serenity-inducing body products, can Americans chew on before the practical disciplines of meditation lose their meaning? Memory serves, but only if it produces healthy doses of self-criticism and canny self-awareness. American seekers have a lot more to bring to the table than their own hunger, an emptiness waiting to be filled by whatever spiritual treasures or tangible goods they can grab from others. But to be bearers of gifts more than shoppers in a marketplace requires acquaintance with proximate, not fictive, pasts, with histories thick with conflict and deferral, not golden with perfection and realization. Perchance it even means studied companionship with one or more of those flawed seekers, ardent strivers, and occasional saints who helped make American spirituality what it is today: Ralph Waldo Emerson or Margaret Fuller, Henry David Thoreau or Thomas Wentworth Higginson, Lydia Maria Child or Ralph Waldo Trine, Sara Bull or Sarah J. Farmer, Rufus M. Jones or W. E. B. Du Bois, Thomas R. Kelly or Howard Thurman, Christopher Isherwood or Max Ehrmann.[24]

Of course, given the fact that this American spirituality of seeking arose in tandem with religious liberalism, the mantle of this tradition will necessarily be worn lightly. Read Walt Whitman, and then recall that Whitman disavowed his own authority to speak for traveling souls: "Not I, not any one else can travel that road for you, / You must travel it for yourself." Then read Whitman again, and recall that in his very disavowal of authority, he insists that obligation, virtue, and duty remain within "this field of individuality" and within the "spirituality" of America's sublime religious democracy. "This is what you shall do," he wrote in his preface to *Leaves of Grass* in 1855:

> *Love the earth and sun and the animals, despise riches, give alms to every one that asks, stand up for the stupid and crazy, devote your income and labor to others, hate tyrants, argue not concerning God,... take off your hat to nothing known or unknown or to any man or number of men, go freely with powerful uneducated persons and with the young and with the mothers of families,...*

dismiss whatever insults your own soul, and your very flesh shall be a great poem.

"Meditation, the devout ecstasy, the soaring flight"—these hallowed forms of "interior consciousness" were not at odds with Whitman's politics, but were instead the religious wellspring for the trenchant reform of "our materialistic and vulgar American democracy."

For all of Whitman's grandiose vision of "the poet of the modern" as the nation's source of salvation, for all his manifest nationalism in the very interchangeability of *America* and *democracy,* he spoke, too, as a social and religious critic. A stalwart champion of diversity and freedom as core values of the American experiment, Whitman also imagined the "spiritualization" of social and civic bonds as a necessary part of liberty's amplitude. "Not that half only, individualism, which isolates," Whitman avowed in *Democratic Vistas.* "There is another half, which is adhesiveness or love, that fuses, ties and aggregates, making the races comrades, and fraternizing all. Both are to be vitalized by religion, (sole worthiest elevator of man or State)." And here Whitman pushed the point with particular ardor and excess: "For I say at the core of democracy, finally, is the religious element. All religions, old and new, are there. Nor may the scheme step forth, clothed in resplendent beauty and command, till these, bearing the best, the latest fruit, the spiritual, shall fully appear." Whitman's turn to the spiritual, to spirituality, was not a flight from social equity and solidarity, but part of his hopeful vision for America's democratic experiment and for God's "divine aggregate, the People."[25]

So, if we really want to do something about narcissism and selfishness, about loose religious and civic connections, about the intolerant narrowness of fundamentalist orthodoxies, about the hubris of empire, we need to work with what got us here—a robust liberal tradition with strong religious elements. At its best that tradition has effectively joined mystical openness and social justice, spiritual seeking and political emancipation, globalism and localism, universality and variety. The spirituality that those principles have produced revels in the religious experience of free and equal individuals, in the development of meditative interiority, in the cultivation of solitude and silence, in artful lives of creative self-expression. At the same time, it has also been committed to the search for community, the mutual understanding of differences, the constitution of meaningful identities, and the creation of unifying alliances across global divides. Filled with tensions and paradoxes, that spirituality has highlighted democracy's contradictions, even as it has sought to reconcile them into nearly impossible harmonies. It offers a prospect—not of the finished work of salvation, but of the incomplete labor of democratic freedom and cosmopolitan progressivism. Be gentle with yourself. You'll need to be, since traveling an open road, as Max Ehrmann well knew, is always harder than never embarking at all.

NOTES

Introduction

1. Wade Clark Roof, *Spiritual Marketplace: Baby Boomers and the Remaking of American Religion* (Princeton, NJ: Princeton Univ. Press, 1999), 139; Jeremiah Creedon, "God with a Million Faces," *Utne Reader,* July–August 1998, cover; Carol Lee Flinders, *At the Root of This Longing: Reconciling a Spiritual Hunger and a Feminist Thirst* (San Francisco: HarperSanFrancisco, 1998), 24–25.

2. For journalistic appraisals and social commentary, see the issue of the *Utne Reader* cited in the previous note. See also Robert Owens Scott, "Are You Religious or Spiritual?" *Spirituality and Health* 4 (Spring 2001): 26–27; George Gallup Jr. and Timothy Jones, *The Next American Spirituality: Finding God in the Twenty-first Century* (Colorado Springs: Cook, 2000), 41–64; and David Brooks, *Bobos in Paradise: The New Upper Class and How They Got There* (New York: Simon and Schuster, 2000), 218–54. Important sociological treatments, in addition to Roof's *Spiritual Marketplace,* include Robert Wuthnow, *After Heaven: Spirituality in America Since the 1950s* (Berkeley: Univ. of California Press, 1998); and Wade Clark Roof, *A Generation of Seekers: The Spiritual Journeys of the Baby Boom Generation* (San Francisco: HarperSanFrancisco, 1993). The commentator on the "new eclecticism" with the most historical breadth is Robert C. Fuller; see his *Spiritual but Not Religious: Understanding Unchurched America* (New York: Oxford Univ. Press, 2001). Another basic resource is *American Spiritualities: A Reader,* ed. Catherine L. Albanese (Bloomington: Indiana Univ. Press, 2001).

3. Wayne Teasdale, *The Mystic Heart: Discovering the Universal Spirituality in the World's Religions* (Novato, CA: New World Library, 1999), 10.

4. Walt Whitman, *Democratic Vistas,* in *The Portable Walt Whitman,* ed. Mark Van Doren (New York: Viking Penguin, 1973), 353; Walt Whitman, *Notebooks and Unpublished Prose Manuscripts,* ed. Edward F. Grier, 6 vols. (New York: New York Univ. Press, 1984), 6:2069–70; George Santayana, *The Works of George Santayana,* 15 vols. (New York: Scribner's, 1936), 4:142–43. For metaphysical usages, see "Short Reflections on the Spirituality of the Soul," *Episcopal Magazine* 1 (1820): 87–88; and John Tillotson, *The Remaining Discourses, on the Attributes of God: Viz. His Goodness, His Mercy, His Patience, His Long-Suffering, His Power, His Spirituality, His Immensity, His Eternity, His Incomprehensibleness, God the First Cause, and Last End* (London: Chiswell, 1700). For an example of a more personal or devotional usage, see "On Spirituality," *Hopkinsian Magazine* 1 (1825): 515–18.

5. Thomas Paine, *The Age of Reason* (Secaucus, NJ: Citadel, 1974), 50; Ralph Waldo Emerson, "Circles" (1841), in *The Spiritual Emerson,* ed. David M. Robinson (Boston: Beacon Press, 2003), 163.

6. Harold Bloom, *The American Religion: The Emergence of the Post-Christian Nation* (New York: Simon and Schuster, 1992), 52. See also his companion commentary on a universal mysticism: Harold Bloom, *Omens of Millennium: The Gnosis of Angels, Dreams, and Resurrection* (New York: Riverhead, 1996). For the Christian flip side of Bloom's mythologizing of American Gnosticism, see James A. Herrick, *The Making of the New Spirituality: The Eclipse of the Western Religious Tradition* (Downers Grove, IL: InterVarsity Press, 2003); and Philip J. Lee, *Against the Protestant Gnostics* (New York: Oxford Univ. Press, 1987). To be fair, there is also plenty of evenhanded, sharp-eyed scholarship in this domain, though the line between esotericism and the wider religious culture still needs to become a lot fuzzier. See especially Alex Owen, *The Place of Enchantment: British Occultism and the Culture of the Modern* (Chicago: Univ. of Chicago Press, 2004); Joy Dixon, *Divine Feminine: Theosophy and Feminism in England* (Baltimore: Johns Hopkins Univ. Press, 2001); and Wouter J. Hanegraaff, *New Age Religion and Western Culture: Esotericism in the Mirror of Secular Thought* (Albany: State Univ. of New York Press, 1998).

7. Auguste Sabatier, *Religions of Authority and the Religion of the Spirit* (New York: McClure, Phillips, 1904). Though I am taking in these pages a broader view of religious liberalism than much of the scholarship on liberal Protestantism does, that literature remains absolutely critical as a foundation for this discussion. See especially Richard Wightman Fox, "The Culture of Liberal Protestant Progressivism, 1875–1925," *Journal of Interdisciplinary History* 23 (1993): 639–60; William R. Hutchison, *The Modernist Impulse in American Protestantism* (Oxford: Oxford Univ. Press, 1982); and Gary Dorrien, *The Making of American Liberal Theology: Imagining Progressive Religion, 1805–1900* (Louisville: Westminster John Knox, 2001).

8. John W. Chadwick, "Paine Versus Spirituality," *Conservator* 2 (March 1891): 2–3.

9. Jenny Allen and Martha Fay, "A Seeker's Guide to Faith," *Real Simple* 10 (December 2002–January 2003): 151, 158; W. F. Allen, "Emerson," *Dial* 3 (May 1882): 3.

10. Elizabeth Lesser, *The New American Spirituality: A Seeker's Guide* (New York: Random House, 1999), 16–18, 25; *New York Times,* 7 December 1925, 11; Hazrat Inayat Khan, *The Heart of Sufism* (Boston: Shambhala, 1999), 78–80; Sirkar van Stolk and Daphne Dunlop, *Memories of a Sufi Sage, Hazrat Inayat Khan* (Wassenaar, Holland: East-West Publications, 1967), 35–36; Martin Kellogg Schermerhorn, *Universal Worship* (Poughkeepsie, NY: Barnes, 1906); Martin Kellogg Schermerhorn, *Hymns and Prayers of World-Religion* (Cambridge, MA, 1914).

11. On Wiccan and neo-pagan reservations about the "New Age," see Sarah Pike, *Earthly Bodies, Magical Selves: Contemporary Pagans and the Search for Community* (Berkeley: Univ. of California Press, 2001), 145–46. For the "vaporhead" remark, see Brooks, *Bobos in Paradise,* 224.

12. John Henry Newman, *Apologia Pro Vita Sua* (New York: Longmans, Green, 1908), 191–92; William James, "Address of the President Before the Society of Psychical Research," *Science* 3 (1896): 887. Intellectual historians have contributed much to my understanding of liberalism, religious and secular. See particularly William R. Hutchison, *Religious Pluralism in America: The Contentious History of a Founding Ideal* (New Haven, CT: Yale Univ. Press, 2003); James T. Kloppenberg, *The Virtues of*

Liberalism (New York: Oxford Univ. Press, 1998); and David A. Hollinger, *Postethnic America: Beyond Multiculturalism* (New York: Basic, 1995). The care with which Hollinger distinguishes among universalist, cosmopolitan, and pluralist perspectives is especially fruitful; his defense of "the venerable cosmopolitan project"—including its embrace of diversity and its grounding of religious and social identities in voluntary affiliations—is stellar (75, 84–86). For notably robust philosophical defenses of the virtues of the Emersonian tradition, see Jeffrey Stout, *Democracy and Tradition* (Princeton, NJ: Princeton Univ. Press, 2004); and Cornel West, *The American Evasion of Philosophy: A Genealogy of Pragmatism* (Madison: Univ. of Wisconsin Press, 1989).

13. Horatio W. Dresser, *A History of the New Thought Movement* (New York: Crowell, 1919), 4, 8, 12.

14. Walt Whitman, *Leaves of Grass: Comprehensive Reader's Edition,* ed. Harold W. Blodgett and Sculley Bradley (New York: New York Univ. Press, 1965), 79.

15. Thomas Jefferson to James Smith, 8 December 1822, in *Jefferson's Extracts from the Gospels,* ed. Dickinson W. Adams (Princeton, NJ: Princeton Univ. Press, 1983), 409. Jefferson did not capitalize the word *states* in the original, but I have done so for clarity's sake.

16. As is evident from the list of figures prominently featured in these pages, focusing on the conjunction of liberalism and spirituality makes it harder to take due measure of Roman Catholic contributions. For most of the nineteenth and twentieth centuries, *Catholicism* and *liberalism* were routinely constituted in mutual opposition to one another—in Catholic-Protestant, Catholic-secular, and intra-Catholic polemics. See the astute analysis of these tensions in John T. McGreevy, *Catholicism and American Freedom: A History* (New York: Norton, 2003). Likewise, my foregrounding of "spirituality" may also act to minimize Catholic elements of the story. Robert A. Orsi has recently remarked on the religious and cultural antagonisms embedded in the American crafting of the term *spirituality.* It has become, he says, a "disciplinary word" to distinguish "good religion" from "bad religion"; as such, it is designed especially, he claims, to marginalize popular Catholic practices and prevent serious attention to them. The normative dimensions of the term certainly contain exclusionary elements alongside the cosmopolitan imperatives. Catholic-Protestant antagonisms were, indeed, important undercurrents in shaping the initial bounds of American "spirituality," the incessant juxtapositions of authority and spirit, church and soul, institutional hierarchy and democratic individuality. See Robert A. Orsi, *Between Heaven and Earth: The Religious Worlds People Make and the Scholars Who Study Them* (Princeton, NJ: Princeton Univ. Press, 2005), 187–88. Increasingly, though, American Catholics have themselves embraced "spirituality" as a construct to overarch traditionally more prevalent terms such as "the spiritual life," "prayer," "devotionalism," "spiritual direction," or "holiness of life." That belated and only partial shift, evident mostly since World War II, can be seen as a byproduct of nineteenth-century liberal trends hitherto effectively resisted. (Catherine Albanese notes, e.g., that the Dominican periodical *Cross and Crown,* founded in 1949, changed its name only in 1977 to *Spirituality Today.* See Albanese, *American Spiritualities,* 4.) The universalized notion of "spirituality" has come to enjoy such cultural sway that American Catholics have appropriated it as their own in an effort to traditionalize the term through emphasizing the "classics" of the Christian life. Yet, a continuing preference for prior devotional categories is also quite apparent—evident, for example, in the studied avoidance

of the term *spirituality* in James M. O'Toole, ed., *Habits of Devotion: Catholic Religious Practice in Twentieth-Century America* (Ithaca, NY: Cornell Univ. Press, 2004). What counts are the routine habits of prayer embodied in the Rosary, the recurrent meditations on the sufferings of Jesus through the Stations of the Cross, the everyday devotions to the Virgin Mary and the saints, or the solemnities of sacramental participation. For the nineteenth-century background on American Catholic devotionalism, see especially Ann Taves, *The Household of Faith: Roman Catholic Devotions in Mid-Nineteenth-Century America* (South Bend, IN: Univ. of Notre Dame Press, 1986). For a broader survey, see Joseph P. Chinnici, *Living Stones: The History and Structure of Catholic Spiritual Life in the United States* (New York: Macmillan, 1989).

17. Dean J. G. Palfrey quoted in Thomas Wentworth Higginson, "Cheerful Yesterdays, IV," *Atlantic Monthly* 79 (1897): 241; "Mysticism and Discipline," *Church Quarterly Review* 62 (1906): 332.

18. William James, *The Varieties of Religious Experience* (New York: Penguin, 1982), 383.

19. James, *Varieties of Religious Experience,* 406.

20. Geoffrey Nunberg, "Lattes, Limousines and Lefties: How Conservatives Pigeonholed Those Poor Liberals," *New York Times,* 2 March 2003, sec. 4, p. 4.

21. Woodbridge Riley, *The Meaning of Mysticism* (New York: Smith, 1930), 8–9.

22. The Emerson ad is in the author's possession; the Thoreau ad is discussed in Kimberly J. Lau, *New Age Capitalism: Making Money East of Eden* (Philadelphia: Univ. of Pennsylvania Press, 2000), 138.

23. Michael Lerner, *Spirit Matters: Global Healing and the Wisdom of the Soul* (Charlottesville: Hampton Roads, 2000), 165–94. On liberal alliances, see especially Spencer Lavan, *Unitarians and India: A Study in Encounter and Response* (Chicago: Exploration, 1991), 143–96; Peter van der Veer, *Imperial Encounters: Religion and Modernity in India and Britain* (Princeton, NJ: Princeton Univ. Press, 2001), 46–48, 69–70; and George D. Bond, *The Buddhist Revival in Sri Lanka: Religious Tradition, Reinterpretation and Response* (Columbia: Univ. of South Carolina Press, 1988), 45–61. Accenting the anti-imperial elements of liberal history and the fruitful cross-cultural alliances that have occasionally developed is not to deny the exclusionary dimensions of liberal theory and practice in various colonial settings. For an extremely effective critique in this regard, see Uday Singh Mehta, *Liberalism and Empire: A Study in Nineteenth-Century British Liberal Thought* (Chicago: Univ. of Chicago Press, 1999). I would argue, though, that Mehta's own "cosmopolitanism of sentiments" and his vision of cross-cultural exchange as a perilous mutuality are retrievable from within the liberal tradition rather than in opposition to it (22–23). For a recent defense of a cosmopolitanism explicitly rooted in liberal political philosophy, see Kwame Anthony Appiah, *The Ethics of Identity* (Princeton, NJ: Princeton Univ. Press, 2005).

Chapter One

1. C. H. A. Bjerregaard, *Lectures on Mysticism and Nature Worship* (Chicago: Corbitt and Burnham, 1897), 11, 13, 25.

2. Bjerregaard, *Mysticism and Nature Worship,* 68–71, 107–11.

3. Bjerregaard, *Mysticism and Nature Worship,* 108–10. For a parallel description of his enthrallment, see C. H. A. Bjerregaard, "Greenacre of Beauty and Peace," *Greenacre Voice,* 11 July 1896.

4. William James, *The Correspondence of William James, July 1899–1901* (Charlottesville: Univ. Press of Virginia, 2001), 501; C. H. A. Bjerregaard, *Lectures on Mysticism and Talks on Kindred Subjects* (Chicago: Corbitt and Burnham, 1896), 19.

5. William James, *The Varieties of Religious Experience* (New York: Penguin, 1982), 419; Robert Alfred Vaughan, *Hours with the Mystics: A Contribution to the History of Religious Opinion*, 5th ed., 2 vols. (London: Slark, 1888), 1:54.

6. Charles Morris Addison, *The Theory and Practice of Mysticism* (New York: E. P. Dutton, 1918), 106, 150–51.

7. Ralph Waldo Emerson, *The Journals and Miscellaneous Notebooks of Ralph Waldo Emerson, 1835–1838*, ed. Merton M. Sealts Jr. (Cambridge, MA: Belknap Press of Harvard Univ. Press, 1965), 502; Joel Myerson, "A Calendar of Transcendental Club Meetings," *American Literature* 44 (1972): 202; John Weiss, *Life and Correspondence of Theodore Parker*, 2 vols. (New York, 1864; New York: Da Capo, 1970), 2:455–56, 481; Larry A. Carlson, ed., "Bronson Alcott's 'Journal for 1838,' " in *Studies in the American Renaissance*, ed. Joel Myerson (Charlottesville: Univ. of Virginia Press, 1993), 232–33. For Alcott's own record of his inspired educational experiments, see A. Bronson Alcott, *Conversations with Children on the Gospels*, 2 vols. (Boston: Munroe, 1836). For an excellent overview of historical writing on Transcendentalism, see Charles Capper, " 'A Little Beyond': The Problem of the Transcendentalist Movement in American History," *Journal of American History* 85 (1998): 502–39. Capper aptly emphasizes the importance of recovering the "religious sensibility" of Transcendentalism as its "animating center" (526). For a comprehensive, richly annotated, and up-to-date anthology of the movement, see Joel Myerson, ed., *Transcendentalism: A Reader* (New York: Oxford Univ. Press, 2000). For three superb recent studies of principal figures of the movement, each of which is highly attuned to religion's importance, see Lawrence Buell, *Emerson* (Cambridge, MA: Belknap Press of Harvard Univ. Press, 2003); Dean Grodzins, *American Heretic: Theodore Parker and Transcendentalism* (Chapel Hill: Univ. of North Carolina Press, 2002); and Alan D. Hodder, *Thoreau's Ecstatic Witness* (New Haven, CT: Yale Univ. Press, 2001).

8. Ralph Waldo Emerson, *Nature, Addresses, and Lectures*, ed. Robert E. Spiller (Cambridge, MA: Belknap Press of Harvard Univ. Press, 1979), 71–93.

9. Thomas Blount, *Glossographia; or, A Dictionary, Interpreting All Such Hard Words, Whether Hebrew, Greek, Latin, Italian, Spanish, French, Teutonick, Belgick, British, or Saxon; As Are Now Used in Our Refined English Tongue. Also the Terms of Divinity, Law, Physick, Mathematicks, Heraldry, Anatomy, War, Musick, Architecture; and of Several Other Arts and Sciences Explicated, with Etymologies, Definitions, and Historical Observations on the Same* (London: Newcomb, 1656), unpaginated; Serenus Cressy, *Exomologesis; or, A Faithfull Narration of the Occasion and Motives of the Conversion unto Catholique Unity of Hugh-Paulin de Cressy* (Paris, 1647), 635–36.

10. Ephraim Chambers, *Cyclopædia; or, An Universal Dictionary of Arts and Sciences*, 7th ed., 2 vols. (London: Innys, 1751–1752), unpaginated.

11. Henry Coventry, *Philemon to Hydaspes; or, The History of False Religion in the Earlier Pagan World, Related in a Series of Conversations* (Glasgow: Urie, 1761), 44, 56, 60.

12. Jonathan Swift, *A Tale of a Tub* (Oxford: Oxford Univ. Press, 1986), 140–41; Coventry, *Philemon*, 48, 55.

13. Coventry, *Philemon*, 47, 51, 55, 61, 121; James, *Varieties of Religious Experience*, 10.

14. William Warburton, *The Doctrine of Grace; or, The Office and Operations of the Holy Spirit Vindicated from Insults of Infidelity, and the Abuses of Fanaticism* (London: Millar and Tonson, 1763), 223.

15. William Hurd, *A New Universal History of the Religious Rites, Ceremonies, and Customs of the Whole World; or, A Complete and Impartial View of All the Religions in the Various Nations of the Universe* (London: Hogg, 1782), 670–71.

16. *Encyclopædia Britannica; or, A Dictionary of Arts, Sciences, and Miscellaneous Literature*, 3rd ed., 18 vols. (Edinburgh: A. Bell and C. Macfarquhar, 1797), 12:598.

17. Hannah Adams, *A Dictionary of All Religions and Religious Denominations, Jewish, Heathen, Mahometan, and Christian, Ancient and Modern*, 4th ed. (New York: Eastburn, 1817), 188–90; Noah Webster, *An American Dictionary of the English Language*, 2 vols. (New York: Converse, 1828), unpaginated; A. Bronson Alcott, *Tablets* (Boston: Roberts Brothers, 1868), 142.

18. Joseph Priestley, *The Theological and Miscellaneous Works*, ed. John Towill Rutt, 25 vols. (London: Smallfield, 1817–1832), 5:340, 354–55.

19. John Fletcher, "An Essay on Mysticism," *Methodist Magazine* 27 (1804): 114–16, 158–61.

20. Thomas Hartley, *Paradise Restored; or, A Testimony to the Doctrine of the Blessed Millennium with Some Considerations on Its Approaching Advent from the Signs of the Times to Which Is Added, A Short Defence of the Mystical Writers* (London: Richardson, 1764), 358, 371, 373, 377.

21. Arthur Versluis, "Bronson Alcott and Jacob Böhme," in *Studies in the American Renaissance*, ed. Joel Myerson (Charlottesville: Univ. Press of Virginia, 1991), 153–54; Kenneth Walter Cameron, ed., *Transcendental Curriculum or Bronson Alcott's Library* (Hartford, CT: Transcendental Books, 1984), 66; Bronson Alcott, *The Journals of Bronson Alcott*, ed. Odell Shepard (Boston: Little, Brown, 1938), 136.

22. Cameron, *Transcendental Curriculum*; Samuel Taylor Coleridge, *Aids to Reflection*, ed. John Beer (Princeton, NJ: Princeton Univ. Press, 1993), 40.

23. A. Bronson Alcott, *Concord Days* (Philadelphia: Saifer, 1872), 237; Alcott, *Journals*, 530.

24. *A Brief Account of the Life of Emanuel Swedenborg, a Servant of the Lord and the Messenger of the New-Jerusalem Dispensation* (Cincinnati: Looker and Reynolds, 1827), 18; *Encyclopædia Britannica; or, A Dictionary of Arts, Sciences, and General Literature*, 8th ed., 21 vols. (Boston: Little, Brown, 1858), 15:758.

25. Ralph Waldo Emerson, *Representative Men: Seven Lectures*, ed. Douglas Emory Wilson (Cambridge, MA: Belknap Press of Harvard Univ. Press, 1996), 76.

26. Emerson, *Representative Men*, 79.

27. Robert N. Hudspeth, ed., *The Letters of Margaret Fuller*, 6 vols. (Ithaca, NY: Cornell Univ. Press, 1983–1994), 1:347–48; 2:172–73; Deshae Elizabeth Lott, " 'The Mutual Visionary Life': The Mystical Model of Margaret Fuller" (Ph.D. diss., Texas A & M Univ., 1999), 3–4, 58; Margaret Fuller, *The Writings of Margaret Fuller*, ed. Mason Wade (New York: Viking, 1941), 167.

28. Samuel Johnson, *Lectures, Essays, and Sermons with a Memoir by Samuel Longfellow* (Boston: Houghton Mifflin, 1883), 12, 14–16, 18.

29. Samuel Johnson Letters, box 1, folder 2, Samuel Johnson Papers, Phillips Library, Peabody Essex Museum, Salem, MA; Paschal Reeves, "The Making of a Mystic: A Reconsideration of the Life of Jones Very," *Essex Institute Historical Collections* 103 (1967): 14–16, 21; Robert D. Richardson Jr., *Emerson: The Mind on Fire* (Berkeley:

Univ. of California Press, 1995), 301–6; Ralph Waldo Emerson, William Henry Channing, and James Freeman Clarke, eds., *Memoirs of Margaret Fuller Ossoli*, 2 vols. (New York: Franklin, 1972), 1:308.

30. Henry Ware Jr., "The Mystical Element in Religion," *Christian Examiner and Religious Miscellany* 37 (1844): 309–11, 316.

31. Robert Alfred Vaughan, *Essays and Remains of the Rev. Robert Alfred Vaughan*, 2 vols. (London: Parker, 1858), 1:xvii; Vaughan, *Hours with the Mystics*, 1:27; 2:8. On Emerson's hybridizing relationship with Persian Islamic poetry, see Wai Chee Dimock, "Deep Time: American Literature and World History," *American Literary History* 13 (2001): 764–70.

32. Vaughan, *Hours with the Mystics*, 1:21; 2:351; John Bernard Dalgairns, *The German Mystics of the Fourteenth Century* (London: Richardson, 1858), 7.

33. Octavius Brooks Frothingham, "Mystics and Their Creed," *Christian Examiner* 79 (1861): 202–4, 211–12, 229; Octavius Brooks Frothingham, *Recollections and Impressions, 1822–1900* (New York: Putnam's Sons, 1891), 115–32, 272–88; Octavius Brooks Frothingham, *Transcendentalism in New England: A History* (Philadelphia: Univ. of Pennsylvania Press, 1972), 249–83, 303–4.

34. James Freeman Clarke, *Events and Epochs in Religious History*, 3rd ed. (Boston: Ticknor, 1887), 276; James, *Varieties of Religious Experience*, 419.

35. Kenneth Walter Cameron, ed., *Transcendentalists in Transition: Popularization of Emerson, Thoreau and the Concord School of Philosophy in the Greenacre Summer Conferences and the Monsalvat School (1894–1909)* (Hartford, CT: Transcendental Books, 1980), 10.

36. Wentworth Webster, "The English Mystics," *Academy* 43 (1893): 367; "Mysticism," *Methodist Quarterly Review* 60 (1878): 412; Henry David Thoreau, *Journal, 1852–1853*, ed. Patrick F. O'Connell (Princeton, NJ: Princeton Univ. Press, 1997), 469.

37. Charles C. Everett, "Mysticism," *Unitarian Review and Religious Magazine* 1 (1874): 8, 10–11, 23.

38. Frothingham, "Mystics," 229; Francis Greenwood Peabody, "Mysticism and Modern Life," *Harvard Theological Review* 7 (1914): 476; George W. Cooke, "American Mysticism," *Current Literature* 15 (1894): 75; James, *Varieties of Religious Experience*, 368; Rufus Jones, *New Studies in Mystical Religion* (New York: Macmillan, 1927), 52, 55.

39. John Wright Buckham, *Mysticism and Modern Life* (New York: Abingdon, 1915), 154, 244; Howard H. Brinton, *Ethical Mysticism in the Society of Friends* (Pendle Hill, PA: Sowers, 1967), 5. For another liberal domain where this same convergence was in evidence, see Stanton Coit, "Ethical Mysticism," in *Aspects of Ethical Religion: Essays in Honor of Felix Adler,* ed. Horace J. Bridges (New York: American Ethical Union, 1926), 28–29.

40. James, *Varieties of Religious Experience*, 155, 160–61; James Bissett Pratt, "The Religious Philosophy of William James," *Hibbert Journal* 10 (1911): 233–34.

41. Rufus Jones, "Mysticism in Present-Day Religion," *Harvard Theological Review* 8 (1915): 161, 165; Washington Gladden, *Recollections* (Boston: Houghton Mifflin, 1909), 36–38; Vida Dutton Scudder, *On Journey* (New York: Dutton, 1937), 50. For a superb historical account of the growing interest in mysticism in late Victorian America, see T. J. Jackson Lears, *No Place of Grace: Antimodernism and the Transformation of American Culture, 1880–1920* (Chicago: Univ. of Chicago Press, 1994), 142–215. Lears presents the return to mysticism as part of an antimodern, particularly

Anglo-Catholic turn; whereas this account locates it within the long-running streams of religious liberalism. Many of the same cultural forces and psychological needs, however, joined these diverse figures in their parallel aspirations (whether the medievalist Ralph Adams Cram or the modernist Rufus Jones). In effect, Lears highlights figures moving from liberal Protestantism back toward Anglo-Catholic traditionalism; I emphasize figures moving in the other direction. Given her contemplative preoccupation with the "Indian mystics" as well as her Quaker ties, I would even place Scudder as much in the cosmopolitan modernist camp as in the antimodernist Anglo-Catholic camp (387).

42. Thomas Wentworth Higginson, "My Creed So Far As I Have One," bMS Am 784, box 6, Houghton Library, Harvard University. The manuscript is undated, but Higginson himself added a note later that it was "written probably between 1870 & 1880." It resembles in some details a short piece he published in 1874. See Thomas Wentworth Higginson, "Law and Love," *Index* 5 (1874): 187.

43. James, *Varieties of Religious Experience*, 66, 230, 380, 395; David Atwood Wasson, *Poems* (Boston: Lee and Shepard, 1888), 137; Joel Myerson, "Convers Francis and Emerson," *American Literature* 50 (1978): 24; Orestes Brownson, "Spirituality of Religion," *Unitarian* 1 (1834): 410–13. Lowell is one of James's cases.

44. Bjerregaard, *Mysticism and Nature Worship*, 27; "Is the Core of Religion to Be Found in Sex Mysticism?" *Current Opinion* 58 (1915): 193; Wayne Teasdale, *The Mystic Heart: Discovering a Universal Spirituality in the World's Religions* (Novato, CA: New World Library, 1999), 3; Phil Jackson and Hugh Delehanty, *Sacred Hoops: Spiritual Lessons of a Hardwood Warrior* (New York: Hyperion, 1995), 4, 45–47.

Chapter Two

1. Henry David Thoreau, *Walden* (New York: Quality Paperback, 1997), 147, 173–75, 178, 184. After a mixed reception in his own day, Thoreau is now, ironically, an industry unto himself. For the fullest treatment of his religious world, see Alan D. Hodder, *Thoreau's Ecstatic Witness* (New Haven, CT: Yale Univ. Press, 2001). For a basic sketch of Thoreau's place among saints and recluses, see Peter France, *Hermits: The Insights of Solitude* (New York: St. Martin's Griffin, 1996), 90–113. For two excellent accounts of the cultus that gradually took shape around his experiment at Walden, see Lawrence Buell, *The Environmental Imagination: Thoreau, Nature Writing, and the Formation of American Culture* (Cambridge, MA: Belknap Press of Harvard Univ. Press, 1995); and W. Barksdale Maynard, *Walden Pond: A History* (New York: Oxford Univ. Press, 2004).

2. Ralph Waldo Emerson, *The Journals and Miscellaneous Notebooks of Ralph Waldo Emerson*, 16 vols. (Cambridge, MA: Belknap Press of Harvard Univ. Press, 1960–1982), 2:326; David M. Robinson, ed., *The Spiritual Emerson* (Boston: Beacon, 2003), 24–25; Thoreau, *Walden*, 115, 117, 293–94.

3. Thoreau, *Walden*, 283–84, 297–99; Henry David Thoreau, *A Week on the Concord and Merrimack Rivers* (New York: Quality Paperback, 1997), 24.

4. William Rounseville Alger, *The Solitudes of Nature and of Man* (Boston: Roberts Brothers, 1867), 329; Thoreau, *Week on the Concord*, 78; William James, *The Varieties of Religious Experience* (New York: Penguin, 1982), 383.

5. [Henry Adams], review of *Transcendentalism in New England*, by O. B. Frothingham, *North American Review* 123 (1876): 470–71; Alger, *Solitudes*, 174; Barbara Er-

akko Taylor, *Silent Dwellers: Embracing the Solitary Life* (New York: Continuum, 1999), 47.

6. *Encyclopædia Britannica* (Edinburgh: 1797; Philadelphia: Dobson, 1798), s.v. "hermit, or eremit"; Edward Gibbon, *The Decline and Fall of the Roman Empire,* 6 vols. (New York: Knopf, 1994), 4:3–4, 9, 12–13, 18.

7. *Encyclopedia Americana,* s.v. "Anachorets, or Anchorets," "Hermit"; Henry Ruffner, *The Fathers of the Desert; or, An Account of the Origin and Practice of Monkery Among Heathen Nations,* 2 vols. (New York: Baker and Scribner, 1850), 1:2–3, 5, 18.

8. Robert Alfred Vaughan, *Hours with the Mystics,* 2 vols. (London: Slark, 1888), 1:109–11; Anna Jameson, *Sacred and Legendary Art,* 2 vols. (London: Longman, 1857), 2:739–79.

9. W. B. O. Peabody, "The New Commandment," *Liberal Preacher* 1 (1831): 125; Alexis de Tocqueville, *Democracy in America,* 2 vols. (New York: Vintage, 1945), 2:106.

10. *Life and Adventures of Robert Voorhis, the Hermit of Massachusetts, Who Has Lived 14 Years in a Cave, Secluded from Human Society* (Providence: Trumbull, 1829), 6–8, 10, 17, 26.

11. *Narrative of the Extraordinary Life of John Conrad Shafford, Known by Many by the Name of the Dutch Hermit* (New York: Carpenter, 1841), title page, 6, 19–22; Alger, *Solitudes,* 42.

12. S. G. Goodrich, *Recollections of a Lifetime; or, Men and Things I Have Seen,* 2 vols. (New York: Miller, Orton, 1857), 1:292–99; Mark Van Doren, ed., *The Portable Walt Whitman* (New York: Viking Penguin, 1977), 549.

13. *Life and Adventures,* 5; James Buckland, *The Wonder of Wonders; or, The Remarkable Discovery of an American Hermit* (Kennebunk, ME: Remich, 1815), 14; Harriet Morrison Irwin, *The Hermit of Petræa* (Charlotte, NC: Hill and Irwin, 1871), 14; Thoreau, *Walden,* 201.

14. Harry E. Resseguie, "Stewart Wilson: The Hermit of Sacandaga Park," *New York Folklore Quarterly* 28 (1972): 43–60; Sue Halpern, *Migrations to Solitude* (New York: Vintage, 1993), vii.

15. *The Pennsylvania Hermit: A Narrative of the Extraordinary Life of Amos Wilson* (Philadelphia, 1839; Beaver Springs, PA: Aurand and Son, 1919), 5–6, 19, 26, 29, 31, 50, 59.

16. John G. Zimmerman, *Solitude* (Philadelphia: Leary, 1850), 16, 32–33; Robert Sattelmeyer, *Thoreau's Reading: A Study in Intellectual History* (Princeton, NJ: Princeton Univ. Press, 1988), 295.

17. John Norris, *A Collection of Miscellanies* (Oxford: Crosley, 1687), 159, 161–62; James Meikle, *Solitude Sweetened; or, Miscellaneous Meditations on Various Religious Subjects* (Albany, NY: Dodge, 1811).

18. Thomas Parnell, *The Hermit* (Andover, MA: Flagg and Gould, 1816), 1, 7; John Eyre, ed., *The Life of Gregory Lopez, a Hermit in America* (New York: Eyre, 1841), iv–v, ix.

19. Eyre, *Life of Gregory Lopez,* iv–ix, 86–93.

20. Orestes Brownson, "The Fathers of the Desert," *Brownson's Quarterly Review* 10 (1853): 383, 387, 396–97; Richard Challoner, *The Lives of the Fathers of the Eastern Deserts* (New York: Saddler, 1852), xv.

21. Johannes Kelpius, *A Short, Easy, and Comprehensive Method of Prayer* (Philadelphia: Miller, 1761), 8, 11, 18, 24. For an excellent account of the group, see

Elizabeth W. Fisher, " 'Prophecies and Revelations': German Cabbalists in Early Pennsylvania," *Pennsylvania Magazine of History and Biography* 109 (1985): 299–333.

22. Robert Ellis Thompson, "The German Mystics as American Colonists," *Pennsylvania Monthly Magazine* 2 (1871): 402–3; Julius F. Sachse, *The German Pietists of Pennsylvania, 1694–1708* (Philadelphia: Stockhausen, 1895), frontispiece, 72–73, 196–97, 202–3, 211–15; Julius F. Sachse, *Justus Falckner, Mystic and Scholar* (Philadelphia: New Era, 1903), 1–2, 32–33; John Greenleaf Whittier, *The Poetical Works of Whittier* (Boston: Houghton Mifflin, 1975), 106. ·

23. Whittier, *Poetical Works,* 39–44.

24. Henry Wadsworth Longfellow, *The Poetical Works of Longfellow* (London: Oxford Univ. Press, 1906), 718–19; B. O. Flower, *Whittier: Prophet, Seer and Man* (Boston: Arena, 1896), 105, 123; George W. Cooke, "American Mysticism," *Current Opinion* 15 (1894): 75; Jayne K. Kribbs, ed., *Critical Essays on John Greenleaf Whittier* (Boston: Hall, 1980), xxiii–xxiv, xxix, 89. Oliver Wendell Holmes even suggested that Whittier's influence on "the religious thought of the American people has been far greater than that of the occupant of any pulpit." See William M. Salter, "Whittier's Influence on Religion and Life," *Conservator* 4 (1893): 103.

25. William Rounseville Alger, *The Poetry of the Orient* (Boston: Roberts Brothers, 1866), v–vii. For the definitive detective work on Alger's career, see Gary Scharnhorst, *A Literary Biography of William Rounseville Alger (1822–1905): A Neglected Member of the Concord Circle* (Lewiston, NY: Edwin Mellen Press, 1990). Scharnhorst reprints the letter from Emerson to Alger on pp. 19–20. For another helpful sketch of Alger's place in these circles, see Arthur Versluis, *American Transcendentalism and Asian Religions* (New York: Oxford Univ. Press, 1993), 148–52, 269–76.

26. Alger, *Poetry of the Orient,* vii, 64–66, 124.

27. James Martineau, *Endeavors After the Christian Life* (Boston: Beacon, 1866), 159–67; Alger, *Solitudes,* 23.

28. Alger, *Solitudes,* 31, 34–35, 38. Alger's companion intellectual passion at the time was the "History of Friendship," making his labors a neat embodiment of the larger solitude and society problematic in Transcendentalist writing. See William Rounseville Alger, *Friendships of Women,* 10th ed. (Boston: Roberts Brothers, 1882), vii.

29. Henri J. M. Nouwen, *Out of Solitude: Three Meditations on the Christian Life* (Notre Dame, IN: Ave Maria, 1974), 14, 18–20; Alger, *Solitudes,* 141–42, 169, 408.

30. Alger, *Solitudes,* x, 168; Henry Ward Beecher, *Eyes and Ears* (Boston: Ticknor and Fields, 1864), 363–64.

31. Alger, *Solitudes,* 168, 332–33, 337–38, 398–99, 407–8.

32. Alger, *Solitudes,* 147, 151–52, 170–71, 174; William R. Alger to Frederic Henry Hedge, 4 September 1864; Alger to Hedge, 15 May 1882; Poor Family Papers, A–132, box 5, Schlesinger Library, Radcliffe Institute for Advanced Study, Harvard University.

33. Van Doren, *Portable Walt Whitman,* 229; Scharnhorst, *Literary Biography,* 31–32; Franklin Benjamin Sanborn, *Transcendental Horizons: Essays and Poetry,* ed. Kenneth Walter Cameron (Hartford, CT: Transcendental Books, 1984), 7–9; John Burroughs, *Indoor Studies* (Boston: Houghton Mifflin, 1889), 214–16; Clifford Hazeldine Osborne, *The Religion of John Burroughs* (Boston: Houghton Mifflin, 1930), 6, 42. On Hotham, see also Kenneth Walter Cameron, "Thoreau's Disciple at Walden: Edmond S. Hotham," *Emerson Society Quarterly* no. 26 (1962): 34–45; and Maynard, *Walden Pond,* 165–70.

34. Elizabeth Cady Stanton, *Solitude of Self* (Ashfield, MA: Paris Press, 2001), 1–6, 21. On spirituality in the late-nineteenth-century suffrage movement, see Joy Dixon, *Divine Feminine: Theosophy and Feminism in England* (Baltimore: Johns Hopkins Univ. Press, 2001), 177–205.

35. "Johnny Appleseed: A Pioneer Hero," *Harper's New Monthly Magazine* 43 (1871): 834.

36. *A Report of the Society, Formed Some Years Ago at Manchester, for Printing, Publishing and Circulating the Writings of the Honourable Emanuel Swedenborg* (Manchester, England: Courier, 1817), 6; "Johnny Appleseed," 830–36; Lindsay quoted in Robert Price, *Johnny Appleseed: Man and Myth* (Gloucester, MA: Peter Smith, 1967), 260; Ednah Silver, *Sketches of the New Church in America* (Boston: Massachusetts New Church Union, 1920), 47–48; Robert Matheson, "In Memoriam Johnny Appleseed," *New-Church Messenger* 61 (1891): 83.

37. W. H. Bushnell, *The Texan Herdsman; or, The Hermit of the Colorado Hills* (New York: Starr, 1874), 3, 18–19, 34. The novel's original title of 1864 is as given in the text.

38. P. C. Mozoomdar, *The Oriental Christ* (Boston: Ellis, 1894), 9; P. C. Mozoomdar, *Lectures in America and Other Papers* (Calcutta: Navavidhan, 1955), 52.

39. Mozoomdar, *Lectures in America*, v, x–xi, 27; P. C. Mozoomdar to Samuel June Barrows, 11 August 1900, Barrows Family Papers, bMS 1807 (357), Houghton Library, Harvard University.

40. P. C. Mozoomdar, *Heart-beats* (Boston: Ellis, 1894), xvi, xl–xli, 28, 206, 227–30; P. C. Mozoomdar, *The Silent Pastor: Words, Precepts and Experiences of Spiritual Life* (Calcutta: Bengal, 1899), 169–71, 180–84.

41. Paul Brunton, *A Hermit in the Himalayas* (New York: Dutton, 1937), 10, 14, 19, 29, 43, 134–35.

42. Thomas Merton, *A Search for Solitude* (New York: HarperCollins, 1996), 240; Thomas Merton, *Thoughts in Solitude* (New York: Farrar, Strauss and Giroux, 1987), 12, 14; William Bly, "The Hermit Days of Henry Thoreau and Thomas Merton," *Thoreau Society Bulletin* 130 (Winter 1975): 2–3; Thomas Merton, *Raids on the Unspeakable* (New York: New Directions, 1964), 12–13, 15.

43. Halpern, *Migrations to Solitude*, 84–85. On Merton's place in the longer tradition of American bohemianism, see James Terence Fisher, *The Catholic Counterculture in America, 1933–1962* (Chapel Hill: Univ. of North Carolina Press, 1989), 205–47.

44. Alger, *Solitudes*, 51; James, *Varieties of Religious Experience*, 31.

45. Alfred North Whitehead, *Religion in the Making* (New York: Macmillan, 1926), 16–17, 74.

46. Roger Housden, *Retreat: Time Apart for Silence and Solitude* (San Francisco: HarperSanFrancisco, 1995), 139, 167, 183. The discussion of Sargent depends on Sally M. Promey, *Painting Religion in Public: John Singer Sargent's Triumph of Religion at the Boston Public Library* (Princeton, NJ: Princeton Univ. Press, 1999), 258–60.

Chapter Three

1. Moncure D. Conway, "Walt Whitman: My Little Wreath of Thoughts and Memories," *Open Court* 6 (1892): 3199–3200; Carleton Noyes, *An Approach to Walt Whitman*

(Boston: Houghton Mifflin, 1910), 132. Conway, like many of his fellow travelers, made his way through various religious identities, including a post-Transcendentalist phase as a freethinking materialist, which, in turn, was modified by the end of his life.

2. "At the Graveside of Walt Whitman," *Conservator* 3 (April 1892): supp., i–iv; Walt Whitman, *Leaves of Grass: Comprehensive Reader's Edition*, ed. Harold W. Blodgett and Sculley Bradley (New York: New York Univ. Press, 1965), 328–37. The funeral liturgy also appeared in a stand-alone volume: Horace L. Traubel, ed., *At the Graveside of Walt Whitman* (Philadelphia: Billstein and Son, 1892).

3. "At the Graveside," i–iv; Whitman, *Leaves of Grass*, 157, 727; Henry David Thoreau, *Walden* (New York: Quality Paperback, 1997), 140; Whitman, *Democratic Vistas*, in *The Portable Walt Whitman*, ed. Mark Van Doren (New York: Viking Penguin, 1973), 365. For an account of the poet's death and funeral, see Gay Wilson Allen, *The Solitary Singer: A Critical Biography of Walt Whitman* (New York: Macmillan, 1955), 540–44. For a basic work focusing on Whitman's religion, see David Kuebrich, *Minor Prophecy: Walt Whitman's New American Religion* (Bloomington: Indiana Univ. Press, 1989). The best contextualization of his ideas about religion is to be found in David S. Reynolds, *Walt Whitman's America: A Cultural Biography* (New York: Knopf, 1995), esp. 251–78.

4. Whitman, *Leaves of Grass*, 75, 78–79, 83, 715.

5. Francis Howard Williams, "The Whitman Cult," *Conservator* 12 (1901): 119; Richard Maurice Bucke, "Walt Whitman and the Cosmic Sense," in *In Re Walt Whitman,* ed. Horace L. Traubel, Richard Maurice Bucke, and Thomas B. Harned (Philadelphia: McKay, 1893), 347; Paul Griswold Huston, "Whitman as a Mystic," *Conservator* 9 (1898): 133, 135; "At the Graveside," iv.

6. "At the Graveside," iii; Whitman, *Leaves of Grass*, 50.

7. Thomas Wentworth Higginson (TWH), *Contemporaries* (Boston: Houghton Mifflin, 1899), 77–79, 84; TWH to William Lloyd Garrison, 19 March 1856, in *Liberator,* 9 May 1856; TWH, 17 March 1856, Houghton Library, Harvard University, bMS Am 784, box 4, no. 546; Mary Thacher Higginson, *Thomas Wentworth Higginson: The Story of His Life* (Boston: Houghton Mifflin, 1914), 328, 411–12.

8. TWH, "The Sympathy of Religions," *Radical* 8 (1871): 2, 20. Sympathy is the subject of a considerable literature, especially in the history of ethics. For two accounts that are particularly relevant, see Jennifer A. Herdt, *Religion and Faction in Hume's Moral Philosophy* (Cambridge: Cambridge Univ. Press, 1997); and Elizabeth B. Clark, " 'The Sacred Rights of the Weak': Pain, Sympathy, and the Culture of Individual Rights in Antebellum America," *Journal of American History* 82 (1995): 463–93. For an incisive examination of the extensions—and limits—of sympathy in nineteenth-century America, see Robert S. Cox, *Body and Soul: A Sympathetic History of American Spiritualism* (Charlottesville: Univ. of Virginia Press, 2003).

9. TWH, "Cheerful Yesterdays," *Atlantic Monthly* 79 (1897): 53, 56, 241, 251.

10. The best biographical account of Higginson as activist and reformer remains Tilden G. Edelstein, *Strange Enthusiasm: A Life of Thomas Wentworth Higginson* (New Haven, CT: Yale Univ. Press, 1968). Edelstein is skimpy, though, in his attention to Higginson's religious thought and does not discuss "The Sympathy of Religions."

11. TWH, "The Return of Faith," 1854–1856, Houghton Library, Harvard University, bMS Am 1081.3 (12). The manuscript is scattered through thirteen folders, some of which include other early religious writings and sermons of TWH. The collec-

tion has not been reordered to fit TWH's short outline of eleven chapters in folder 7, no. 91, so it takes some careful reconstruction in reading the chapter notes that do survive. For the cited quotations, see folder 7, nos. 94–95; folder 8, no. 113; folder 11, no. 169; and folder 12, nos. 177, 179.

12. TWH, *Scripture Idolatry* (Worcester, MA: John Keith, 1854), 7–8, 11–12, 14–15; TWH to Garrison.

13. TWH, *Scripture Idolatry*, 16; TWH, "Extra-Christian or Anti-Christian," *Index* 3 (1872): 37.

14. TWH, *The Results of Spiritualism* (New York: Munson, [1859]), 19, 21; TWH, *The Rationale of Spiritualism* (New York: Ellinwood, 1859), 3–4.

15. TWH, diaries, 24 January to 19 February 1870; 5 January 1871, bMS 1162; TWH, clippings on "The Sympathy of Religions," in scrapbooks, bMS Am 1256.2; TWH, 15 December 1871, bMS Am 784, box 6, no. 1077; inscribed frontispiece, TWH to Eva S. Moore, in *The Writings of Thomas Wentworth Higginson,* 7 vols. (Boston: Houghton Mifflin, 1900), Houghton Library, Harvard University, *AC85.H5358.C900wb v.7.

16. Octavius Brooks Frothingham, *Recollections and Impressions, 1822–1890* (New York: G. P. Putnam's Sons, 1891), 120; M. T. Higginson, *Thomas Wentworth Higginson,* 268; TWH, *The Sympathy of Religions* (Boston: Free Religious Association, 1876); *Unity Church-Door Pulpit,* 16 June 1885. The standard work on the FRA remains Stow Persons, *Free Religion: An American Faith* (New Haven, CT, 1947; Boston: Beacon, 1963). Also very helpful on the FRA's importance as a link between Transcendentalism and the World's Parliament is Carl T. Jackson, *The Oriental Religions and American Thought: Nineteenth-Century Explorations* (Westport, CT: Greenwood, 1981), 103–22.

17. TWH, "Sympathy of Religions," 1–2.

18. TWH, "Sympathy of Religions," 2–5.

19. TWH, "Sympathy of Religions," 3, 12–13, 16, 18, 20–22. TWH prefaced his inclusion of "Galla Negroes" with the condescending adjective *ignorant.* That disparaging wording was intended as descriptive of their lack of formal knowledge of "technical Christianity" (which might well be, in Higginson's view, a good thing). Elsewhere he spoke of "the beautiful prayers of the Gallas" and attributed "an inspiration akin to genius" to their songs. See TWH, "The Use of Religion," *Index* 4 (1873): 209.

20. TWH, "Sympathy of Religions," 3, 12–13, 16, 18, 20–22.

21. John W. Chadwick, "Universal Religion," *New World* 3 (1894): 405, 416, 418. For evidence of the extent of this perspective, see Ralph Waldo Emerson, "Essential Principles of Religion," in *The Later Lectures of Ralph Waldo Emerson, 1843–1871,* ed. Ronald A. Bosco and Joel Myerson, 2 vols. (Athens: Univ. of Georgia Press, 2001), 2:266–73; David Wasson, *Christianity and Universal Religion* (Boston: Parker Fraternity, 1865); Samuel Longfellow, "The Unity and Universality of the Religious Ideas," *Radical* 3 (1868): 433–57; Samuel Johnson, "The Natural Sympathy of Religions," *Proceedings at the Third Annual Meeting of the Free Religious Association* (Boston: Wilson, 1870), 59–83; Minot J. Savage, *Life* (Boston: Ellis, 1890), 211–23; C. A. Bartol, "Cosmopolitan Religion," *New World* 2 (1893): 51–60; John W. Chadwick, *The Friendship of Religions* (Boston: Ellis, 1893); Ednah Dow Cheney, *Reminiscences* (Boston: Lee and Shepard, 1902), 162–65; Martin K. Schermerhorn, *Universal Worship*

(Poughkeepsie, NY: Barnes, 1906); R. Heber Newton, *Catholicity: A Treatise on the Unity of Religions* (New York: G. P. Putnam's Sons, 1918).

22. Lydia Maria Child, *Aspirations of the World: A Chain of Opals* (Boston: Roberts Brothers, 1878), 1–2, 8, 48, 257–58; Lydia Maria Child, "The Intermingling of Religions," *Atlantic Monthly* 28 (1871): 395.

23. William J. Potter, "'Sympathy of Religions,'" *Index* 3 (1872): 329; W. Creighton Peden and Everett J. Tarbox Jr., eds., *The Collected Essays of Francis Ellingwood Abbot (1836–1903), American Philosopher and Free Religionist*, 4 vols. (Lewiston, NY: Edwin Mellen Press, 1996), 1:321–24; Francis E. Abbot, "A Study of Religion: The Name and the Thing," *Index* 4 (1873): 109; Joseph Henry Allen, "The Alleged Sympathy of Religions," *New World* 4 (1895): 312, 320; William Wallace Fenn, "The Possibilities of Mysticism in Modern Thought," *New World* 6 (1897): 201. Potter's manuscript sermons also contain recurrent reflections on these themes. See William J. Potter, "The Bibles of the World as Showing the Antipathies and Sympathies of Religions," 4 November 1877; "One Spirit, Many Manifestations," 10 July 1870; "Unity of the Spirit: The Progress of Mankind toward Spiritual Unity," 9 October 1870; and "The East and the West in Religion," 1 November 1874, New Bedford Free Public Library Archives, New Bedford, MA.

24. TWH, "Opening Address of the President," *Proceedings at the Twenty-eighth Annual Meeting of the Free Religious Association* (Boston: Free Religious Association, 1895), 6–7; Solomon Schindler, "The Present Tendencies in the Religious World," *Proceedings at the Twenty-eighth Annual Meeting of the Free Religious Association* (Boston: Free Religious Association, 1895), 24, 30. For Schindler's biography, see Arthur Mann, "Solomon Schindler: Boston Radical," *New England Quarterly* 23 (1950): 453–76. Emil G. Hirsch in Chicago was another radical Jewish rabbi who thought carefully about the importance of preserving differences amid the prophecies of oneness: "To point out these differences is not a sin against the holy spirit of liberalism." See Hirsch, "Reform Judaism and Unitarianism," 1905, in *Twenty Discourses* (New York: Bloch, n.d.), 2. The phrase "colorless cosmopolitanism" is also from that discourse (2).

25. Potter, "'Sympathy of Religions,'" 329; Peden and Tarbox, *Collected Essays*, 1:321–24.

26. TWH, "Sympathy of Religions," 23; TWH to Garrison; TWH, 22 November 1855, bMS Am 784, box 4, no. 528; TWH, "Fayal and the Portuguese," *Atlantic Monthly* 6 (1860): 533–35. "Faial" is now the accepted spelling, but for historical purposes I have retained the nineteenth-century spelling. On Higginson's interest in health regimens and open-air devotion, see TWH, "Saints, and Their Bodies," *Atlantic Monthly* 1 (1858): 582–95.

27. S. G. W. Benjamin, *The Atlantic Islands as Resorts of Health and Pleasure* (New York: Harper, 1878); Albert L. Gihon, *The Azores and Madeira Islands, the Great Sanitarium of the World: Sketches of Interest to Tourists and Travelers* (Boston: Bartlett, [1877]); Herman Canfield, "The Azores as a Health Resort," *Around the World* 1 (1893–1894): 163–64; C. Alice Baker, *A Summer in the Azores with a Glimpse of Madeira* (Boston: Lee and Shepard, 1882), 3–4.

28. TWH, 23 July 1855, bMS Am 784, box 4, no. 505; TWH, "Fayal and the Portuguese," 526; TWH, 9–13 November 1855, bMs Am 784, box 4, nos. 520, 525, 527.

29. Henrique de Aguiar Oliveira Rodrigues, ed., "The Diary of Catherine Green

Hickling, 1786–1788," *Gávea-Brown* 15–16 (January 1994–December 1995): 122–23, 130, 141, 145–46, 148, 160, 178.

30. Silas Weston, *Visit to a Volcano; or, What I Saw at the Western Islands* (Providence, RI: Weston, 1856), 12–15, 25.

31. Robert Steele, *A Tour Through Part of the Atlantic; or, Recollections from Madeira, the Azores (or Western Isles), and Newfoundland* (London: Stockdale, 1810), 42, 52–54, 103, 118–19; Edward Boid, *A Description of the Azores, or Western Islands* (London: Bull and Churton, 1834), 57–58; John Fowler, *Journal of a Tour in the State of New York, in the Year 1830; with Remarks on Agriculture in Those Parts Most Eligible for Settlers: And Return to England by the Western Islands* (London: Whittaker, Treacher, and Arnot, 1831), 269–70.

32. Joseph May, ed., *Samuel Longfellow: Memoir and Letters* (Boston: Houghton Mifflin, 1894), 24–37; Roxana Lewis Dabney, comp., *Annals of the Dabney Family in Fayal, 1806–1871,* 3 vols. (Boston: Mudge, [1892]), 1:456, 476–79; 2:533, 608, 643, 649–51, 715–16; 3:1364, 1398, 1483.

33. May, *Samuel Longfellow,* 38–40; TWH, "Fayal and the Portuguese," 540–41. For analysis of Protestant spectating, see especially Jenny Franchot, *Roads to Rome: The Antebellum Protestant Encounter with Catholicism* (Berkeley: Univ. of California Press, 1994).

34. TWH, 13 November 1855, no. 527; 25 November 1855, no. 529; 8 December 1855, 16 December 1855, no. 531; 26 December 1855, no. 533; 31 December 1855, no. 536; 5 February 1856, no. 543; 14 March 1856, no. 549.

35. TWH, 18 February 1856, no. 546; 20–22 March 1856, no. 550; TWH, "Fayal and the Portuguese," 541.

36. TWH, 18 February 1856, no. 546.

37. TWH, "Fayal and the Portuguese," 533, 540–43; TWH, 5 March 1855, no. 499; 6 December 1855, no. 531.

38. TWH, "Sympathy," 23.

39. TWH, "Sympathy," 18, 23; TWH, "Fayal and the Portuguese," 543.

40. TWH, *Army Life in a Black Regiment* (New York: Norton, 1984), 122. Another practical instance where Higginson took the Catholic side against Protestant opinion was on the composition of the Boston School Board. See TWH, "Roman Catholics on the Defensive," *Index* 6 (1885): 146–47.

41. TWH, *Army Life,* 41, 71. Higginson was acknowledged "above all others" as the critical supporter of the first book-length collection of spirituals. See William Francis Allen, Charles Pickard Ware, and Lucy McKim Garrison, *Slave Songs of the United States* (New York: A. Simpson, 1867), xxxvii. His contributions are especially evident in the notations to the songs (pp. 4–6, 19–21, 38, 45, 48, 72, 93, 114–15).

42. TWH, *Army Life,* 41, 45, 48, 55, 70–72, 187–213, 241; TWH, "Negro Spirituals," *Atlantic Monthly* 19 (1867): 685–94; TWH, "Use of Religion," 209; TWH, "Remarks," *Report of Addresses at a Meeting Held in Boston, May 30, 1867 to Consider the Conditions, Wants and Prospects of Free Religion in America* (Boston: Adams, 1867), 51. For the prejudices of other abolitionists toward African-American evangelical worship, see Anna M. Speicher, *The Religious World of Antislavery Women: Spirituality in the Lives of Five Abolitionist Lecturers* (Syracuse, NY: Syracuse Univ. Press, 2000), 104–5.

43. TWH, *Army Life,* 70–71; Christopher Looby, ed., *The Complete Civil War Journal and Selected Letters of Thomas Wentworth Higginson* (Chicago: Univ. of

Chicago Press, 2000), 218. Higginson apparently added the comparisons to mysticism and Transcendentalism upon further reflection. Note their absence from the relevant passage in Looby's critical edition of Higginson's wartime journal (p. 86) versus Higginson's published version in *Army Life* (pp. 70–71).

44. W. E. B. Du Bois, *The Souls of Black Folk*, ed. Henry Louis Gates Jr. and Terri Hume Oliver (New York: Norton, 1999), 154, 157, 161, 214.

45. Du Bois, *Souls of Black Folk*, 136, 217. Higginson's failure to stand up for the National Negro Conference and the organization of the NAACP is discussed in Edelstein, *Strange Enthusiasm*, 391–93. Two days before his death in 1911, though, Higginson sent a supportive note of inquiry to the leader of the Boston NAACP, which suggests he may have seen the error of his initial stance in 1909 (400).

46. TWH, "A Correction," *Index* 6 (1875): 697; Octavius Brooks Frothingham, "Address of the President," *Proceedings at the Third Annual Meeting of the Free Religious Association* (Boston: Wilson, 1870), 16, 22; Johnson, "Natural Sympathy," 60–61; TWH, "Address," *Proceedings at the Sixth Annual Meeting of the Free Religious Association* (Boston: Cochrane and Sampson, 1873), 60–61.

47. TWH, "Address," *Proceedings at the Tenth Annual Meeting of the Free Religious Association* (Boston: Free Religious Association, 1877), 86–88.

48. *Proceedings at the Twenty-Sixth Annual Meeting of the Free Religious Association* (Boston: Free Religious Association, 1894), 12–13, 22–23; TWH, "The Sympathy of Religions," in *The World's Parliament of Religions*, ed. John Henry Barrows, 2 vols. (Chicago: Parliament, 1893), 1:780–84. Excellent accounts of the negotiation of religious difference and unity at the parliament can be found in Richard Hughes Seager, *The World's Parliament of Religions: The East/West Encounter, Chicago, 1893* (Bloomington: Indiana Univ. Press, 1995); and Carrie Tirado Bramen, *The Uses of Variety: Modern Americanism and the Quest for National Distinctiveness* (Cambridge, MA: Harvard Univ. Press, 2000), 250–91.

49. Lewis G. Janes, "Address," in *Proceedings at the Thirtieth Annual Meeting of the Free Religious Association* (New Bedford: Free Religious Association, 1897), 6–14; Lewis G. Janes, "The Study of Comparative Religions," *Greenacre Voice*, 8 July 1896; "Program of the Summer Lectures at Greenacre-on-the-Piscataqua," 1897, box 6, Sarah J. Farmer Papers, National Bahá'í Archives, Wilmette, IL.

50. Swami Saradananda, "The Sympathy of Religions," *Journal of Practical Metaphysics* 1 (1897): 318–19.

51. "The Greenacre Lectures," *Boston Evening Transcript*, 4 September 1897; Alfred W. Martin, *Great Religious Teachers of the East* (New York: Macmillan, 1911), 3–4; Alfred W. Martin, *Seven Great Bibles* (New York: Stokes, 1930), v–viii; "Autograph Book," 1904, box 3, Farmer Papers.

52. William Norman Guthrie, "Whitman and the American of the Future," 31 May 1912, noted in *Walt Whitman Fellowship Papers* (Philadelphia: The Fellowship, 1912); William Norman Guthrie, *Modern Poet Prophets* (Cincinnati: Clarke, 1897), 246, 250, 254, 257, 331; William Norman Guthrie, *Offices of Mystical Religion* (New York: Century, 1927), xxiv; William Norman Guthrie, ed., *Leaves of the Greater Bible: A Spiritual Anthology* (New York: Brentano's, 1917). Tisa Wenger, who has done wonderfully balanced research on Guthrie's various entanglements, first alerted me to him. See Tisa J. Wenger, "The Practice of Dance for the Future of Christianity: 'Eurythmic Worship' in New York's Roaring Twenties," in *Protestants in Practice: Histories of the Christian Life*

in America, ed. Laurie Maffly-Kipp, Leigh Schmidt, and Mark Valeri (Baltimore: Johns Hopkins Univ. Press, forthcoming).

53. Guthrie, *Offices of Mystical Religion,* xxiii; Guthrie, *Leaves of the Greater Bible,* unpaginated foreword.

54. Coleman Barks, *The Essential Rumi,* rev. ed. (San Francisco: HarperSanFrancisco, 2004), xvii, 32, 99. I give the quote from Whitman as it appears in the original; Barks slightly misquotes it, transposing school and church, and leaving out "own." Barks has a nice phrase for the kinds of observations that academics tuck away in endnotes, "chew-toys for the intellect," but accuracy remains a virtue worth gnawing on (xxiv). For the fullest treatment of Rumi and his multiple incarnations since the thirteenth century, including Barks's rendition, see Franklin D. Lewis, *Rumi, Past and Present, East and West* (Oxford: Oneworld, 2000), esp. 589–94.

Chapter Four

1. "Address of Prof. Felix Adler," *Proceedings of the Ninth Annual Meeting of the Free Religious Association* (Boston: Free Religious Association, 1876), 76–77. For Adler's biography, including his embrace of Emerson and Parker, see Benny Kraut, *From Reform Judaism to Ethical Culture: The Religious Evolution of Felix Adler* (Cincinnati: Hebrew Union College Press, 1979), 106–7, 134.

2. Felix Adler, *The Essentials of Spirituality* (New York: Pott, 1905), 1–2, 4–5, 15.

3. Adler, *Essentials of Spirituality,* 11, 14, 26.

4. Philip Schaff, *America: A Sketch of Its Political, Social, and Religious Character* (Cambridge, MA: Belknap Press of Harvard Univ. Press, 1961), 94–95, 140, 210–11.

5. For traditional forms of Christian meditation, see Charles E. Hambrick-Stowe, *The Practice of Piety: Puritan Devotional Disciplines in Seventeenth-Century New England* (Chapel Hill: Univ. of North Carolina Press, 1982), 161–75; Leigh Eric Schmidt, *Holy Fairs: Scotland and the Making of American Revivalism,* 2nd ed. (Grand Rapids, MI: Eerdmans, 2001), 134–45; and Ann Taves, *The Household of Faith: Roman Catholic Devotions in Mid-Nineteenth-Century America* (South Bend, IN: Univ. of Notre Dame Press, 1986), 74–82.

6. William James, *Varieties of Religious Experience* (New York: Penguin, 1982), 406; Horatio W. Dresser, *The Religion of the Spirit in Modern Life* (New York: Putnam's, 1914), 153–77.

7. Ralph Waldo Trine, *In Tune with the Infinite: Fullness of Peace, Power, and Plenty* (London: Thorsons, 1995), 28.

8. The standard history of the movement remains Charles S. Braden, *Spirits in Rebellion: The Rise and Development of New Thought* (Dallas: Southern Methodist Univ. Press, 1963). For works of sharper focus and keener analysis, see Beryl Satter, *Each Mind a Kingdom: American Women, Sexual Purity, and the New Thought Movement, 1875–1920* (Berkeley: Univ. of California Press, 1999); and R. Marie Griffith, *Born Again Bodies: Flesh and Spirit in American Christianity* (Berkeley: Univ. of California Press, 2004).

9. Henry Wood, *The New Thought Simplified: How to Gain Harmony and Health* (Boston: Lee and Shepard, 1903), 13, 147.

10. Horatio W. Dresser, *A History of the New Thought Movement* (New York: Crowell, 1919), iv, 8, 177–91; Braden, *Spirits in Rebellion,* 153–54. For the wealth of alliances among New Thought leaders, liberal Protestants, and progressive reformers, see Satter, *Each Mind a Kingdom,* 8–9, 181–216.

11. Peirce was the only one who remembered the prior Metaphysical Club, belatedly noting its erstwhile existence in 1907. See Louis Menand, *The Metaphysical Club: A Story of Ideas in America* (New York: Farrar, Straus and Giroux, 2001), 201, 203. Peirce's memory, which went back thirty-five years at that point, may have been colored by the ongoing presence in Boston of Dresser's more prominent Metaphysical Club. The young Dresser was a presence around Harvard from the early 1890s through 1907, when he finally received his Ph.D. in philosophy after years of various New Thought diversions. See Braden, *Spirits in Rebellion,* 158–60. Another Metaphysical Club, longer lived than Peirce's and shorter lived than Dresser's, arose in Boston in 1883 and was spearheaded by Julia Ward Howe's daughter, Julia Romana Anagnos, whose death in 1886 spelled the end of this venture. It offered talks on such topics as "Nirvana," "Transcendentalism," and the "Newest Phases of Christianity"; its agenda, speakers, and clientele were part and parcel of the liberal Unitarian, comparativist milieu. See *Proceedings of the Metaphysical Club, at a Meeting Held March 24, 1886* (Boston: Clark, 1886), 69–74.

12. Braden, *Spirits in Rebellion,* 155; Dresser, *History,* 171.

13. Henry Wood, *Ideal Suggestion Through Mental Photography: A Restorative System for Home and Private Use* (Boston, 1893; Boston: Lee and Shepard, 1899), 8, 24, 69.

14. Wood, *Ideal Suggestion,* 70–71, 103.

15. Wood, *Ideal Suggestion,* 108–9, 111, 113, 117, 132, 145, 161.

16. See Louis Schneider and Sanford M. Dornbusch, *Popular Religion: Inspirational Books in America* (Chicago: Univ. of Chicago Press, 1958), 162.

17. For a basic portrait of Trine, see Charles Brodie Patterson, "Ralph Waldo Trine; A Biographic Sketch," *Mind: Science, Philosophy, Psychology, Metaphysics, Occultism* 9 (1902): 325–29. For his animal-welfare work, see Ralph Waldo Trine, *Every Living Creature; or, Heart-Training Through the Animal World* (New York: Crowell, 1899); and Trine, "An Open Letter to the People of the State of New York, on a Certain Species of Legalized Cruelty," broadside, c. 1902, Huntington Library, Rare Books and Manuscripts, San Marino, CA. For his most sustained discussion of progressive social and political reforms, see Ralph Waldo Trine, *In the Fire of the Heart* (New York: McClure, Phillips, 1906). There is also a small collection of Trine's correspondence at the Huntington Library from which additional biographical details can be gleaned as well as evidence of the extent of his popularity as a self-help writer.

18. Trine, *In Tune with the Infinite,* 2, 10, 14, 16, 29–30.

19. Trine, *In Tune with the Infinite,* 77–78, 89–90, 169–70; Ralph Waldo Trine, *What All the World's A-Seeking* (Boston: Ellis, 1896), 16–18; Trine, *Every Living Creature,* 7, 11, 34–38.

20. Trine, *In Tune with the Infinite,* 49–52, 80–81, 190–94, 205–7; Ralph Waldo Trine, *On the Open Road* (New York: Crowell, 1908), 1.

21. Trine, *In Tune with the Infinite,* 182–89; F. Max Müller to Ralph Waldo Trine, 29 March 1898, Ralph Waldo Trine Collection, Huntington Library, San Marino, CA; *New York Times,* 20 June 1926, 3.

22. On the history of the Theosophical Society, see Bruce F. Campbell, *Ancient*

Wisdom Revived: A History of the Theosophical Movement (Berkeley: Univ. of California Press, 1980).

23. See Campbell, *Ancient Wisdom Revived*, 31–87; Stephen Prothero, *Purified by Fire: A History of Cremation in America* (Berkeley: Univ. of California Press, 2001), 25–42, 87–88; and Stephen Prothero, *The White Buddhist: The Asian Odyssey of Henry Steel Olcott* (Bloomington: Indiana Univ. Press, 1996).

24. Henry S. Olcott, *The Buddhist Catechism* (London: Theosophical Publishing Society, 1915), xii, 1, 7, 9–10, 26, 41, 66, 71. Prothero offers a good reading of *The Buddhist Catechism* in terms of liberal Protestantism and academic Orientalism; see Prothero, *White Buddhist*, 101–6.

25. Olcott, *Buddhist Catechism*, 10, 49, 94.

26. H. P. Blavatsky, *The Voice of the Silence* (Wheaton, IL: Theosophical Publishing House, 1973), 68.

27. Annie Besant, *Four Great Religions* (Chicago: Theosophical Press, 1897), 10; Annie Besant, *Thought Power: Its Control and Culture* (Wheaton, IL: Theosophical Publishing House, 1966), 94–95; Annie Besant, *Esoteric Christianity* (New York: Lane, 1902), 291. For an excellent recent analysis of Besant's journey, see Mark Bevir, "Annie Besant's Quest for Truth: Christianity, Secularism and New Age Thought," *Journal of Ecclesiastical History* 50 (1999): 62–93.

28. Besant, *Thought Power*, 71, 76, 81–84, 100.

29. Annie Besant, *An Introduction to Yoga* (Adyar, India: Theosophical Publishing House, 1959), 117; Swami Vivekananda, *Complete Works*, 8 vols. (Calcutta: Advaita Ashrama, 2001), 1:24; 2:24–37. See also Carl T. Jackson, *Vedanta for the West: The Ramakrishna Movement in the United States* (Bloomington: Indiana Univ. Press, 1994), 28–30; and Carrie Tirado Bramen, *The Uses of Variety: Modern Americanism and the Quest for National Distinctiveness* (Cambridge, MA: Harvard Univ. Press, 2000), 255–56, 258–59, 269–71.

30. Vivekananda, *Complete Works*, 1:119–313, 503–21; 2:37; 4:218–49; 6:37–40; Jackson, *Vedanta for the West*, 29–30, 72–73; Satish K. Kapoor, *Cultural Contact and Fusion: Swami Vivekananda in the West* (Jalandhar, India: ABS, 1987), 209–16.

31. Swami Paramananda, *Emerson and Vedanta* (Cohasset, MA: Vedanta Centre, 1985), 55.

32. Swami Paramananda, *Vedanta in Practice* (Cohasset, MA: Vedanta Centre, 1985), 70–71; Swami Paramananda, *Book of Daily Thoughts and Prayers* (Cohasset, MA: Vedanta Centre, [1926]), 125; Mabel Potter Daggett, "The Heathen Invasion," *Hampton Columbian Magazine* 27 (1911): 400. For Paramananda's far-flung venues, see Jackson, *Vedanta for the West*, 61–65; and Polly Trout, *Eastern Seeds, Western Soil: Three Gurus in America* (Mountain View, CA: Mayfield, 2001), 71–107.

33. Ananda Guruge, ed., *Return to Righteousness: A Collection of Speeches, Essays and Letters of the Anagarika Dharmapala* (Ceylon: Government Press, 1965), 684–85. For an excellent analysis of Dharmapala's negotiation of his in-between identity, see Gananath Obeyesekere, "Personal Identity and Cultural Crisis: The Case of Anagarika Dharmapala of Sri Lanka," in *The Biographical Process: Studies in the History and Psychology of Religion,* ed. Frank E. Reynolds and Donald Capps (The Hague: Mouton, 1976), 221–52. Another Buddhist contributor to this wider recommendation of meditation to Americans was the Japanese monk Soyen Shaku, who lectured across the continent in 1905–1906 from San Jose and Oakland to Philadelphia and Boston. For a collection of his American lectures, including one on the disciplines of contemplation

or introspection, see Soyen Shaku, *Sermons of a Buddhist Abbot: Addresses on Religious Subjects,* trans. Daisetz Teitaro Suzuki (Chicago: Open Court, 1906), 146–59.

34. "Diary Leaves of the Late Ven. Anagarika Dharmapala," ed. Sri D. Valisinha, *Maha Bodhi* 63 (1955): 53–56, 436–39.

35. Dharmapala, "Diary Leaves," 438–39; Dharmapala, "Diary Leaves," *Maha Bodhi* 64 (1956): 25, 48, 103, 296–97, 302, 349–50; Dharmapala, "Diary Leaves," *Maha Bodhi* 65 (1957): 48, 123; Dharmapala, "Diary Leaves," *Maha Bodhi* 66 (1958): 34. On the organization of the Procopeia Club, an offshoot of the Greenacre summer community and a precursor to the Metaphysical Club, see Dresser, *History,* 179–80.

36. Dharmapala, "Diary Leaves," *Maha Bodhi* 65 (1957): 362–67.

37. Guruge, *Return to Righteousness,* xlix, 313; Dharmapala, "Diary Leaves," *Maha Bodhi* 64 (1956): 52, 460; Dharmapala, "Diary Leaves," *Maha Bodhi* 65 (1957): 476–79.

38. Dharmapala, "Diary Leaves," *Maha Bodhi* 65 (1957): 476–79.

39. Robert H. Sharf, "Buddhist Modernism and the Rhetoric of Meditative Experience," *Numen* 42 (1995): 247–48, 251–53, 257–59. Another highly suggestive context within which to read the history of modern meditation is the history of modern attention (and the disciplining of its various deficits). For a brilliant history of attention to art that displays a notable inattention to religion, see Jonathan Crary, *Suspensions of Perception: Attention, Spectacle, and Modern Culture* (Boston: MIT Press, 1999).

40. Vivekananda, *Complete Works,* 4:230.

41. Annie Payson Call, *Power Through Repose* (Boston: Roberts Brothers, 1891), 12–13, 129–42.

42. Besant, *Thought Power,* 101–4; Dhan Gopal Mukerji, *Daily Meditation; or, The Practice of Repose* (New York: E. P. Dutton, 1933), 13.

43. William James, *The Principles of Psychology,* 2 vols. (New York: Dover, 1950), 1:294, 330, 391–93; Trine, *In Tune with the Infinite,* 58.

44. Joshua L. Liebman, *Peace of Mind* (New York: Citadel, 1994), 186–87. For an excellent recent interpretation of Liebman's significance, see Andrew R. Heinze, *Jews and the American Soul: Human Nature in the Twentieth Century* (Princeton, NJ: Princeton Univ. Press, 2004), 195–239.

45. Mukerji, *Daily Meditation,* 14–24.

46. Vivekananda, *Complete Works,* 1:509, 511; Besant, *Thought Power,* 96.

47. Besant, *Thought Power,* 109; Trine, *In Tune with the Infinite,* 158–73.

48. Joseph Goldstein and Jack Kornfield, *Seeking the Heart of Wisdom: The Path of Insight Meditation* (Boston: Shambhala, 1987), 159.

49. Goldstein and Kornfield, *Seeking the Heart of Wisdom,* 159–70.

50. Daniel Goleman, *The Meditative Mind: The Varieties of Meditative Experience* (Los Angeles: Tarcher, 1988), ix, xii, xvi–xvii.

Chapter Five

1. Mohammed Alexander Russell Webb, *Islam in America* (New York: Oriental Publishing, 1893), 5–6, 11.

2. Webb, *Islam in America,* 7–9; Mohammed Alexander Russell Webb, *The Three Lectures* (Madras: Lawrence Asylum, 1892), 53.

3. Webb, *Islam in America,* 11–14.

4. Webb, *Islam in America,* 33, 41, 52; Mohammed Alexander Russell Webb, *A*

Guide to Namaz: A Detailed Exposition of the Moslem Order of Ablutions and Prayer with a Review of the Five Pillars of Practice (New York: Moslem World Publishing, 1893), 3.

5. Esther Davis, "The Great Discovery," *Star of the West* 21 (1931): 330–31, 334.

6. The scholarly literature on Greenacre is surprisingly sparse, and mostly what has been written is by Bahá'í historians doing American Bahá'í history. See James Douglas Martin, "The Life and Work of Sarah Jane Farmer, 1847–1916" (M.A. thesis, Univ. of Waterloo, 1967); Anne Gordon Atkinson [Perry], *Green Acre on the Piscataqua* (Eliot, ME: Green Acre Bahá'í School Council, 1991); and Robert H. Stockman, *The Bahá'í Faith in America: Early Expansion, 1900–1912* (Oxford: Ronald, 1995), 142–48, 217–19. Historians of Vedanta have also shown an occasional interest in the community. See especially Pravrajika Prabuddhaprana, *Saint Sara: The Life of Sara Chapman Bull, the American Mother of Swami Vivekananda* (Calcutta: Sri Sarada Math, 2002), 82–121, 138–44.

7. Sarah Farmer's address book, 1895, Green Acre Fellowship Records, box 4, f. 4, National Bahá'í Archives, Wilmette, IL; Albert Le Baron (communicated by William James), "A Case of Psychic Automatism, Including 'Speaking with Tongues,'" *Proceedings of the Society for Psychical Research* 12 (1896): 277–97; Richard Hodgson to Farmer, 14 July 1896, Sarah J. Farmer Papers, box 1, f. 23, National Bahá'í Archives, Wilmette, IL. For James's part in offering advice on Farmer's treatment, see his two letters that survive in the court records over the contestation of Sara Bull's will and her half-million-dollar estate. In that case, Farmer's distress was used to further impugn Bull's own mental stability. See York County Probate Court, Alfred, Maine, Sara C. Bull Records, 1911, case no. 54667, 4 vols., 1:66–67, 77, 81; 2:457, 466, 468–69.

8. Stockman, *Bahá'í Faith in America,* 148; Peter Smith, "The American Bahá'í Community, 1894–1917: A Preliminary Survey," in *Studies in Bábí and Bahá'í History,* ed. Moojan Momen (Los Angeles: Kalimát Press, 1982), 162. For the religious quest of one exemplary seeker of the period, who passed from Catholic to Theosophist to Buddhist to Bahá'í to Vedantist identities, see Thomas A. Tweed, "Inclusivism and the Spiritual Journey of Marie de Souza Canavarro (1849–1933)," *Religion* 24 (1994): 43–58.

9. "The Diary Leaves of the Late Ven. Anagarika Dharmapala," ed. Sri D. Valishna, *Maha Bodhi* 66 (1958): 35.

10. Augustine Caldwell, *The Rich Legacy: Memories of Hannah Tobey Farmer, Wife of Moses Gerrish Farmer* (Boston: Ellis, 1892), 62–64, 82–83, 98–99, 218–19, 430–33; Sarah Farmer, "Diary Notes," box 4, f. 10, Farmer Papers; Margaret Ford, "Sarah Jane Farmer, 1847–1916," unpublished memoir, 1947, 4, box 3, f. 36, Farmer Papers; Farmer to unidentified correspondent, 14 March 1902, box 1, f. 49, Farmer Papers; Richard M. Gipson, *The Life of Emma Thursby, 1845–1931* (New York: New York Historical Society, 1940), 357–59, 364–70. Ford, also of the Bahá'í faith, did invaluable work in compiling Farmer's papers, canvassing old friends, and sketching out her life in a manuscript biography, which was never published. All that survives of Farmer's diary is a transcribed outline that Ford undertook in 1942. The original has disappeared, and the copy appears to be a bare summary of the autograph.

11. Caldwell, *Rich Legacy,* 565, 568–69; Sarah Farmer to Phoebe Hearst, 25 April 1904; Farmer to Hearst, 25 November 1904; Phoebe Apperson Hearst Papers, Bancroft Library, University of California, Berkeley. Farmer later claimed to have

discerned her vision for Greenacre in June 1892 before her trip to Chicago. It is possible, but the parliament seems the clearest catalyst. For her memory of a prior vision, see Myron H. Phelps, "Green Acre," *Word* 1 (November 1904): 55. Her diary suggests February 1894 as the "turning point," the occasion of a "solemn vow" to the new enterprise. See Farmer, "Diary Notes," 4 February 1894.

12. Ford, "Sarah Jane Farmer," 5; Sarah Farmer to W. S. Key, 9 May 1900, box 1, f. 28, Farmer Papers.

13. Ford, "Sarah Jane Farmer," 1, 5–6; Martin, "Life and Times," 58; Emma Thursby to Ralph Waldo Trine, 10 September 1930, Ralph Waldo Trine Collection, Huntington Library, San Marino, CA; Swami Vivekananda, *The Complete Works of Swami Vivekananda*, 8 vols. (Calcutta: Advaita Ashrama, 1989), 6:259–62. For the particular form of hydrotherapy in fashion at Greenacre in the late 1890s, see Sebastian Kneipp, *The Kneipp Cure* (New York: Kneipp Cure Publishing, [1896]).

14. "Buddhism and Other Religions Taught in New England," *Boston Sunday Journal*, 19 July 1903, 3.

15. Lewis G. Janes, *Our Nation's Peril: Social Ideals and Social Progress* (Boston: West, 1899), 24–27; Lewis G. Janes, "The Comparative Study of Religions: Its Pitfalls and Its Promise," *Sewanee Review* 7 (1899): 7; "The Monsalvat School for the Comparative Study of Religion: Sixth Annual Session," 1901, box 7, f. 33, Farmer Papers; *Lewis G. Janes: Philosopher, Patriot, Lover of Man* (Boston: West, 1902), 35–40, 167–68.

16. Lewis Janes to Sarah Farmer, 21 September 1898; Farmer to Janes, 10 June 1899; Janes to Farmer, 22 December 1899, box 21, f. 24, 28, 30, Farmer Papers. An extensive correspondence between Farmer and Janes survives, amply documenting their disagreements, small and large, and also their shared enthusiasms. For third-party accounts of the conflicts, see Sara Bull to Farmer, 31 May 1900, box 1, f. 10; John Fretwell to Lewis Janes, 30 March 1901, box 2, f. 39; Rena R. Haskell to Janes, 30 May 1901, box 2, f. 43; Farmer Papers.

17. Sarah Farmer, "The Green Acre Ideal," 1898, box 6, pamphlets, Farmer Papers; "Monsalvat School," 1901.

18. Kurt Leidecker, "Amos Bronson Alcott and the Concord School of Philosophy," *Personalist* 23 (1952): 250–51, 25; Martin, "Life and Work," 101–7; "Home of Soul Culture," 2 May 1899, newspaper clipping, box 5, f. 28, Farmer Papers; "Greenacre, 'Home of Soul Culture,' and Its Founder," *Phrenological Journal and Science of Health* 108 (1899): 239–44.

19. Franklin B. Sanborn, ed., *Familiar Letters of Henry David Thoreau* (Cambridge, MA: Riverside, 1894), v–vi, 1; Robert P. Richardson, "The Rise and Fall of the Parliament of Religions at Greenacre," *Open Court* 46 (1931): 134–35. For Malloy's popular lectures on Emerson and his other activities on the bard's behalf, see Charles Malloy, *A Study of Emerson's Major Poems*, ed. Kenneth Walter Cameron (Hartford, CT: Transcendental Books, 1973); and Benjamin O. Flower, *Progressive Men, Women and Movements of the Past Twenty-five Years* (Boston: New Arena, 1914), 178–79.

20. Franklin Benjamin Sanborn, *Table Talk: A Transcendentalist's Opinions on American Life, Literature, Art and People from the Mid-Nineteenth Century Through the First Decade of the Twentieth*, ed. Kenneth Walter Cameron (Hartford, CT: Transcendental Books, 1981), 170, 234; Kenneth Walter Cameron, ed., *Transcendentalists in Transition: Popularization of Emerson, Thoreau and the Concord School of Philosophy in*

the *Greenacre Summer Conferences and the Monsalvat School (1894–1909)* (Hartford, CT: Transcendental Books, 1980).

21. William Innes Homer, ed., *Heart's Gate: Letters between Marsden Hartley and Horace Traubel, 1906–1915* (Highlands, NC: Jargon Society, 1982), 39.

22. "Program of the Summer Lectures at Greenacre-on-the-Piscataqua," 1896, box 6, f. 34, Farmer Papers; Fenollosa quoted in Carl T. Jackson, *The Oriental Religions and American Thought: Nineteenth-Century Explorations* (Westport, CT: Greenwood, 1981), 215–18; Ernest Fenollosa, *East and West* (New York: Crowell, 1893), v–vi, 54–55.

23. Marsden Hartley, *Somehow a Past: The Autobiography of Marsden Hartley,* ed. Susan Elizabeth Ryan (Cambridge, MA: MIT Press, 1998), 21, 67, 181, 188; Homer, *Heart's Gate,* 41; Townsend Ludington, *Seeking the Spiritual: The Paintings of Marsden Hartley* (Ithaca, NY: Cornell Univ. Press, 1998), 28–29; Charles C. Eldredge, "Nature Symbolized: American Painting from Ryder to Hartley," in *The Spiritual in Art: Abstract Painting, 1890–1985,* ed. Maurice Tuchman (New York: Abbeville, 1986), 118–19. For an indication of how important this congruence continues to be, see Robert Wuthnow, *Creative Spirituality: The Way of the Artist* (Berkeley: Univ. of California Press, 2001).

24. Sarah Farmer, "The Abundant Life," in *The Spirit of New Thought,* ed. Horatio Dresser (New York: Crowell, 1917), 29–36; Charles Brodie Patterson, "Helen Van-Anderson: A Biographic Sketch," *Mind: Science, Philosophy, Psychology, Metaphysics, Occultism* 10 (1902): 245; Vivekananda, *Complete Works,* 6:260.

25. Horatio Dresser, "Metaphysics at Greenacre," *Journal of Practical Metaphysics* 2 (1897): 56–57.

26. Horatio Dresser, *A History of the New Thought Movement* (New York: Crowell, 1919), 214–15.

27. Farmer to unidentified correspondent, 14 March 1902; Farmer to Horatio Dresser, 14 March 1902, box 1, f. 49, Farmer Papers.

28. Rena R. Haskell to Lewis Janes, [1901], box 2, f. 45; Farmer to Helen Cole, 22 August 1902, box 1, f. 12, Farmer Papers.

29. Farmer to Helen Cole, 31 May 1903, f. 2, Helen Cole Papers, National Bahá'í Archives, Wilmette, IL; "Program of the Twelfth Season of Summer Conferences," 1905; Charles Mason Remey, "Reminiscences of the Summer School Green-Acre, Eliot, Maine," 2 vols., Dartmouth College Library, 1:27–30.

30. Mohi Sobhani, ed. and trans., *Mahmúd's Diary: The Diary of Mírzá Mahmúd-i-Zarqání Chronicling 'Abdu'l-Bahá's Journey to America* (Oxford: Ronald, 1998), 216. For an early attempt by an American lawyer and Greenacre supporter to identify the "essential nature" of the Bahá'í "attitude toward other religions," see Myron H. Phelps, *Life and Teachings of Abbas Effendi* (New York: Putnam's Sons, 1912), 127–48.

31. 'Abdu'l-Bahá to Sarah Farmer, July 1906, trans. Ali Kuli Khan; 'Abdu'l-Bahá to Farmer, 19 March 1901; 'Abdu'l-Bahá to Farmer, 1 July 1908, box 5, 'Abdu'l-Bahá Collection, National Bahá'í Archives, Wilmette, IL; Marie Hopper, "Recollections of Sarah Farmer," 7–8, box 3, f. 39; Charles Remey to unidentified correspondent, 19 August 1916, box 2, f. 3, Farmer Papers.

32. Sanborn, *Table Talk,* 280, 305, 315; Rena Haskell to Lewis Janes, [1901], box 2, f. 47, Farmer Papers; Sarah Farmer to St. Cecilia, 19 July 1914, Emma Thursby Papers,

New York Historical Society, New York City; Richardson, "Rise and Fall," 148; "Miss Farmer and Greenacre," *Open Court* 29 (1915): 572.

33. A fairly good picture of the care Farmer received in these years can be pieced together from the Farmer letters in the Emma Thursby Papers.

34. *Boston Post,* 4 August 1913; *Portsmouth Herald,* 10 August 1913; Carrie Kinney, "Account of the Rescue of Sarah Farmer," box 3, f. 40, Farmer Papers; Ivy Drew Edwards, "Diary," 30 July 1915, 3 August 1915, 14 August 1915, 20 November 1916, Eliot Bahá'í Archives, Eliot, ME.

35. Kinney, "Account of the Rescue"; Richardson, "Rise and Fall," 156–57; *New York Times,* 10 January 1921, 15; *New York Times,* 30 September 1921, 2; *New York Times,* 18 April 1927, 16; Urbain Ledoux, *Mr. Zero?* (New York, 1931), A7–A9; Hari G. Govil, "Urbain Ledoux: His Message to Mankind," *Reality: A Magazine Devoted to the Elimination of Prejudice, Religious, Racial and Class* 5 (August 1922), reprinted in Urbain Ledoux, *Prophecies in Blue: Zero's Scrap Book* (New York, 1932), 9, 12–21.

36. Kinney, "Account of the Rescue"; Richardson, "Rise and Fall," 156–57; Mary Sanford to Phoebe Hearst, 23 October 1916, Hearst Papers; Ford, "Sarah Jane Farmer," 2, 19–21; *Boston American,* 10 August 1913.

37. "Sarah Farmer Dies," unlabeled newspaper clipping, box 6, f. 9, Farmer Papers; Horace Holley, "Green Acre," *Star of the West* 21 (1926): 117; Richardson, "Rise and Fall," 161, 165–66; Robert P. Richardson, "The Persian Rival to Jesus and His American Disciples," *Open Court* 29 (1915): 481.

38. Ford, "Sarah Jane Farmer," 16; 'Abdu'l-Bahá to Farmer, 16 February 1907; 'Abdu'l-Bahá to Farmer, 23 July 1907; Sobhani, *Mahmúd's Diary,* 220; Farmer to Phoebe Hearst, 16 June 1904, Hearst Papers.

39. Sobhani, *Mahmúd's Diary,* 211; 'Abdu'l-Bahá, *The Promulgation of Universal Peace: Talks Delivered by 'Abdu'l-Bahá During His Visit to the United States and Canada in 1912* (Wilmette, IL: Bahá'í Publishing Trust, 1982), 264; John Weiss, *American Religion* (Boston: Roberts Brothers, 1871), 83; William James, *The Varieties of Religious Experience* (New York: Penguin, 1982), 310–11.

40. Ellen V. Beecher, "Vision Given to Mother Beecher," 1905, box 11, Louise and John D. Bosch Papers, National Bahá'í Archives, Wilmette, IL; Bahá'u'lláh, *The Seven Valleys,* trans. Ali Kuli Khan (Chicago: Bahai Publishing Society, 1906), 10–11, 13–14. Another important devotional text, with many of the same themes, appeared a year earlier. See Bahá'u'lláh, *Hidden Words* (Chicago: Bahai Publishing Society, 1905). For wider background on the movement's publishing ventures, see Roger M. Dahl, "American Bahá'í Publishing: 1896–1922," *World Order* 29 (Spring 1998): 31–47. For the family background of Ellen Beecher, see Dorothy Freeman, *From Copper to Gold: The Life of Dorothy Baker* (Oxford: George Ronald, 1984), 15–20.

41. Stanwood Cobb, "Memories of 'Abdu'l-Bahá," in *In His Presence: Visits to 'Abdu'l-Bahá* (Los Angeles: Kalimát Press, 1989), 25–29, 34–35; Stanwood Cobb, "Visit to Rabbi Fleischer," 15 February 1906, box 37; Stanwood Cobb, lecture notes, 1906, box 10; Stanwood Cobb, "The Green Acre Story," 20 July 1958, box 39; Stanwood Cobb, "A Tribute to Sarah Farmer," undated, box 23; Cobb Family Papers, Special Collections Research Center, Bird Library, Syracuse Univ., Syracuse, NY. A good sense of his pained soul-searching before 1906 is to be found in Stanwood Cobb, "A Spasmodic Diary or Record of Impressions," 1903–1904, box 37, Cobb Family Papers.

42. Stanwood Cobb, journal, 13 October 1909, box 37, Cobb Family Papers; Stanwood Cobb, "The Spirituality of the East and the West," *Open Court* 27 (1913): 306.

43. Paul Carus to Anagarika Dharmapala, 26 February 1896, quoted in Harold Henderson, *Catalyst for Controversy: Paul Carus of Open Court* (Carbondale: Southern Illinois Univ. Press, 1993), 116; Paul Carus, "The Spirituality of the Occident," *Open Court* 27 (1913): 316–17; Paul Carus, *The Dawn of a New Religious Era and Other Essays* (Chicago: Open Court, 1916), 20–21; Paul Carus, "The Religion of Resignation," *Open Court* 3 (1890): 2051–52; Paul Carus, "Is Religion a Feeling of Dependence?" *Open Court* 13 (1899): frontispiece, 563–65; "Schleiermacher as a Man," *New Englander* 21 (1862): 429–30, 437. For a classic elaboration of Schleiermacher's feeling of dependence in American liberal theology, see Newman Smyth, *The Religious Feeling: A Study for Faith* (New York: Scribner, Armstrong, 1877), esp. 29–52.

44. Cobb, "Memories of 'Abdu'l-Bahá," 31; Cobb, journal, 19 January 1910.

45. Octavius Frothingham, "The Religion of Humanity," in *Proceedings at the Fifth Annual Meeting of the Free Religious Association* (Boston: Cochrane, 1872), 72; James, *Varieties of Religious Experience*, 46–47, 49.

46. James, *Varieties of Religious Experience*, 51, 210; Stanwood Cobb, "Religiosity Versus Spirituality," undated manuscript, box 23, Cobb Family Papers.

47. Carol Lee Flinders, *At the Root of This Longing: Reconciling a Spiritual Hunger and a Feminist Thirst* (San Francisco: HarperSanFrancisco, 1998), 60–61, 84–85.

Chapter Six

1. Octavius Brooks Frothingham, "What Is Religion, and What Is It For?" *Radical* 7 (1870): 433–34, 437–38; Frothingham, "Address of the President," *Proceedings at the Third Annual Meeting of the Free Religious Association* (Boston: Wilson, 1870), 22; Minot J. Savage, "Unity in Religion," *Proceedings at the Twenty-sixth Annual Meeting of the Free Religious Association of America* (Boston: Free Religious Association, 1894), 52–53.

2. Ralph Waldo Emerson, *Essays: First and Second Series* (New York: Gramercy, 1993), 165, 168; James Freeman Clarke, "Why I Am Not a Free-Religionist," *North American Review* 145 (1887): 378. Appropriately, the "endless seeker" epigram was also reprinted as a hallowed piece of "Concord Wisdom" in the *Greenacre Voice*, 15 August 1896.

3. Ephraim Pagitt, *Heresiography; or, A Description of the Hereticks and Sectaries of These Latter Times* (London: Wilson, 1646), unpaginated dedicatory epistle, 141. For an excellent overview, see J. F. McGregor, "Seekers and Ranters," in *Radical Religion in the English Revolution,* ed. J. F. McGregor and B. Reay (New York: Oxford Univ. Press, 1984), 121–39. His summary conclusion is: "There is little objective evidence that either Seekers or Ranters formed coherent movements or that they existed in any considerable numbers." Both categories were "largely artificial products of the Puritan heresiographers' methodology" (p. 122).

4. On the impact of Jones on Thurman, see Thurman's own account in Howard Thurman, *With Head and Heart: The Autobiography of Howard Thurman* (San Diego: Harcourt Brace, 1979), 74–77. See also Luther E. Smith Jr., *Howard Thurman: The Mystic as Prophet* (Washington, DC: Univ. Press of America, 1981), 27–30. For one of Thurman's early essays demonstrating the convergence, see Howard Thurman, "Mysticism and Social Change," *Eden Seminary Bulletin* 4 (1939): 3–34.

5. Elizabeth Gray Vining, *Friend of Life: The Biography of Rufus M. Jones* (Philadelphia: Lippincott, 1958), 87; Rufus M. Jones, "Why I Enroll with the Mystics," in *Contemporary American Theology: Theological Autobiographies,* ed. Vergilius Ferm (New York: Round Table, 1932), 196; William James, *The Varieties of Religious Experience* (New York: Penguin, 1982), 7. For Jones as popularizer, see Matthew S. Hedstrom, "Rufus Jones and Mysticism for the Masses," *Cross Currents* 54 (2004): 31–44. Jones and Thurman as the mystical wing of liberal Protestantism are also helpfully surveyed in Gary Dorrien, *The Making of American Liberal Theology: Idealism, Realism, and Modernity, 1900–1950* (Louisville: Westminister John Knox, 2003), 364–71, 559–66.

6. Vining, *Friend of Life,* 38–39; Jones, "Why I Enroll with the Mystics," 191–95; Rufus M. Jones, *Some Exponents of Mystical Religion* (London: Epworth, 1930), 176–77, 202–4. The portrait painted here of Jones's office is from various photographs taken of him at his desk about 1915. See Rufus M. Jones Papers, box 136, Mss. Collection no. 1130, Haverford College Library, Haverford, PA. A room-sized facsimile of Jones's office is still on display at the Haverford Library; it includes the various images discussed here.

7. Walt Whitman, "Elias Hicks," in *Walt Whitman: Poetry and Prose* (New York: Library of America, 1996), 1245–46, 1256–58. Jones's copy of the Binns's biography of Whitman is in Jones's reproduced study at Haverford.

8. Jones, "Why I Enroll with the Mystics," 191–97; Rufus M. Jones, *Studies in Mystical Religion* (London: Macmillan, 1909), v, xxxiii–xxxv; Rufus M. Jones, "Prayer and the Mystic Vision," in *Concerning Prayer: Its Nature, Its Difficulties, and Its Value* (London: Macmillan, 1921), 123. For detailed background on the multiple fault lines running through nineteenth-century Quakerism as well as the liberal response of Jones and company, see Thomas D. Hamm, *The Transformation of American Quakerism: Orthodox Friends, 1800–1907* (Bloomington: Indiana Univ. Press, 1988); and Hugh Barbour and J. William Frost, *The Quakers* (Westport, CT: Greenwood, 1988).

9. Jones, *Studies in Mystical Religion,* 452, 454; Rufus M. Jones, preface to *A Philosophical Study of Mysticism,* by Charles A Bennett (New Haven, CT: Yale Univ. Press, 1931), x.

10. Jones, *Studies in Mystical Religion,* 452, 458–59.

11. Rufus M. Jones, *Mysticism and Democracy in the English Commonwealth* (Cambridge, MA: Harvard Univ. Press, 1932), x–xi, 58–59; Vernon L. Parrington, *Main Currents in American Thought,* 3 vols. (New York: Harcourt Brace, 1927–1930), 2:379, 381. The impact of Jones and Parrington on the historical imagination was especially evident in the reinvention of the seventeenth-century New Englander Roger Williams as both "transcendental mystic" and consummate "Seeker" in the early 1930s. See James Ernst, *Roger Williams: New England Firebrand* (New York: Macmillan, 1932), 490–92. As Edmund S. Morgan subsequently pointed out, nowhere did Williams embrace the "Seeker" label as a self-description. See Morgan, *Roger Williams: The Church and the State* (New York: Harcourt, Brace and World, 1967), 152–53.

12. Thomas Kelly, *The Eternal Promise* (New York: Harper and Row, 1966), 18, 93, 100–105.

13. Thomas R. Kelly to Rufus M. Jones, 23 April 1938, box 37, Jones Papers. The most important biographical work on Kelly is by his son, who was only four at the time of his father's death but who, as an adult, worked valiantly to collect his father's papers and to make sense of his life. See Richard M. Kelly, *Thomas Kelly: A Biography*

(New York: Harper and Row, 1966). For other portraits, see Douglas V. Steere, "A Biographical Memoir," in *A Testament of Devotion,* by Thomas R. Kelly (New York: Harper and Row, 1941), 1–28; Douglas V. Steere, "Thomas Kelly: A Brother Lawrence for Our Time," in *The Lamb's War: Quaker Essays to Honor Hugh Barbour,* ed. Michael L. Birkel and John W. Newman (Richmond, IN: Earlham College Press, 1992), 211–22; Mary Kelly Farquhar and T. Canby Jones, *Thomas R. Kelly: A Sketch of His Life* (Wilmington, OH: Wilmington College, 1962); T. Canby Jones, *Thomas R. Kelly As I Remember Him* (Wallingford, PA: Pendle Hill, 1988); and Kyle Lolliffe, "A Bright Comet Appears: The Canadian Sojourn of Thomas Kelly, 1914–1916," *Canadian Quaker History* 57 (1995): 3–14. Farquhar was Kelly's sister; Canby Jones was a devoted student of Kelly's at Haverford; and Steere was a colleague and friend. Besides *Testament of Devotion* and *Eternal Promise,* the one other essay of Kelly's still in circulation (as a Pendle Hill pamphlet) is Thomas R. Kelly, *Reality of the Spiritual World* (Wallingford, PA: Pendle Hill, 1942).

14. Thomas R. Kelly to Edgar Thompson, 4 January 1929; Kelly to Thompson, 24 September 1930; Kelly to Arthur Gillett, 14 March 1932, box 4, Mss. Collection no. 1135, Thomas R. Kelly Papers, Haverford College Library, Haverford, PA.

15. Thomas R. Kelly to Arthur Gillett, 1 June 1932; Kelly to J. H. Woods, 30 November 1932; Clarence Lewis to Lael Kelly, 12 January 1935, box 4, Kelly Papers.

16. Thomas R. Kelly to Arthur Gillett, 22 November 1935; Kelly to "Folks," 21 February [1935], box 4, Kelly Papers. The Meyerson research did eventually appear, despite the financial hurdles, in a run of five hundred copies. See Thomas R. Kelly, *Explanation and Reality in the Philosophy of Émile Meyerson* (Princeton, NJ: Princeton Univ. Press, 1937).

17. Thomas R. Kelly to Rufus M. Jones, 9 May 1936, box 37, Jones Papers; Kelly to Clarence Lewis, 11 May 1935; Kelly to Jones, 30 May 1935, box 4; Kelly, "Oriental Philosophy Courses," box 7, Kelly Papers.

18. Thomas R. Kelly to Arthur Gillett, 22 March 1936, box 4, Kelly Papers; Kelly, *Thomas Kelly,* 90–91. On Steere, see E. Glenn Hinson, *Love at the Heart of Things: A Biography of Douglas V. Steere* (Wallingford, PA: Pendle Hill, 1998).

19. Kelly, *Thomas Kelly,* 54–55, 79; Thomas R. Kelly, "Spiritual Autobiography," sent to Rufus M. Jones, 7 April 1928, box 27, Jones Papers; Thomas R. Kelly, "What Is the Mystic's Experience?" 1925–1930, box 5, Kelly Papers. A copy of Kelly's autobiographical manuscript is also in box 4, Kelly Papers.

20. Kelly, "Spiritual Autobiography."

21. Thomas R. Kelly, "Master, Where Dwellest Thou?" unpublished sermon, 1930, box 8, Kelly Papers.

22. Kelly, "Master, Where Dwelleth Thou?"; Kelly, "Spiritual Autobiography."

23. Thomas R. Kelly to Rufus Jones, 30 May 1935; Kelly to Arthur Gillett, 22 November 1935, box 4, Kelly Papers.

24. Kelly, *Eternal Promise,* 38–39; Abraham Joshua Heschel, *Man's Quest for God: Studies in Prayer and Symbolism* (Santa Fe, NM: Aurora, 1998), 135, 139. This work actually closes with an address that Heschel first gave to German Friends in Frankfurt-am-Main in 1938 (147–51).

25. Thomas R. Kelly to family, 31 August 1938; Kelly to family, 16 August 1938, box 4, Kelly Papers; Kelly to Jones, 26 September 1938, Jones Papers; Kelly, *Testament of Devotion,* 97–100.

26. Thomas Kelly to family, 16 August 1938; Merrill Root to Kelly, 10 May 1936, box 4, Kelly Papers.

27. Jones, *Thomas Kelly As I Remember Him*, 37–40; Fran Bacon to Thomas R. Kelly, 1 May 1939, box 4, Kelly Papers; Kelly, *Thomas Kelly*, 118–21; Kelly, *Testament of Devotion*, 29, 54, 122.

28. Rufus M. Jones, "Thomas R. Kelly," *Meeting* 72 (February–March 1941): 3–4. Jones's paragraph endorsement was on the front cover of the first edition in 1941.

29. Elton Trueblood, *While It Is Day: An Autobiography* (New York: Harper and Row, 1974), 25; Elton Trueblood, *The Essence of Spiritual Religion* (New York: Harper and Brothers, 1936), 3; Richard J. Foster, introduction to *A Testament of Devotion*, by Thomas R. Kelly (New York: HarperCollins, 1992), x. The *Christian Century* endorsement was on the back of the 1941 and 1992 editions.

30. Kelly, *Testament of Devotion*, 20, 36. Page references from here on are to the more widely available 1992 edition, with Richard Foster's introduction, rather than the first edition of 1941.

31. Kelly, *Testament of Devotion*, 3, 5, 9, 27, 95.

32. Kelly, *Testament of Devotion*, 5, 8, 12, 33–34, 53, 72. The "take all of me" prayer is from Kelly, "Have You Ever Seen a Miracle?" which was added to the expanded edition of *The Eternal Promise* (Richmond, IN: Friends United Press, 1977), 154. Except for reference to this added meditation, all other citations refer to the pagination of the first edition.

33. Kelly, *Testament of Devotion*, 38, 40–41, 45–46, 77, 100; Kelly, *Eternal Promise*, 15.

34. Christopher Isherwood, *Diaries, 1939–1960*, ed. Katherine Bucknell (New York: HarperCollins, 1997), 162, 170. Bucknell's introduction to the diaries is masterful.

35. Isherwood, *Diaries, 1939–1960*, 198, 211–12, 217; Christopher Isherwood, *My Guru and His Disciple* (Minneapolis: Univ. of Minnesota Press, 2001), 25–26, 49, 90–95.

36. Isherwood, *My Guru*, 88, 92; Isherwood, *Diaries, 1939–1960*, 186–87, 204.

37. Eugene Exman to Thomas R. Kelly, 4 January 194[1], box 12, Kelly Papers; Kelly, *Thomas Kelly*, 122; Eugene Exman, Thomas E. Powers, and Douglas V. Steere, *Search for Meaning* (Rye, NY: Wainwright House, 1961), vi, 1. Writing just after the New Year, Exman misdated his above letter as 1940.

38. Christopher Isherwood, *My Guru*, 11; Gerald Heard, ed., *Prayers and Meditations* (New York: Harper and Brothers, 1949), 9.

39. Huston Smith, *Beyond the Postmodern Mind: The Place of Meaning in a Global Civilization*, rev. ed. (Wheaton, IL: Quest, 2003), 236–44; Phil Cousineau, ed., *The Way Things Are: Conversations with Huston Smith on the Spiritual Life* (Berkeley: Univ. of California Press, 2003), 2–4, 80–82.

40. Gerald Heard, *A Quaker Mutation* (Wallingford, PA: Pendle Hill, [1939]); Isherwood, *My Guru*, 96–97; Christopher Isherwood, "Trabuco," September 1942, box 51, no. 1140, Christopher Isherwood Papers, Huntington Library, San Marino, CA; Douglas Steere, *Time to Spare* (New York: Harper and Brothers, 1949), 18. The Heard-Steere connections are well documented in Hinson, *Love at the Heart of Things*, 272–75, 279–91, though Hinson downplays Heard's eclecticism and misidentifies him as "an Anglican mystic" (272). The records on the Conference on the Nature and Laws of the Spiritual Life, also known as the Conference on Religion and Psychol-

ogy, are in the Friends Historical Library of Swarthmore College, Swarthmore, PA. The bulk of these files cover the years from 1943 to 1997. Steere spoke the first year; Heard spoke in 1945 and 1950, and his devotional guides featured prominently on the group's reading list; D. T. Suzuki lectured in 1954. The spread of the new retreats can also be followed in the pages of *Inward Light,* which often published reports from around the country. The Spring 1949 issue was devoted to the subject. On the Catholic dimensions of the retreat movement, see Joseph P. Chinnici, *Living Stones: The History and Structure of Catholic Spiritual Life in the United States* (New York: Macmillan, 1989), 157–71; and Brigid O'Shea Merriman, *Searching for Christ: The Spirituality of Dorothy Day* (South Bend, IN: Univ. of Notre Dame Press, 1994), 131–69.

41. On Palmer, see Parker J. Palmer, *Let Your Life Speak: Listening for the Voice of Vocation* (San Francisco: Jossey-Bass, 2000), 23–24; and Parker J. Palmer, *A Hidden Wholeness: The Journey Toward an Undivided Life* (San Francisco: Jossey-Bass, 2004). The Pendle Hill records, many of them administrative files, run through 112 boxes at the Friends Historical Library at Swarthmore.

42. Isherwood, *My Guru,* 51–52. By the 1960s, sociologists of religion had begun to use the term *seekers* to characterize people who inhabited a cultural space somewhere between "believers" and "nonbelievers." That sociological trend culminated in Wade Clark Roof's depiction of the baby boomers in *A Generation of Seekers* (1994). See Margit Warburg's overview of the emergence of that literature in "Seeking the Seekers in the Sociology of Religion," *Social Compass* 48 (2001): 91–93. By now, it should be clear that there is a considerable history behind the sociological appropriation of this category.

43. Thurman, *With Head and Heart,* 74–77; George K. Makechnie, ed., *Howard Thurman: His Enduring Dream* (Boston: Boston Univ. Howard Thurman Center, 1988), 21–22; Kelly, "Have You Ever Seen a Miracle?" 160.

44. Anne Spencer Thurman, ed., *For the Inward Journey: The Writings of Howard Thurman* (Richmond, IN: Friends United Meeting, 1984), 207; Makechnie, *Howard Thurman,* 21–22, 80.

Epilogue

1. Robert N. Bellah, Richard Madsen, William M. Sullivan, Ann Swidler, and Steven M. Tipton, *Habits of the Heart: Individualism and Commitment in American Life* (New York: Harper and Row, 1985), vii, 55, 63–64. Bellah's view of religious individualism was in part a self-critique of his own idiosyncratic journey that only belatedly returned him to settled membership in the Episcopal Church: "A period of seeking, when one tries out various options, would seem normal in our kind of society," he commented in 1990, "but I would not recommend my protracted process." See Robert N. Bellah, "Finding the Church: Post-Traditional Discipleship," *Christian Century,* 14 November 1999, 1061.

2. Bellah et al., *Habits of the Heart,* 81, 221, 226, 235.

3. Bellah et al., *Habits of the Heart,* 46, 81, 235, 248. For two carefully balanced and mediating perspectives, see the discussion of "a practice-oriented spirituality" in Robert Wuthnow, *After Heaven: Spirituality in America Since the 1950s* (Berkeley: Univ. of California Press, 1998), 16–17, 168–98; and the subtle ethnographic reflections on New Age spirituality in Michael F. Brown, *The Channeling Zone: American Spirituality in an Anxious Age* (Cambridge, MA: Harvard Univ. Press, 1997). For the ne

plus ultra of critical accounts of privatized spirituality as a capitalist, corporate, colonial, and consumerist tool, see Jeremy Carrette and Richard King, *Selling Spirituality: The Silent Takeover of Religion* (London: Routledge, 2005). Carrette and King, predictably, present Sheilaism as one of the shorthands for the reviled privatization of religion (p. 55).

4. Max Ehrmann, *A Farrago* (Cambridge, MA: Co-Operative Publishing Co., 1898), 113–14; Bertha K. Ehrmann, *Max Ehrmann: A Poet's Life* (Boston: Humphries, 1951), 46.

5. Max Ehrmann, *Jesus: A Passion Play* (New York: Baker and Taylor, 1915), unpaginated preface; Bertha K. Ehrmann, ed., *The Journal of Max Ehrmann* (Boston: Humphries, 1952), 249–50. For a generous review of Ehrmann's various literary efforts, see Vandervoort Sloan, "Max Ehrmann," *Drama* no. 28 (November 1917): 485–91. I am quoting throughout the epilogue from the published version of Ehrmann's journal, but it also exists in manuscript and typescript forms in the Max Ehrmann Papers, DC 21–22, Archives of DePauw University and Indiana United Methodism, Greencastle, IN. There are layers of additions, corrections, omissions, and other textual variations from one version to another. Ehrmann made many of these changes himself when he started thinking of his journal as something that might be published; his wife (whom he married only near the end of his life) did more editorial work as she readied the text for publication after her husband's death. The published version is largely reliable, though additional passages and materials (including Ehrmann's own indexing apparatus) are recoverable only through the collections at DePauw.

6. "Framed Prayer Stolen from Indiana Building"; "News Item: The Theft of a Prayer"; "Daring Souvenir 'Fiend' Steals Famous Prayer at World's Fair," 1904, clippings, Ehrmann Papers.

7. "Max Ehrmann's Work," Dodge Publishing Company advertisement, n.d., clippings, Ehrmann Papers. Many of the pop-culture myths about the "Desiderata" are now instantly traceable on the Internet. See also Barbara J. Katz, "Popular Prose-Poem Is No Work of the Ages," *Washington Post,* 27 November 1977, B1, B3. On Niebuhr's prayer and its wider context, see Elisabeth Sifton, *The Serenity Prayer: Faith and Politics in Times of Peace and War* (New York: Norton, 2003).

8. For the Protestant book of sermons on Ehrmann's poem, see Granville T. Walker, *Go Placidly amid the Noise and Haste: Meditations on the "Desiderata"* (St. Louis: Bethany, 1975). Hendra's double life as religious satirist and troubled soul can be followed in Tony Hendra, *Father Joe: The Man Who Saved My Soul* (New York: Random House, 2004); and Tony Hendra and Sean Kelly, *Not the Bible* (New York: Ballantine, 1983).

9. Max Ehrmann, *The Poems of Max Ehrmann* (New York: Dodge, 1910), 188.

10. Ehrmann, *Journal,* 11, 130–31.

11. Ehrmann, *Journal,* 302.

12. Max Ehrmann, *The Desiderata of Faith* (New York: Crown, 1996), 12–13, 20–21, 30; Ehrmann, *Journal,* 185.

13. Ehrmann, *Journal,* 22, 112, 273, 276–77, 288, 335, 344; Ehrmann, *Poems,* 175.

14. Ehrmann, *Journal,* 92–93. On Sanctuary House and its part in a larger community of eclectics, see Laura Chester, *Holy Personal: Looking for Small Private Places of Worship* (Bloomington: Indiana Univ. Press, 2000), 170–77.

15. Ehrmann, *Journal*, 23, 127, 255. For a careful evaluation of the limits of liberal Protestant progressivism on race matters in one bellwether movement, see Andrew C. Reiser, *The Chautauqua Moment: Protestants, Progressives, and the Culture of Modern Liberalism* (New York: Columbia Univ. Press, 2003), 10–11, 128–60. The story is not all one of limits, evident in a number of interracial alliances that emerged in the early twentieth century, including support for the NAACP from such leading white progressives as Jane Addams, Emil Hirsch, Felix Adler, Edwin Mead, and Jenkin Lloyd Jones. See Ralph E. Luker, *The Social Gospel in Black and White: American Racial Reform, 1885–1912* (Chapel Hill: Univ. of North Carolina Press, 1991), 266–67, 312–13; see also Ronald C. White Jr., *Liberty and Justice for All: Racial Reform and the Social Gospel (1877–1925)* (Louisville: Westminster John Knox, 2002).

16. Max Ehrmann, "A Re-Evaluation of the Sex-Life," *U.S. Public Health Bulletin*, n.d.; "Talk," *Birth Control Review*, n.d., clippings, Ehrmann Papers; Max Ehrmann, "Preachments: Christianity and Sex," in *Scarlet Sketches* (Terre Haute: Indiana Publishing Co., 1925), unpaginated.

17. "Tribute to Eugene V. Debs," *American Socialist*, 21 October 1916, clippings, Ehrmann Papers; Max Ehrmann, "Inceptions: A Footnote to the Psychology of Play-Writing," *Drama* no. 34 (May 1919): 85. The dialogue between "Socialist" and "Bourgeois" also appeared as an entry in his *Journal* (27) the year before. For Ehrmann's pained disagreement with Debs as revolutionary, see Ehrmann, *Journal*, 23–24, 50–51.

18. Ehrmann, *Journal*, 255–56, 296–97; Bellah et al., *Habits of the Heart*, 22.

19. Ehrmann, *Journal*, 263, 266, 300–301, 334.

20. Ehrmann, *Journal*, 309; A. Roy Eckardt, "The New Look in American Piety," *Christian Century*, 17 November 1954, 1395; Will Herberg, *Protestant-Catholic-Jew* (Garden City, NY: Anchor, 1960), 266, 268–69.

21. David Brooks, "Hooked on Heaven Lite," *New York Times*, 9 March 2004, A25; Martin E. Marty, "Me, My Church and I," *Christian Century*, 25 January 2005, 47. Brooks predictably cited "Sheilaism" in *Bobos in Paradise* as an example of "spirituality without obligation," but he did so within a more balanced argument on the ongoing tensions between autonomy and community, freedom and connection. See David Brooks, *Bobos in Paradise: The New Upper Class and How They Got There* (New York: Simon and Schuster, 2000), 235–36. For the piece that provoked Marty, see Cathleen Falsani, "Etheridge: 'I Am and Always Have Been a Healer,'" *Chicago Sun-Times*, 14 November 2004.

22. LaTonya Taylor, "The Church of O," *Christianity Today*, 1 April 2002; James A. Herrick, *The Making of the New Spirituality: The Eclipse of the Western Religious Tradition* (Downers Grove, IL: InterVarsity Press, 2003), 14–15, 25; Kate Meaver, "Oprah Winfrey and Her Self-Help Saviors: Making the New Age Normal," *Christian Research Journal* 23 (2001): 2; Amy Wellborn, "The Feel-Good Spirituality of Oprah," *Our Sunday Visitor*, 13 January 2002. I have been assisted in my understanding of current debates about Oprah Winfrey's religion through the work of Kathryn Lofton, who graciously shared some of her research with me. See Kathryn Lofton, "Practicing Oprah; or, The Prescriptive Compulsion of a Spiritual Capitalism," *Journal of Popular Culture* (forthcoming).

23. Bellah et al., *Habits of the Heart*, 152–55; Jonathan Alter, "Barack Obama: 'The Audacity of Hope,'" *Newsweek*, 3 January 2005, 78–79.

24. For balanced accounts of Euro-American appropriations of Native American spirituality, see Philip J. Deloria, *Playing Indian* (New Haven, CT: Yale Univ. Press,

1998), 154–80; and Philip Jenkins, *Dream Catchers: How Mainstream America Discovered Native Spirituality* (New York: Oxford Univ. Press, 2004). For the less-balanced version of the scholarly analysis of New Age appropriations, see Kimberly J. Lau, *New Age Capitalism: Making Money East of Eden* (Philadelphia: Univ. of Pennsylvania Press, 2000).

25. Mark Van Doren, ed., *The Portable Walt Whitman* (New York: Viking Penguin, 1973), 11–12, 90, 321, 337, 369, 374.

INDEX

⟡⟡⟡⟡

Page references followed by *p* indicate a photograph; followed by *i* indicates an illustration.

Hartley, Marsden, 202, 203
Hartley, Thomas, 42
Harvard Divinity School: Emerson's
controversial speech at, 33; mystics
coming out of, 15
Haverford College, 231, 232, 233, 243
Heard, Gerald, 19, 231, 260–61, 262,
263, 264
Hearst, Phoebe, 193
Heart-beats (Mozoomdar), 95, 96
Hebrew Union College, 248
Hendra, Tony, 275
Herberg, Will, 283
*Heresiography; or, A Description of the
Hereticks and Sectaries of These Lat-
ter Times* (Pagitt), 230
hermitage: Catholic perspective on,
78–79; Chapter of Perfection use of,
79–80; *Encylopædia Britannica* defi-
nition of, 67–68; nineteenth-century
Protestant imagination on, 69–73;
sensational tales of, 73–75. *See also*
solitude
The Hermit of the Colorado Hills:
(Bushnell), 93–94
Hermit in the Himalayas (Brunton),
96, 97
"Hermit" (Parnell), 76
The Hermit of Petræa (Irwin), 73
Hermit of Sacandaga Park, 74
The Hermit (Sargent painting), 99p–100
Hermits of the Wissahickon, 79–80
Herrick, James A., 284
Herron, George D., 195
Heschel, Abraham Joshua, 248
Hickling, Catherine, 121, 122
Hickling, Thomas, 121–22
Hicks, Elias, 234
Hicks, Mary, 201–2
Hidden Words (Baháu'lláh), 215
Higginson, Thomas Wentworth: anti-
slavery activism by, 108–9; apprecia-
tive view of Eastern religions by, 134;
background and writings of, 106–7,
108; as cosmopolitan piety architect,
107p; exposure to Catholicism during
Fayal trip, 119–29; FRA (Free Reli-
gious Association) participation by,

106, 112–13, 133–36; friendship between Ehrmann and, 272; health reform efforts of, 120; on Holy Week
(Portuguese Catholic) rites, 126, 128;
"My Creed" as written by, 59, 133;
relationship with African Americans,
130–33; religious authority reinter-
preted by, 110–11; sympathy of religions approach by, 111–38;
Transcendentalism movement role by,
108–11; World's Parliament of Reli-
gions participation in, 135p–36
Hindu philosophy: incorporation into
Western spirituality, 64, 66, 94–96,
100; Kelly's studies of, 243. *See also*
Eastern religions
*History of the Corruptions of Christian-
ity* (Priestley), 41
"Holy Obedience" (Kelly), 251
Holy Week (Portuguese Catholic),
126, 128
homosexuality, 258–59
Hook and Ladder Club, 82
Hotham, Edmond Stuart, 89
Hours with the Mystics (Vaughan), 29,
51, 69, 233
Housden, Roger, 100
Howe, Julia Ward, 149
Howells, William Dean, 202
Hull House, 188
Hume, David, 37, 38
Hurd, William, 39
Hutchinson, Anne, 270
Huxley, Aldous, 19, 178, 179, 231, 257,
262
Hymns and Spiritual Songs
(Maxwell), 4

Inayat Khan, 8
independence-dependence issue,
215–16, 221–25, 255–56
"Indian Mystic Offers One Religion for
All" (*New York Times*), 9
Ingersoll, Robert G., 105–6
Insight Meditation Center (Massachu-
setts), 177
International Metaphysical League
(Boston, 1899), 204

International New Thought Alliance, 157

An Introduction to Yoga (Besant), 162

In Tune with the Infinite (Trine), 153, 154, 155, 199

Inward Light (magazine), 261

Irwin, Harriet Morrison, 73

Isherwood, Christopher, 19, 231, 256–59, 261, 263*p*–64, 265–66

Islam: Higginson's appreciative view of, 134; Sufis sect of, 83, 184, 262; Webb's adoption of, 181–84

Islam in America (Webb), 182

"Is Religion a Feeling of Dependence?" (Carus), 221

Jackson, John, 236, 237

Jackson, Phil, 61–62

Jameson, Anna, 69

James, William: complaint about sexualizing mysticism, 38; correspondence between Sarah Farmer and, 189–90; exploration of altered stated of consciousness by, 179; on independence-passivity tensions in spiritual life, 215–16, 222–25; influence on Ehrmann by, 277; on life worth living question, 57–58; on mysticism, 28, 53–54, 56, 60; on practice of meditation, 147, 174; religion as defined by, 98; Rufus Jones and, 232

Janes, Lewis G., 136, 195–96, 209, 315n.16

Jefferson, Joseph, 202

Jefferson, Thomas, 5, 13

Jesus and the Disinherited (Thurman), 268

Jewish people: Cooperative College Workshop work resettling, 257–58; Kelly's reaction to Nazi violence against, 248–49

Jewish Theological Seminary, 248

Johnny Appleseed, 91–93, 92*i*

Johnson, Samuel, 48–49, 115, 124

Jones, Jenkin Lloyd, 188

Jones, Rufus M.: association between Kelly and, 231, 238–40, 247, 248–49, 251; correspondence between James and, 232; early life of, 231–32; influence and accomplishments of, 232–34; on influence of Whitman, 234–35; photographs of, 233*p*, 239*p*; prolific writings on mysticism by, 56; Quakers transformed by, 230–31; study of "seekers" by, 18, 236–38; Thurman on his love of, 266–67; on writers who influenced him, 233–35

Jones, Stephanie, 8

"Journal of Mysticism and Idealism" (proposed journal), 44

Julian of Norwich, 43, 225

Jung, Carl, 264

Kallen, Horace M., 138

Kandinsky, Wassily, 203

karma, 159

Keen, Sam, 268

Kelly, Lael, 256, 257*p*

Kelly, Thomas R.: association between Rufus Jones and, 231, 238–40, 247, 248–49, 251; biographical work done by son of, 320n.13; death of, 256; denied Harvard Ph.D., 243–44; early life and career of, 238–45; god-seeking spirituality of, 249–56; on his few interracial friendships, 267; photographs of, 241*p*, 257*p*; practice heart of testimony by, 254–55; reaction to Nazi violence by, 248–49; religious alienation experienced by, 246–47; "Secret Seekers" meditation by, 238; shift to spiritualized liberalism by, 244–47; as twentieth-century seeker, 18, 19

Kelpius, Johannes, 79, 80

Khan, Hazrat Inayat, 9

Khan, Pir Vilayat Inayat, 8

King, Martin Luther, Jr., 22, 57, 268, 287

King, Thomas Starr, 123

Kneipp, Sebastian, 194

Kornfield, Jack, 177–78

Krishnamurti, Jiddu, 179

Larson, Sheila, 270–71, 275, 283, 284, 285

Laubach, Frank, 250

Migrations to Solitude (Merton), 97
mind-cure, 148, 149
Monsalvat School (Greenacre colony), 136, 195–97, 207
Moore, Fillmore, 210
morality vs. religion discussion, 60
Mosher, Thomas Bird, 200, 203
Moslem World (journal), 182
Moyers, Bill, 262
Mozoomdar, Protap Chunder, 14, 94–96
Mr. Norris Changes Trains (Isherwood), 257
Muir, John, 67
Mukerji, Dhan Gopal, 173, 175
Müller, F. Max, 107, 157, 196
Musical Theme (Hartley painting), 202*p*, 203
"My Creed So Far As I Have One" (Higginson), 59, 133
My Guru and His Disciple (Isherwood), 259, 265
My Pilgrimage to the Wise Men of the East (Conway), 101
mystical theology, 35–36
Mystic Club: founded by Alcott, 30*p*, 31; purpose of, 44
mysticism: connection between political activism and, 56–57; debate over mystical theology vs., 35–36; development and growth of, 14–15; embraced as new spirituality, 57–58; formation of modern, 58; Kelly on paradox of true, 256; as part of eighteenth-century critique of Protestant enthusiasm, 36–45; Transcendental Club discussions on, 29, 35, 41, 43, 60; Transcendentalist transformation of, 14–15, 29–62
"Mysticism in Modern Art" (Hicks lecture), 201–2
Mysticism and Modern Life (Buckham), 56
The Mystic Rock (Greenacre colony), 199
"Mystics" (*Encyclopædia Britannica*), 40, 45
"The Mystic's Experience" (Kelly lecture notes), 245
"The Mystic" (Wasson), 60

NAACP (National Association for the Advancement of Colored People), 133, 195
National American Woman Suffrage Association, 89
National Lampoon, 275
National Union for Practical Progress, 188
Nature (Emerson), 34, 64
New Age spirituality, 6
The New American Spirituality: A Seeker's Guide (Lesser), 8
New England Tract Society, 76
Newman, John Henry, 10
New Spirituality: Bjerregaard's, 53; Oprahfication of, 285–87; religious liberalism of, 13
New Thought movement: Eddy's desire to control, 148–49; Greenacre colony inclusion of, 203–7; intersection of Theosophy and, 161–62; meditation reinvented in, 147–49; Metaphysical Club discussions on, 149, 150; restoration of physical health at heart of, 155; rift between Greenacre Bahá'í groups and members of, 206–10. *See also* Protestantism
Newton, R. Heber, 115
New Universal History of the Religious Rites, Ceremonies, and Customs of the Whole World (Hurd), 39
New York Times, 9, 10
Nicene Creed, 184
Niebuhr, Reinhold, 173, 274
Nietzsche, Friedrich, 280
Norris, John, 76
Nouwen, Henri, 86

Obama, Barack, 287
Offices of Mystical Religion (Guthrie), 139
"Off-the-Cuff Philosophy" bracelet, 20–21
"Of Solitude" (Norris), 76
Olcott, Henry Steel, 158, 159–60
Omega Institute (New York), 8
On the Spiritual in Art (Kandinsky), 203

258–59; Kelly's liberal understanding of, 244–45; Kelly's visit through Europe with, 248–49; mysticism of, 40; Pendle Hill founded by, 18–19; spiritual seeking of the, 230–31, 235–36; transformed by influence of Rufus Jones, 230–31. *See also* Pendle Hill

Quimby, Phineas P., 148, 149

Radical (periodical), 112
Raja-Yoga, 164, 172, 175. *See also* yoga
Ramakrishna, 162, 165
Real Simple (magazine), 7
Recollections (Gladden), 58
religion: American liberalism role in, 10–11; Frothingham on imagining future of, 52–53; Hindu/Eastern, 64, 66, 94–96, 100; independence-passivity tensions over, 215–16, 221–25; James's definition of, 98; questioning nature of, 227–28; spirituality distinguished from, 4; Transcendental Club discussion on morality vs., 60; universal, 114–16, 118, 138–39, 141, 157; Whitehead's definition of, 98–99. *See also* Christianity; Eastern religions; Protestantism; sympathy of religions
Religion in the Making (Whitehead), 98
religious authority: conflict between feminist beliefs and, 224–25; Higginson's reinterpretation of, 110–11
religious liberalism. *See* liberalism
Religious Right, xii, 19
"Remarkable Discovery of an American Hermit" (pamphlet), 73
Remey, Charles Mason, 209
Representative Men (Emerson), 45
Retreat: Time Apart for Silence and Solitude (Housden), 100
"The Return of Faith and the Decline of the Churches" (Higginson), 109, 111, 127, 304n.11
Reveries of a Solitary Walker (Rousseau), 80
Riley, Woodbridge, 20
Ripley, George, 29, 30, 31
Robert the Hermit, 71, 73

Roman Catholic Church: hermitage as perceived by, 78–79; Higginson's exposure to Portuguese, 119–29; liberalism and, 293n.16–94n.16; Vaughan's mysticism condemned by, 52
Rousseau, Jean-Jacques, 80
Royce, Josiah, 232
Ruffner, Henry, 68–69
ar-Rumi, Jalal al-Din, 82–83, 140–41

Sacred Anthology (Conway), 101
Sacred Books of the East (Müller), 157
Sacred Hoops (Jackson), 61
Sacred and Legendary Art (Jameson), 69
Sanborn, Franklin, 44–45, 54, 109, 169, 198–200, 198*p*
Sanger, Margaret, 281
Santayana, George, 5, 272
Saradananda, Swami, 136, 137
Sargent, John Singer, 99, 100
Satprakashananda, Swami, 262
Savage, Minot, 115
Schaff, Philip, 146
Schermerhorn, Martin Kellogg, 9, 115
Schindler, Solomon, 118, 195
Schleiermacher, Friedrich, 221
Schmidt, Nathaniel, 209
School for Applied Metaphysics (Greenacre colony), 204
Schudder, Vida D., 58
Schweitzer, Albert, 57
Science and Health (Eddy), 148
Scripture Idolatry (Higginson), 110
Search for Meaning (essay collection), 260
seekers: as seventeenth-century term for heresy, 229–30; community-building efforts supporting, 262–68; Emerson as self-described, 228–29, 265; Isherwood's description of, 265–66; Kelly's transfer from self-seeking to god-seeking, 249–56; multitude of nineteenth-century, 229; Parrington's notion of, 237–38; Quakers as spiritual, 230–31, 235–36; questions about nature of religion by, 227–28; Rufus Jones's study on, 18, 236–38. *See also* spirituality